THE HOUGHTON MIFFLIN

RADIO BROADCASTING SERIES

Albert Crews

EDITOR

RADIO

THE FIFTH ESTATE

Judith C. Waller

DIRECTOR OF PUBLIC SERVICE
CENTRAL DIVISION
THE NATIONAL BROADCASTING COMPANY

32507

HOUGHTON MIFFLIN COMPANY
BOSTON · NEW YORK · CHICAGO · DALLAS · ATLANTA · SAN FRANCISCO
The Riverside Press Cambridge

The Riverside Press
CAMBRIDGE · MASSACHUSETTS
PRINTED IN THE U.S.A.

To

HARRY CLIFFORD KOPF

whose vision and foresight made possible
the National Broadcasting Company-
Northwestern University Summer Radio
Institute, I dedicate this volume in gratitude and appreciation.

FOREWORD

The National Broadcasting Company is very proud to endorse this, the second in a series of books on broadcasting to emanate from the Radio Institute which has been conducted for several years by the Company in co-operation with Northwestern University.

The author, Judith Waller, has been the central figure in the organization and development of the Institute; and in her book she has brought together the ripe fruits of her many years of broadcasting experience, while availing herself also of the lessons which the Institute has taught concerning the requisites for a complete and intelligible picture of American radio. In this task she has naturally enjoyed the assistance of many of her colleagues in the Company, as well as that of the members of the staff of the University.

The result is a lucid and well-balanced presentation of a highly complex agency which crucially affects the lives of almost the entire population. In its pages the layman will find himself introduced to a world of which he has commonly the most superficial and fragmentary impressions, while not a few persons engaged in the industry will discover in the book fresh and unfamiliar information of value.

As a text for young people desirous of entering one or another of the fields of radio, the book should prove invaluable, shortening by months or even years the time ordinarily required to understand the scope and complications of the business.

Here one can learn about the different national forms for the administration of radio, about the organization of American radio stations, large and small; about how the networks are put together and operated; about program planning: the work of script writers, announcers, studio producers, actors, musicians, and sound effects men; about recordings; about time sales, station contracts, promotion and publicity about news gathering and transmission; about religious programming; about radio in schools and colleges; about listener groups and methods of determining individual listening; about programs for women and for children; about forums and round tables; about the engineering problems of broadcasting, including control of radio traffic on telephone wires; about regulations and their enforcement in compliance with federal, state, industrial and company requirements. In fact, no item of real consequence has been overlooked, and although conditions change from time to time, and the coming of television and the increased use of frequency modulation will alter the picture in some respects, the basic factors, set forth in the text are likely to hold valid for a long time to come.

Radio is part theatre, part concert hall, part newspaper, part pulpit, part school, part forum — no other single medium serves so many and so divergent purposes; none exercises potentially so tremendous an influence upon the thought and feeling of millions of people. This book is an admirable introduction to all this area of human activity, and should greatly improve the public understanding of the important issues involved.

JAMES ROWLAND ANGELL

Public Service Counselor,
New York City.   *National Broadcasting Company*

WHEN radio was in its infancy a brief quarter century ago, its broadcasters were inexperienced and learned by "doing." But radio is now a highly recognized industry in its own right, and it must meet the challenge of a modern world. It has become necessary for broadcasters to receive training and background. It was to meet this need that the NBC Summer Radio Institutes were formed, the first of which was the NBC-Northwestern University Summer Radio Institute offered in 1942. Those of us who were responsible for the instructional courses of that and subsequent Institutes took it upon ourselves to get together the necessary information and materials, thinking that they might well grow into a series of standard textbooks for other radio courses.

For a number of reasons it was not practical to bring out such a series of books in 1942 in published form. On the other hand, it occurred to us that we might edit the notes we used that year and put them into shape for use by the students in the three Summer Radio Institutes being given in 1943 by the National Broadcasting Company in collaboration with Northwestern University, Stanford University, and the University of California at Los Angeles. By so doing, we could see whether the information was practical and usable and whether too much had been omitted that should have been included. In the light of this tryout, the material might then be re-edited for publication.

This book is an outgrowth of the work-study book on Public Service, which was brought out in that series. Because there seemed to be a greater need for a more comprehensive survey of the field than for one dealing solely with the subject of radio's public service, the book was expanded to include the many fields covered in this volume. Much of the material deals with various phases of radio with which many of my colleagues at NBC are more familiar than I. Through the good offices of my associates it is now possible to present this volume.

All of us realize its many inadequacies; almost every chapter

could be expanded into a volume in its own right. It was impossible to cover any of the subjects in their entirety. All we
could hope to do in the short space of five hundred pages was
to give a general survey of the different problems that are involved in the business of radio broadcasting. There are, of
necessity, many omissions of activities going on in radio stations all over the country; of excellent work being accomplished by many people; of historical incidents that should
have a place; of the most recent developments in a fast-chang-
ing industry; of certain features that could only be touched
upon in passing. Perhaps at some future time there may be an
opportunity to atone for these omissions.

Between the time when the manuscript went into proof-
form and the time when the actual publication of the book
occurred, peace has again returned to the world, which means
that a number of the restrictions noted in various chapters will
no longer apply. It was found to be impractical to make all the
necessary corrections to bring the material in this book completely up to date. It will be ever thus in radio because its
medium is so fluid that changes could be made even from day
to day and week to week, and still the information would never
be completely current and timely.

It will be apparent to any reader of this book that much of
it is concerned directly with the NBC way of doing things.
This naturally results from the fact that all the people associated with me in the development of this volume are or were
NBC people. If they are to speak with any authority at all, it
must be on ground with which they are thoroughly familiar;
and, of course, we are more familiar with our own network
than with the others. We do not intend to suggest that ours is
the only way of doing business or that it is even the best way.
However, it is true that the procedures outlined are generally
characteristic of the entire broadcasting field. This is due to
several factors; for one thing, NBC was the pioneer in network
broadcasting, and naturally many of its procedures have
furnished the pattern for what has followed throughout the
industry. The sameness of pattern that prevails in the broad-

casting industry is also undoubtedly due to the fact that existing conditions impose logical and uniform methods of conduct
throughout any industry.

It is with profound gratitude that I thank all of those who
have been so helpful and cooperative in this venture: Joseph
McDonald, formerly Assistant Legal Counselor of NBC and
now Legal Counsel of the American Broadcasting Company,
Incorporated, who gave so much of his time and thought in all
the formative stages and to his fine contribution in the first
section of the book; Clarence L. Menser, Vice President in
charge of Programming for NBC, for his chapters on programming; Frank Chizzini, Director of Radio Recording for
NBC, Central Division, for the chapter on "Transcriptions and
Recordings"; Margaret Cuthbert, Director of Women's and
Children's Programs for NBC, and Harriet Hester, formerly
Educational Director, Station WLS, Chicago, for their contributions to the chapter on "Women's Programs"; William Drips,
Director of Agriculture for NBC, and Everett Mitchell, Director of Agriculture for Station WMAQ, Chicago, for their able
help on the chapter on "Agricultural Programs"; William Wed-
dell and Oliver Morton of the NBC Central Division Sales Staff
for their chapters on "Sales Organization for Radio"; Emmons
Carlson, Director of Advertising and Promotion, NBC, Central
Division, for his two chapters on "Sales Promotion" and "Audience Measurement"; John F. Ryan, Director of Press and Publicity, NBC, Central Division, for his chapter on "Press and
Publicity"; Eric Danielson, Head of Traffic, NBC, Central
Division, for his help on the chapter on "Communications and
Traffic"; and the whole staff of the Engineering Department,
NBC, Central Division, and especially to Howard Luttgens
and Walter Lanterman, Mr. Luttgens for his able organization
of the material and Mr. Lanterman for his untiring efforts in
coordinating and writing the chapter on "Radio Engineering";
Albert Crews for his counsel, guidance, and editorship on the
book as a whole; and the many others, both in and out of the
Company, who have aided along the way. Without each and

every one of these people the book would not have been
written.

If within its pages the student or the layman interested in
the subject of radio finds information that is both helpful and
useful from a historical as well as a guidance angle, our labors
will not have been in vain.

JUDITH C. WALLER

CHICAGO, ILLINOIS

CONTENTS

SECTION FOUR
THE SALES ORGANIZATION

SECTION FIVE
THE AUDIENCE

SECTION SIX
SERVICING THE PROGRAM

SECTION SEVEN
ENGINEERING

SECTION EIGHT
EDUCATIONAL BROADCASTING

APPENDIX

1

THE STRUCTURE OF BROADCASTING

CHAPTER 1

THE WORLD SYSTEMS OF BROADCASTING

RADIO BROADCASTING is not just a business; it is also an art. It is the newest means of mass communication, and it is one of the most potent of present-day forces. It follows in the footsteps of the press and goes beyond it. It has become the Fifth Estate, a factor in the life of the world without which no one can reckon.

~ In the technical sense, broadcasting is essentially an electronic system for re-creating sound at many places simultaneously. In the social sense, however, broadcasting has developed in the short span since 1920 into a force which in many ways has impinged on and influenced the lives of most of the civilized peoples of the world. There is room in the available bands of frequencies for only a limited number of broadcasting stations. There is, by the same token, room for only a limited number of "broadcasters." Radio is too important to be allowed to develop as it will; its very nature requires that it be adequately supervised and controlled.

It is interesting to note that as radio developed in various countries, methods of control which came into being were a direct outgrowth of national philosophies and racial characteristics. From a welter of chaos and experimentation, there emerged three main systems of broadcasting control.

The methods of controlling radio form the logical point of departure in any study of radio broadcasting, because what radio has become in various parts of the world has been a direct result of the systems under which it has grown. These three systems are usually classified as the "State-Owned System," the "British System," and the "American System." Each has its own peculiar characteristics and its own line of development in keeping with the temperament of the peoples involved. There is no country in which radio is not government-controlled, but there is considerable variation in the kind and amount of regulation under the various systems.

<h2>THE STATE-OWNED SYSTEM</h2>

The state-owned system of control operates in nearly every country in the world except the British Commonwealth of Nations and the United States. Under such a system, the ownership and control of broadcasting is completely in the hands of the government and usually is delegated to a special department. Financing is done by appropriation of government funds. In a few European countries prior to 1939, notably Luxembourg, the government-owned stations sold time to commercial advertisers, and the proceeds were used as general government funds.

The objectives of a state-owned system are to furnish the people with a means of contact with their government and to give them some kind of entertainment and education, but more important, to give the government a means of contact with the people of their own country and of other lands as well. Programming under these circumstances has a definitely bureaucratic tinge and is subject to the whims of those in power. However, in most cases at least some pretense is made of offering a full program service to listeners of the country.

Under this system, radio has never flourished as it has in England and America. As might be expected, the percentage of radio-equipped homes in countries where benevolent state ownership exists is not very high. Part of this is due to general educational and economic standards, and part of it to the fact that programs generally do not offer the potent pulling power of American radio. In spite of these conditions, audiences were growing and ownership of radio sets was on the increase in most countries immediately preceding the outbreak of the second World War.

In the totalitarian states, where dictatorship is in effect, radio is under the strictest control. It is considered of the highest importance and is given the most scrupulous attention. The peoples of totalitarian countries must conform strictly to the desires of their dictator, and dictators learn very quickly to appreciate the propaganda and control value of radio. In Germany, prior to VE Day, and in all the formerly occupied countries, there were a great many radios in operation. It is true that most sets were built with a limited tuning device so that they could receive only the station or stations for which they were designed — Axis stations in every case. Still, there were more radio-equipped homes in Germany than in many countries where a more benevolent kind of ownership existed.

Radio in dictator-controlled countries was financed completely by the government. Control was rigid, since the entire purpose of all radio output was to influence the people, inform them of the state's wishes, and keep them loyal to the government. This does not mean that all programs had propaganda content, but their over-all effect was to propagandize. Consequently, the development of radio in most dictator-controlled nations was carefully fostered by the government. It offered another avenue of approach to the ears and minds of the people, and this avenue was controlled and used to the utmost.

THE BRITISH SYSTEM

In Great Britain, broadcasting is carried on by the British Broadcasting Corporation, which operates under a Royal Charter subject to renewal by Parliament at the end of ten years. This is commonly regarded as an example of government operation, but in reality there are important distinctions. In peacetime, British radio is not government-controlled except in a very indirect manner. The BBC is not a government department but an autonomous public corporation. It is on a non-profit basis and is entrusted with the task of supplying broadcasting services for the domestic listener, although it has also developed services for the Empire, Europe, and many other areas. Under the Charter, the Postmaster General has the right to exercise certain powers in an emergency; in wartime these powers were transferred to the Minister of Information, and, in practice, constituted guidance on matters of wartime national policy, without involving any direct control or supervision over operations or programs.

A most important feature of the system is that the Royal Charter under which the BBC operates is an exclusive one. There is no competition for the BBC from rival networks or stations in England. A second feature of the British system is that in peacetime it is supported solely by license fees from listeners. Each household with a radio receiving set or sets pays a charge of ten shillings ($2.00) a year. About a quarter of the income thus derived is retained by the Post Office, and the remainder is turned over to the BBC. In wartime, however, because of greatly expanded overseas services, the BBC received its funds from the Treasury on a vote by Parliament. For the year 1943-44 the grant was £10,000,000.

The British system aims to give the listeners the best kind of programming, with an emphasis on cultural standards, educational values, and good taste, which leads most Americans to suspect that the British audience does not always get what it likes. On the other hand, the BBC has through its Listener Research Department claimed to have established an effective index and barometer of listener interest as a guide to program policy.

Sponsors and sales managers, advertising agencies and network or station commercial operators have never been a part of the British system of broadcasting. In wartime the BBC, like American radio, worked closely with the government in all matters having to do with the implementation of rationing and other administrative controls. Parliament, which controls renewal of the BBC Charter, has ultimate control over the BBC, just as Congress through the Federal Communications Commission has ultimate control over American radio. The government, however, has not been disposed to interfere any more than Congress has in America, and for the most part the BBC has had a comparatively free hand.

As a result and because of lack of competition, the programs of the BBC tend to be conservative, and often they seem dull and a little stodgy to Americans. Freedom from commercial pressure and competition, on the other hand, has allowed BBC program planners to attempt many experimental kinds of programs.

There is a high saturation of set ownership in Britain, where the figures, proportional to population, are second only to the United States. English audiences turn to radio with great avidity, according to surveys. During the latter days of the war, at 6 P.M. each day, fourteen to fifteen million people, excluding children, was the average radio audience in Britain. At 9 P.M. this figure rose to sixteen million out of a total adult population of thirty million. This is evidence that the British turned to radio more and more during the trying days of war, partly because of such wartime conditions as the blackout which prevented large numbers of people from leaving their homes at night, and partly because in war reporting no other medium was able to give an equivalent service.

THE AMERICAN SYSTEM

American broadcasters have developed a system of radio which is suited to the temperament of the American people. Radio in the United States is privately owned and privately operated. There are no exclusive franchises. Radio is highly competitive, and it pays its own bills out of its own income. American radio, as every listener is well aware, is financed by the sale of time to advertisers. There is no taxation of receiving sets, and there is no subsidy by the government. Radio in America is as independent of control as it is possible for a self-limiting medium like radio to be.

While the ownership of radio in the United States is completely private, there is some measure of government control. There has been a tendency during the last few years for this control to become more stringent, but, compared to other systems of broadcasting in the world, it is free. Licensing remains in the hands of the government in a manner which will be discussed in detail later in this book. Certain broad regulatory power is held by the government, but except for these controls, American radio has little to do with the government. Even in a time of national emergency, radio continued in private hands and did a remarkable job of co-operating with the government in helping to co-ordinate and further the war effort. Operating under wartime conditions is the supreme test of privately owned radio, and American broadcasters did a good voluntary job. Many hours of the broadcast day were made available for government messages of various types, without charges.

In dictator-controlled countries the objective of broadcasting is to give the people what the state wants them to have; in Great Britain the objective seems to be to give the people what they ought to have; in America broadcasters give the audience what it wants. The primary desire of American broadcasters is to get and hold listeners. In order to do this, they will go to almost any decent extreme. Because radio is operated for profit and because it is highly competitive, the quality and variety of most of the programs in this country can be equaled nowhere else in the world. Because broadcasting is, for the most part, a very lucrative business, finances are available to make the best in radio programs available to listeners.

The size of the United States and the comparatively large number of stations work together to give audiences a great deal of choice in their listening. Competition creates pressures which are always operating to improve the quality of programs from the point of view of popular acceptance. The programming is catholic in range, and the choice of subject matter is almost completely free.

The percentage of radio-equipped homes in the United States is greater than in any other country. There are many more radio-equipped homes than telephone-equipped homes. The audience runs from top to bottom in the social and economic scale and includes everything in between. It may almost be said that the radio audience is the whole American people.

It has been argued that in countries where radio is supported by a tax on receiving sets, the payment of a license fee may be said to vest a certain amount of control over program standards in the radio audience, by virtue of the fact that if programs were not popular, support would not be forthcoming. However, it would seem that in practice such control proves much too indirect to be of importance. Under an advertising-supported system, however, the control is direct and effective. If a commercial program does not prove popular, lack of audience acceptance is reflected in the sale of the product, which in turn will result in a change in the quality or the type of the program. All indications are that the American system of broadcasting has built the largest and the most loyal listening audience in the world.

The three major systems of broadcasting, as outlined very briefly here, have many variations. For example, the license-fee method of supporting radio is used in some countries where radio is state-owned. The amount of these fees naturally varies and is based on several factors. Among these are the distance of the receiver from the transmitter, the value of the receiving set, and whether it is operating in a public or a private place. The fee, usually in the form of an annual tax, varies roughly from $2 to $10 per year for sets in private homes, and from $3 to $15 for sets in public places. Some countries depend in part on contributions from listeners, the giving of public concerts, the management of talent, the sale of records, and other sources of income. There are even some countries in which two or more of these major systems of operation work side by side.

A detailed study of the various broadcasting systems cannot be made here. However, a general classification by way of summary may be made as follows:

Private ownership of facilities — the United States
Private ownership and public ownership existing side by side — Australia, Canada, and, before the war, France
Ownership and operation by the government — prewar Germany, prewar Italy, and the Soviet Union
Ownership and operation by a public corporation under government franchise — Great Britain
Technical operation by the state; programs produced by a state-controlled society — Sweden and Switzerland
Ownership and operation by an organization international in aspect — the League of Nations and the Vatican

Ownership by associations of listeners — the Netherlands

Ownership and operation by the government plus ownership of the receiving sets themselves, which are rented to listeners and are maintained and repaired by the government — Iceland

This variety of treatment of broadcasting reflects local differences in economic, cultural, and political life and indicates the complexity of the problem of dealing on a world-wide basis with this powerful force which, while national in origin, knows only scientific and not political boundaries. Broadcasting is so sensitive to changes in political control that this postwar period may see important departures from the foregoing analysis.

INTERNATIONAL ALLOCATION OF FREQUENCIES

By international convention or by agreements between governments the entire range of useful frequencies is divided and allocated to various types of services such as broadcasting, radio telephone, government services, amateur, ship communication, and airplane communication circuits, in order to channelize the services and avoid chaos. The first regulation on assignment of call letters to various countries came at the International Radiotelegraph Conference held at Berlin in 1906. The convention was signed on November 3, 1906, and was later ratified by the United States. Conventions in London in 1912, Washington in 1927, Madrid in 1932, and Cairo in 1938 successively changed and brought up to date the various subjects dealt with in the agreements. The Madrid Convention combined for the first time the radio-telegraph and telegraph conventions, which latter had previously been covered by separate conventions beginning with that of St. Petersburg in 1875.

In 1925, the International Broadcasting Union was formed in Geneva by representatives of various countries, semi-official bodies, and private organizations, to exchange information and co-ordinate the broadcasting interests of each. The IBU, or, as it is generally known by its French initials, the UIR (Union Internationale de Radiodiffusion), acts as a clearing house for international relations in radio, with its headquarters in Geneva.

Under the Madrid Convention, as modified by the Cairo regulations, the frequencies allocated to broadcasting throughout the world are from five hundred and fifty to fifteen hundred kilocycles. In addition, the 540-kilocycle channel was allocated for use in Canada, and the band from fifteen hundred to sixteen hundred kilocycles was made available for allocation in North America pursuant to agreements joined in by the governments in the region.

Owing to the characteristics of radio waves, broadcasting stations operating on the medium wave length, corresponding to frequencies between five hundred and forty kilocycles and sixteen hundred kilocycles are not subject to any significant amount of interference from stations located on other continents. However, in a single continent the interference between stations of various countries would make broadcasting impossible unless a detailed allocation of each specific frequency was agreed upon by the governments concerned. In Europe the allocation is effected by the European Broadcasting Convention of Lucerne (1933).

In North America the allocation of frequencies available to stations in Canada, the United States, Mexico, and Cuba was established in the Havana Treaty of 1937, which became effective on March 29, 1941. The frequencies allocated by the Havana Treaty are classified with various attendant restrictions, such as power, time of operation, and the location and number of stations to which they may be assigned for use.

The conventions and treaties do not grant licenses to particular persons or groups. They merely make certain frequencies available for assignment by each government for use by stations located in its territory and subject to its jurisdiction. The frequencies available for broadcasters in the United States, within the limits set by the Madrid Convention and the allocations made by the Havana Treaty, are assigned to various licensees by the Federal Communications Commission under the authority of the Federal Communications Act and in accordance with the regulations promulgated by the Commission.

Among the powers given the Federal Communications Commission by the Communications Act of 1934 are the authority to classify radio stations and prescribe the nature of the service to be rendered by each, to assign bands of frequencies to the various classes of stations, to assign frequencies for each individual station and determine the power and call letters which each station shall use and the time during which it may operate, and to make such regulations not inconsistent with law as it may deem necessary to prevent interference between stations in keeping with the provisions of the Act. The Commission is enjoined by the statute to study new uses for radio, to provide for experimental uses of frequencies, and generally to encourage the larger and more effective use of radio in the public interest. It also has authority to make special regulations applicable to radio stations engaged in network broadcasting, and to make general rules and regulations requiring stations to keep such records of programs, transmissions of energy, communications, or signals as it may deem desirable. In addition, it is authorized to prescribe the qualifications of station operators, to classify them according to the duties to be performed, to fix the forms of such licenses, and to issue them to such citizens of the United States as it finds qualified. The Commission is also empowered to make such rules and regulations and prescribe such restrictions and conditions, not inconsistent with law, as may be necessary to carry out the provisions of the Act, or of any international radio or wire communications treaty to which the United States is a party. Under the Act all radio stations in the United States must hold licenses issued by the Federal Communications Commission. At the present time such licenses are granted for a three-year term.

ALLOCATION OF FACILITIES

There are three classes of standard broadcast channels identified in the regulations of the FCC — clear, regional, and local.

A clear channel is one on which the dominant station or stations render service over wide areas, and which are cleared of objectionable interference within their primary service areas, and over all or a substantial portion of their secondary service areas. A regional channel is one on which several stations may operate with powers not in excess of five kilowatts; a local channel is one on which several stations may operate with powers not in excess of two hundred and fifty watts; the primary service area of a station operating on either such channel may be limited, as a consequence of interference, to a given field of intensity contour.

The stations which may be assigned to these available channels are classified in five groups — Class I, Class II, Class III, and Class IV, with Class III being subdivided into III-A and III-B. A Class I station is a dominant station operating on a clear channel and designed to render primary and secondary service over an extended area and at relatively long distances. Its primary service area is free from objectionable interference from other stations on the same and adjacent channels, and its secondary service area free from interference except from stations on the adjacent channel and from stations on the same channel in accordance with the channel designation in certain cases. The operating power of Class I stations is not less than ten kilowatts nor more than fifty kilowatts.

A Class II station is a secondary station which operates on a clear channel and is designed to render service over a primary service area which is limited by and subject to such interference as may be received from Class I stations. A station of this class operates with power of not less than two hundred and fifty watts nor more than fifty kilowatts. Whenever necessary, a Class II station must use a directional antenna or other means to avoid interference with Class I stations or other Class II stations.

A Class III station is one which operates on a regional channel and is designed to render service primarily to a metropolitan district; that is, a principal center of population in any locality and the rural area contiguous thereto. Class III stations are subdivided into two classes as indicated above. A Class III-A station operates with power of not less than one kilowatt nor more than five kilowatts, and its service area is subject to interference in accordance with the engineering standards of the Commission. A Class III-B station operates with power of not less than five hundred watts nor more than one kilowatt at night or five kilowatts during the daytime, and its service area is subject to interference in accordance with the Commission's standards.

A Class IV station is a station operating on a local channel and designed to render service primarily to a city or town and the suburban and rural areas contiguous thereto. The power of a station of this class shall not be less than one hundred watts nor more than two hundred and fifty watts and its service area is subject to a certain amount of interference in accordance with the Commission's regulations.

The several classes of standard broadcast stations are licensed to operate for unlimited time, limited time, daytime, on a shared-time basis, or for a specified number of hours.

Limited time is applicable to Class II (secondary) stations operating on a clear channel. It permits operation of the secondary station during daytime and until local sunset if located west of the dominant station on the same channel, or if located east thereof until sunset at the dominant station, and in addition during night hours, if any, not used by the dominant station on the channel. A daytime license permits operation during the hours between average monthly local sunrise and average monthly local sunset.

A shared time license permits operation during hours which are fixed by agreement with the one or more other stations using the same channel. A license for specified hours, as the description indicates, permits operation during only the exact hours specified in the license.

An authorization for a new standard broadcast station or an increase in facilities of an existing station will be issued only after a satisfactory showing has been made that the proposed assignment will tend to effect a fair, efficient, and equitable distribution of radio service among the several states and communities; that objectionable interference will not be caused to existing stations; or that if interference will be caused, the need for the proposed service outweighs the need for the service which will be lost by reason of such interference. In addition, it must be established that the proposed station will not suffer interference to such an extent that its service would be reduced to an unsatisfactory degree, and that the applicant is financially qualified to construct and operate the proposed station.

It must also be shown that the applicant is legally qualified; that the applicant, or the person or persons in control of an applicant corporation or other organization, is of good character and possesses other qualifications sufficient to provide a satisfactory public service; that the technical equipment proposed, the location of the transmitter, and other technical phases of operation comply with the regulations, and with the requirements of good engineering practice; and that the facilities sought are subject to assignment as requested under existing international agreements and the rules and regulations of the Commission. Furthermore, it is necessary to meet the over-all test of general welfare by showing that the public interest, convenience, and necessity will be served through operation under the proposed assignment.

CHAPTER 2

THE ORGANIZATION OF A BROADCASTING STATION

CONSIDERING American radio stations, big and little, any observer is bound to conclude that broadcasting is a functional business indeed. Regardless of a station's wattage, there is a pattern of similarity in the organization of them all, a pattern impressed by the basic requirements of broadcasting.

Form follows function, and in broadcasting the form of a station's organization follows the four-fold function of the broadcasting business. Any commercial station finds its organization divided to perform the duties of management, engineering, programming, and sales. In the higher wattage stations these functions are carried on by separate staffs, but even in a one-hundred-watter the functions are the same, although two or more of them may be performed by a single individual. The individual who does "everything around the place except sweep out the station" is a familiar figure in the low-power radio field, but the multiplicity of his jobs inevitably falls into the same kind of pattern that would be familiar around a big station.

Considering now the question of how an individual station comes into being and is organized thereafter, it is probable that in most cases management is the first factor. If it is necessary to decide which came first, the chicken or the egg, in this case it was probably the egg — as symbolic of the considerable nest egg that management and ownership must possess before attempting to enter the commercial broadcasting field. A fair gauge of this is the fact that it is not uncommon to hear of sale prices ranging upward to one hundred thousand dollars for going stations in the two hundred and fifty-watt class. Therefore, with physical properties of this value at stake, it is obvious that management must be vested in an individual of considerable business acumen. It is the responsibility of management to handle a station's fiscal affairs, to undertake the over-all supervision of its personnel, to negotiate whatever network contracts the station may enter into, to handle its labor situation, to make the necessary decisions for station expansion or improvement, to handle its affairs with the Federal Communications Commission, and to have an intimate knowledge of all functions in the broadcasting unit.

In a typical station setup engineering bulks large as a prime factor. It is a simple fact that a radio station cannot be operated without an FCC licensed engineer. In the early days of broadcasting, he was often a graduate from the amateur operator ranks. Today he is usually the product of a technical school, specifically trained in handling the complicated details that fall to the lot of a broadcasting engineer. In the final analysis, it is the engineer who determines whether or not a program goes on the air, and it is therefore vital that the closest liaison be maintained between his department and other branches of the broadcasting organization. He must be thoroughly familiar with everything that turns on, shuts off, or burns out around the station.

Programming is the next most vital category in station organization. With management having made a station possible through financing, and with engineering ready and able to put the station on the air, the station is still incapable of fulfilling its charter to serve the public interest, convenience, and necessity without adequate programming. As in the case of engineering, entire departments are concerned with this phase of broadcasting in larger stations. In a typical small station, the programming job may be a portion of the manager's duties, shared with other members of the staff. It is usual, however, to name some one individual as program manager and vest in him the decision as to what shall go on the air and at what time. Ideally, the program manager must have a good working knowledge of "show business"; it will be his job to decide what type of program will be of interest to local listeners, and then to arrange the details of script, talent, and program content necessary to put such programs on the air. He must have a good budgetary sense in order to work with the station's sales department to plan shows meeting the specific requirements of specific sponsors. He must also have a good working knowledge of several broadcast engineering factors, since the production of sound is his personal domain.

It is obvious, or should be, that it takes money to operate a broadcasting station. This money comes either from a subsidy, as in the case of the BBC, or from selling time on the air, as is the case of the American system. The sales unit, therefore, is that portion of a station organization most likely to keep the station on the air once broadcasting has begun. Whether or not a station will have an individual bearing the title of Sales Manager depends on its size. In smaller broadcasting units this title may be one of several held by an individual member of the staff, although everyone from the office boy to the manager may have some participation in making time sales.

It is obvious in smaller stations that there is considerable overlapping between these various functions; it is interesting to note that this overlapping obtains to a degree even in major network organizations. This simply emphasizes the fact that the various operations of a broadcasting organization are very closely knit and are highly interdependent upon one another.

Considered in the mass, there seems to be an infinity of differentiation between the more than nine hundred radio broadcasting stations in the United States. However, for all practical purposes these stations can be considered from an organizational standpoint by breaking them down into three different groups — non-affiliated commercial stations, stations with network affiliations, and stations maintained by educational and religious organizations and often operated on a non-commercial basis. Station organization within these various groups will now be considered.

Non-Affiliated Commercial Stations

Stations not affiliated with any network range in power from one hundred to one thousand watts, though, generally speaking, they average from one hundred to two hundred and fifty watts and cover small areas in their listening range.

Out of the 913 stations in the United States, slightly fewer than one-fourth, or 212, are not affiliated with the major networks. However, a number of those 212 are affiliated with state networks composed of stations of similar power. All these small stations share time with stations operating in other sections of the country, and many of them are on the air for limited times, often only from sunup to sundown.

In the main, these small stations attempt to serve only their own communities and act as an advertising medium for the local merchant. All their income is derived from this source and from such national spot advertising as comes their way.[1] The income of the small station is not large, but neither are its costs, and such a station is likely to make a comfortable profit. The local merchant has found this means of advertising very effective, and the local housewife becomes as dependent on radio advertisements for bargain news as she is on the newspaper.

While program sources are not as accessible to the small station as to the large, the program director can build a varied schedule through the use of transcriptions and recordings and of a staff pianist or a hillbilly trio as the occasion demands. News, too, is accessible through arrangement with the local paper or through subscription to one of the national press services, such as the International News Service or the United Press Service. Another standard feature of any station is the woman's program, broadcast by a staff member. This feature can readily become an important service to the women in the community as well as a distinct asset to the station.[2]

Any small non-affiliated station has, of course, more time to make available to local, civic, and community groups than does the larger affiliated station. The possibilities of presenting educational and cultural programs of real information and service are endless. By working with all types of organizations, a well-rounded public service program can easily be developed.[3]

[1] See Chapter 18 for information on spot advertising.
[2] See Chapter 9 on Women's Programs.
[3] See Chapter 11.

WLDS JACKSONVILLE, ILLINOIS
250 WATTS

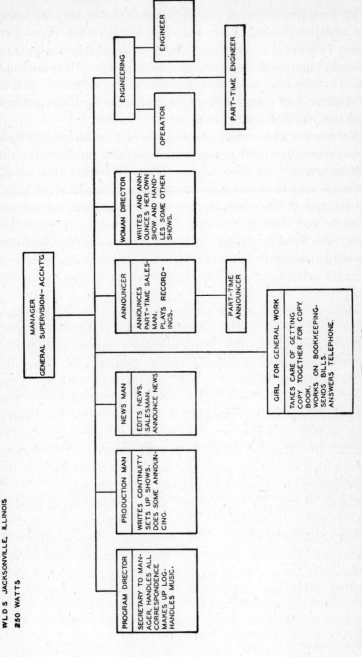

Figure 1

The organization of a typical two-hundred-and-fifty-watt station is shown in the chart of station WLDS at Jacksonville, Illinois (Figure 1). Here the owner of the station acts also as the manager, with over-all supervision of every function and activity, including programming. While his secretary, in this instance, also acts as the program director, the owner directs her activities. The secretary is also responsible for making up the log sheet and handling the music and its clearance as well as for taking care of all correspondence. The production man writes continuity, sets up shows, and does some announcing; the announcer is a part-time salesman and plays recordings; the newsman is also a salesman as well as editor and announcer of the news. The value of working on a small station is the opportunity it offers to learn every part of the radio business through handling all types of jobs.

NETWORK-AFFILIATED STATIONS

Stations with network affiliations may differ only slightly from non-affiliates, depending, of course, on their power and the size of the community they serve. At this writing there are six hundred and fifty-five stations affiliated with one or the other of the four major networks. The breakdown finds NBC with one hundred and forty-four affiliates; Columbia with one hundred and forty-six; the ABC has one hundred and ninety and Mutual lists two hundred and twenty-one.[4] About fifty stations of the total are affiliated with more than one of the national networks at the same time. This dual affiliation is made possible under recent FCC regulations designed to permit a station multiple affiliations if it so desires.

In the lower power brackets there are at least two points of difference discernible between affiliated and non-affiliated stations. The word "traffic" starts taking on more importance, and some member of the staff will have a good-sized job keeping up with the constant flood of communications from and to the network, dealing with program offerings, timing, cues,

[4] These figures vary slightly between day and night operation.

availabilities, and a hundred other items connected with the traffic or movement of shows along the network.[5]

Programming usually presents the second point of difference from an organizational standpoint, and can be either a simple or complicated phase of staff activity depending on how the individual station chooses to operate. It is obvious that the program function of an affiliated station can be very simple if the station elects to be programmed entirely by the network. However, most stations have a logical desire to establish identity as a servant of the community, and the program manager's job can become a highly specialized and time-consuming activity if the station desires to maintain a standard of program excellence reasonably comparable to its network offerings.

There is, of course, less time to fill locally on a network-affiliated station, as the network programs, commercial or sustaining, will undoubtedly consume at least six hours of the station's daily time, depending on the length of time the station is on the air.

In the larger stations, those from five kilowatts to fifty kilowatts, the organization becomes more complicated. Program standards are higher; there is more likelihood of the station's building programs approximating network caliber if such stations are in an area where talent is available, such as Chicago, Cincinnati, Denver, Dallas, Nashville, and so on. An increase in power always carries with it the added responsibility of serving a larger listening audience with more varied tastes and interests. The competition is greater, as usually there will be more than one high-powered station within the region, and program directors are, therefore, forced to greater creative efforts. In Nashville, for example, station WSM has long been conscious of its obligation, not only to Nashville and the surrounding territory, but also to the country as a whole, and has held the same high standards in program building as are held by the networks themselves. As a result, many of the station's programs have become weekly network features. The same

[5] See Chapter 24 on Communications and Traffic.

holds true of station WJR in Detroit, station KYW in Philadelphia, and a dozen others which might be mentioned.

In the building of programs of network caliber, the station
has made it possible for the sales department of either the
station itself or of the network to sell such program to national
advertisers for release on the networks. The "Grand Old Opry"
of WSM and the "Lone Ranger" of WXYZ are cases in point.
Both programs originated with the local stations and attained
such popularity within their own listening area that it was
only natural that the station should seek a larger audience; the
result was national sponsorship for the programs over a coast-
to-coast hookup of long years' duration.

RELIGIOUS STATIONS

There are in the United States today fourteen radio stations
owned by religious organizations. Most were established to
further the doctrine of the faith held by the group responsible
for the station, and they are serving the adherents to
their faith with a varied program of inspiration, information, and entertainment. In some instances, these stations
sell time for commercial programs to help defray the
costs of operation. In other cases, the license is still held by
the religious group, but the station is managed and operated
entirely by other interests. Such a station is WWL of New
Orleans, owned by the Jesuits of Loyola University, but managed by W. H. Summerville. On the other hand, WMBI is
owned and operated entirely by the Moody Bible Institute in
Chicago, all the program offerings being religious, inspira-
tional, or informational in nature. The cost of operation is
borne entirely by funds appropriated by the Institute or by
gifts from interested listeners. The chart on page 24 shows
the station's simplicity of organization as compared with a
station selling time and having network affiliation.

WMBI — 5000 Watts, 1110 kc.
WDIM — 1000 Watts, 47.5 meg.

Stations Owned and Operated by the Moody Bible Institute

Non-commercial. Types of programs include sacred and classical music, talks, dramatizations, church services, news, educational features, etc.

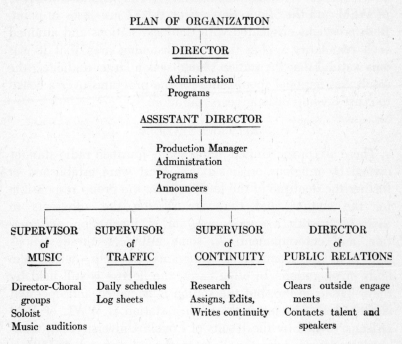

PLAN OF ORGANIZATION

DIRECTOR

Administration
Programs

ASSISTANT DIRECTOR

Production Manager
Administration
Programs
Announcers

SUPERVISOR of MUSIC	SUPERVISOR of TRAFFIC	SUPERVISOR of CONTINUITY	DIRECTOR of PUBLIC RELATIONS
Director-Choral groups	Daily schedules	Research	Clears outside engagements
Soloist	Log sheets	Assigns, Edits,	Contacts talent and
Music auditions		Writes continuity	speakers

PERSONNEL

1. STAFF — 10
2. ANNOUNCERS — 10
3. WRITERS — 7
4. MUSIC TALENT — 85
5. SECRETARY AND TYPISTS — 7
6. STUDIO ASSISTANTS — 5

LIST OF RADIO STATIONS OWNED BY RELIGIOUS INSTITUTIONS IN THE UNITED STATES

STATE	CITY	STATION	FREQ.	POWER	OWNER
CALIFORNIA	Los Angeles	KFSG	1150	2,500–LS	Echo Park Evangelistic Assn.
	Pasadena	KPPC	1240	100	Presbyterian Church
COLORADO	Denver	KPOF	910	1,000	Pillar of Fire
ILLINOIS	Chicago	WMBI	1110	5,000	Moody Bible Institute
IOWA	Boone	KFGQ	1260	250–D	Boone Biblical College
LOUISIANA	New Orleans	WWL	870	50,000	Loyola University
MICHIGAN	Lapeer	WMPC	1230	250	Liberty Street Gospel Church
MISSOURI	St. Louis	KFUO	850	5,000	Evangelical Lutheran Synod
NEW JERSEY	Zarephath	WAWZ	1380	5,000–LS 1,000–N	Pillar of Fire
NEW YORK	Brooklyn	WBBR	1330	1,000	Watchtower Bible and Tract Society
VIRGINIA	Richmond	WBBL	1240	100	Grace Covenant Presbyterian Church
WASHINGTON	Seattle	KTW	1380	1,000	First Presbyterian Church
WISCONSIN	Appleton	WHBY	1230	250	Fr. James Wagner
	Green Bay	WTAQ	1360	5,000	Fr. James Wagner

CHAPTER 3

THE ORGANIZATION OF A NETWORK

RADIO NETWORK broadcasting probably dates from January 4, 1923, when a land line telephone circuit was used to hook up WEAF in New York and WNAC in Boston for an experimental broadcast heard in both cities at the same time. This was the first attempt to achieve the mass audience which is one of the major factors responsible for the success of network broadcasting today. However, possibly due to the fact that the potentialities of network operation were not realized at the time, the mass of the listening public had to wait nearly four years before anything resembling a regular network was established.

Throughout the remainder of 1923 and sporadically through the years until mid-December of 1926, network hookups were attempted on something like a catch-as-catch-can basis. President Harding's start on a westward tour, the inauguration of Calvin Coolidge carried on a twenty-four-station hookup in 1925, and the Dempsey-Tunney world championship fight in 1926 were characteristic of the events for which these informal early networks were hurriedly thrown together.

On November 1, 1926 the National Broadcasting Company was organized as the first radio network service, and on the following January 1 NBC carried the Rose Bowl game from Pasadena, California as the first established network program in radio history. At the time, NBC had two stations of its own, WEAF and WJZ, both in New York City. The remainder of the network was composed of independent stations scattered from coast to coast and connected to the broadcasting company only by virtue of signed agreements to take a stipulated number of programs from the network. This is the pattern on which other networks have subsequently been formed, and it can be used to serve as a definition — a radio network is a business

NATIONAL BROADCASTING COMPANY, INC.

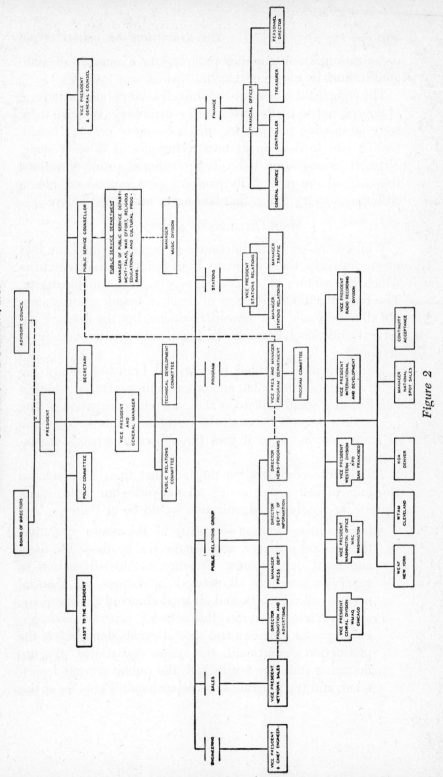

Figure 2

organization which supplies programs to a number of affiliated stations by means of telephone wires.

The complexities of a network broadcasting organization are,
of course, not so easily stated as the definition. Because there
were no existing patterns for such a business, network broadcasting had to develop its own techniques as it went along.
Network organization today is a combined result of shrewd
thinking on the part of its pioneers, plus experience, plus a
willingness to try things that had never been tried before.

Main Divisions of a Network

While there are some differences in organization of the four
major networks, there are many basic points of similarity from
which the picture of a network organization can be drawn.
The four functional elements of a single broadcasting station
are all to be found in a network company, but the network has
several additional branches to handle its greater variety of
activity.

Management is divided into several branches as are the
fields of engineering, sales, and programming. Traffic, which is
handled at a small affiliate as the part-time occupation of one
person, in a network becomes the vastly important full-time job
of many people. Thus it goes throughout a network organization.

Taking into consideration the fact that there are essential
elements of difference among all networks, an approximate
pattern for a network organization would be as follows:

Administrative Division — consists of the major executive,
the general manager, and usually the heads of the fiscal
and legal departments. Function of this division is to
supervise generally all network operations, all financial
matters, all contracts, and all legal affairs of the company.

Program Division — under the network program manager,
encompasses the news and special events department, the
production department, the script department, the announcing staff, the music staff, the public service department, and the program sales department. Function of this

division is to plan, produce, and schedule the network's programs, to supervise all programs heard on the network but produced by outside agencies, to determine the policies which govern broadcasts for the network, to supervise employment and payment of talent, and to provide for the writing or purchase of all needed script.

Sales Division — divides itself into two specialized departments, each under individual management, but with both reporting to one general sales manager. The two subdivisions are network sales department and the local and spot sales department. The network sales department is responsible for time sales to national advertisers. The local and spot sales department handles local station business for the network's own stations, much in the same manner that an independent station would sell its time locally as distinct from network time.

Engineering Division — under divisional management, is divided into studio and field engineering, transmitter engineering, research and development, and maintenance engineering. It is responsible for everything that happens between microphone and loud-speaker.

Public Relations Division — This is a grouping of several departments, all of which are concerned with the impact which the network and its programs makes on the radio audience, the advertiser, and the public in general. Under this general heading, although not necessarily under the same general management, come the press department, the promotion department, the guest relations department, and the audience relations department. The chief duty of the press department is to keep the reading public informed about the network, its programs, and its performers. The promotion and advertising department has the function of presenting the network and its services to the trade groups and, through various advertising media, to the public in general. Guest relations is concerned with the monumental job of caring for the scores of visitors who come to the key stations of the network; and audience relations has a multiplicity of jobs concerned with the listening public, not the least of which is handling the vast collection of fan mail which comes to a network every year.

Station Relations Division — This is exclusively a network operation, developed to maintain a vital liaison between the network and its affiliates aside from fiscal affairs. Work of the traffic department is generally classified as an operation of station relations, since this department must maintain daily close co-operation with the affiliates in order that program schedules may be maintained.

Office Management Division — As distinct from network management as represented in the administrative group, networks employ numerous business personnel, have routine business office requirements, and need routine business supplies and services. All functions which would be common to any large business institution are common to a network's office management division.

These are the major divisions of almost any network broadcasting organization. In the main, they will be found fairly typical of the ABC and CBS as well as NBC. There are several points of variation in Mutual due to the peculiarity of this particular network operation. Instead of being set up as a nation-wide production and time-marketing agency under a national management and with all associated employees working for the same firm, Mutual operates in large part as a function of its affiliated members. From point to point along its network it depends on the sales and production functions of its individual affiliates.

There are many other subdivisions of a network organization, such as the placement, records, and employee relations groups that fall within the scope of the NBC personnel department. In the main, these are branches of organization likely to be found in any large business and are not peculiar to broadcasting alone, so they will not be discussed here.

WHAT CONSTITUTES THE NET?

One key item of network operation which has not been discussed up to this point is found in the question of what makes the net in the network? Going back to the original definition, we used the words "supplies . . . programs . . . by means of telephone wires." [1] These wires, owned by the American Telephone and Telegraph Company, form the network which carries the programs from station to station across the country.

This arrangement for carrying programs has existed since the earliest days of network broadcasting. At one time, the Telephone Company itself was in the broadcasting business and WEAF, original key station of the NBC Red network, was a property of AT&T before the formation of NBC. Originally, established long-distance lines were used to carry the programs, but with the further development of broadcasting on a network plan, specially engineered wire circuits were leased on a reasonably permanent basis for the exclusive use of broadcast operations. Rental of these lines represents a considerable part of a network's operating cost. In a single month NBC's bill for this wire service is approximately $300,000.

The process of growing up to such a monthly telephone bill as this looks logical and orderly in retrospect, but its actual development was a point to point evolution based on the practical necessities of the moment. No network has ever sprung to life fully developed. The ABC is a possible exception, since it was detached as a successful unit of the parent National Broadcasting Company in 1942. However, even in this case there are great differences in the ABC today as compared with the form it took when it was originally set up as an independent unit. Some study of network broadcasting growth is essential for an understanding of how network organizations developed.

As originally construed by practically all operators, broadcasting stations were usually set up to advertise a service or a product of the individual broadcaster. One of the first experiments in the sale of time to an outside interest was the AT&T sale of air time to the Queensboro Corporation, a Long Island real estate firm, for the reported sum of $100. This program

[1] Chapter 3, page 28.

was heard on August 28, 1922. In a comparatively short time, other business firms, realizing the potentialities of this new medium, were clamoring to purchase time on the air; and the broadcasting industry for the first time seemed to have an answer to the question, "How is broadcasting going to be financed?"

The next step in the progression was brought about by requests for time from advertisers with national distribution. Advertisers in this group were interested in having their programs heard across the country wherever there was adequate local distribution of their product. While this desire was natural, the goal was not very easy to attain. Local stations more often than not had their program schedules filled with favorite features and could not always find it convenient to change those schedules to accept a network program. It was obvious that some arrangement had to be made between the network and individual stations, so that the network could guarantee that an advertiser would be able to purchase a specific group of stations at a specific time.

This necessity led to the establishment of affiliation contracts under which the stations granted the network the right to use the station as an outlet during certain hours of the day and evening. While this seemed to solve one problem, it immediately presented another. Since wire-line facilities were set up on a permanent basis through certain cities, it was obvious that there would be a loss of revenue to intermediate stations if a sponsor chose to have his program heard only on the key stations in New York, Cleveland, and Chicago. Such an arrangement also produced dissatisfaction on the part of stations that wanted a national program of high quality but were not able to get it. To overcome this situation, NBC set up a so-called "basic" network, composed of stations in twenty cities, and any advertiser buying time on the network had to take all twenty stations as a nucleus for any network program.

Eventually, telephone line facilities were extended to the Pacific coast and also north and south from the network's key points, so that today a sponsor may purchase radio time to cover every state in the Union. Usually the size of a sponsor's network has a direct bearing on the distribution of his product. Hence, it is a general practice to purchase time on a full network of stations if the product advertised has national distribution. In cases where a product has only sectional distribution, a sponsor usually purchases time on the basic network plus such supplementary "legs" of the network as may be most closely co-ordinated with his distribution area. It is also a general rule that sponsors expand to additional legs of the network as the area of product distribution increases.

CONTRACTUAL RELATIONSHIPS BETWEEN A NETWORK AND AFFILIATED STATIONS

It seems appropriate at this point to discuss the general subject of the contractual relationships that exist between networks and their affiliated stations, since these contracts are the business links that make the network a network.

Under the rules of the FCC such affiliation contracts may not exceed two years in length. The purpose of such contracts is to make available to the network a certain number of hours per day at designated times. The contract between a network and an individual affiliate also establishes the rate of compensation which the network pays the station for portions of its time sold commercially. The network also agrees to supply the affiliate with program service covering a specific number of hours each day. Such program service contains both commercial and sustaining programs. In the case of commercial offerings, the station is required to accept the program if it falls specifically within the period of the day covered by the affiliation contract. It may or may not accept the sustaining offerings, either within the hours of contract coverage or at other times during the broadcasting day.

The rate which an individual station charges usually varies in direct proportion to the size of its audience. Various factors are considered in establishing the rate, however. The power of the station, its geographic location, the electrical and physical conditions of the surrounding terrain, the density and type

of population in the area, and the general popularity of the
station's programs all enter into the decision. It is customary
in commercial broadcasting to evaluate the total effect of all
these elements by conducting surveys among the people in the
station territory. Two or more stations operating within the
same area may have entirely different coverage and popularity
ratings, and only by actual measurement of the audience can
a true basis for a station's commercial rate structure be established. Methods of audience measurement will be discussed in
greater detail in Chapter 20.

Prior to the ruling of the federal court in 1943 which upheld
the FCC Network Regulation promulgated on May 2, 1941, the
networks had exclusive arrangements with stations; that is,
when a station became an affiliate of one of the networks,
it agreed thereby not to permit the sale of its time by any other
network. This arrangement was adhered to by practically all
the stations affiliated with the networks other than Mutual.
The FCC, fearing that such an arrangement might work a hard-
ship on some stations, forbade the use of the exclusive clause;
and it is possible, therefore, for any station to signify its willingness to accept programs from any of the networks. By and
large, however, most of the stations which have heretofore been
associated with a certain network continue that association
though they are not now bound to do so.

The network regulations of the FCC also forbade stations
to obtain commitments from a network not to make its program
service available to other stations in the same market. They
prohibited affiliation contracts of longer duration than two
years and contracts which tended to deprive an affiliate of its
discretion in passing on the public-interest value of network
programs sent to it, or which would limit in any way the
station's right to fix its local rate.

Other regulations forbade the operation of two networks by
any organization, or the ownership by a network of two stations
in one market, or of one station in a market in which ownership
by the network might constitute an unfair economic advantage.

Originally the network regulations prohibited stations from

giving options on any period of time. This would have eliminated the so-called network option-time system. Under this system stations had made a practice of granting options to networks on periods of time between certain hours of the day or up to a specified maximum throughout each day. For example, NBC network option time was from 1:00 A.M. to 12:00 Noon, 3:00 P.M. to 6:00 P.M., 7:00 to 7:30 P.M., and 8:00 to 11:00 P.M. on weekdays, and from 1:00 to 4:00 P.M., 5:00 to 6:00 P.M., and 7:00 to 11:00 P.M. on Sundays. In the case of CBS the option time was not confined to any specific portion of the clock, but an over-all limit per week was placed on the amount of time the network could obtain under the option.

After further consideration of the problem the FCC modified the regulations to the extent of providing for a modified form of option time. The day is divided into four segments, namely 8:00 A.M. to 1:00 P.M., 1:00 to 6:00 P.M., 6:00 to 11:00 P.M., and 11:00 P.M. to 6:00 A.M. The station may grant to networks what are termed "non-exclusive options" on not more than a total of three hours within each of these segments. In practice, then, non-exclusive options amount to a right on the part of a network to have its network programs considered first by an affiliated station to which they are offered. Time other than network option time is called "station time."

The networks must now make special arrangements in each case with affiliates for the sale of any programs. The stations can, if they so desire and deem it within the public interest to do so, sell more than the specified three hours to any network and may, therefore, sell some of their "station time." This is especially advantageous when high-quality programs are available to a station that finds it difficult to build good local programs, or when it is difficult to sell the time locally.

A network, of course, endeavors to secure affiliates located strategically in various parts of the country, so that all areas of the population are covered. It will be found, therefore, that any network will, in all probability, have affiliated stations in the majority of the large cities from coast to coast and in all other areas where population warrants it. There are some stations, however, small in power and limited in coverage, which are not affiliated with any network and find through lack of availability of talent an inability to command as large an audience as they had hoped for. It is often possible for these stations to make arrangements with a network to become affiliated on a "bonus" basis. "Bonus" stations are, therefore, those stations that cover a limited area, pay their own facilities costs (the telephone wires from their stations to the nearest network affiliate), and receive no fee from the network for time used by the network for commercial programs. Through this arrangement, a small station is able to build prestige and render a public service to the listener within its coverage range, thereby enlarging its audience. Eventually such stations arrive at the point where their coverage justifies an increase in rates large enough to make it worth while for the network to accept the stations on a regular affiliated basis.

The network organizations have contracts with the various broadcasting stations comprising the network which under the usual arrangement, provide for the payment by the network to the station of a percentage of the rates established for the station for the use of its facilities. The network, in turn, makes a time charge to the advertiser using the network facilities which is composed of the total of the applicable charges established by all the stations on the network which are used. This total time charge is subject to such discounts as may be established by the network for quantity or continuity of use. In addition, since practically all advertising is placed through advertising agencies, the charge is subject to an advertising commission at a rate of 15 per cent. The amount which is left after deducting from the gross charge to the advertiser the various discounts, the agency commission, and the payment by the network to the station under the affiliation contract, is retained by the network organization to cover its own operating expenses, including such specific items as the lease of the wire-line facilities connecting the stations,[2] the production of sustaining programs, and the maintenance of the manifold necessary activities such as engineering, research and development,

---

[2] Some networks require the station to pay its own network circuit costs.

program planning, network sales efforts, and the maintenance and improvement of large studio facilities for the origination of the network programs.

The number of network programs carried by each station on a network varies, but a substantial amount of the station's time is available for its own local sustaining programs and for commercial programs which are sponsored either locally or over a regional network with which the station may be affiliated. The revenue of the individual station with network affiliation, therefore, is made up of the receipts from its own sale of its time locally and its share of the receipts of the network or networks with which it is affiliated.

Each station is free to fix its own charges for the use of its facilities. The usual arrangement involves the placing of a value on one hour in the evening and then making the charge for shorter periods of time and for periods of time in other parts of the day bear a percentage relationship to the one-hour evening rate. Most common is considering a half hour as equivalent to 60 per cent of one hour and 15 minutes as equivalent to 40 per cent of an hour. Daytime rates, for time prior to 6:00 P.M. local time, are usually one half of the evening rates, and other multipliers such as one third and three quarters are used for other parts of the day in some cases. The variety of these charges and the amounts in which they are fixed are entirely independent of government regulation. The operation of a broadcasting station is a private business within the framework of the Communications Act, in contrast to the operation of a telephone or telegraph company, which are common carriers whose rates are subject to regulation by the Federal Communications Commission.

The relationship between the charges made for various services of a station and the discounts which are allowed for the quantity of use or the continuity of use are not subject to the laws relating to price control, either from the standpoint of the establishment of so-called ceiling prices or, as under the Robinson-Patman Act, from the standpoint of making reductions in price to large users depend upon the amount of the reduction in cost involved. It is likely, however, that unequal treatment

of advertisers using the same type and amount of service would
be an unfair practice under the federal Fair Trade Act. Therefore, having established charges at any particular time, the
broadcaster's duty with respect to such charges is merely to
apply them equally to all advertisers who use the same type
and amount of service. Since this constitutes no more than
sound business practice, it is readily apparent that the widest
possible latitude is given to American broadcasters in this
respect.

THE BENEFITS OF NETWORK ORGANIZATION

As the study of station and network rate cards will reveal, it
is obvious that an affiliate receives less for the sale of its time
to the network than the same station would receive if it sold
the air time to an advertiser direct. However, there are positive
benefits to the station from its network affiliation, and in scope
these are sufficient to offset any seeming disparity in the
amounts of money received from sales to the network as compared to direct time sales.

One of the major benefits of such an affiliation is that the
station is enabled to sell a far greater portion of its daily time
than would be possible otherwise. Equally important is the
fact that it would be practically impossible for most local
stations to produce shows as large in caliber or fine in quality
as the productions that are possible on a network. This latter
fact is true of both commercial and sustaining ventures – a
glance at the annual talent bill for any network will reveal the
fact that it usually bulks larger than the combined annual income of several of its leading affiliates. With a central network
organization and a large budget, events of national importance
can be delivered to a local station for only a small fraction of
the cost that would be entailed if the station were to attempt
such coverage by itself. The station therefore is able to receive
credit because of having rendered better service to its listeners
– a vital and ponderable fact in the success story of any radio
station.

Another point worth noting is that the delivery of network
service is not all one-sided. Under a network organization, it is

possible for many a local station to acquire national note by providing special broadcast features for airing on other stations of the network. Network pickups are by no means limited to what might be considered the national talent centers. Thus, in the case of NBC's "Grand Old Opry," as already mentioned, the national listening audience knows that WSM, Nashville, Tennessee is the point of program origin. Hence, WSM acquires fame far beyond its primary radiating area.

One benefit generally appreciated by the affiliates, but not readily apparent from the outside, is found in what might be termed the "relief" factor. Since the network program schedule considerably relieves the pressure on local production managers, production men at the affiliated stations are able to give more time to the consideration of whatever individual local program problems may exist. The net result is that local program quality tends toward a higher plane of content and performance than would be possible if the harried program manager were responsible for creating all details of the entire broadcasting day.

As any "D-Day," "VE-Day," or "VJ-Day" listener can testify, radio acquitted itself magnificently on the score of world-wide news coverage. This performance record was possible only because of network organization. No single station in the United States could have underwritten the cost entailed in any one of those days' service, let alone the continuing cost of news coverage that was maintained by the networks as a daily wartime routine. In other words, the maintenance of a world-wide news organization is one of the benefits of network affiliation.

To summarize, the direct benefits of network affiliation include better talent and programs, better listener service, a chance for a local station to become known nationally, relief and time to develop better local programs, opportunity to use the services of a world-wide news staff, fewer problems from a time-sales standpoint, and lower talent and production costs.

To conclude this chapter on network organization, a chart of the National Broadcasting Company is shown in Figure 2. It gives a fair idea of the scope of this network's activities and is fairly representative of the organization plan followed by both CBS and the Blue.

CHAPTER 4

CONTROL OF BROADCASTING

SOUND POLICIES are the foundation of every successful business. This is especially true in broadcasting, for a radio station has but little opportunity to avoid criticism of its policies. What it broadcasts is audible to all who can receive its signals, and the policies underlying those broadcasts are correspondingly apparent. The policies are subject, therefore, to the appraisal of a group of critics of widely diverse sentiments and qualifications.

Radio stations are licensed by the Federal Communications Commission to operate pursuant to a showing that the licenses will serve the "public interest, convenience, or necessity," and the renewal of those licenses is dependent upon the same test applied to what has been done in actual practice. The words "public interest, convenience, or necessity" are not defined by statute, and they present somewhat the same difficulty in definition as the word "reasonable." The phrase may be regarded as approximately equivalent to "the welfare of a substantial portion of the population regularly to be served."

The "public interest, convenience, or necessity" test, like the Golden Rule, is readily subscribed to and generally approved. However, in practice it is often extremely difficult to decide whether a particular action will meet the test, and for that reason it is necessary for the management of a broadcasting station to formulate a set of policies which will clearly express the management's conception of what is right and what is wrong. Such a statement of policies serves to guide not only the management and the employees of the station but also the commercial program producers, advertising agencies, and advertisers who use the station's facilities.

There are some policies which are imposed by law and are, therefore, clearly mandatory upon the station. The Communications Act itself establishes certain specific requirements which must be a part of any station's policy. For example, Section 315 of the Communications Act requires impartial treatment by the station in making its facilities available to candidates for public office, and Section 316 of the Act prohibits the broadcasting of any information concerning lotteries or contests offering prizes determined upon the basis of chance.

These and other provisions of the Act are in turn amplified in certain respects by the Rules and Regulations of the Federal Communications Commission. In the case of candidates for public office, the regulations define the terms used in the statute, set up a procedure for the keeping of records by stations concerning political broadcasts, and emphasize that the rates charged shall be uniform. However, even under the regulations, which are quite specific, interpretations by the licensee are continually necessary in the light of each political campaign and each station's rate structure and practices.

Based on an analysis of this and comparable problems, it may be said that the source of a broadcaster's decision on a matter of policy as to any particular question may lie in one or more of the following:

1. The Federal Communications Act
2. The regulations of the Federal Communications Commission
3. The federal and state laws applicable in the states in which the studio and transmitter are located and in those states regularly served by the station
4. The Code of the National Association of Broadcasters
5. The postal regulations, insofar as an incidental use of the mails is anticipated
6. In wartime, the Code of Wartime Practices issued by the Office of Censorship and the regulations of the Office of War Information and of the military services
7. The broadcaster's own statement of policies

In short, it is good policy to observe all the rules of the game, and in broadcasting the principal rules of the game are found in the applicable statutes, regulations, and statements of policy. The salient policies required by each of the seven sources itemized above will now be considered.

THE FEDERAL COMMUNICATIONS ACT

Political Broadcasts. Section 315 of the Communications Act requires that if a candidate for public office is permitted to use a broadcasting station, equal treatment must be accorded to all other candidates for the same office. The text of this section is:

> If any licensee shall permit any person who is a legally qualified candidate for any public office to use a broadcasting station, he shall afford equal opportunities to all other such candidates for that office in the use of such broadcasting station, and the Commission shall make rules and regulations to carry this provision into effect: Provided, That such licensee shall have no power of censorship over the material broadcast under the provisions of this section. No obligation is hereby imposed upon any licensee to allow the use of its station by any such candidate.

A careful reading of this section reveals certain important questions which are answered in part in the regulations of the Federal Communications Commission, dealt with in the next section of this chapter.

Contests. Section 316 of the Act prohibits the broadcasting of any information concerning "any lottery, gift enterprise, or similar scheme offering prizes dependent in whole or in part upon lot or chance, or any list of the prizes drawn . . . " This prohibition is not amplified in the regulations of the FCC. The determination of whether a proposed radio contest is acceptable for broadcast is essentially a legal question and one that would ordinarily involve a comparison of the proposed contest with plans which have been found lawful or unlawful by courts under the statute. No cases have been decided under Section 316 of the Commission's Act; nevertheless, guidance is available from the decisions whch have been rendered under a corresponding statute in the U.S. Criminal Code dealing with matter sent through the mail. Of these cases there are many, and as a practical matter, even though the Post Office Department has no jurisdiction over broadcasting, the attitude of the Post Office Department toward contests in general is given great weight in considering contests proposed for radio. One reason for this is that most radio contests involve the incidental use of the mails, and even though the FCC should not take action with respect to a particular contest, the Post Office Department might step in and refuse to handle any mail concerning or resulting from the contest, thereby upsetting costly plans at a late hour in the campaign.

It is difficult to give general rules which will adequately cover the many variations devised by the authors of radio contests. Basically, it should be remembered that there are three elements of an illegal contest. They are:

1. Consideration
2. Chance
3. Prize

By consideration is meant the doing by contestants of something which they are not bound to do. Normally this involves the expenditure of money, but consideration may also result from the expenditure of effort, and according to some views it may even be composed of a benefit flowing to the sponsor of the contest. This latter contention, that a benefit flowing to the sponsor is consideration, is not generally subscribed to, but it is important to note that whether or not consideration is found to exist depends as a practical matter upon how much chance is involved in the contest.

The question of whether chance exists is fascinating, and in many cases it is difficult to determine. At one extreme is the clear-cut case of chance in the drawing of numbers from a hat. At the other extreme is the quiz program or the written examination. The criticism may be made that chance is present in any written examination because of the possibility that some contestants may happen to be asked questions familiar to them and thus be enabled by luck to do better than others in the contest. It is generally felt that this objection is specious and that there is a certain amount of chance in all undertakings, which must be regarded as merely incidental and negligible. Between these two extremes there is a wide variation in the degree of chance present. In each case, the rules of the contest must be studied with a view to two principal factors — the extent to which chance enters into the determination of the outcome of the contest, and also the nature of the consideration which is required of the contestants to enable them to enter. A contest which clearly requires no expenditure on the part of the contestant will usually be acceptable even though chance is present to some degree, whereas a contest requiring the purchase of goods or the sending in of money must be very carefully scrutinized to see that practically no chance is involved. On this score it is generally conceded that the writing of letters or slogans, if they are conscientiously judged, does not involve the element of chance even though there is, as a practical matter, some chance present by virtue of the personality of the judges, the correct anticipation of exactly what the judges are seeking, and the possible misrouting of entries before they reach the sponsor or while they are in his hands.

Identification of Sponsorship. Section 317 of the Communications Act requires that all commercial programs, defined as those for which "money or any other valuable consideration is directly or indirectly paid, or promised to or charged or accepted by the station" must be announced as paid for or furnished, as the case may be, by the person paying for the program or furnishing the program. This section has not often been called into play, because the obvious purpose of the vast majority of sponsored programs is to call attention to the sponsor and his product. However, there are cases in which persons have wished to sponsor broadcast programs anonymously, and it would be a clear violation of the Act not to mention the fact of sponsorship and to identify the sponsor.

The problem of anonymity has serious implications in the case of propaganda material of one kind or another, political or economic. Propaganda labeled as to source is immediately suspected and is viewed askance by the very people whom it is designed to influence.

A question which might be raised under this section with respect to regular commercial programs is whether it is suffi-cient to refer to the product or service only and not give the sponsor's name. Brand names play a highly important rôle in American advertising. In many cases listeners and users of a product do not know the actual name of the manufacturer or distributor of the product. They order it by its brand name because they see it and hear it advertised as such. It is gen-erally satisfactory to permit the identification of sponsorship in such cases to consist of the mention of the product and not to require that the exact firm or corporate name of the sponsor be formally announced.

Other Problems

Section 325 prohibits the broadcasting of any false or fraud-ulent signal of distress, and it also prohibits the rebroadcasting by any station of any part of the program of another broad-casting station without the expressed authority of the station originating the program. In network broadcasting the specific authority of the originating station exists insofar as affiliated stations on the network are concerned, but several cases have been decided under this section condemning the unauthorized broadcasting of the programs of one station by another. From the standpoint of program policy the reasonableness of these restrictions requires no argument. Care should be taken in recognizing and detecting the presence of "signals of distress" in program material because, aside from the violation of the Act, untold harm could result from the broadcasting of such misinformation.

Section 326 of the Act prohibits the broadcasting of "any obscene, indecent, or profane language." What constitutes in-decent language must be judged from the viewpoint that the words are being heard by all ages and types of audiences, and a mere avoidance of criminal responsibility under this section is not the aim of any conscientious broadcaster.

THE REGULATIONS OF THE FEDERAL COMMUNICATIONS COMMISSION

Many of the regulations of the Federal Communications Commission are primarily of an engineering or operating nature, as distinguished from program policy. However, some are the particular concern of the program department, and they will be briefly reviewed in the order in which they occur in the regulations.

Program Logs. Regulation 3.404 requires the keeping of program logs in which must be entered:

1. The time each station identification announcement (call letters and location) is made
2. A brief description of the program broadcast, such as "music," "drama," "speech," etc. with the program title, the name of the sponsor, if any, the time of the beginning and ending of the program, whether records or transcriptions were used, and if so, the time they were announced as such. (In the case of a political candidate, the name and political affiliations of the sponsor must be listed.)
3. A statement that each sponsored program has been announced as sponsored as required by Section 317 of the Communications Act

Regulation 3.405 requires that the logs shall be retained for a period of two years, but in certain circumstances logs must be retained for a longer period. Logs incident to or involved in any claim or cause of which the licensee has notice must be retained by the licensee until the claim has been disposed of or until the time within which a suit might be brought on the claim has expired. Logs concerning communications incident to a disaster or involving statements incidental to an investigation by the Commission, concerning which the licensee of the station has been notified, must be retained until the licensee is specifically authorized by the Commission to destroy them.

Station Identification. Regulation 3.406 requires that the call letters and location of the station shall be announced each time the station comes on the air and leaves the air and also, (1) on the hour, and (2) either on the half hour or at the quarter hour following the hour, and at the quarter hour preceding the next hour, with the provision that the identification announcement need not be made on the hour if to do so would interrupt a single consecutive speech, play, religious service, symphony concert, or operatic production of longer duration than thirty minutes. In such cases, the identification announcement shall be made at the beginning of the program, at the first interruption of the entertainment continuity, and at the conclusion of the program. The identification announcements required on the half hour or quarter hour are similarly excused to avoid interrupting the continuity of program material, in which case the identification must be made at the first interruption of the entertainment continuity and at the conclusion of the program. In general, two minutes' latitude each side of the points at which the identification announcements are to be made is allowed, and in some special cases the latitude is increased to five minutes.

Records and Transcriptions. Regulation 3.407 deals with programs using mechanical records; that is, phonograph records or electrical transcriptions. In the case of electrical transcriptions a descriptive announcement must be made which includes the words, "transcription," "electrical transcription," "transcribed," or "electrically transcribed." When phonograph records are used, they must be announced as "records." These announcements must be made at the beginning and at the end of each such program of this type and, in the case of programs greater than thirty minutes in length, at each thirty-minute interval. A mechanical record not longer than five minutes must be identified immediately preceding its use. In any event a licensee must not attempt to create the impression that any mechanical reproduction consists of live talent. No identification is needed in the case of mechanical records used for background music, sound effects, station identification, theme music of short duration identifying programs, or identification of sponsorship.

Rebroadcasts. Regulation 3.408 defines "rebroadcast" as the "reception by radio of a program of a radio station and the simultaneous or subsequent retransmission of such program." Broadcasters are permitted to rebroadcast programs, provided the Commission is notified of the call letters of the originating station and has certified to it by the rebroadcasting station that express authority has been received by the rebroadcasting station from the originating station.

Political Broadcasts. Regulations 3.421 and 3.424 provide in detail for the handling of broadcasts of legally qualified candidates for public office. After restating the requirement of equality set forth in Section 315 of the Communications Act and the requirement that the licensee shall have no power of censorship over the material broadcast by any such candidate, the regulations define a legally qualified candidate as a person who has publicly announced that he is a candidate for nomination or election, who meets the qualifications prescribed by the applicable laws to hold the office for which he is a candidate, and who has qualified for a place on the ballot or is eligible to be voted on by a write-in campaign, provided he has been duly nominated by a political party or makes a substantial showing that he is a bona fide candidate for nomination or election.

Regulation 3.423 particularizes with respect to equality for the rates charged for political time and specifies that no licensee shall make contracts for so much of his time that he is unable to comply with the orders for time of other legally qualified candidates for the same office. It should be noted that the emphasis is placed in all cases on "the same office." It is clear that having allowed a candidate for County Treasurer to speak, the station is obligated to afford all other candidates for County Treasurer in the same county equal access to the microphone, but there is no requirement that it permit candidates for any other office to use its facilities.

Regulation 3.424 requires that the licensee must keep and permit public inspection of a complete record of requests for broadcast time made by or on behalf of candidates for public office, with an appropriate notation showing the disposition made by the licensee of such requests and the charges made, if any, in connection with the requests which have been granted.

STATE LAWS

Advertising Problems. The application of state laws to program policies is a broad subject essentially legal in character and one which must be worked out in practice in each particular situation in the light of the applicable statutes and local laws. There may be statutes regulating or prohibiting particular types of advertising, such as that for insurance, hard liquor, beer, cigarettes, or certain medicinal preparations. There are also in some states laws regulating the making of offers if such offers require the submission of proof of purchase. These statutes, commonly referred to as the trading-stamp statutes, were enacted in many states in the early part of this century to control the conduct of the very popular trading-stamp device, and while they do not present an active problem at the present time, they should be studied and taken into consideration by the broadcaster in the states where they exist.

In view of the fact that under the laws of a number of states it is unlawful to use a person's name for advertising purposes without his consent, and that in at least one state it is prescribed that such consent must be in writing, it is highly desirable, in connection with scripts containing testimonials or other use of a person's name for commercial purposes, that definite proof of the written authorization of such use should be furnished.

For the same reason, when living persons are impersonated, written authorization of the impersonation should be obtained. Departure from this strict requirement may occasionally be permissible, as for example when the impersonation is one of a series of impersonations given as part of an act, particularly when the subjects are in the entertainment industry or otherwise in the public eye.

Defamation. The problem of preventing the making of defamatory statements is a large and important one. It goes without saying that the broadcaster is anxious to avoid defaming anyone. On the other hand, there is as a practical matter little opportunity in many cases for him to prevent the utterance of defamatory matter even if he has time to formulate an opinion as to whether or not it is defamatory in the eyes of the law.

At the present time, the character of the legal consequences of a derogatory statement made over the radio is a local question; that is, it is governed by the laws of the individual states, there being no federal law on the subject. In some states an opportunity must be offered to the broadcaster to make a retraction before suit is brought because of defamatory statements. If such retraction is made, the damages are limited to actual damages as distinguished from punitive or exemplary damages. In another state the broadcaster is not liable if he can show that he used due care in preventing the broadcasting of the libelous statement. Just what constitutes due care cannot be told with any certainty until cases are decided under the statute. One state had for a short time a law relieving the broadcaster from all liability unless he affirmatively stated that he adopted the defamatory statements as his own. As a practical matter, this would make it impossible in almost every case to hold the broadcaster responsible, and the statute was held to be unconstitutional. In another state the broadcaster is relieved from liability if he can establish that as soon as possible after the defamatory statement he cut the speaker off the air. This poses a delicate question for broadcasters and in the hands of a timid operator might result in the interruption of many programs in an effort to play safe.

In still another state the broadcaster is not responsible for any defamatory statements made over his facilities during political broadcasts unless actual malice on the part of the broadcaster can be proved, and in that state it is provided that stations on a network are not responsible for defamatory statements broadcast by them unless they originated the program in question. In this connection it is interesting to note that in at least one case in another jurisdiction the network outlet was held to be fully responsible for the defamatory material it broadcast, even though the program originated at a key station of the network.

This maze of conflicting limitations on the liability of broadcasters with respect to a single problem points to the great desirability of establishing a uniform standard of the broadcaster's liability in such cases through the enactment of a federal statute on the subject.

The Code of the National Association of Broadcasters

In many industries federal regulation is the outgrowth of inadequate self-regulation on the part of the industry. Broadcasters have taken important strides in self-regulation, and in this respect the work of the trade association known as the National Association of Broadcasters has been exceedingly valuable.

The code of the National Association of Broadcasters enunciates as a cardinal principle in American radio the provision of time by stations, without charge, for the presentation of public questions including those of a controversial nature. At the same time, it advises against the sale of time for the presentation of controversial issues except in the case of political broadcasts during political campaigns. The basic foundation for the prohibition against the sale of time for the presentation of controversial issues is the public duty of broadcasters to present such issues, regardless of the willingness of others to pay for their presentation. If time were sold for that purpose, it would have to be sold to all with the ability to pay, and as a result the advantage in any discussion would rest largely with those having the greater financial means to buy broadcasting time.

In excepting political broadcasts, recognition is given to the practice which has been established since the very beginning of commercial broadcasting, of permitting the use of broadcasting facilities in a manner similar to the use of advertising space in newspapers; that is, on a commercial basis in full keeping with the Communications Act and the Regulations of the Communications Commission.

The Code stresses the desirability of care in the selection

and control of material for children's programs, educational broadcasts, and religious broadcasts. It also deals briefly with the presentation of news in a fair and accurate manner. In general, the handling of news largely consists in the accuracy and speed with which it is gathered and distributed, with freedom from editorial bias in its selection and presentation.

Another salient feature of the Code is a limitation on the length of commercial announcements. A schedule of the limitations, which have been effective in meeting the criticism formerly heard of alleged over-commercialization of time on the air, follows:

LENGTH OF PROGRAM	TOTAL LENGTH OF COMMERCIAL ANNOUNCEMENTS (Daytime Programs)	TOTAL LENGTH OF COMMERCIAL ANNOUNCEMENTS (Nighttime Programs)
Five minutes — news	1:45	1:30
Five minutes — other than news	2:00	1:45
Ten minutes	2:30	2:00
Fifteen minutes	3:15	2:30
Twenty-five minutes	4:15	2:45
Thirty minutes	4:30	3:00
Sixty minutes	9:00	6:00

Excepted from the above programs are participation programs, "musical clocks," shoppers' guides, and other local programs falling within this general classification.

The Code emphasizes that care must be taken in accepting various types of business, confining clients to those engaged in legitimate commerce whose products, services, and advertising practices comply with legal requirements, fair-trade practices, and accepted standards of good taste.

The phrase, "accepted standards of good taste," is clarified by a list of thirteen items regarded as unacceptable, as follows:

1. Any spirituous or "hard" liquor
2. Any remedy or other product the sale of which or the method of sale of which constitutes a violation of law
3. Any fortune-telling, mind-reading, or character-reading by

handwriting, numerology, palm-reading, or astrology, or advertising related thereto

4. Schools that offer questionable or untrue promises of employment as inducements for enrollment
5. Matrimonial agencies
6. Offers of "homework" except by firms of unquestioned responsibility
7. Any "dopester," tip-sheet, or race-track publications
8. All forms of speculative finance (Before member stations may accept any financial advertising, it shall be fully ascertained that such advertising and such advertised services comply with all pertinent federal, state, and local laws.)
9. Cures and products claiming to cure
10. Advertising statements or claims member stations know to be false, deceptive, or grossly exaggerated
11. Continuity which describes repellently any functions or symptomatic results of disturbances, or relief granted such disturbances through use of any product
12. Unfair attacks upon competitors, competing products, or upon other industries, professions, or institutions
13. Misleading statements of price or value, or misleading comparisons of price or value

Operation within the framework of the Code of the National Association of Broadcasters gives reasonable assurance that the broadcaster will avoid the pitfalls which often beset those who employ a hit-or-miss approach to questions of policy.

THE POSTAL REGULATIONS

The application of the postal regulations to any use of the mails incident to an advertising campaign is clear. These various restrictions need not be reviewed here. The most important phase of the Post Office Department's regulation of mail matter, insofar as it has a bearing on radio programs, is that dealing with contests as outlined above in the discussion of Section 316 of the Communications Act.

THE CODE OF WARTIME PRACTICES

During the war, it was, of course, very necessary to prevent the transmission of information which could have been of value

to the enemy. To this end the Office of Censorship published
a Code of Wartime Practices. The first edition was released
in January, 1942, and it was kept up to date in the light of the
experience of broadcasters and the Office of Censorship and
in keeping with international developments by the issuance of
new editions and directives dealing with specific subjects.

The general scope of the Code may be indicated briefly by
listing some of the phases of broadcasting with which it dealt:
News Broadcasts and Commentators; Programs — Request Programs, Quiz Programs, Forums and Interviews, Special Events
and Other Ad-lib Reporting, Commercial Continuity; Foreign
Language Broadcasts; and Military Personnel on Programs.

THE OFFICE OF WAR INFORMATION

The Office of War Information was created in June, 1942, to
formulate and carry out informative programs concerning the
war effort and the policies, activities, and aims of the Government, to co-ordinate the informational activities of all federal
departments and agencies, and to clear and approve all programs dealing with war information. The regulations of the
Office of War Information clarified the responsibility for various
types of programs and provided for the review of all proposed
radio programs sponsored by federal departments and agencies,
whether they bore upon the war effort or not. In essence, the
OWI acted as the point of clearance and contact for the broadcasting industry in its relations with all federal departments
and agencies.

THE BROADCASTER'S OWN POLICIES

To supplement the policies required by law, federal regulations, and the industry code, certain individual policies are
desirable. These should be developed by each broadcaster in
the light of his local situation and needs. Particularly are they
necessary for the reduction to concrete examples of situations
which are not dealt with definitely enough in the code and
regulations. A few such examples will be discussed under
this heading.

It is desirable to have a deadline, in advance of broadcast, of at least twenty-four hours for the submission of all continuities, in order that they may be checked for compliance with policy. As a separate subject, a description of the musical compositions to be incorporated in a program should be submitted at least one week in advance, in order that the right of the broadcaster to perform them may be checked.

In the case of new programs, the right should be reserved to require a complete performance in recorded or live form, so that the effect of the program as played may be observed, something which might prove greatly different from the effect produced by a mere reading of the script.

Point-to-point communication is prohibited by the Communications Act, not specifically, but on the theory that broadcasting stations have been licensed in the general public interest, and that it is not proper, therefore, to carry messages intended for individuals or small groups. Under some circumstances, of course, matters of general interest may be couched in language ostensibly directed to individuals or groups, but only under the most exceptional circumstances should messages be broadcast that are of interest to but a few.

The discussion of pending litigation should be avoided because of the danger of committing contempt of court, but factual statements on news programs are entirely proper.

Testimonials ought to reflect the authentic experiences of competent persons, and claims which would not be accepted in any other copy should not be permitted merely because they are included or incorporated in testimonials. The manner in which testimonials are presented on the air is important, and in cases where the individual giving the testimonial is impersonated that fact should be clearly indicated. From a long-range standpoint nothing is more important to the broadcasting industry than to maintain the confidence of the listening audience in the integrity and honesty of those programming radio stations.

It is well to have certain minimum requirements in dealing with radio contests. Primarily the statement of the contest rules should be clear and unambiguous. It is advisable to specify in each announcement that the opinion of the judges shall be final and that duplicate prizes will be awarded in the event of ties. In order to avoid any misunderstanding, the closing date of the contest should be clearly announced at the outset or, in the case of long-term contests, announced well in advance of the final closing date. The types of prizes should be subject to the approval of the broadcaster to avoid adverse public reaction, and provision should be made for supplying the broadcaster with a complete list of the names of winners and other related information, in case inquiries are made by public authorities or contestants.

Care should be exercised in scrutinizing the details of offers of premiums, whether or not a charge is made, and in avoiding situations in which an inadequate supply of premiums is available; the offer under such circumstances is reduced to a point where it consists merely of a contest to see who gets his reply in first.

The preparation of a workable set of policies is difficult, and the enforcement of the policies in individual cases often presents delicate problems of client relationship which must be handled with the utmost tact. Nevertheless, careful attention on the part of the broadcaster to the composition and application of his broadcasting policies will pay substantial dividends not only in the revenue derived from sound business but also in the full measure of the public interest which will thereby be served.

CHAPTER 5

PARTICIPATING ORGANIZATIONS

To THE NOVICE looking at radio from the outside, it may seem to be a simple combination of talent, announcer, a microphone, and an engineer combining their efforts to put a program on the air. Sometimes it seems as simple as that. Sometimes it is! Unfortunately there are a great many complicating factors behind this seemingly simple and straightforward process. Lines must be written; music must be procured, paid for, and performed; recordings must be made; time must be purchased; someone must be persuaded to pay for all this activity, to mention only a few of the complications.

To fulfill these myriad functions there have come into being many new organizations and new departments in already existing organizations, which we shall call, for want of a better term, participating organizations. These organizations are not a part of any radio station or network, but their function is to supply a service which the station or network needs.

Some of these organizations are labor unions; some are individual businesses, organized for profit; still others are trade associations which help to set policy and outline the procedure of their member organizations. All these various groups are more or less directly concerned with the creation and broadcasting of various kinds of programs, each contributing its special service which, when combined with all the others, helps to create the daily radio program output.

ADVERTISING AGENCIES

One of the largest and most important of these organizations is the group of advertising agencies. The novice may or may not know that a great many commercial programs which are broadcast daily are not originated by any radio station or network. Many of these programs are designed, written, cast, and produced under the direct supervision of advertising agencies. Having built the program, the agency simply buys time on the air from a station or network and uses that time to broadcast the program. That statement is, of course, an over-simplification of what actually happens, but basically it is true. Whether or not the agency actually builds the program, nearly all advertising business of a network nature, and much local radio advertising business as well, is placed through advertising agencies. In other words, the station or network seldom deals directly with a client; it deals usually with the client's representative, the advertising agency.

The advertising agency assumes the responsibility for counseling a client on the type and amount of advertising that client should use to promote his products. In addition, the agency usually acts as purchasing agent for all time on the air for the client. To the amount they spend for the purchase of radio time, they add a 15 per cent charge when they bill the client, and this charge constitutes their major source of income. Finally, the agency may actually build the complete program. In this case they bill the client for all talent outlay and usually add a charge for their service in building the program. There are, of course, several variations on the way in which the agency collects from the client for its services, but the methods here mentioned are the more or less standard procedure.

In order to make the situation completely clear, let us take an example. Suppose that a shoe company decides to spend a certain amount of money for advertising their product. They feel that they need the expert advice of an advertising agency on the possibilities of the various advertising media to handle the advertising program. The advertising department of the shoe company would, in that case, consult with and finally make a contract with an advertising agency to handle the spending of their advertising appropriation.

The advertising agency would then set about a complicated process of product analysis, market analysis, and sales analysis and, as a result of all this research, present a plan of advertising and promotion for this particular product. Their plan might include the use of newspapers, magazines, billboard advertising, and a considerable amount of radio advertising.

For the simplification of the example, the activities in other advertising media will be ignored, and the discussion will center on what happens in the radio field. Here, the radio department of the advertising agency will study the promotion plan outlined by the executive of the agency who handles the client's account. On the basis of these findings, he will decide what territory needs to be covered by radio, what times are available on the stations or networks for effective coverage, and what kinds of programs would best reach and move the audience with which the client wishes to make contact.

As the result of all this investigation, the radio department of the advertising agency might conceive and submit for approval a plan for a radio program which they believe would sell the product. Plans would be made to buy the necessary time on the stations or networks which would be the most suitable for the purpose. When the plans were approved, the advertising agency might hire a script writer, a production director, and a cast, or whatever other talent were needed for the program, and proceed to build a program and put it on the air. They would, of course, receive the full co-operation of the network or station involved.

All the costs of building this program – the fee for the writers, the production director, the actors, and the announcers, and all the other services connected with building the program – would be totaled and billed to the client. In addition, the station or network would bill the advertising agency for the full amount of the time on the air.

The advertising agency would then, in turn, submit the bill for the radio time and talent and all other costs to the client. However, when the advertising agency paid the station or network for the time, they would pay them only 85 per cent of the bill, keeping 15 per cent for their profit on the transaction.

In some cases the advertising agency neither designs, creates, nor produces the program. This work may remain in the hands of the station or network, and the advertising agency simply acts as a time buyer and consultant for the client. In this case, of course, the agency submits no bill for talent or production and derives its entire profit from the 15 per cent deduction on the time sales.

There are some two hundred advertising agencies in the country that do a more or less significant amount of business in the field of radio advertising. However, most of radio's largest network accounts are handled by perhaps three dozen of the largest agencies in the country. Even much of the spot advertising and local advertising which is aired on smaller stations around the country is handled by advertising agencies. They are so much an inextricable part of the broadcast picture that no consideration of radio can be complete without them. They are, for the most part, the creators of the large bulk of commercial programs on American radio.

TRADE ORGANIZATIONS OF ADVERTISERS

The American Association of Advertising Agencies is one of the important trade organizations which is characteristic of American business. Competitors, who are keen rivals in their search for business, find it wise to sit down at a conference table and draw up certain rules and regulations for the conduct of that competition. This kind of trade association is common in the United States. The American Association of Advertising Agencies is one of the best examples of such an organization.

The Association is concerned with all branches of advertising and has a special committee to deal with and present problems arising in the field of broadcast advertising. Some of the outstanding executives in American advertising agencies make up the membership of this committee. The Association maintains offices in New York City and concerns itself with the establishment of certain standards of practice to which most of the reputable advertising agencies conform. It also furnishes a common meeting ground for the discussion of mutual problems and the consideration of solutions. Its importance to the broadcast picture is a secondary one and makes itself felt only in the actions of the advertising agencies.

There are several other such organizations in the field which have the same general purpose and serve somewhat the same function. Such an organization is the Advertising Federation of America with headquarters in New York City. The Association of National Advertisers is another group which has some influence on the setting of policy and the creation of procedure in radio advertising. There are several specialized advertising associations and several regional associations which bring some influence to bear on the procedure of radio advertising.

FREE-LANCE PRODUCTION AGENCIES

In some of the larger broadcasting centers, there have grown up alongside the advertising agencies organizations which call themselves production agencies. These agencies specialize only in the design and production of radio programs and do not help the client to buy time or place advertising. Their function is a still more highly specialized function of producing programs. Such production agencies are useful mostly to two classes of clients. They may be of considerable help to a very large concern with its own advertising agency, which can buy time but which may be unable to produce programs. On the other hand, they may also be useful to a very small advertising agency which does not maintain a large enough staff in the field of radio to go about the actual building and production of programs, but which can supervise the work of a production agency.

Most production agencies make their money by engaging some special talent, putting that talent on the agency payroll, and selling it at a profit to a client. For example, a production agency may be able to acquire the services of a top-flight writer and an excellent production director, and any client who wants the services of these two people will have to get them through the production agency. Sometimes the agency is little more than an office presided over by a man with an intimate knowledge of production methods who has contacts through which he can pick up writers, production directors, and actors as he needs them for his work.

Such agencies are highly specialized and are found, for the most part, only in New York, Chicago, and Hollywood, where the centers of network activity are the largest. These production agencies deal primarily with "package" jobs. For a fixed sum, they agree to deliver a script written, rehearsed, and directed, and acted by talent which they supervise, thus furnishing to the client a complete show, ready to put on whatever network or local time he buys, or to put on a recording in case he wishes to handle his coverage in that way.

TALENT AGENCIES

The *Broadcasting* magazine *Yearbook* lists 160 agencies that handle radio talent. These agencies take upon themselves the task of supplying to the users of radio talent all kinds and varieties of people. Most such agencies work on a percentage basis, taking their profit out of the artist's earnings. The artist, in return for this fee, is represented by the agency, which does its best to place him in the various jobs for which he is fitted. These talent agencies furnish a central point to which directors and station managers can apply for talent, and they also furnish to the talent a contact point with the various agencies that might be able to use his services. The agencies handle all kinds of talent — actors, announcers, masters of ceremonies, vocalists, and all sorts of specialty artists.

The radio talent agency is a good example of the kind of subsidiary organizations which have been created as a part of and dependent on the parent industry of radio for their support. Some talent agencies work with theater and movie talent as well. A few of these organizations are largely parasitic in nature, but most of them do a real, honest service to the industry.

One of the branches of the talent agency business which deserves special note is the band-booking organization. Agencies such as the Music Corporation of America have become extremely powerful factors in the entertainment world by virtue of their control of complete musical organizations. Most orchestras that are "free lance" groups, that is, orchestras that are under contract to no particular network or radio station, are managed by some talent agency or some talent-handling group, and through such an agency all bookings for these musical units are made. Most of the national "name" orchestras are handled by various talent agencies which, because of their control over these musical units, are important factors in the entertainment world, of which radio is a significant part.

TRANSCRIPTION AGENCIES

A rather large and profitable business has developed in the making of recordings and transcriptions for radio use. There are two main types of service offered by transcription agencies. The first kind of organization, which is typified by the World Broadcasting System, is an organization which is set up to produce and record transcription programs, which can then be duplicated on as many records as are needed to send out to specific stations. Such organizations as this are used by advertising agencies that do not have their own transcription facilities.

The second type of transcription service is that which records musical numbers and other kinds of program material on a wholesale basis for distribution directly to the station. Such organizations as Lang-Worth will record, on 33 1/3 r.p.m. platters, all kinds of music which can be used by local stations to build up musical programs. These transcriptions are furnished complete with card catalogs and cross-index references so that any desired kind of music may be found very quickly. A great many smaller stations which do not have a staff of musicians depend largely on recordings and transcriptions for their music.

Discussion of the function and operation of transcription agencies will be found in Chapter 10 of this book.

LICENSING ORGANIZATIONS

Every composer of a piece of music who elects to copyright his work is protected by law from the indiscriminate use of this music. In order to provide a channel through which permission to use music may be secured, the licensing organization came into being. It provides a clearing house, a common middle ground on which the composer and the user of music can meet and do business; it issues permission to use the music of its clients and collects whatever fees result therefrom.

Some of these licensing agencies were in existence some time before the advent of radio broadcasting; and so when radio began to use the staggering amounts of music which it now uses, the means for clearing its use was already in existence. Since that time, others have been created which service radio exclusively.

The largest, and perhaps the best known, of these organizations is ASCAP, the American Society of Composers, Authors, and Publishers. This organization acts as the legal and financial representative for a large pool of composers and lyric writers who place their work in the hands of ASCAP for handling. ASCAP, in turn, will make contracts with radio stations and networks for the use of this copyrighted material. Some of it is made available on a blanket-fee basis, whereby the station or network pays a yearly fee which entitles him to the unlimited use of an agreed amount of music. Some of the more desirable music is made available only on the payment of specific individual fees. Other arrangements may sometimes be made.

Because of a radical disagreement between the radio networks and ASCAP in 1941 the networks pooled their resources to create a new licensing organization which they called Broadcast Music, Incorporated. BMI collected a considerable amount of music that was in the public domain, made new contracts with composers and in a comparatively short time built up a rather impressive library of material that was not controlled by other existing licensing organizations. Even since the disagreement with ASCAP was resolved, BMI has continued in active existence and is operating as a regular licensing organization in the same manner as its older predecessors.

The Society of European Stage Authors and Composers is

the licensing organization which controls most of the copyrights of foreign music, and it does an active business with radio in this country. It is organized on the same basic lines as ASCAP and serves the same function.

It is easy to see what a complex matter it is to arrange for performance rights on so many miscellaneous pieces of music. Such a clearing house as these licensing organizations provide is the only feasible answer to the problem yet developed. It is still necessary, in the field of literary rights, to deal individually with authors, their publishers, or their agents.

UNIONS

As radio has expanded, a great many of the workers in the field have chosen to organize themselves into guilds or trade unions. In some cases, unions already in existence moved into the radio field. There are still some spheres of activity in which no unions exist in radio, but for the most part radio is "organized."

Long before radio existed, the American Federation of Musicians, or AFM, was looking out for the interests of musicians. When radio began to use large numbers of musicians, it was natural that AFM should extend its jurisdiction over that field also. It is still the only bargaining agency of any importance representing musicians. All the major networks have contractual agreements with AFM which govern wages and working conditions of radio musicians. As radio has become an increasingly bigger business, the musicians who play such a prominent part in its programming have benefited. Each new contract negotiated has usually resulted either in pay increases or improvement in working conditions. Contracts also dictate the number of staff musicians which each station or network shall maintain. AFM has jurisdiction over all instrumentalists, but not vocalists. In a few isolated spots, notably Chicago and St. Louis, the AFM also has jurisdiction over turntable operators, although that is being currently contested by the National Association of Broadcast Engineers and Technicians.

The AFM is a semi-closed shop, which means that it is not

always possible to obtain membership in it at will. This condition gives AFM very strict control over the personnel which stations and networks may hire. AFM has consistently been a militant organization and has so far successfully imposed nearly all of its demands on broadcasters.

Actors, announcers, sound effects men, and vocalists are organized under a guild known as the American Federation of Radio Artists, or AFRA. AFRA is strictly a guild organization; that is to say, no actor, announcer, or singer may appear on any network or station program which has an agreement with AFRA unless that person is a member of AFRA. However, AFRA agrees to take into membership anyone that the station or network wishes to employ. Therefore, strictly speaking, it is not a closed shop, but it is a union arrangement.

The history of the relationship between AFRA and the networks has been a remarkably peaceful and amicable one. While AFRA has made certain very definite demands on the networks for the protection and payment of its personnel, it has been fairly well aware of network problems, and the degree of co-operation between the networks and AFRA has always been rather high. So far, the influence of AFRA has been confined, for the most part, to the three major broadcasting centers, New York, Chicago, and Hollywood, although chapters are being organized in the large subsidiary centers of broadcasting, and the influence of AFRA is gradually spreading.

Another group which is coming into increasing importance is the Radio Writers Guild. This organization of radio writers is similar to the American Newspaper Guild and has similar objectives. It is part of the Authors' League of America, Inc., and is one of the most recent organizations. It still has much more "guild" influence than "union" influence. Some stations have separate contracts with the Radio Writers Guild, covering staff continuity writers and staff news writers; others have contracts covering news writers with the American Newspaper Guild.

Other unions are the representatives of various groups of staff employees. One of the most important of such groups is the broadcast engineers, who are represented by the International Brotherhood of Electrical Workers, the American Communications Association, or the National Association of Broadcast Engineers and Technicians. IBEW is affiliated with the American Federation of Labor; The American Communications Association is a CIO organization. In addition, some broadcasters have contracts with the International Alliance of Theatre Stage Employees (IATSE) representing the stage electricians, carpenters, and property men when the use of theaters is involved in the origination of programs.

All these union organizations have as their primary purpose the protection of their members and the improvement of their working and wage conditions. They act as collective bargainers for the group, representing them in negotiations with stations and networks. It is interesting that there have been no major interruptions in broadcast service in the United States due to labor difficulties. While relations between broadcasters and unions have not always been of the best, there usually has been a basically sound working agreement which was acceptable to both groups.

It is impossible here to go into detail about the functions of these various organizations. More reference will be made to them in succeeding chapters, but it is wise to know what these organizations are and what use they serve, in order to bring them into focus in the complete picture. Most of these so-called participating organizations are a direct outgrowth of the needs created by radio broadcasting. Some of them are businesses; some are trade unions; some are trade associations; but all serve a purpose, and function more or less usefully and efficiently in the day-to-day operation of radio broadcasting.

2

PROGRAMMING

CHAPTER 6

PROGRAM PLANNING

BASIC TO THE UNDERSTANDING of how to plan a program schedule is an understanding of a station's audience at every hour of the broadcasting day. This involves not only numerical considerations, which are reasonably easy to check, but much more complex factors, such as sex and age of the listener mass, the time of day, the season of the year, national or international events which may have a bearing on listener habits, the intelligence norm of the group, and listener likes and dislikes in the way of program material.

To employ a rough-hewn illustration, the mind of a station program-planner must function with much the same kind of understanding that motivates the manager of a neighborhood movie house. The local movie proprietor knows exactly what kind of fare will bring people into his cinema house, and he knows what type of picture will keep them away. He knows his audience by temperament and often by sight; he knows what kind of picture to book for what kind of weather; he knows how much variety to offer and whether or not his customers want single, double, or triple features.

Similarly, in radio the people in the audience are a guide to a program manager's selections. In planning a day which may be regarded as fairly typical, he will probably decide to offer his awakening audience a service program which will wake them up, tell them the time, report on weather prospects, give them the news, and, in general, get the family through breakfast and off to school and work. Time signals, useful to get the family on its schedule, will not have much importance once the children and the breadwinners have left the house. The daytime hours, therefore, will probably be devoted to programs that have appeal to women — drama, music, household helps, etc., depending on the desires of the local audience.

By late afternoon children are home from school, and again the character of the schedule will change to accommodate this audience. Through the evening mealtime most program schedules will follow a neutral motif sometimes highlighted by news, dinner music, and kindred program offerings.

Starting with the evening schedule, it can generally be assumed that age classifications are not a determining factor in program selection, and programs will usually be planned for general audience appeal. Still later in the evening a good portion of the audience will retire for the night, and the programs must be redesigned to fit the needs of remaining listeners.

At this point a financial consideration enters the picture. In commercial broadcasting the amounts of money to be spent on production at given times of the day will vary with the character and size of the audience. It should be fairly obvious that the people who pay for the programs would not desire to pay premium hour prices for a program in a period that would reach, say, only ten per cent of the listeners available at a peak evening hour. Thus, in the case of late evening programs, the usual procedure is to aim for productions that will be reasonable in cost and still coincide with the entertainment desires of remaining listeners.

Aside from network offerings which, of necessity, must have universal appeal, there are many localized conditions which have to be considered by a radio station in making its plans. A case in point is furnished by KROC at Rochester, Minnesota. This city is the home of a great medical center, and large portions of its transient and resident groups are well-to-do. The station schedule, therefore, carries a rather heavy complement of programs having literary, educational, and musical elements specifically appealing to such a group.

This preamble is a relatively simple picture of a very complex affair. For a proper understanding of radio programming, the subject should be considered from the standpoint of its setting in the general radio structure, rather than as an isolated phase of radio. After viewing the pattern of which programming is only one part, it should be possible to approach the main subject more closely and examine it more specifically.

As has been suggested, the network audience is likely to be much more heterogeneous than the audience for a single station. While it is probably true that the fundamentals of human nature are much the same throughout the United States, it is also true that various sections or localities have developed customs which are an inherent part of their own culture and which are quite foreign to other sections of the country. Local stations in these sections can achieve great popularity by programming to suit the particular desires of the local audience, as in the previously mentioned case of KROC. Network programs can do much less of this sort of thing. They must have a common denominator. If they are to hold a vast coast-to-coast audience, they must do it on the basis of elements which are universally accepted. With these considerations taken properly into account in network programming and the local considerations taken properly into account by the individual stations, there is a happy solution to the problem of meeting both the general and the specific requirements of the listener.

For this reason, the program policies for a network are set upon very broad and general lines. They have to do with maintaining a program structure which is always "in the public interest." It is interesting to note that in announcing the formation of the National Broadcasting Company, the Radio Corporation of America published a newspaper advertisement on September 14, 1926 which contained the following significant statements:

> Any use of radio transmission which causes the public to feel that the quality of the programs is not the highest, that the use of radio is not the broadest and best use in the public interest, that it is used for political advantage or selfish power will be detrimental to the public interest in radio and, therefore. to the Radio Corporation of America.

> The purpose of the (National Broadcasting) Company will be to provide the best programs available for broadcasting in the United States.

In order that the National Broadcasting Company may be advised as to the best type of program, that discrimination may be avoided, that the public may be assured that the broadcasting is being done in the fairest and best way, always allowing for human frailties and human performance, it has created an Advisory Council.[1]

It was with the advice of the Advisory Council that the National Broadcasting Company's methods of operation and program standards took form, setting the pattern, not only for itself, but for all broadcasting networks that were to come.[2]

All the network programs presented on NBC must, therefore, conform to the program policies and practices of the company. This is true of programs sponsored by commercial institutions as well as by various organizations which are given sustaining time. These program policies and practices have been designed for the sole purpose of providing programs which will not offend the listener, regardless of his age, sex, race, or religion. These principles are thus set forth because of the specific obligations which the network feels to the homes and the family circles in which programs are heard.[3]

In addition to insistence upon good taste, these policies specifically provide that "no program should lower the moral standards of those who received it"; that "law, natural and divine, must not be belittled, ridiculed, nor must a sentiment be created against it"; that "as far as possible, life should not be misrepresented, at least not in such a way as to place in the minds of youth false values on life and human behavior."[4]

As broadcasting experience has grown, program policies have been subjected to revision in the light of that experience, but always with a sound concept of public service. The National Broadcasting Company also subscribes to the code of the National Association of Broadcasters, which governs the ethical and business standards of the broadcasting industry.

[1] *New York Times*, September 14, 1926, p. 27.
[2] *NBC Program Policies and Working Manual*, 1944, pp. 7-8.
[3] *Ibid.*, p. 9.
[4] *Ibid.*

Network Program Organization

In order that we may understand how these policies become effective, let us examine the NBC program organization which is charged with the responsibility for putting them into practice. The organization of the program department follows that of the Company generally in that there are three divisions — the Eastern Division, the Central Division, and the Western Division. Each of these divisions of the Company is headed by a vice president and general manager. So in the program department there is an Eastern Division program manager, a Central Division program manager, and a Western Division program manager; there is also a vice president in charge of programs. Functionally, the various division program managers report to their own vice presidents on all matters of operation within the division. They report to the vice president in charge of programs on all matters of general company program policies and on all program matters affecting interdivision operations. In general, the organization and the operation under each division program manager is the same. An examination of the setup in New York will suffice, therefore, to show the division operation and also will make it possible to see how the full network operation, under the vice president in charge of programs, co-ordinates and extends the work of the various Division program managers.

The work of the program department falls into two general classes: one is getting things done; the other is planning the things to do. The latter is creative; the former is chiefly service. The department as a whole is made up of divisions, and the person in charge is designated as the head of the division. At present, in New York, there is a program development division, a script division, a sports division, a music division, a package-sales division, a booking division, and a production division. For purposes of organization, the head of the announcers and the head of the sound effects technicians both report to the production manager.

The heads of all these various divisions constitute a network

NBC PROGRAM DEPARTMENT

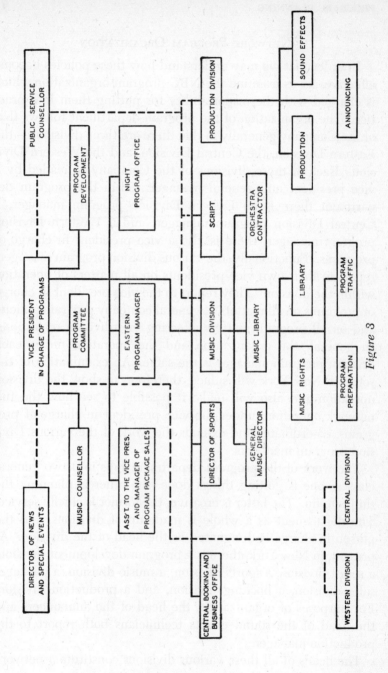

Figure 3

program board. It meets regularly once each week or more frequently on call. It is a planning and discussion group. It reviews programs currently on the air; it discusses and makes recommendations on new program ideas which are submitted; and it checks the schedules with the purpose of keeping a balanced program structure. Its meetings are visited by representatives of the sales department, who acquaint the board with contemplated sales, get the board's approval for programs which are scheduled to appear under the commercial sponsorship, receive program presentations which are recommended to specific clients, discuss problems in connection with current commercially sponsored programs; in short, provide a liaison between the activities of the sales department and those of the program department.

In much the same way, these meetings are visited by representatives of the press department, of news and special events, and of the public service department, for discussions which will co-ordinate their various activities with those of the program department.

Once each month the members of the program board, together with the heads of sound technicians and of announcers and the head of the booking division, hold a staff operations meeting for the sole purpose of discussing interdivision operational problems. Thus, there is set up a regular system for dealing with the problems arising from either program content or program operation.

All programs, of course, fall into two classes; namely, "sustaining," those for which the company arranges payment for both the facilities and the talent, and "commercial," those for which the cost is borne by a commercial sponsor. The same program policies are made to apply to both; the only difference is one of method. The fact that NBC creates most of its sustaining programs while the commercially sponsored programs come from many sources merely means that with the former the method is a little more direct in the matter of maintaining balance. When policy problems arise in commercial programs, both the sales department and the program department are

called into conference since they are both involved. Another
department which, in order to be perfectly neutral, reports
neither to the sales department nor to the program department,
is also brought into the discussion. It is a continuity acceptance
department whose duty it is to check all commercial scripts, of
whatever nature, and approve them for policy before they are
allowed on the air. This approval covers not only program and
sales policies, but those restrictions which are listed under the
head of client acceptance, product acceptance, the provisions
of the Federal Trade Commission, etc. In other words, before a
commercial program goes on the air, it must be given an inspection which will guarantee that it does not violate any of the
company's policies.

The maintenance of a proper schedule, which involves both
commercially sponsored and sustaining programs, brings up for
consideration a wide variety of points. One such point alone
has caused much perplexity; any decision on it is openly questioned: it is the simple point of program sequence. Is it better
to keep a sequence of programs all of the same general type,
or is it better to break the sequence with different types of
programs, such as music followed by drama? Since every
station wishes to hold its audience, should it follow a program
having a high rating with a similar program, thereby opening
itself to the charge of monotony, or should it follow with a
program of a different type, thereby running the risk of losing
part of its audience? It is a comparatively simple question, but
the answer is highly complex. Some of the reasons for this
complexity will be discussed in the next chapter.

The NBC network opens at 8:00 A.M. EST. It closes full
network operations at 1:00 A.M. EST. This means that the
network must be programmed for seventeen hours each day.
The most commonly used unit of program time is fifteen
minutes; this is particularly true throughout the daytime hours.
In the evening there are a large number of thirty-minute programs. Once in a while there is a program of forty-five
minutes and there are a few of one hour's duration. The job
of programming for a network is, therefore, a job of filling

every fifteen or thirty-minute period for a seventeen-hour day during seven days a week. That is a lot of programming. Add to this the number of local stations opening at 6:00 A.M. or 6:30 A.M. and those which run all night, and you greatly expand the total. No other medium in the world does anything comparable to it. The figures for one network alone are staggering. When one considers the radio industry as a whole, it is incomprehensible. A single figure may serve to prove the point. In June of 1943 the radio industry as a whole contributed eighteen thousand hours in announcements and programs dedicated to the war effort. That means some twenty days more than two years of solid listening. All of it had to be programmed, and all of it had to be fitted into other program schedules. All of this was at no cost to the government or to radio's millions of listeners — a fact for which the American system of broadcasting can take great credit.

It may be taken for granted that these schedules are no more and no less complicated than kindred time tables of other networks. It has been noted in the preface to this volume that the discussions are primarily concerned with NBC methods; however, the same general problems confront all networks and the solutions are roughly similar.

To illustrate the magnitude of the problem, the program schedules for two days of NBC network operations are given. Monday is typical of the schedules for five days of the week, Monday through Friday. Sunday has its special characteristics, as will be noted in the schedules shown on the following pages (pages 80 to 100).

NBC PROGRAMS SCHEDULED BY CHICAGO STATIONS

ISSUED BY "PROGRAM AND TRAFFIC" — SUNDAY, JANUARY 23, 1944

OPENING UNTIL 5:00 P.M.

WMAQ 670 kc   WENR — WLS 890 kc   WCFL 1000 kc

LEGEND: Items in CAPS: Originate in Chicago
Items in lower-case: Originate outside Chicago
CGM: Chicago Chimes
PUM: Chimes from Pickup
NBC: This is the NBC

TIME	STUDIO	FEED	NTW FACILITIES	PROGRAM	ANNCR-PRODN
A.M.					
7:00–7:05		O	Net	European News (s)	
7:05–7:30		O	Net	Organist (s)	
7:30–8:00		O	Net	Boone County Neighbors (s)	
8:00–	C	WMAQ	LCL	SIGN ON WMAQ	FITZPATRICK
8:00–8:15	C	WMAQ	Net	World News Roundup (s)	FITZPATRICK
8:15–8:30	C	WMAQ	Net	Commando Mary (s)	FITZPATRICK
					(OPEN)
					DOWNS
8:30–	ET-C	WMAQ	LCL	HILLS BROS T.S. (C)	DOWNS
8:30–8:43:30	C	WMAQ	LCL	RADIO PARADE (S)	HOLTMAN
					FITZPATRICK
					BEAN
8:30–9:00		O	Net	The Melody's the Thing (s)	
8:43:30–8:44:30	ET-C	WMAQ	LCL	MESSAGE OF THE DAY (S)	DOWNS
8:45–9:00	ET-C	WMAQ	LCL	REBDCST RELIGION IN THE NEWS (S)	
					DOWNS
9:00–9:30	F	WMAQ	NET NY & CHGO	NAT'L RADIO PULPIT (S)	HOLTMAN
					LATEAU

SUNDAY, JANUARY 23, 1944

TIME	STUDIO	FEED	NTW FACILITIES	PROGRAM	ANNCR-PRODN
A.M.					
9:30–	ET-C	WMAQ	LCL	AMER. CHICLE T. S. (C)	DOWNS
9:30–10:00	G	O	NET	WORDS & MUSIC (S)	FITZPATRICK
(B)ORTH FILE (P. S.)				CGM	BEAN
9:30–10:00	ET-C	WMAQ	LCL	CHGO HERALD AMERICAN (C)	DOWNS
				(Turning the Pages)	
10:00–	ET-C	WMAQ	LCL	FITZPATRICK T. S. (C)	DOWNS
10:00–10:30		O	Net DENVER	Rhapsody of the Rockies (s)	
				PUM	
10:00–10:30	ET-C	WMAQ	LCL	SIMONIZ (C)	HOLTMAN
				(Sunshine Serenade)	
10:30–	ET-C	WMAQ	LCL	AMER. CHICLE T. S. (C)	HOLTMAN
10:30–10:45		O	Net	News (s)	
10:30–10:45	G	WMAQ	LCL (MVX)	CLOYD HEAD (S)	DOWNS
	ET-C STDBY			(News Commentary)	
10:45–11:00		O	Net	Modern Foods (c)	
				(Olivio Santoro)	
10:45–11:00	T	O	NET	CAROL SISTERS (S)	HOLTMAN
				CGM-R	LATEAU
10:45–10:59:40	U	WMAQ	LCL	EVANS FUR CO. (C)	FITZPATRICK
				(Johnny Betts)	BEAN
10:59:40	ET-C-U	WMAQ	LCL	AMER. CHICLE T. S. (C)	FITZPATRICK
11:00–11:30	M		Net CINCINNATI	Bunte Bros (c)	DOWNS
	G-STDBY			(World Front)	
	(ORGAN)			"NBC" FM P. U. (5 SEC PAUSE)	
				CGM	
11:00–11:30		WMAQ	Net	Bunte Bros (c)	FITZPATRICK
			JOB	(TIE IN ANNCT)	BEAN
11:30–	U	WMAQ	LCL	MUSTEROLE T. S. (C)	FITZPATRICK

SUNDAY, JANUARY 23, 1944

TIME	STUDIO	FEED	NTW FACILITIES	PROGRAM	ANNCR-PRODN
A.M.					
11:30-12:00			Net	Prince Matchabelli (c) (Stradavari Orch)	
11:30-12:00	U	WMAQ	Net	Prince Matchabelli (c) (TIE IN ANNCT)	FITZPATRICK (OPEN) HOLTMAN
P.M.					
12:00–	U	WMAQ	LCL	GOLDENROD T. S. (C)	HOLTMAN
12:00-12:15 (A) ORTH SALE #2055 (R. R.)	H	WMAQ	NET	AMER DAIRY ASSN (C) (Voice of the Amer Dairy) CGM	FITZPATRICK BEAN
12:15-12:30	U	WMAQ	Net	Labor for Victory (s)	HOLTMAN
12:30-1:00 (B) ORTH	Nemo–U H-STDBY (HAMM) U of C	WMAQ	NET MITCHELL TOWER	UNIV OF CHGO ROUND TABLE(S) CGM	ELDER (P.U.) HOLTMAN
FILE (P. S.)					
1:00–	T	WMAQ	LCL	GENERAL ELECTRIC T. S. (C)	FITZPATRICK
1:00-1:30	T	WMAQ	Net COAST JOB	General Foods (c) (Those We Love) PUM	FITZPATRICK
1:30–	T	WMAQ	LCL	PLOUGH T. S. (C)	FITZPATRICK
1:30-2:00	T	WMAQ	Net COAST JOB	Westinghouse Electric (c) (The Westinghouse Program) PUM	FITZPATRICK (OPEN) DOWNS
2:00–	T	WMAQ	LCL	BEAUMONT T. S. (C)	DOWNS
2:00-2:15	T	WMAQ	Net	Candy Council (c) (Washington Reports on Rationing)	DOWNS

SUNDAY, JANUARY 23, 1944

TIME	STUDIO	FEED	NTW FACILITIES	PROGRAM	ANNCR–PRODN
P.M.					
2:15–2:30	T	WMAQ	Net COAST & NY	Sheaffer Pen (c)	DOWNS (OPEN)
			JOB	(World News Parade) PUM	HOLTMAN
2:30–	T	WMAQ	LCL	GOLDENROD T. S. (C)	HOLTMAN
2:30–3:30	D		Net NY & JOB SPECIFIED POINTS	This Is the Army Hour (s)	DOWNS (OPEN) HOLTMAN
2:30–3:30	D–U	WMAQ	Net JOB	This is the Army Hour (s)	FITZPATRICK (OPEN) DOWNS
3:30–	U	WMAQ	LCL	CHUCKLES T. S. (C)	DOWNS
3:30–3:55	U	WMAQ	Net	Lands of the Free (s)	DOWNS (OPEN) BENSON
3:55–4:00	H	O	Net	News (s)	FARRALL
3:55–4:00	G–STDBY (ORGAN)	WMAQ	LCL (MVX)	HENRY C. LYTTON & SONS (C) (News)	
4:00–5:00	T	WMAQ	Net	General Motors (c) (Symphony of the Air)	BENSON

Program and Traffic Schedules
Sunday, January 23, 1944 — 5:00 P.M.-1:00 A.M.

Time	Studio	Feed	NTW Facilities	Program	Anncr-Prodn
P.M.					
5:00—	T	WMAQ	LCL	HUEBINGER T. S. (C)	BENSON
5:00-5:30	T	WMAQ	Net	Catholic Hour (s)	BENSON
					(OPEN)
					FARRALL
					FARRALL
					FARRALL
					ROEN
5:30-6:00	T	WMAQ	Net COAST / JOB	Kraft (c) (TIE IN ANNCT) PUM	
5:30-6:00			Net COAST	Kraft (c) (The Great Gildersleeve) PUM	
6:00-6:30	U	WMAQ	Net COAST / JOB	General Foods (c) (Jack Benny) PUM	DONOVAN
6:30—	U	WMAQ	LCL	BULOVA T. S. (C) (20)	DONOVAN
6:30-7:00	U	WMAQ	Net	F. W. Fitch (c) (Fitch Bandwagon)	DONOVAN
7:00—	U	WMAQ	LCL	BULOVA T. S. (C) (10)	DONOVAN
7:00-7:30	U	WMAQ	Net COAST &	Standard Brands (c)	DONOVAN
					(OPEN)
6 SEC SW. TO NY APPX 7:28:29 ON CUE: "THIS IS BILL GOODWIN SAYING GOODNIGHT FM HLYD'S RADIO CITY."			JOB NY	(Edgar Bergen & Charlie McCarthy)	BENSON
7:30-8:00	U	WMAQ	Net COAST / JOB	Standard Brands (c) (One Man's Family) PUM	BENSON

SUNDAY, JANUARY 23, 1944

TIME	STUDIO	FEED	NTW FACILITIES	PROGRAM	ANNCR-PRODN
P.M.					
8:00–	U	WMAQ	LCL	BULOVA T. S. (C) (20)	BENSON
8:00–8:30	T	WMAQ	Net	R. L. Watkins (c) (Manhattan Merry Go Round)	FARRALL
8:30–9:00	T	WMAQ	Net	Bayer Aspirin (c) (Amer. Album of Fam Music)	FARRALL
9:00–9:30	T	WMAQ	Net	General Electric (c) (Hour of Charm)	FARRALL
9:00–10:00	M	WMAQ	Net COAST JOB	P. Lorillard Co. (c) (Bob Crosby) PUM	DONOVAN
10:00–	M	WMAQ	LCL	BULOVA T. S. (C) (10)	DONOVAN
10:00–10:15		O	Net	Press News (s)	
10:00–10:15	T H-STDBY (PIANO)	WMAQ	LCL (MVX)	GROVE LAB (C) (News)	BENSON
10:15–10:30	G	WMAQ	NET NY & CHGO	MILES LAB (C) (News of the World)	LYON DONOVAN GILLIS
10:30–	G	WMAQ	LCL	DRUGGIST (S) (25)	DONOVAN
10:30–10:45	G	WMAQ	LCL	LITTLE CROW MILLING (C) (Coco Wheats Melody Time)	DONOVAN KIRBY GILLIS
10:30–11:00	M	O	Net COAST & JOB PHILA.	The Pacific Story (s) PUM	

(A) ORTH REBDCST WMAQ
11:15–11:45 P.M. (P.S.)

SUNDAY, JANUARY 23, 1944

TIME	STUDIO	FEED	NTW FACILITIES	PROGRAM	ANNCR-PRODN
P.M.					
10:45-11:00	ET-C	WMAQ	LCL	RHUMBA TIME (S) / OWI #1 (S) (ET) (100) / OWI WAC (S) (100)	BENSON
11:00-	ET-C	WMAQ	LCL	AMER CHICLE T. S. (C)	BENSON
11:00-11:05		O	Net	News (s)	
11:00-11:10	C	WMAQ	LCL (MVX)	CHGO SUN (C) (News)	DONOVAN
11:05-11:30	ET-STDBY	O	Net COAST	Thomas Peluso & Orch (s) PUM	
11:10-11:15	ET-C	WMAQ	LCL	MOMENT MUSICALE (C-S) / ILL BELL (C) (100) / CORONET (C) (ET) (100)	DONOVAN
11:15-	C	WMAQ	LCL	BRIGGS. T. S. (C)	DONOVAN
11:15-11:45	ET-C	WMAQ	LCL	REBDCST-PACIFIC STORY (S)	DONOVAN
11:30-11:55		O	Net	Francis Craig & His Orch (s)	
11:45-11:55	ET-C	WMAQ	LCL	A LITTLE NIGHT MUSIC (S) / OWI #2 (S) (ET) (100) / INFANTILE PARALYSIS (S) (100)	DONOVAN
11:55-12:00	T	WMAQ	Net	News Reports (s)	BENSON
A.M.					
12:00-12:30	Nemo-T H-STDBY (PIANO)	WMAQ	LCL PUMP ROOM	AMBASSADOR EAST (S) (Emile Petti)	BENSON
12:30-12:55	ET-C	WMAQ	LCL (MVX)	POT LUCK (S) / OWI #4 (S) (ET) (100) / SAFETY (S) (100)	DONOVAN
12:55-1:00	C	WMAQ	LCL (MVX)	NEWS (S)	DONOVAN
1:00-	C	WMAQ	LCL	SIGN OFF WMAQ	DONOVAN
1:00-1:01	ET-C	WMAQ	LCL	NATIONAL ANTHEM (S)	DONOVAN

MONDAY, JANUARY 24, 1944 — OPENING UNTIL 5:00 P.M.

TIME	STUDIO	FEED	NTW FACILITIES	PROGRAM	ANNCR-PRODN
A.M.					
5:30–	C	WMAQ	LCL	SIGN ON WMAQ	ALLEN
5:30–5:35	C	WMAQ	LCL (MVX)	NEWS (S)	ALLEN
5:35–5:59	ET-STDBY ET-C	WMAQ	LCL (MVX)	THE EARLY BIRD (S) OWI #1 (S) (ET) (100) OWI-WAC (S) (100) SAFETY (S) (100)	ALLEN
5:59–6:00	ET-C	WMAQ	LCL	MARCH OF DIMES (S) (ET) (5 min) MESSAGE OF THE DAY (S)	ALLEN
6:00–6:15	ET-C	WMAQ	LCL (MVX)	NEWS (S) (ET & LIVE)	ALLEN
6:15–6:45	ET-C	WMAQ	LCL	OWI #2 (S) (ET) (100) TOWN & FARM (S) (ET & LIVE) (Everett Mitchell)	ALLEN
6:45–6:55	ET-C	WMAQ	LCL	MORNING JUBILEE (C-S) MARYLAND (C) (ET & LIVE) (100) MARLIN (C) (ET) (100) OWI #4 (S) (ET) (100)	ALLEN
6:45–7:00 RING CHIMES TO NET PRECEDING PROGRAM	D	O	NET	GROVE LAB (C) (Reveille Roundup) CGM	KIRBY GIBBS
6:55–7:00	ET-C	WMAQ	LCL (MVX)	WALGREEN (C) (ET & LIVE) (News)	ALLEN
7:00–7:15 (A) ORTH REBDCST KOA 8:30–8:45 AM(SD)	G	WLS	NET (MVX)	SKELLY OIL (C) (News-Alex Dreier) CGM	ROEN
7:00–7:15		O	Net	World News Roundup (s)	
7:00–7:55	ET-C	WMAQ	LCL	CHGO N. W. RR (C) (ET & LIVE) (The "400" Hour)	ALLEN
7:15–7:45		O	Net	Do You Remember (s)	

MONDAY, JANUARY 24, 1944

TIME	STUDIO	FEED	NTW FACILITIES	PROGRAM	ANNCR-PRODN
A.M.					
7:45–8:00	D	O	Net	Associated Press News (s)	KIRBY
7:45–8:00		O	NET	GROVE LAB (C)	GIBBS
(A) ORTH REBDCST WED				(Reveille Roundup)	
WMAQ 11:45–12:00 (SD)				CGM	
7:55–8:00	H	WMAQ	LCL (MVX)	QUAKER OATS (C)	ROEN
				(News–Clifton Utley)	
				(TEL FILTER)	
8:00–8:30		O	Net	Mirth and Madness (s)	
8:00–8:30	ET-C	WMAQ	LCL	WIEBOLDTS INC (C) (ET & LIVE)	ALLEN
				(Your Neighbor Program)	
8:30–	ET-C	WMAQ	LCL	HILLS BROS T. S. (C)	ALLEN
8:30–8:40	ET-C	WMAQ	LCL	PEARSALL BUTTER CO (C)	HOLTMAN
				(Music To Your Taste)	
8:30–8:45		O	Net		
8:30–8:45	ET-K	KOA		REBDCST–SKELLY OIL (C)	ROEN
				(News–Alex Dreier)	SHAHEEN
				CGM–R	
8:40–8:44:40	T	WMAQ	LCL (MVX)	WILSON COMPANY (C)	KIRBY
				(U. P. News)	
8:44:40–	ET-C	WMAQ	LCL	AMER CHICLE T. S. (C)	HOLTMAN
8:45–9:00		O	Net	Special Assignment (s)	
8:45–9:00	ET-C	WMAQ	LCL	EVANS FUR CO (C) (ET & LIVE)	HOLTMAN
				(Songs in Fashion)	
9:00–	C	WMAQ	LCL	MUSTEROLE T. S. (C)	HOLTMAN
9:00–9:15	M	WMAQ	Net	B. T. Babbitt (e)	ROEN
				(Lora Lawton)	
9:15–9:30	H	WMAQ	NET	STORY DRAMAS BY OLMSTED (S)	HOLTMAN
				CGM	BUBECK

MONDAY, JANUARY 24, 1944

TIME	STUDIO	FEED	NTW FACILITIES	PROGRAM	ANNCR-PRODN
A.M.					
9:30–9:45	G-U	WMAQ	NET	CUDAHY PACKING CO (C) (Helpmate) CGM-SYN	LYON GILLIS
9:30–9:45	D	O	NET	GROVE LAB (C) (Reveille Roundup) CGM-SYN	KIRBY CAVALLO
9:45–10:00	M	WMAQ	Net COAST JOB	P & G (Dreft) (c) (Star Playhouse) PUM	ALLEN
9:45–10:00	V-G	O WMAQ CHGO RCDG	Net NET	Music Room (s) P & G (DUZ) (C) (Road of Life) (TEL FILTER)	LYON (G) HOLTMAN GILLIS
10:00–10:14:40 NO MUSIC TO CHGO RCDG					
10:14:40– NO STATN IDENT.	G	WMAQ	Net	"NBC" NO CHIMES P & G (Drene) Annct (c)	LYON
10:15–10:30	H-F		NET CHGO & NY	P & G (CRISCO) (C) (Vic and Sade) CGM	KIRBY HECK (F) GIBBS (H) ROEN BUBECK
10:15–10:30 (A) ORTH SALE #2210 (RR)	F-C	IOA NBR	Net JOB	P & G (CRISCO) (C) (IVORY FLAKES TIE IN)	
10:15–10:30	F-U	WMAQ	Net JOB	P & G (Crisco) (c) (AMER FAMILY TIE-IN)	ALLEN CAVALLO FITZPATRICK
10:30–10:45	M	WMAQ	Net	P & G (Ivory) (c) (Brave Tomorrow)	
10:30–10:45 (B) NON ORTH SALE #2026 (RR)	T	IOA NBR	Net	P & G (Ivory) (c) (WHITE LAUNDRY TIE-IN) CGM R	HOLTMAN GILLIS

MONDAY, JANUARY 24, 1944

TIME	STUDIO	FEED	NTW FACILITIES	PROGRAM	ANNCR-PRODN
A.M.					
10:45–11:00	M	WMAQ	Net	B. T. Babbitt (c) (David Harum)	FITZPATRICK
11:00–	M	WMAQ	LCL	CHUCKLES T. S. (C)	FITZPATRICK
11:00–11:15	G	O	NET	WORDS & MUSIC (S) CGM	HOLTMAN BUBECK
11:00–11:15	ET-C	WMAQ	LCL	KROGER STORES (C) (ET & LIVE) (Editor's Daughter)	LYON OBERG
11:15–11:30	G	O	NET	WORDS & MUSIC (S) CGM	HOLTMAN BUBECK
11:15–11:30	ET-C	WMAQ	LCL	KROGER STORES (C) (Linda's First Love)	LYON OBERG
11:30–	ET-C	WMAQ	LCL	AMER CHICLE T. S. (C)	LYON
11:30–11:45	H	WMAQ	LCL (MVX)	CHGO DAILY NEWS (C) (News Commentary)	ROEN
	G-STDBY (ORGAN)			U. S. Navy Band (s)	
11:30–12:00		O	Net		
11:45–12:00	ET-C	WMAQ	LCL	REBDCST-GROVE LAB (C) (Reveille Roundup)	FITZPATRICK
P.M.					
12:00–12:01	F	WMAQ	LCL	COM. EDISON (C)	ROEN HART
12:00–12:15 NO BREAK		O	Net DENVER	Sketches in Melody (s)	
12:01–12:15	F	WMAQ	LCL (MVX)	ELIZABETH HART PRESENTS (S)	ROEN GILLIS
	G-STDBY (ORGAN)				
12:15–12:30		O	Net DENVER	Sketches in Melody (s) PUM	

MONDAY, JANUARY 24, 1944

TIME	STUDIO	FEED	NTW FACILITIES	PROGRAM	ANNCR-PRODN
P.M.					
12:15-12:30	ET-C	WMAQ	LCL	TUNES & TIPS (C-S) POTTER (C) (ET) (100) COLGATE (C) (ET) (100) MARYLAND (C) (ET) (100) CONTINENTAL (C) (ET) (100) PILLSBURG (C) (ET) (100)	FITZPATRICK OBERG
12:30-	C	WMAQ	LCL	WASTE PAPER T. S. (C)	FITZPATRICK
12:30-12:45	T	O	NET	ECHOES FROM THE TROPICS (S) CGM (ECHO)	ROEN CAVALLO
12:30-12:44:40	H ET-C STDBY	WMAQ	LCL (MVX)	MENTHOLATUM (C) (News)	ELDER
12:44:40	ET-C	WMAQ	LCL	AMER CHICLE T. S. (C)	KIRBY
12:45-1:00		WCFL	Net	Carey Longmire (s)	
12:45-12:59:30	ET-C	WMAQ	LCL	OMAR INC (C) (Ranch House Jim)	
12:59:30-	ET-C	WMAQ	LCL	FITZPATRICK T. S. (C)	KIRBY OBERG KIRBY
1:00-1:15	V-G	WMAQ	NET	GENERAL MILLS (C) (The Guiding Light)	LYON CREWS
CONCL CUE: "LISTEN TO TODAY'S CHILDREN" NO CHIMES OR STATN IDENT. (2) (A) ORTH REBDCST (SD)					
1:15-1:30	B-G	WMAQ	NET	GENERAL MILLS (C) (Today's Children)	LYON HECK
CONCL CUE: "10 SEC PAUSE FOR STATN IDENT. NO CHIMES (A) ORTH REBDCST (SD)					

MONDAY, JANUARY 24, 1944

TIME	STUDIO	FEED	NTW FACILITIES	PROGRAM	ANNCR-PRODN
P.M.					
1:30–1:45 (A) ORTH REBDCST (SD) CONCL CUE: "HYMNS OF ALL CHURCHES WHICH FOLLOWS IMMED." NO CHIMES OR STATN IDENT.	M	WMAQ	Net	General Mills (c) (Light of the World)	HOLTMAN
1:45–2:00 (A) ORTH REBDCST (SD)	D	WMAQ	NET	GENERAL MILLS (C) (Hymns of All Churches) CGM	LYON GIBBS
2:00–	M	WMAQ	LCL	GENERAL ELECTRIC T. S. (C)	FITZPATRICK
2:00–2:14:30 CONCL CUE: "NBC" NO CHIMES	M	WMAQ	Net	P & G (Ivory) (c) (A Woman of America)	FITZPATRICK
2:14:30– NO STATN IDENT.	M	WMAQ	Net	P & G (Pres. Birth. Ball) Annct (s)	FITZPATRICK
2:15–2:30 NO MUSIC TO DFS	C-G	WMAQ DFS	NET	P & G (OXYDOL) (C) (Ma Perkins) CGM	KIRBY (C) LYON GILLIS
2:30–2:44:40 CONCL CUE: "NBC" NO CHIMES			Net	P & G (Camay) (c) (Pepper Young's Family)	
2:30–2:44:40 CONCL CUE: "NBC" NO CHIMES	U	WMAQ	Net	P & G (Camay) (c) (AMER FAMILY TIE-IN)	FITZPATRICK HECK
2:44:40– NO STATN IDENT.			Net	P & G (Crisco) Annct (c)	
2:44:40– NO STATN IDENT.	U	WMAQ	Net	P & G (Crisco) Annct (c)	FITZPATRICK

MONDAY, JANUARY 24, 1944

Time	Studio	Feed	NTW Facilities	Program	Anncr-Prodn
P.M.					
2:45–3:00	M	WMAQ	Net	P & G (Ivory) (c) (The Right to Happiness)	LYON (OPEN)
3:00–	M	WMAQ	LCL	PLOUGH T.S. (C)	FITZPATRICK
3:00–3:14:40 OPENS NY TO CHGO APPX 3:00:20 ON CUE: "GET DOUBLE DANDERINE TODAY."	V		NET NY & CHGO	R. L. WATKINS (C) (Backstage Wife) "NBC" NO CHIMES	FITZPATRICK LYON GILLIS
3:00–3:14:40 CONCL CUE: "NBC" NO CHIMES	V-M	WMAQ	Net JOB	R. L. Watkins (c) (Backstage Wife)	FITZPATRICK
3:14:40– NO STATN IDENT.	V		Net	R. L. Watkins Annct (c)	LYON
3:14:40– NO STATN IDENT.	M	WMAQ	LCL	CAL ASPERIN ANNCT (C)	FITZPATRICK
3:15–3:30	M	WMAQ	Net	Chas. H. Phillips (c) (Stella Dallas)	FITZPATRICK
3:30–3:45 NO CHIMES OR STATN IDENT.	M	WMAQ	Net	Chas. H. Phillips (c) (Lorenzo Jones)	FITZPATRICK
8:45–4:00	M	WMAQ	Net	Bayer Co (c) (Young Widder Brown)	FITZPATRICK
4:00–4:14:30 CONCL CUE: "NBC" NO CHIMES	M	WMAQ	Net	General Foods (c) (When A Girl Marries)	FITZPATRICK
4:00–4:14:30 CONCL CUE: "NBC" NO CHIMES	G	IND IOA NBR	Net	General Foods (c) (TIE IN ANNCT)	LYON HECK

MONDAY, JANUARY 24, 1944

TIME	STUDIO	FEED	NTW FACILITIES	PROGRAM	ANNCR–PRODN
P.M.					
4:14:30– CONCL CUE: NO STATN IDENT.	M	WMAQ	Net	General Foods Annct (c)	FITZPATRICK
4:14:30– CONCL CUE: NO STATN IDENT.	G	IND IOA NBR	Net	General Foods Annct (c)	LYON
4:15–4:30	M	WMAQ	Net	General Foods (c) (Portia Faces Life)	FITZPATRICK
4:30–4:45 NO CHIMES OR STATN IDENT.	M	WMAQ	Net	American Home Products (c) (Just Plain Bill)	FITZPATRICK (OPEN) FARRALL
4:45–5:00	M	WMAQ	Net	American Home Products (c) (Front Page Farrall)	FARRALL

PROGRAM AND TRAFFIC SCHEDULES

MONDAY, JANUARY 24, 1944 — 5:00 P.M. TO CLOSING

TIME	STUDIO	FEED	NTW FACILITIES	PROGRAM	ANNCR-PRODN
P.M.					
5:00–	ET-C-G	WMAQ	LCL	SCHUTTER T.S. (C)	ELDER
5:00–5:05	G	WMAQ	LCL (MVX)	CAMPBELL CEREAL (C)	ELDER
	STDBY			(News-Don Elder)	
5:00–5:15		O	Net	News (s)	
5:05–5:15	ET-C	WMAQ	LCL	MUSIC AT FIVE-O-FIVE (C–S)	FARRALL
				COLGATE (C) (ET) (100)	HART
				CONTINENTAL (C) (ET) (100)	FOOTE
				RIT (C) (ET) (100)	
5:15–5:20	ET-C	WMAQ	LCL (MVX)	WALGREEN CO (C) (ET & LIVE)	NOBLE
	ET-STDBY			(War Commentary)	
5:15–5:40	T	O	Net	Serenade to America (s)	
5:20–5:25		WMAQ	LCL	KITCHEN ART FOODS (C)	DOWNS
				(Happy Jack)	BUBECK
5:25–5:30	ET-C	WMAQ	LCL	SEECK & KADE (C)	FARRALL
				(Singing Neighbor)	FOOTE
5:30–	ET-C	WMAQ	LCL	THOS J. WEBB T.S. (C)	FARRALL
5:30–5:40	ET-C	WMAQ	LCL	MUSICAL MEMORIES (C–S)	FARRALL
				JOHNSON (C) (ET) (100)	HART
				MARYLAND (C) (ET) (100)	FOOTE
				WILCOX GAY (C) (100)	
5:40–5:45	J	O	Net	Presenting Jim Boring (s)	NOBLE
5:40–5:45	ET-C	WMAQ	LCL	PATRIOTS ON PARADE (S)	HECK
	STDBY				
5:45–	ET-C	WMAQ	LCL	BEAUMONT T.S. (C)	FARRALL

MONDAY, JANUARY 24, 1944

TIME	STUDIO	FEED	NTW FACILITIES	PROGRAM	ANNCR-PRODN
P.M.					
5:45–6:00		O	Net	Sun Oil (c) (Lowell Thomas)	
5:45–6:00	G G–STDBY (PIANO)	WMAQ	LCL (MVX)	PETER PAUL INC (C) (News–Dick Noble)	DOWNS
6:00–6:15		O	Net	Liggett & Myers (c) (Fred Waring)	
6:00–6:15	ET–C	WMAQ	LCL	SWEET & SPANISH (C–S) POTTER (C) (ET) (100) RIT (C) (ET) (100) LEVER (C) (ET) (100) MARYLAND (C) (ET) (100) ORANGE CRUSH (C) (ET & LIVE) (100)	FARRALL HART OBERG
6:15–6:30	G	WMAQ	NET NY CHGO JOB & COAST	MILES LAB (C) (News of the World)	LYON BUBECK
6:30–	T	WMAQ	LCL	BULOVA T.S. (C) (10)	DOWNS
6:30–6:45	F	O	NET	THE CAROL SISTERS (S) CGM	FARRALL GILLIS
6:30–6:45	T	WMAQ	LCL	MCLAUGHLIN (C) (Supper Interlude) (1–77A & 1–77B) (ECHO)	MURPHY CAVALLO
6:45–7:00	M	WMAQ	Net	Pure Oil (c) (H. V. Kaltenborn)	BENSON
7:00–7:30	T	WMAQ	Net	DuPont (c)	FARRALL (OPEN) BENSON
				(Cavalcade of America)	

MONDAY, JANUARY 24, 1944

TIME	STUDIO	FEED	NTW FACILITIES	PROGRAM	ANNCR–PRODN
P.M.					
7:30–8:00	T	WMAQ	Net HOUSTON	Firestone (c)	BENSON
	G-STDBY (PIANO)		JOB	(The Voice of Firestone) NBC FM. PU CGM	(OPEN) DOWNS
8:00–	T	WMAQ	LCL	BULOVA T. S. (C) (20)	DOWNS
8:00–8:30	T	WMAQ	Net	Bell Telephone System (c)	DOWNS (OPEN)
8:30–9:00	T	WMAQ	Net	(The Telephone Hour) Vicks Chemical Co (c) (Dr. I. Q.)	FARRALL FARRALL
9:00–	T	WMAQ	LCL	BULOVA T. S. (C) (20) CARNATION (S)	FARRALL DOWNS
9:00–9:30	A	WMAQ	NET (SRS)	(Contented Hour) CGM (ECHO & 6–77B)	BEAN
9:30–10:00	M	WMAQ	Net	H. J. Heinz (c) (Information Please)	FARRALL
9:30–10:00 (A) PROC. ORTH SALE #3060 (RR)	F		JOB	LONE RANGER PGM. FM C. Q.	
10:00–	M	WMAQ	LCL	BULOVA T. S. (C) (10)	FARRALL
10:00–10:15	M	WMAQ	Net	Liggett & Myers (c) (Fred Waring)	FARRALL
10:00–10:15	T	O	NET (MVX)	ASSOCIATED PRESS NEWS (S) CGM-R	DOWNS
10:15–	G-STDBY (PIANO) ET–H	WMAQ	LCL	PARAMOUNT T. S. (C) (ET & LIVE)	BENSON

MONDAY, JANUARY 24, 1944

TIME	STUDIO	FEED	NTW FACILITIES	PROGRAM	ANNCR–PRODN
P.M.					
10:15–10:30		O	Net	Harkness of Washington (s)	
10:15–10:30	H	WMAQ	LCL (MVX)	RICHMAN BROS (C)	BENSON
	G–STDBY (PIANO)			(News–Kleve Kirby)	KIRBY
10:30–	H	WMAQ	LCL	DRUGGIST T. S. (C) (25)	BENSON
10:30–10:45	U	WMAQ	LCL	ATLANTIC BREWING INC (C)	DOWNS
				(Tavern Pale Playtime)	BEAN
10:30–11:00		O	Net	DuPont (c)	
				(Cavalcade of America)	
10:30–11:00	D	O	NET	ESCAPE (S)	KIRBY
(A) ORTH REBDCST				(ECHO & FILTER)	FARRALL
11:15–11:45 PM WMAQ (PS)				CGM–R	JACOBSON
SAFETY COPY TO FILE					
10:45–10:59:40	ET–C	WMAQ	LCL	BEAUMONT LAB (C)	GIBNEY
				(Guest Star Theater)	LAWRENCE
10:59:40	ET–C	WMAQ	LCL	AMER CHICLE T. S. (C)	BENSON
11:00–11:05	T	O	NET (MVX)	NEWS REPORTS (S)	NOBLE
	G–STDBY (PIANO)			CGM	
11:00–11:10	C	WMAQ	LCL (MVX)	CHGO SUN (C)	BENSON
	ET–STDBY			(News)	
11:00–11:30		O	Net	Bell Telephone System (c)	
				(The Telephone Hour)	
11:05–11:30	T	O	Net ST LOUIS	St. Louis Serenade (s)	NOBLE
	G–STDBY (PIANO)		JOB	"NBC" FM PU	
				CGM–R	
11:10–11:15	ET–C	WMAQ	LCL	MOMENT MUSICALE (C–S)	DOWNS
				SEECK & KADE (C) (ET) (100)	
				ILL BELL (C) (100)	

MONDAY, JANUARY 24, 1944

TIME	STUDIO	FEED	NTW FACILITIES	PROGRAM	ANNCR-PRODN
P.M.					
11:15–					
11:15–11:45	C	WMAQ	LCL	BRIGGS T. S. (C)	DOWNS
11:15–11:55	ET-C	WMAQ	LCL	REB'CST-ESCAPE (S)	BENSON
11:30–11:55		O	Net	Three Suns Trio (s)	
11:45–11:55	ET-C	WMAQ	LCL	A LITTLE NIGHT MUSIC (S)	BENSON
				OWI #7 (S) (ET) (100)	
				OWI NAVY (S) (100)	
11:55–12:00	T	WMAQ	Net	News Reports (s)	DOWNS
A.M.					
12:00–12:30	Nemo–T G-STDBY (PIANO)	WMAQ	LCL PUMP ROOM	AMBASSADOR EAST (S) (Emile Petti)	FARRALL(PU) DOWNS
12:30–12:55	ET-C	WMAQ	LCL (MVX)	POT LUCK (S)	BENSON
				OWI #8 (S) (ET) (100)	
				SAFETY (S) (100)	
				OWI WAR FOOD (S) (100)	
				INFANTILE PARALYSIS (S) (100)	
12:55–1:00	C	WMAQ	LCL (MVX)	NEWS (S)	BENSON
1:00–	C	WMAQ	LCL	SIGN OFF WMAQ	BENSON
1:00–1:01	ET-C	WMAQ	LCL	NATIONAL ANTHEM (S)	BENSON

Legend for NBC Program Schedules

LCL	Local Program
NET	Network Program
MVX	Memovox (Paper recording)
SRS	Sound Reinforcing System (Loud-Speaker for Audience Shows)
ET	Electrical Transcription
ET & LIVE	Employing both transcribed and live talent
REBDCST	Rebroadcast (Program recorded off network and rebroadcast locally by electrical transcription)
KOA	Leg of Blue Network
IND	
IOA	Legs of NBC Network
NEB	
TEL FILTER	Telephone Filter (Microphone used to give effect of telephone conversation)
ECHO	Echo Chamber (Used for resonating effects)
T. S.	Time Signal
(C)	Commercial Program
(S)	Sustaining Program
(100)	100 Word announcement
(30)	30 Word announcement
(10)	10 Word announcement
ORTH	Orthacoustic
NON ORTH	Non-Orthacoustic $\Big\}$ These are all terms used in recording and
FILE	Recording for file $\quad$ transcribing programs.
NEW DISC	Unused recording disc
STDBY	Standby (Music ready to fill time in case of emergency)
77 B	
77 A	Special Microphones
JOB	Special incoming channel (There are four in all)
PU	Pickup
NY	New York origination
SW	Switch
HAMM	Hammond Organ
CGM–SYN	Synchronized chimes (When two programs originate from the same place and conclude at same time, chimes in the two studios are rung simultaneously.)
FACILITIES COLUMN	Any listing appearing in this column, except MVX or SRB, indicates origination point of program.

If the National Broadcasting Company's network were merely a line of stations all tied together throughout the day and evening, the operation would be comparatively simple. A radio network, however, is much like a railroad network. There are lines running straight across the country, but there are also subsidiary lines which run in many directions. Over all these lines go through trains and locals. Indeed, the comparison might be carried further by saying that the services run all the way from deluxe accommodations to freight. They all are essential in that they provide a type of service which is in demand. So the varied types of radio programs even on a network are booked on a wide variety of network operations. A program leaving the New York studios may go clear through to the Pacific coast and be broadcast simultaneously by every station on the network. The program immediately following it, however, may be broadcast under very different circumstances. Suppose the sponsor does not have distribution for his product throughout the entire United States or suppose that he knows one section of the country to be very favorable to his product while another section is not so favorable. He may then originate a program in Chicago which he sends only to the eastern market. That leaves the networks open beyond Chicago. So while the one program is going east, it becomes necessary to build a program for the western end of the network, either in Hollywood or San Francisco, or Denver; or perhaps Chicago builds two programs, one to go east and one to go west at the same time. Suppose further that a local merchant in Chicago wishes to buy time on WMAQ for this identical period for a local program only. In that case Chicago might have to build three programs for the same fifteen-minute period. In fact, because of the peculiarities of the network setup and because Chicago is in a strategic position with respect to the NBC network, there have been times when the Chicago studios had four programs operating at exactly the same time, all being broadcast to different sections of the country. This means that for that particular period the programming effort is not merely being duplicated, as it is in a great many instances during the day, but is being quadrupled and must all come from one point.

Such an extreme case as the one just referred to does not happen often, but instances in which two different programs are being put out at the same time are extremely numerous.

One of the factors which causes duplication of program effort and which always must be considered in network programming is the time differential. This means, in simple terms, that when it is 8:30 P.M. in New York, it is 5:30 P.M. in Hollywood. If a sponsor feels that he wants an 8:30 audience, he simply cannot get it in all portions of the United States by a single broadcast. If he is willing to allow for an hour's difference, he can solve his problem by repeating the same program at two different times during the evening. In other words, if he broadcasts from New York at 8:30 and goes as far as Chicago, it is then 7:30 in Chicago and through the Middle West. If he does a second broadcast later in the evening, he can reach Denver and the Inter-Mountain country at 8:30 while reaching the West Coast in the western time zone at 7:30. This procedure is frequently followed. Some years ago NBC had a children's program, originating in Chicago, which had three broadcasts each day in order that it might be heard at the same time in three different time zones. Many instances might be given. They all emphasize the fact that the time differential and the problems incident to it become just one more factor to complicate the matter of network schedules.

Some of the inherent difficulties of split network operation can be eliminated by having numerous production centers along the network. With the exception of Mutual, the major networks all operate stations of their own at key points across the country, and these stations can be called upon to produce for the entire network or for portions of it. NBC has six such stations; CBS has nine; and the ABC has four.

The following example will show how this multiple production setup works in the case of NBC: while New York is originating a program to go as far west as Chicago and through the eastern zone except, perhaps, for the Southeast, that latter part of the country can be taken care of by a program from Washington. At the same time Chicago can be originating a program for the Middle West while San Francisco sends a program to the Coast network, and Denver may be originating something for the territory between Chicago and the Coast; or if Chicago should be busy with another type of operation, Cleveland may be called upon to originate a program.

In addition, there are other points throughout the network from which programs can originate without setting up additional facilities. These are points where NBC has affiliated stations whose personnel and facilities are often employed to bring in programs originating in their cities. Sometimes they furnish programs in the regular sustaining schedule. In addition to being familiar with the facilities set up at these points, it is also important that the New York office should know what talent units are available for these affiliates in the event that they are to be asked to furnish a sustaining program.

PROGRAM ORGANIZATION OF AFFILIATED STATIONS

In general, affiliated stations are of two types. One is the station which is in large demand by sponsors because of its strategic location in a center of population and which finds itself with a very heavy schedule of network commercial programs. The other is the station which is somewhat less in demand because of either its location or its low power and which by virtue of the fact that it has less time devoted to network commercials, either takes a higher percentage of network sustaining programs or originates more of its own programs independently.

The machinery for program control in a station follows the same general pattern as that of a network; the chief difference is, perhaps, the size of the staff. Most of the functions which are carried on in a large non-affiliated station are carried on also in a smaller station; the main variation is that in the latter case one person may be charged with the responsibility for jobs which would be given to several people in a larger setup. The very large affiliated stations have staffs covering nearly

all the departments which a network operates. In a very small
station some phase of nearly all of these activities is carried on
by someone, but in some cases the general manager may also
be the program manager, the chief announcer, the script writer,
and on occasion the baritone soloist! If a station carries a large
number of network programs, the amount of local program
activity is curtailed, of course. But no station is so far sold out
that it does not have an abundance of local programming to do
and, therefore, extensive application of program policy.

In order that a comparison may be made between a network
schedule and a similar schedule for a large network affiliate, a
schedule for Sunday and Monday is given herewith for WFAA,
Dallas, Texas.

STATION WFAA, DALLAS, TEXAS

SUNDAY, JANUARY 7, 1945

TIME	STUDIO	PROGRAM	NTW	ANNC'R	PRDCTN
7:00–7:05	E	News Summary	(Blue)	HV	
7:05–7:30	E	Woodshedders	(Blue)	HV	
7:30	E SPOT —	Clabber Girl	(50)	HV	
7:30–8:00	E	Baptist Hour (Fm. WSB Atlanta to WFAA via SPEC CKT)	(Nemo)		HV
8:00	E SPOT —	OWI — Wacs	(SX)	HV	
8:00–8:15	E	Morning News (Transit Grain)	(Talk)	EB/PH	PH
8:15	E SPOT —	Program Promotion	(SX)	HV	
8:15–8:30	E	Commando Mary	(NBC)	HV	
8:30	B	OWI — Careless Talk	(ET #2)	HV	
8:31–8:45	E SPOT —	Books — Old & New	(Talk)	PH	PH
8:45	E	News Promotion	(SX)	HV	
8:45–9:00	E	Hear Southland Singing	(ET)	HV	HV
9:00	E SPOT —	Program Promotion	(SX)	HV	
9:00–9:15	E	Harry C. Withers	(Talk)	PH	PH
9:15	E SPOT —	Gas Co	(50)	PH	PH
9:15–9:30	E	Voice of the Army	(ET #226)	PH	PH
9:30	C SPOT —	Dallas Railway	(100)	PH	
9:31–9:59	C	Dr. David Lefkowitz	(Talk)	HV	HV
9:59	C SPOT —	OWI — Combat Aircrews	(SX)	HV	
		(10:00–12:00 — STATION WBAP)			
12:00–12:14	D	Waltz Lives On	(ET)	HV	HV
12:14	D SPOT —	B. C. Remedy	(ET #AG-12)	HV	
12:15–12:30	E	America United	(NBC)	HV	
12:30	E SPOT —	OWI — Tin Salvage	(SX)	HV	
12:30–12:45	C	Tendersweet Musical Interlude (Iowa Canning)	(Music)	BS	KL
12:45	E SPOT —	Program Promotion	(SX)	EB	

SUNDAY, JANUARY 7, 1945

TIME	STUDIO	PROGRAM	NTW	ANNC'R	PRDCTN
12:45–1:00	E	News (Texas Textile)	(Talk)	HV/PH	PH
1:00	SPOT—	Nat'l Candy	(ET #4)	BS	
1:00–1:30	E	Memory Lane (D P & L)	(ET)	EB	EB
1:30	SPOT—	Rem	(ET #S3)	BS	
1:30–2:00	E	John Charles Thomas (Westinghouse)	(NBC)	BS	
2:00	SPOT—	Dr. Pepper	(ET S1 #8)	BS	
2:00–2:30	E	World Parade (Schaeffer Pen)	(NBC)	BS	
2:30	SPOT—	Rauscher Pierce	(50)	BS	
2:30–3:30	E	(Joint) Army Hour	(NBC)	HV	
3:30	SPOT—	OWI — Wacs	(SX)	HV	
3:30–4:00	E	Showtime (Interstate) (Fm. KPRC to WFAA & TQN)	(QC)	BS	
4:00	SPOT—	Linz Bros	(ET #1)	BS	

(4:00–6:00 — STATION WBAP)

TIME	STUDIO	PROGRAM	NTW	ANNC'R	PRDCTN
6:00–6:30	E	Jack Benny (Lucky Strike)	(NBC)	WE	
6:30	SPOT—	Burleson Honey	(25)	WE	
6:30–7:00	E	Bandwagon (F. W. Fitch)	(NBC)	WE	
7:00	SPOT—	Linz Bros	(ET #2)	WE	
7:00–7:30	E	Charlie McCarthy (Chase & Sanborn)	(NBC)	WE	
7:30	SPOT—	Beechnut Gum	(25)	WE	
7:30–8:00	E	One Man's Family (Standard Brands)	(NBC)	WE	
8:00	SPOT—	Doc Jackson	(25)	WE	
8:00–8:30	E	Manhattan Merry Go Round (Sterling Dr Lyons)	(NBC)	WE	
8:30	SPOT—	Penetro Nose Drops	(ET 6-1535 #16)	WE	
8:30–9:00	E	Album of Familiar Music (Sterling-Bayer)	(NBC)	WE	
9:00	SPOT—	Bulova Watch	(25)	WE	

(9:00–12:00 — STATION WBAP)

TIME	STUDIO	PROGRAM	NTW	ANNC'R	PRDCTN
10:00–10:15	E	News (Groves Labs)	(Talk)	WE/JS	JS

STATION WFAA, DALLAS, TEXAS

MONDAY, JANUARY 8, 1945

Texas Farm & Home Pgm (Fm. WTAW for WBAP & TQN)

TQN 6:02–6:15

TIME	STUDIO	PROGRAM	NTW	ANNC'R	PRDCTN
7:00	A	Early Birds Sign On	(½M)	AI	
7:00½–7:10½	E	Morning News (Peter Paul)	(Talk)	EB/PH	PH
7:10½–7:14	A	Early Birds	(Music)	NS/JJ	IW
7:14	A SPOT—	W. A. Green	(100)	NS	
7:15–7:30	A	Early Birds (Mentholatum)	(QC)	NS/JJ	IW
7:30	A SPOT—	Republic Bank	(25)	NS	
7:30–7:45	A	Early Birds (Wm. Cameron)	(QC)	NS/JJ	IW
7:45	A SPOT—	Peter Paul Choclettos	(50)	EB	
7:45½–8:00	E	Today's News (Griffin Mfg)	(ET #3)	JS/PH	PH
8:00	E SPOT—	A. Harris	(25)	EB	
8:00–8:15	A	Date at 8 with Birds (Purity)	(Music)	NS/JJ	IW
8:15–8:29	A	Early Birds	(Music)	NS/JJ	IW
	SPOTS—				
8:29	8:25 A SPOT—	Church & Dwight	(100)	NS	
		Tyler Comm College	(100)		

(8:30–10:30 — STATION WBAP)

TQN 8:45–9:00

TIME	STUDIO	PROGRAM	NTW	ANNC'R	PRDCTN
8:45–9:00	D	Rhythm Rally (Imperial Sugar) (NOTE: Fm. WFAA to TQN)	(QC)	PH	KL
q					
10:30–10:45	D	Star Playhouse (P&G Dreft)	(NBC)	PH	PH
10:45	D SPOT—	Gas Co	(25)	JS	
10:45–11:00	D	David Harum (B. T. Babbitt)	(NBC)	JS	
11:00	D SPOT—	Chamberlain Lotion	(1M)	JS	
11:01–11:06	E	News for Women (Producers Creamery)	(NBC)	PH	PH

MONDAY, JANUARY 8, 1945

TIME	STUDIO	PROGRAM	NTW	ANNC'R	PRDCTN
11:06	E SPOT—	Program Promotion	(SX)	WE	
11:06–11:15	E	Novelette	(ET)	WE	WE
	SPOTS—				
11:09		Super Suds	(ET 13 #3)		
11:11		Wonder Bread	(ET 4 #1)		
11:15	E SPOT—	Rit Dyes	(1M)	WE	
11:16–11:29	E	Texas School of the Air	(QS)	WE	
		(Fm. WBAP to KPRC SPEC CKT)			
11:29	E SPOT—	Cuticura	(ET S16 #10)	WE	
11:30–11:45	D	Life Can Be Beautiful (P&G Oxydol)	(ET 1646)	JS	JS
11:45	D SPOT—	Gas Co	(25)	WE	
11:45–12:00	C	Servess Program (W. H. Allen) (To KPRC & WOAI on SPEC CKT)		EB	IW
12:00	C SPOT—	Skidoo	(25)	WE	
12:00–12:15	E	Noon Day News (Fant Milling)	(Talk)	JS	JS
12:15	E SPOT—	Pepsi Cola	(ET 128 #5)	PH	
12:15–12:30	C	Mrs. Tucker's Smile (Int. Cotton Oil)	(ET #9)	NS	KL
12:30	C SPOT—	Sewell Motors	(25)	PH	

(12:30–3:00 — STATION WBAP)

TQN

TIME	STUDIO	PROGRAM	NTW	ANNC'R	PRDCTN
12:30–12:45		Burrus Mills (Fm. WBAP for WBAP & TQN)	(QC)		
12:45–1:00		Hawk & Buck (Fm. WBAP for WBAP & TQN)	(QC)		
3:00–3:15	E	Backstage Wife (Sterling-Haley's MO)	(NBC)	BS	
3:15–NO BREAK					
3:15–3:30	E SPOT—	Stella Dallas (Sterling-Phillips Cream)	(NBC)	BS	
3:30	E SPOT—	OWI — Tin Salvage	(SX)	BS	
3:30–3:45	E	Lorenzo Jones (Sterling-Bayers)	(NBC)	BS	
3:45–NO BREAK					
3:45–4:00	E	Young Widder Brown (Sterling-Phillips Mag)	(NBC)	BS	

Time	Studio	Program	Ntw	Annc'r	Prdctn
4:00	E SPOT—	Pertussin	(ET 51944–45 #15)	BS	
4:00–4:15	E	When a Girl Marries (Gen Foods-Maxwell House)	(NBC)	JS	
4:15–NO BREAK					
4:15–4:30	E	Portia Faces Life (Gen Foods-Bran)	(NBC)	JS	
4:30	E SPOT—	Bulova Watch	(25)	JS	
4:30–4:45	E	Just Plain Bill (Anacin)	(NBC)	JS	
4:45–NO BREAK					
4:45–5:00	E	Front Page Farrell (Hill's Cold Tablets)	(NBC)	JS	
5:00	E SPOT—	Musterole	(ET #7)	JS	
5:00–5:15	D	Goldbergs (P&G Duz)	(ET #1901)	BS	BS
5:15	E SPOT—	Bordens	(ET #4)	BS	
5:15–5:30	E	News (Planters Peanuts)	(Talk)	JS/HS	JS
5:30	E SPOT—	B. C. Remedy	(ET #PD–11)	BS	BS
		(5:31–6:30 — Station WBAP)			
6:30–6:45	E	Evening News Round Up (Nat'l Biscuits)	(Talk)	WE/JS	JS
6:45	E SPOT—	Dr. Pepper	(ET S1 #9)	BS	
6:45–7:00	E	Headline Time (Grand Prize) (Fm. KPRC)	(QC)	BS	
7:00	E SPOT—	Beich Candy	(ET #6)	BS	
7:00–7:30	E	Cavalcade of America (Du Pont)	(NBC)	BS	
7:30	E SPOT—	Luden's	(25)	BS	
7:30–8:00	E	Voice of Firestone (Firestone)	(NBC)	WE	
8:00	E SPOT—	Bulova Watch	(25)	WE	
8:00–8:30	E	Telephone Hour (Bell System)	(NBC)	WE	
8:30	E SPOT—	Conoco Oil	(25)	WE	
8:30–9:00	E	Information, Please (H. J. Heinz)	(NBC)	WE	
9:00	E SPOT—	Equitable Bldg.	(25)	BS	
9:00–9:30	E	Contented Hour (Carnation)	(NBC)	BS	
9:30	E SPOT—	Baird's Bakery	(ET #1)	BS	
9:30–10:00	E	Dr. I. Q. (Mars, Inc.)	(NBC)	BS	
10:00	E SPOT—	Wm. Cameron	(25)	BS	
10:00–10:15	E	News (Southern Select)	(Talk)	WE/JS	JS
10:15	E SPOT—	Listerine Tooth Powder	(ET 4130 #2)	BS	
		(10:15–12:00 — Station WBAP)			

PROGRAM ORGANIZATION OF LOCAL INDEPENDENT STATIONS

The operation of a local independent station is, naturally, much simpler than that of a large station, whether or not that station is affiliated with a network.

In a typical 250-watt station there will be very few "live talent" shows, with the exception of a woman's feature broadcast, generally, by a woman member of the staff, possibly some hillbilly music by local talent, and programs by a staff pianist. Otherwise, the schedule is made up of transcribed musical shows interspersed with commercial spot announcements. These announcements are written by the manager of the station, the salesman, or the announcer. Very often there is no one whose sole job is writing continuity.

The small station or the station in a small town or city has an opportunity to do a better public service job than is possible for a larger station in a larger community where there is likely to be a greater preponderance of commercial programs. Every civic organization has access to the station in its community, and the manager of the station is glad and eager to work with these groups. Such co-operation builds good will for the station and, in turn, helps out the daily program schedule. Often schools and colleges in these towns are able to build and present educational programs for in-school listening, and frequently broadcast programs merely of a promotional or public relations nature. These stations, too, more often than not carry a religious service broadcast by one of the local churches, sometimes selling time for this purpose, but frequently giving the time in exchange for the program. Many broadcasters and religious groups are trying to discourage the practice of selling time for religious programs; but inasmuch as well as over a million dollars was spent by religious groups in 1943 on local stations, it is hard to persuade stations to give up this source of revenue.[5]

The whole programming problem of a local non-affiliated station is centered in the resources available within the com-

[5] See Chapter 14.

munity. A station with network affiliations, of course, has the additional and considerable resource stemming from the network. To achieve a lasting place in the community, the policy of the station must be to build programs of high standard from the basic material available at home.

It will be apparent at this point that any discussion of program planning by networks or local stations must take into account a great many factors which are unpredictable as to number and a great many people who are often unpredictable as to action. Let us turn to the next chapter to see how this highly complex setup really works.

CHAPTER 7

THE MACHINERY OF PROGRAM PRODUCTION

THE JOB OF MAKING the machinery of program production actually work is a good deal like making a constantly changing picture out of a jigsaw puzzle, yet keeping it always intact. The figure is even more pertinent if you consider a jigsaw puzzle in which the over-all pattern is made up of numerous smaller pictures, each of which must be changed frequently, but when viewed at any given instant must seem to be in perfect shape. In other words, each program must be so fashioned as to accomplish its own purpose, yet fit in with the variety of other programs around it in such a way as to complete a larger pattern. However, since the unit is always the individual program, let us turn our attention to that.

MOTIVATION OF A PROGRAM

A program may get into the schedule in one of several ways. The most elementary way is that the program manager suddenly discovers that a period has to be filled. Perhaps a commercial program has been canceled. Perhaps a sustaining series is being concluded. The program manager and the other members of the program board have immediately to take into account a number of considerations. The most obvious is the time of day or night of the period which is to be filled. Another is whether it is to go to a limited network or whether it is to go coast-to-coast. Still another is the program sequence in which the period occurs; that is to say, what type of programs are ahead of it and what type will follow it? Availability of talent must be considered also.

Suppose, for example, it were a fifteen-minute period which came at a time when all the staff musicians were rehearsing for a symphony program. Those musicians simply would not be available for another program at that time. A still further consideration would be the possible origination point; that is, is the schedule of the network at this period such as would make it possible to originate a program in Hollywood or Chicago or New York, or must its origination be confined to only one of these three places? These are typical of the problems that must be taken into account in planning any kind of program to fill a particular period. When the motivation for program activity is merely that of having a period to fill, the answers to many questions of this type must be sought immediately.

Perhaps the program machinery is set in motion by the approach of a holiday. The NBC program board together with the heads of various departments spent weeks in planning the three-hour Christmas-afternoon program of 1943. Again, all sorts of questions were asked and answered. Since Christmas fell on Saturday and since NBC had no commercial programs on Saturday afternoon, the problem of canceling commercials was not involved. Had Christmas fallen on any other day, this would have been a consideration, though not a serious one, since this project was so important to the network that commercials would have been canceled anyway, as indeed they are for many special programs having to do with holidays.

Another motivation might have come from a special occasion. Sometimes these plans are made well in advance, and sometimes they are made on very short notice. Those made for the exclusive broadcast of the ceremony honoring Orville Wright on the fortieth anniversary of the Kittyhawk flight were planned well in advance. Of the two broadcasts, one was rudely interrupted by a blizzard at Kittyhawk the night before the ceremony, with the result that the whole program plan had to be changed during the night. The broadcast of "Victory, Act I," celebrating the collapse of Italy, was one which was planned and worked out well in advance, but for which the actual time had to be set on short notice.

Another type of motivation to set the program machinery in motion is the subject matter or thesis. An outstanding example of this sort was the broadcast of "The Murder of Lidice," a dramatization of the poem by Edna St. Vincent Millay. The idea of paying tribute to the people of that ill-fated city met with instant favor. When it was discovered that Miss Millay's poem might be available, the result was a feature which was truly memorable.

Perhaps a piece of talent motivates a broadcast. It need not always be performing talent. It may rather be a personality, or perhaps it is merely the circumstance attending the arrival of an unknown. In short, a name or an event in the news may set the machinery in motion.

These various suggestions which call for action in the program department may come from within the organization or from the outside. They usually take one of two forms, either a vague idea or a more or less complete script.

It is, of course, extremely difficult to pay off on the basis of vague ideas. Yet the failure of the general public to understand this principle is partly responsible for the somewhat general feeling that radio is a closed business except for people with influence. The fact is that program managements are wide open to ideas, but they want to be sure that they are workable ideas and that they have not been presented a hundred times before. With respect to these two points, most ideas, especially those presented by people with no technical understanding of the medium, are likely to fail.

When ideas are presented to NBC, the Company asks for a waiver. No consideration is given to the idea until such a waiver has been signed. This is a common protective measure which says in effect that the originator of the idea appreciates the fact that someone else may have had the same idea earlier and presented it to the network for consideration.

The idea is then discussed. Perhaps the originator is called in for a conference. In some instances these conferences develop the fact that the idea as originally submitted is useless, but that with some collaboration it can be made the basis of a program. In hundreds of instances network personnel have given that collaboration with no profit to themselves, but with gratifying results to the other party. It is a fact that ideas as such cannot be broadcast; someone has to translate the idea into a script. This latter activity often becomes the all-important part of the transaction. Ideas embodied in scripts, rather than disembodied ideas, are, therefore, much more usable and, by the same token, much more salable.

When scripts are submitted, the same waiver form must be signed before they are given consideration. The scripts are then read and discussed. When the subject matter is not deemed right, they usually are rejected. If, however, questions arise as to the method of treatment, the authors are called in to confer and perhaps to rewrite, in an effort to correct the difficulty. In some cases final judgment may even be reserved until an audition has been arranged so that the script can be heard exactly as in a broadcast. This treatment naturally represents considerable expenditure of time and money. Its use is referred to here as a further indication that the networks and stations are eager for scripts and ideas which can be broadcast.

In this connection, it may be wise to point out the rather terrifying lack of common sense which some would-be script writers show in making their contacts with the radio industry. The writer who insists that he has a wealth of ideas only waiting for expression, but that he has no way of finding out what length the script should be or what pattern to follow, is simply talking nonsense. Two abilities are all that are needed. One is the ability to turn on a radio set; the other is the ability to tell time. A complete analysis of a radio program of any kind can be made by simply listening to it with a watch in hand. Information as to how the program starts, how long it continues before it changes its pattern, what it does when it does change, and how soon it gets back to another pattern, as well as how it brings the curtain down at the end — all these are simple to note. It is equally simple to decide whether the program was so good that it should be imitated or so terrible that it should be avoided. The prospective author for a radio program will do well to plan some analytical listening in the hope of imitating the things he likes best. That method has been practiced in all the arts for thousands of years. It is still good.

So the program machinery is set in motion in one of the ways indicated, or in still other ways which produce the same result: a program is to be built for broadcasting. Let's see what happens to it.

DEVELOPMENT OF A PROGRAM

Since this is a new project, the program-development division is given responsibility for launching it. These particular functions are considered important enough in the New York Office of NBC to be handled by a special division of the program department. However, it should be noted that the functions exist in every program department, whether or not they are allocated to special people. In fact, in most cases the program manager and perhaps one or two other people whom he selects carry out these functions in the normal course of their activities. The program development division is charged with seeing that the first broadcast gets on the air. If it is a broadcast in a series, the subsequent programs are taken over by other operating departments and continued throughout the series, according to the pattern which has been agreed upon at the start but which may change during the course of the series, after proper discussion and agreement on the points to be changed. In the initial stages, however, the program de· velopment division assembles and co-ordinates personnel from other divisions and supervises their work through the first broadcast.

Among the first people to be brought in is the head of the script division, who not only assigns a writer to the script but also supervises his work. The assignment of a particular writer is dependent upon a number of considerations. The writing may be original or it may be an adaptation. It may be highly specialized or fairly standard. It is the business of the script division manager either to have on his staff or to have available from his card-index file writers who can turn out all types of work. A particular program may be largely musical, yet call for a highly distinctive type of narrative, or it may be a straight dramatic program with no restricting qualifications. Perhaps the time it fills in the schedule demands light comedy treatment. Perhaps the client involved has a limited budget and, therefore, must have an idea program[1] rather than one using expensive talent. It may be that the occasion for the broadcast is such as to require a great deal of research about the people present or the event which it celebrates. All these and many other similar factors make the job of selecting the writer for a particular program an extremely important one. In addition, the script division manager knows that if this is an adaptation, he must clear the literary rights on the original. He knows, too, that before the program goes on the air it must have a title, and that it will fall to him to clear that title against duplication by other programs, which might make it confusing, or by plays or pictures or books, which might make it costly. In addition, he must continue his supervision of the writer until the script is ready in mimeographed form for the preliminary rehearsals, and through such revision as is necessary during the rehearsals. His responsibility ends only when his writer has delivered a completely satisfactory script to the production director.

The production division assembles and co-ordinates all the various elements that go to make up an actual broadcast. The individual production directors who make up this division are, therefore, completely in charge of their programs in the studio. When a production director is assigned, he goes into conference with the script writer on the basic idea and the method by which the idea will be worked out. On the basis of this discussion he proceeds to organize the other elements. He knows the amount and type of music to be involved in the program. In a conference with the head of the music division, the musical setup for the program is arranged.

The music division controls and assigns all performing musi-

---

[1] "The Stradivari Orchestra," an orchestra built entirely of Stradivari violins, presented by Prince Matchabelli Perfumes.

cians on the staff. It handles the music library, with its millions of arrangements and compositions. It has a tremendous record library available, either for consultation or for use on the air. It has a staff of arrangers and copyists. It also has a staff of composers, in case special music is to be composed. The assigning of a given number of men to the orchestra; the assignment of a conductor, who is also brought into the conference on the music; the decision on the type of music to be used, how much of it will be by special arrangement, how much of it will be original composition; perhaps the clearance of rights and the payment of a royalty on a given number; and all the detailed preparation for actually putting the music on the stand in the studio so that it can be played at the time of the broadcast, are set in motion by the conference between the production director and the head of the music division.

The program requires other talent, so the production director becomes a casting director. He sends through his own department a casting sheet showing what artists are to be called, what they are to be paid, and the time and length of each rehearsal. Perhaps a particular bit of research which the writer does as he proceeds with his task requires that the program should have a chorus. The decision as to number and type of the chorus, the engaging of the singers, perhaps the engaging of a vocal arranger, are all done in conference again with the music division.

These varied elements will give a clue to the size of the studio that must be available for the broadcast. Since studio assignments are a part of the production operation, the production director goes again to his own department and reserves the studio for a specific number of hours for rehearsal and broadcast.

This particular broadcast may be on a war theme and, therefore, may involve considerable work from the sound technicians. As soon as it is possible to determine how extensive the sound effects will be, men are assigned who later check the script and bring into the studio all the equipment necessary for effective sound presentation. Special effects are built or devised as needed, and perhaps three men may be employed to operate hundreds of pieces of equipment during a single broadcast. It is not uncommon to have sound rehearsing lasting ten or twelve hours for a single thirty-minute program.

The final element to be assigned to the program is the announcer. His duties may vary all the way from the routine "sign on" and "sign off" to the performance of an all-important narrative throughout the entire program. Again the production director, in conference with the head of the announcing division, suggests the particular qualifications he would like the announcer to have.

When these elements within the program department have been provided for, other departments may be called on for special contributions over and above those of normal operation. For example, if the rehearsal for this program appears merely in a routine way on the daily schedules, the engineering supervisor will assign an engineer to the studio in time for the rehearsal. It may be, however, that special engineering equipment is needed. Perhaps an echo chamber is to be used, or a filter mike. The production director is expected to make his wants known to the engineering department so that they will have ample time to provide special service. Many a broadcast has been made unusually effective by a special engineering device which was available only because notice was given in plenty of time. It is a wise production director who takes his engineer into account.

It is also possible that the production director must confer with the traffic department in the early stages. This is particularly true if the program is to contain a remote pickup. Lines may have to be installed for this. It is not uncommon to have technical pickup problems at remote points change the whole routine of the program. In such cases, it is foolish not to investigate and learn the facts well in advance. It is Production's responsibility to check on all such factors through the engineering and traffic departments.

Arrangements may also have to be made for either or both of two types of recordings. If the program is the first in a series and has not been auditioned, it will be necessary to order a recording of a dress rehearsal far enough in advance so that the program manager may hear it and approve it before it actually goes on the air. When it is broadcast, a reference recording may be needed. The ordering of these recordings is the responsibility of the production director.

It will be apparent from this that the production director's job is a tremendously important one. When he has finished doing all the things previously enumerated he has, however, only begun his real work. The remainder of the work takes place in the studio during rehearsal and broadcast. Then it becomes his business to co-ordinate and blend all the varied contributing elements in such a way that the finished product will be an accurate and artistic reflection of the author's original idea and purpose. The director must be, in effect, expert with both the microscope and the telescope. He must place the microscope over each element of the program while he examines it for perfection of detail. Then he must be able to switch instantly to the telescope in order to see that each element is in proper balance with the others. He must be able to evaluate music and drama and speech and sound. He must know the importance of tempo and climax. He must inspire the confidence of his artists in a way that will bring them to peak performance. He must be prepared for a burst of applause which will run his program thirty seconds over, or a line failure from a remote pickup which will leave him with three minutes to fill. In short, he must be completely in charge of every element that goes to make up that program. His importance is emphasized here because he is the focal point in the functioning of the entire program machinery.

All the varied program activities are quite pointless except as they appear in their proper place in a broadcast. The fine writing which is nullified by a stupid actor, the expert acting which is drowned out by the musical background, the beautiful music that nullifies itself because it is too long or because it does not fit the scene, the overloud sound which places the house inside the telephone instead of the telephone inside the house, all fail to take into account what a radio program really is. Yet the answer is so simple! Every radio program in the world can be reduced to one word — sound. The fact that the sound may come from a human throat or from a violin string or from the bumping of two marbles in an iron skillet merely means that a wide variety of sound is available. To put them together so that they willl create pictures in the mind of the listener requires great skill and great imagination. This is where the art of radio and the science of radio combine.

CHAPTER 8

TYPES OF PROGRAMS

NETWORK PROGRAMS

ON THE WHOLE, the types of programs broadcast over a network are not essentially different from the types of programs broadcast over the local stations, as has been pointed out in an earlier chapter. Availability of funds to engage better writers, to employ more professional talent, both actors and musicians, and to command more expert production are the variables that make the difference. Also, as shown previously, the professionals in all fields of entertainment seem to gravitate toward the three largest producing centers, New York, Chicago, and Hollywood. This is natural, but it is also the prime reason why it is more difficult for local stations in smaller cities and communities to build live-talent programs comparable to those heard on the networks and originating generally from one of the three centers. This is not always true, of course, as is obvious to anyone listening regularly to stations scattered in all parts of the country. You can pick up good live-talent shows from Dallas, Texas, to Portland, Maine or Oregon, but by and large the majority of entertainers, actors, and actresses tend to concentrate in the three cities where most network programs originate.

As has been pointed out before, there are two kinds of programs — commercial and sustaining.

Commercials are those programs broadcast under the sponsorship of some firm or industry as a part of its advertising campaign to promote the sale of products or to stimulate good will. Such programs are built and produced either by an advertising agency or by the radio station or the network. In the case of a network, the greater percentage of programs carried are agency-built. This does not mean that the program departments of networks do not build and sell radio programs, and many are offered to agencies for advertisers as "package shows" — meaning that the whole show is offered together as a complete unit for a given price. In the case of a local station, it is generally the station itself which is responsible for building and producing the program.

Sustaining programs comprise all the other types of programs which can be heard daily, programs that have no sponsorship, which are put on either as pure entertainment or as a public service and are paid for by the station or network. There are few instances, however, in which it would not be possible to offer these programs for sale, and many programs which have been carried on the network as sustainers have been sold later. Before the war, the ratio of sustaining to sponsored programs was about two to one; however, for the year 1944, the tables were practically reversed.

Commercial Programs. Network commercial shows may assume any of a number of forms: variety, dramatic, musical, audience participation, quiz, talks, forums, news, special events, or sports, to name those most frequently heard. The decision on the part of an advertiser to use one form in preference to another may be arrived at in a number of ways. For instance, what type of audience is he interested in reaching; how wide is the distribution of his product; how much can he afford to spend to move the product; and, how quickly must it be moved? If the product has wide distribution and is used generally by the public in rather large quantities, such as cigarettes or coffee, sales would warrant the manufacturer's spending more money for advertising than if he were selling an article with a much less general appeal. Together with his advertising agency, he will try to decide the type of program that will interest all kinds of people from every stratum of society, whether they be rich or poor, highly educated or of an average intelligence. In this case, a variety show probably will be the answer, principally because there undoubtedly will be elements somewhere in the show that will appeal to every listener. There will be classical music and boogie-woogie; there will be comedy and sometimes pathos; there will be funny gags to bring many laughs; and there may be a serious note now and then. In other words:

> A *variety show* is one that is made up of all those elements, music, drama, comedy, and gags held together by an expert master of ceremonies who can catch his audience at once and hold it through the sheer force of his personality, with the support of a fast-moving show composed of the features mentioned. Outstanding examples are "Bob Hope," "Jack Benny," "Fred Allen," or "Charlie McCarthy."

Other types of shows that might be called variety shows are those built around the personalities of two people; in other words, the comedy teams such as "Fibber McGee and Molly," or "Amos 'n' Andy," or "Burns and Allen." In a sense, these programs are variety shows, but they might more truly be called straight comedy, as the whole show is, in reality, a combination of amusing situations, common to everyone, in which two characters find themselves. The main responsibility for keeping the show moving rests on the shoulders of these two principal characters. Through the magnetism of their personalities, their consistency in building and maintaining characters who are bound to appeal to all listeners, and their ability to project the sincerity that goes into the portrayal of their rôles, "Fibber McGee and Molly," "Amos 'n' Andy," "Burns and Allen," and "Abbott and Costello" have had no difficulty in keeping their shows moving rapidly, and in establishing their top-flight positions in the weekly radio listening habits of the American people.

In addition to the comedy teams, many variety programs owe their popularity to an individual artist around whom comedy routines are planned; such artists include Fannie Brice with her "Why, Daddy?", Joan Davis, Red Skelton, Gracie Fields, and Gildersleeve. This type of show is more difficult to build than the average, as it is never a simple matter to find another Fannie Brice, or Marion and Jim Jordan (Fibber McGee and Molly), or a Burns and Allen; these artists are truly born, not made. It requires an infinite amount of time and patience to establish such features; Marion and Jim Jordan had been broadcasting for many years before just the right vehicle was found through which their particular gifts could best be presented.

A *comedy show*, therefore, is one built around a person or team that has an innate facility for catching an audience through many amusing situations and gags, and achieves success through finding the right writer who each week can develop situations which will permit the artist's own natural talent to have full sway.

Turning next to the dramatic program, it is interesting to learn that today this is the most popular form of all radio entertainment. For many years music in the popular vein commanded the largest audience, but drama now tops the polls with at least 65 per cent of all the listeners preferring it.

The dramatic program is not, of course, confined to a single type. There is the straight dramatic show, such as "Lux Radio Theatre," the best-known and most popular of all the straight dramatic shows on the air and the one which probably has had the most expert and careful supervision, over a period of years, of any of them. It is, in all probability, the highest-priced dramatic radio show today.

There are, of course, many other types of dramatic shows, such as "The First Nighter," different from the "Lux Radio Theatre" in that the plays presented each week are written especially for the program and are not adaptations. The same is true of "Dr. Christian," only in this case the drama or play is written around the same character each week, that of Dr. Christian, played by Jean Hersholt. Again, there is the type in which a whole family finds itself either in a different situation each week, such as "Henry Aldrich," or progressively living their normal lives, such as "One Man's Family." The examples of dramatic shows are legion; there are "Sherlock Holmes" and "Mr. District Attorney," "Hot Copy," and "Arthur Hopkins Presents," to recall only a few, as well as the shows where spots of drama are dropped into an informational show to bring to life the historical situations being presented, as, for instance, in the "March of Time." Then there are those especially written for radio by such people as Arch Oboler, Norman Corwin, and Orson Welles, programs experimenting in different and unusual forms. Radio is really beginning to develop its own dramatic literature, which is a sign that radio is growing up.

Of course, there are the dramatic serials which have come to be called, flippantly, "soap operas" because so many of them have been sponsored by concerns selling soap or its derivatives. For the past decade, these short, episodical, dramatic programs have been the daytime radio fare of the American housewife from coast to coast. They are radio's continued story, in which all the emotions and situations that can be gathered together by a versatile pulp writer are presented daily in every conceivable guise. Here are the love stories, the triangles, the tragedies, the mysteries, the problems, the cares, the laughter, and the tears that make up the world of today, lived through the lives of makebelieve people, people who become more real to many a woman than her closest friends or relatives. These serials, which have taken the country by storm, have been praised and damned by people in all walks of life. Nevertheless, they are being listened to daily by 40 per cent of all the women in the country, and no one has ever proved that they are as base and harmful as some radio reformers would like to believe. Mrs. Leda P. Summers, in a published survey of daytime serial listening in Iowa, says: "Two women out of every five who listen regularly to radio serials believe that serial listening helps them solve the problems of their own everyday lives."[1] Surely there is a place for this form of dramatic radio program if it is meeting a need in the lives of so many people. Sometimes one does not stop to think how little drama and variety there are in the lives of thousands of women in America, women not only in rural or isolated areas, but in crowded cities, where the daily routine of housework becomes a bore and where women can become even more lonely than on a farm. If these women can be transported from their humdrum existence and given a mental respite through

[1] "Daytime Serials and Iowa Women," by Leda P. Summers. Des Moines. Iowa: Radio Station WHO.

this means of vicarious living, isn't there something to be said for the daytime serial?

> *Dramatic programs* are divided into several forms: straight dramatic, such as adaptations of stage or screen plays; plays written especially for radio; dramatized spots or black-outs to bring to life certain incidents for purpose of emphasis; and the daytime serial, i.e., the continued episodical story.

A few years ago anyone working in the program department of a radio station would have said that music was the most popular form of radio program that could be presented. Today every poll or survey will reflect a reversal in the popularity of program types and show that during the daytime listening hours drama occupies about 34 per cent of all the time on the air, while music can claim only about 20 per cent. All other types, including news, variety, talks, and audience-participation shows make up the difference, or 46 per cent. At night the percentages vary somewhat, with drama taking about 29 per cent and music about 21 per cent.

Needless to say, however, music is still the popular radio fare of many people, music of all kinds, with dance music heading the list as far as young people are concerned. They still want their swing and jazz and boogie-woogie as played by such leaders as Harry James, Tommy Dorsey, Bob Crosby, and Guy Lombardo, or sung by Frank Sinatra, Bing Crosby, Bob Ebberley, or any particular star of the moment. The favorites come and go, a particular form may change, but the type will always remain. The boys and girls dance to it, study to it, or just listen to it; the adults dance to it, read to it, or play games to it. Whether it is straight jazz, popular, or classical music, it forms the ideal background for many activities and does not, of course, require undivided listening.

Programs of music made up entirely of straight dance bands, picked up from the night spots, from hotels or restaurants across the land, are more likely to be sustaining than commercial. On the other hand, there are the famous "Lucky Strike Hit Parade" and kindred programs owing their popularity to the hit tunes, and they have had no trouble in finding sponsors.

Up a peg or two on the musical ladder come next in popularity those programs that feature light, semi-popular music such as is heard on the "Kraft Music Hall," Bayer's "Album of Familiar Music," "The Carnation Contented Hour," "The Hour of Charm," and "The Pause that Refreshes"; programs made up of ballads and tunes principally from the light operas and the well-known love songs. These programs are favorites with a great many people who "love to listen to music," who "don't know much about music, but know what they like," and who definitely are not interested in jazz. In this field of popular musical programs fall also those programs, such as Kate Smith's, in which the charm and sincerity of the singer builds a personal following not alone for the music, but for a personality. Dinah Shore, Ginny Simms, and Connee Boswell are other cases in point — though all three of these artists are generally heard on variety shows as singing stars, whereas Kate Smith *is* the program.

From the light popular musical program, it is another peg up to the concert type, such as the "Voice of Firestone," or "The Telephone Hour," or "Great Moments in Music," programs composed of a symphony orchestra featuring a famous concert soloist, and lastly up just one more peg to the great symphony orchestras of the country and the Metropolitan Opera.

Both the opera and the symphonies were for many years broadcast on a sustaining basis at great cost to the networks themselves. Finally, however, certain advertisers were convinced that here was a form of radio program appealing to large numbers of people who were interested in the finer things of life and who would be appreciative of the type of product or service that could be rendered by their organizations. First the Metropolitan Opera acquired a sponsor, then the New York Philharmonic, then the NBC Symphony with Arturo Toscanini, and finally the Boston Symphony. It is not quite fair to say "first the Metropolitan Opera," as the San Francisco Symphony had been sponsored on the Pacific Coast network for many years before opera or symphony in the East were broadcast, but as far as the coast-to-coast networks are concerned the opera was the first of the famous musical organizations to acquire sponsorship. In broadcasting the opera or any one of the symphonies as a sponsored program, the form of presentation remains exactly as it is heard in the opera house or concert hall, except that over the air the intermission periods are used by the sponsor in various ways to present his story. Nothing is said or done to detract from the actual presentation in the way of announcements dropped in at odd moments during the playing of a number or immediately following a number; all commercial credit lines occur at the opening or close or during regular intermission periods.

There is no doubt that the presentation of these fine musical organizations has increased radio's prestige in the minds of many people who had looked upon it before as a medium of pure entertainment, and not so pure at that, according to some. That these programs are reflecting good will upon the industry which presents them goes without saying, and they have brought to radio many listeners that hitherto "never bothered to listen."

> *Music programs* are divided into approximately four types of presentations: the popular, that is jazz, swing, or boogie-woogie; light popular, or ballad and light opera; semi-classical studio programs with symphonic orchestras and guest soloists; and straight classical, the opera and the famous symphony orchestras.

Ever since the beginning of World War II, or in fact ever since the momentous days of Munich, the radio public has asked for more and more news. They want it the first thing in the morning when they get up, the last thing at night before going to bed, and at many intervals during the day. They want straight news reports and they want commentators. Because of this widespread interest in the news, it is not surprising that there are more calls for news programs by would-be sponsors with medium-sized appropriations than for any other type of program. Over a network such sponsorship more generally takes the form of commenting on the news than of straight reporting, while on a local station, it is generally the straight news report that is sponsored. The reason is obvious; there is less likelihood in small towns or cities than in large centers that there are people with a background of sufficient knowledge on national and international affairs to appreciate serious discussion of the news, while the press services with their up-to-the-minute news are available to most of the medium-size as well as the large stations throughout the country.

This does not mean, of course, that an advertiser cannot or does not sponsor straight news over a network. There are currently a number of such programs on all four networks, and in most instances these take the form of a round-the-world service, with reports coming in from the capitals of the world. On the other hand, with the close of day the listener turns to his radio for an appraisal of the news by his favorite commentator, someone whom he feels has the background and knowledge to interpret daily events in their proper perspective. That person may be Hans V. Kaltenborn, the dean of the commentators, heard over NBC; or he may be Raymond Gram Swing, the most dispassionate and objective of the commentators, heard over the American Broadcasting Company; or he may be Fulton Lewis with his clear-cut analysis heard over Mutual; or Edward R. Murrow, Columbia's famous London representative; or George Hicks, or William L. Shirer, or John W. Vandercook, or Clifton Utley, or Baukhage. Each has his particular following, and each can be counted on to give an accurate picture of the news as he sees it. Women as well as men have been broadcasting straight news or news summaries over both networks and local stations for some time. The best known are Lisa Sergio with her daily program over WQXR, Bernadine Flynn on CBS, and Jane Cowl on Mutual. In addition to these commentators heard daily, others, such as Dorothy Thompson, Sumner Welles, and Edward Tomlinson, have weekly fifteen-minute broadcasts, generally presenting the background of the principal news events of the week, and in the case of Mr. Tomlinson the events pertaining to South America and Central America. Then, too, there are the weekly gossip reporters like

Walter Winchell, who specialize on the intimate news events in the lives of the celebrities of the day as well as give now and then a high spot of news of national or world interest.

There are advertisers who have sponsored news in round table form; for example, the "World Front News" heard weekly over NBC. During this program three, and sometimes four, well-informed persons discuss among themselves the foremost news events of the week.

> The *News Program* may be a straight recital of the news by an announcer; or the news may be commented on and analyzed by well-known reporters and journalists; or it may be discussed in round table form by a group of well-informed men and women.

A number of years ago program directors, in searching for new program types, hit upon the idea of bringing the radio audience into the picture, first, through a series of questions and answers, which were directed to men-on-the-street or to persons in the studio, and later, through other forms of actual participation. The idea became a success almost overnight, and the air lanes were crowded with all types of "audience participation" shows. There was "Major Bowes' Amateur Hour," one of the first programs employing a participating audience and for years a popular feature over Columbia; there was the "Good-Will Court," on which, during the broadcast, Mr. Anthony tried to help and advise many unhappy people; there were "Vox Pop" and "Treasure Chest" and "Dunninger" and "People are Funny." One could go on indefinitely naming the various programs which feature audience participation. "Man-in-the-street" broadcasts were seldom heard over the networks, except during political conventions or during the broadcasting of some sports event. Until the war, however, this type of broadcast probably filled more minutes a day over many small local stations than did music programs.

It was, of course, an easy mental step from "audience participation" to actual "quiz shows." On the other hand, "Information Please," the quiz show which has probably become the most famous of them all, was carried for many months by NBC

as a sustaining feature. It was impossible to convince a salesman or an advertiser that any program using the word "information" in the title would have the slightest interest for the
majority of people. It sounded "educational," and educational
programs were definitely a drug on the market at that time.
It has taken the sales departments of radio networks and radio
advertising agencies a long time to come to the realization that
sometimes "information" and "education" can be interesting.
The format of "Information Please" is too well-known to need
extended description; a moderator or master of ceremonies
questions a panel of four or five people on many and diverse
subjects sent in by the listeners. These questions, of course,
have not been divulged to the panel before the broadcast, and
if a question cannot be answered by anyone on the panel, a
prize is sent to the person sending it in.

It is not to be wondered at that after the sensational success
of "Information Please," many people who were responsible for
creating program ideas should have attempted to imitate the
program. So along came the "Quiz Kids." In program form,
it was an exact duplicate of "Information Please," except that
the panel was composed of youngsters anywhere from five
to sixteen years of age, instead of adults. "Quiz Kids" was
heard first as a replacement for "Fibber McGee and Molly" on
NBC during the summer months of 1940, while Marion and
Jim Jordan were on vacation. Because of the charm and pre-
cociousness of the children, it became an instant success. It did
not, therefore, require much persuasion on the part of the
owner of the program to convince an advertiser that here was
a show that would command a large audience from week to
week, and so, in the fall, with the return to NBC of "Fibber
McGee and Molly," the "Quiz Kids" moved to the then Blue
Network under the aegis of a sponsor.

Both programs, in the common parlance, were "naturals."
They were and are "naturals" only because they appeal to the
competitive impulse tucked away inside of everyone, that impulse to see whether he can answer the questions before the
"experts." It is a game everyone plays with himself, and only

so long as each listener is interested in his own mental gymnastics, so long will these "quiz" programs maintain their radio popularity.

> *Audience Participation and Quiz Shows* are those in which the audience itself is a very definite part of the show, either as amateur performers, or as persons being interviewed or questioned by a master of ceremonies.

With the exception of political talks or religious programs, it is seldom that an advertiser sponsors a straight talk, the reason being that most straight talks are dull and uninteresting and will not catch the attention of the average radio listener. Then, too, the policy of most of the networks is not to sell time for talks by groups or organizations for the purpose of promoting their own interests, selling memberships in their organizations, or discussing controversial issues. Instead, the networks reserve the right to schedule programs by such groups on a sustaining basis, though, of course, no solicitation of funds is permissible except in the case of the American Red Cross, the Community Chests, or the War Bond Drives. Time is sold by the networks for political talks only during political campaigns. At any other time, the facilities of the networks are made available, at no cost, to persons in governmental capacities for the purpose of presenting information on matters of importance to the country as a whole. During political campaigns, however, the radio law requires that any network or radio station selling time to any one political party shall offer the same amount of time to any other party represented on the ballot.[2]

Two other program types remain to be discussed, "special events" and "sports," and the only "special events" shows that have been sponsored fall in the category of "sports": horse races, prize fights, football, and baseball, to name the important ones. Of these, the only ones that have been sponsored on any of the networks have been the Kentucky Derby, carried yearly by the Columbia Broadcasting System, world-championship

---

[2] See Chapter 4. Also the Radio Act of February 23, 1927, Sec. 18.

prizefights, the world series, and professional football. Unless the sports event has wide national appeal there is no object on the part of an advertiser in sponsoring it. Some events that seem important in local communities are found to have very little appeal outside and do not, therefore, justify sponsorship.

A *Special Event* is a broadcast originating outside of a radio studio and may be any single event or series such as the christening of a ship, the running of a horse race, the dedication of some community enterprise, the description of a flood, the graduation exercises of a university, or any of the pickups that were used in connection with the broadcast of "The Army Hour," to cite only a few examples of the thousand and one that are classified as "special events."

Sustaining Programs. There is little difference between commercial and sustaining programs broadcast over the networks as regards actual types and forms. A variety program on a sustaining basis is made up of music and gags, drama and comedy, and presented by a master of ceremonies in just the same way as it would be if it were commercially sponsored; the only difference may be that the network often does not feel justified in spending as much money on a sustaining show as would be spent if the show were commercial. This difference might mean that the best comedians would not be available, nor the highest-priced gag writers, nor the most versatile master of ceremonies. On the other hand, if the network hoped to sell the variety show, every effort would be made to plan as excellent a show on a sustaining basis as if the program already had a sponsor.

The same is true of dramatic programs. It might be true that a sustaining show could not afford the best-known actors and actresses, and the quality of production might be lessened on that account, but the type of program would be the same. There have been excellent straight dramatic shows on a sustaining basis; for instance, the "Great Plays" series that ran for several years on NBC and the "Shakespeare" series on Columbia, plays that were as carefully cast and produced as any play series now being sponsored. Many of the daytime serials were scheduled as sustaining shows on the networks long before they were sponsored. "Today's Children," almost the first of that type of program, is a case in point, as is "Vic and Sade." "Amos 'n' Andy" is another good example of a fine sustaining show that ran for many months with all the elements that it had when it was bought by Pepsodent, the show's first sponsor. The New York Philharmonic, the Metropolitan Opera, and the Boston Symphony have not changed their manner of presentation, nor their form, one iota since acquiring sponsorship.

There are, of course, some programs carried on the networks as sustaining features, which probably never will be sponsored; some should not be sponsored, while others could be without any loss of prestige or quality. Most of these programs fall in the category of public service or educational features and are discussed in another chapter. But, using "Doctors Look Ahead," the American Medical Association series over NBC, as an example, the dramatic form used to present the show is the same as that used by "Death Valley Days," which is sponsored; and "The Roy Shield Revue" uses the same type of music as it would use if the program were not sustaining.

In broadcasting news, either through straight news reports, by round tables, or commentators, the handling of the news copy itself is the same in every detail as it would be if it were sponsored, and is colored in no way through any influence brought to bear by the advertiser. Great care is taken by the networks to protect the integrity of the news in this respect.

There have been queries from time to time as to whether discussion programs such as the "University of Chicago Round Table" or "America's Town Meeting of the Air" could afford to accept sponsorship. Some schools of thought believe that such discussion shows could not remain free and unbiased under those circumstances. In commenting on the question as it is related to all types of public service shows, Mr. William Burke Miller, then manager of the public service department of NBC, once said, "Any program, excepting the religious programs,[3] would entertain a sponsorship interest providing it had

[3] Mutual is the only network which sells time for religious programs.

dignity, institutional type of announcement, and a product that was generally respected and recognized throughout the country. The sponsor could have no control over the program." Since the fall of 1944 "America's Town Meeting of the Air" has been under the sponsorship of *Reader's Digest*. Mr. George V. Denny, moderator of "America's Town Meeting of the Air," feels that the sponsorship has been eminently satisfactory. In a letter to the author dated February 5, 1945, Mr. Denny says:

> After five months of sponsorship by the *Reader's Digest*, under a contract with the Blue Network which gives Town Hall complete freedom as to the selection of subjects and speakers, with the express provision that the sponsor shall have no control whatever over the selection of speakers and topics or the content of the program, I am pleased to say that sponsorship of a forum program, as we know it, is eminently satisfactory. Instead of 120 stations or less from time to time, we have 181 stations carrying the program with the interest and support of nearly all of these stations, together with the promotion given us by our sponsor, the sponsor's advertising agency, and the news distribution service in the various cities throughout the country. By means of the additional funds made available as a commercially sponsored program, we have enlarged our production staff and have a Research Department of four people, which supplies factual material to all of the speakers in advance of each program.

A sustaining feature that played a big part in the program scheduling of any network during the war was government programs. From the days immediately following Pearl Harbor, dozens of programs were offered to radio stations weekly by the Office of War Information acting as the clearing house for all information from the government. These programs took any number of forms, from straight one-to-five-minute announcement types to the elaborate Sunday afternoon feature on NBC known as "The Army Hour." In 1943 the OWI and the radio stations worked out a plan through which every radio station and all the networks carried important government messages to the nation. The network plan called for the making of an announcement every two weeks by every commercial and sustaining program using its facilities, the subject to depend on the particular service or issue being stressed at the moment. This was in addition to any special programs, such as "The Army Hour," which was broadcast by the United States Army in co-operation with OWI, and "The Man behind the Gun" on Columbia. A discussion of those programs which come under the headings of public service or education will be found in Section III of this book.

LOCAL PROGRAMS

In discussing the difference between the various types of programs broadcast over local stations, it is necessary to divide the local stations into different categories. There are the large fifty kilowatt clear-channel stations affiliated with one or the other of the networks, such as WLW in Cincinnati, KMOX in St. Louis, WMAQ in Chicago, or WOR in New York, whose program schedule is just as complex and is carried out in just as much detail as a network schedule. The program problems are similar in many respects, except that no one of those stations is required as a rule to originate more than several network programs a day and therefore would not need to employ as many artists and musicians as the network origination points. The majority of the time during which a fifty-kilowatt clear-channel station is on the air is occupied by programs built by the station itself and sold to local advertisers or co-sponsored by some civic organization. These include variety shows, dramatic shows, musical shows, and a great many locally sponsored news shows. There are also likely to be many so-called "participation" shows occupying five, ten, or fifteen minutes, during which one-to-five-minute spot announcements are scheduled between the playing of recordings. This type of programming accounts for a great deal of the time on the smaller wattage stations, but every large local station will also have five or six of these periods during the eighteen hours it is on the air.

Next would come the stations ranging from five kilowatts

to twenty-five kilowatts, which are also, in most instances, affiliated with one of the networks and therefore accept many network programs during a day. The program problems of these stations are very likely to be the same as those of the clear-channel stations, though differing somewhat because of their location. If a twenty-five-kilowatt station were situated in the heart of Kansas where real talent was rather scarce, the type of program built and broadcast by the station itself would be decidedly different from a twenty-five-kilowatt station in Los Angeles or Chicago where a good talent market is located and where it would be comparatively easy to plan the same type of dramatic and musical shows as were being broadcast over the networks. The station in Kansas undoubtedly would be inclined to co-operate more fully with civic groups as there would, in all probability, be more time available for sustaining shows. On the other hand, an increase in the demand for radio time is rather general throughout the country, and every type of station is reaping the benefit of this added income. A contributing influence can be found in the fact that because of the paper shortage in 1944-45 magazines and newspapers have been forced to ration their available advertising space; some firms have therefore turned to radio for the first time to sell their products or to keep their trade names alive.

Two other groups make up the remainder of the stations: the thousand-watters and the small, independent local stations of one hundred or two hundred and fifty watts. Many of the former have network affiliations, and a few of the small wattage stations, in areas not served by the larger stations, are also affiliated with the networks. The small stations, for the most part, must depend upon records and transcriptions for the bulk of their programming. Their revenue is obtained principally from the local merchant with his one- and five-minute announcements, often as many as five or ten a day being scheduled from one concern. These announcements are broadcast generally in a woman's activity program, put on by a woman announcer, or form part of a participation hour. In many sections of the country, hillbilly music is still the stand-by of the small station as it is more readily available and more likely to be inexpensive.

In addition to spot announcements and hillbilly music, the principal fare of the small, independent station is news, which is furnished to it by one of the radio news services or through the co-operation of the local newspaper. These news broadcasts are invariably sponsored and furnish a substantial part of the station's revenue.

Before the war, another type of program which had become standard at many of the smaller stations was the man-in-the-street interview; this was a simple program to arrange and it seemed to find favor among the station's audience. This particular type of program was not permitted during the war, and in all likelihood something more interesting will be found to take its place in the future.

Almost all small stations sell time to churches for the broadcasting of their Sunday services. Though this practice has been more or less frowned upon by the NAB, it is still a popular feature in the majority of the stations, large and small, across the land and accounts for a great deal of revenue during the year. The churches like to broadcast, and the stations like to sell the time, and many people see no reason why the custom should be discontinued.

Local political talks, especially during campaigns, are also a well-established feature of all stations, large or small, though undoubtedly one would find more of such talks scheduled on the smaller stations, but only because the smaller stations have more time to sell for this purpose. Politicians have found it easier to reach the voters through radio than through any other medium, and each candidate is anxious, therefore, to broadcast as frequently as he can secure the time and as his funds permit. Most stations will sell as much time as they can for this purpose, with little regard for their program schedules. If one talk follows another, it is too bad, but it can't be helped.

Sustaining features differ only slightly from commercial features on the average station. Generally they consist of recorded music, a staff pianist, a hillbilly trio or duo, plus a few programs of a civic or educational nature broadcast by women's clubs, parent-teacher associations, the local schools, or luncheon groups. During the war a great deal of time was set aside for government-sponsored programs, furnished to the stations by the Office of War Information. Some of these were simple announcements which were read by the station announcer; some were professionally written scripts which could be put on by whatever talent was available, sometimes the dramatic group of the local high school or woman's club; and some were talks prepared to be read by some prominent local citizen. More than sixty-six million dollars' worth of time was given by the radio stations of the country in 1944 for government programs, and the local stations were responsible for a large percentage of that figure.

CHAPTER 9

WOMEN'S PROGRAMS

"Remember that old adage? 'When you want to spread good news in a hurry, telephone, telegraph, tell a woman!' That is the reason for my news program for women," says Rhea McCarty, formerly director of women's programs for station WCOL.

This is the basic philosophy behind nearly every women's program — its appeal to the woman in the home, the consumer. She is the homemaker, the great potential in radio, and radio is acceptable to her. She can summon the world with a twist of the wrist. She can go from station to station, shopping for what she wants to hear, depending on her mood.

Radio entertains her, keeps her up-to-date, gives her advice and information on everything that concerns her home, her family, her community, and herself. Contrariwise, radio provides an escape from her anxieties and her troubles and obliterates the four walls that surround her. Radio helps her to combat a feeling of loneliness. It helps her to meet the normal need for vicarious living. It helps her with her personal problems. Most important of all, it helps her to establish a personal standard of judgment. All this, and more, make radio one of the great social forces of our time, particularly where women are concerned.

The definition, delineation, and constitution of programs for women is a matter for perennial discussion and controversy. The administrative and executive personnel of the radio industry has been almost entirely masculine up to the present time. Consequently, the analysis and anticipation of feminine listening requirements have often been regarded as more than slightly mysterious. The elusive "woman's angle" on account acceptance and commercial presentation of commodities, as well as on program building, has frequently been

sought by the employment of one woman for that specific purpose on the staffs of radio stations, networks, and agencies.

Nevertheless, the vast audience of American women must be
served. It is a known fact that practically the entire audience
available to radio during the daytime hours consists of women
at home. Economic experts tell us that the women of America
spend 80 per cent of the national income, and the largest part
of this expenditure is made for the necessities and the small
luxuries of life. Studies of audience mail and the various types
of marketing research reveal that the daytime audience of
women at home consists largely of persons in the economic
groups having average or less-than-average incomes. These
facts are significant to commercial radio broadcasters. They
point to the daytime hours of radio and the feminine audience
available at those hours as a profitable hunting ground for the
advertiser whose commodity could be classed as a necessity
or which falls into the small-luxury category.

The facts stated above also indicate that all daytime programs are essentially women's programs, whether they be
newscasts, interviews, music, variety shows, serial stories, man-
on-the-street interviews, quiz programs, pots-of-gold, or talks
directed deliberately at women's homemaking and social interests. If they remain on the air any length of time, it is safe
to assume that they are successfully serving the needs of a
certain group of women.

However, in common usage the phrase "women's programs"
has come to mean the various kinds of daytime programs in
which a woman commentator, with or without music, special
features, or inserted newscasts, attempts to meet the special
interests and needs of this specific audience.

In the beginning, women's programs were unwanted children — there to fill the air until something better came along.
Now, they have come of age and can stand on their own feet,
combining, as they do, a well-rounded, complete coverage of
all subjects that concern and interest women. Just as listeners
select their own programs, so does a woman's program select
its own audience, depending on the insight of the woman con-

ducting the program, the people she works with in radio, and the people in the advertising agencies.

Research in the field of women's daytime radio listening reveals many interesting facts. Doctor Paul Lazarsfeld of Columbia University, in a study made in 1941, discovered that while many women who listed their major daytime radio preference as serial stories gave reasons for their choice which indicated that they thought them educational, other factors in their replies consistently bore out the hypothesis that their actual search was for companionship and social contact. This is not strange. Most of the daytime audience, as previously remarked, consists of women whose income level is moderate. They may be country women or city women, but they are restricted to the narrow confines of their homes. This restriction may be due to distance from other people, in the rural areas, or to the responsibility for little children or old people, personal ill health, or some other cause. But ordinarily, it is the woman whose income does not permit frequent movies, clubs, or other diversions that cost money who listens most to the radio during the day. She is the typical American mother and housewife. Regardless of her intellectual level or educational achievement, she is liable to become lonely and bored with her own four walls and her own circumscribed round of thought. Her radio becomes a magic thing which allows her to push out her horizons and to meet people and enjoy experiences beyond her individual physical possibility.

To answer this need for companionship, she chooses the daytime serials, the human-interest programs, the hymn broadcasts, the variety shows, and occasional women commentators. She chooses music for listening when she has something else to do and is not anxious to divert her own thought nor to have to listen to the radio too closely.

In normal times, she rarely hunts for news broadcasts. To the majority of American women, this is still very much a man's world; until the war few of them saw any urgent connection between their immediate, personal problems and interests and events in Washington, London, or Tokyo. During the war women did keep abreast of the news in general, because their own concerns were so obviously entangled with world activities. However, even then, it was not news for the sake of information which they sought, it was simply information which pertained to the activities and welfare of their own particular family and friends. This was partly the fault of the newscasters, who presuppose a background of knowledge of geography, history, and economics on the part of their audience. Housewives generally do not have such knowledge at their finger tips. Consequently they were not impressed by all the newscaster reported and continued to listen specifically for those fields, such as rationing, taxes, warfare in territories where their sons were fighting, which affected them.

If one were to list in order of importance the reasons why women listen to the radio in the daytime, the need for social contact would head the list, followed by desire for entertainment, and occasional use of the radio as a pace setter for other activity, with the craving for information or education a long way down the line. A woman will listen to many types of programs at various times, under various conditions and while engaged in various occupations.

In actual program planning in this field, much more specific information needs to be secured. The local radio station which serves a community largely foreign-born has a different women's audience from the local station which serves a midwest agricultural area, or the sophisticated city station whose listeners may have access to more movies and a wider variety of foodstuffs and whose children play on cement pavements and have no chores to do. If any program is to answer the needs of the audience it serves, it must be built upon a careful analysis of their living habits and interests. When such knowledge is at hand, the next problem is the adaptation of the facilities available to meet these requirements.

The time of day at which a program is scheduled for broadcast has some bearing on this adaptation. The morning is an active work time in most households. The style, pace, content of a morning program should be set to harmonize with such activity. The early afternoon is likely to be a time for relaxation; the baby is asleep and there is mending to be done. Women's programs at that hour do well to take these factors into account. They may influence the decision as to whether or not music should be included. They will have much to do with the choice of the musical selections which are used.

The question of popular versus classical music for these broadcasts — not to mention the innumerable variations in these two classifications, such as hillbilly, salon, light opera, etc. — must be settled in terms of suitability to the time of day, the audience activity, and the materials and flow of the program itself. Bizet's "Agnus Dei" has no more place in the middle of a fast-moving morning program of practical household helps than "The Tiger Rag" has in the quiet time of early afternoon. That does not mean that good music cannot be played in the morning and popular music in the afternoon. It does mean that the same rules of good programming must apply consistently in any show. There are selections among the good music available to fulfill the need for color and action, and there are popular tunes which lean toward the languorously sentimental side.

Women's programs may or may not be sponsored. If they are sponsored, there are two possibilities. A single advertiser may take over an entire program or several advertisers may buy one- or two-minute announcements, known as "spots," in the same program. The second situation is the more common.

On small stations, the woman handling the broadcast very often has to secure her own advertisers. On larger stations, or in agencies, the sales departments of those organizations bring in the accounts. However, it is wise for the person in direct charge of the program to maintain some control over the acceptance of accounts. There are times when the salesman's ardor may overcome his judgment and good taste. There are also times when too many commercials in the same field may keep the general content of the program within too narrow a range.

Advertisers who buy spot announcements on a participation show, as such programs are called, expect a certain amount of support and promotion from the general context of the program. How much they receive depends on the good judgment and diplomacy of the program's director. The more desirable advertisers are the first to understand that a good program in general, attracting women and winning their confidence, will do more to sell their commodity than the garbled show which stretches broadcasting ethics and good programming in order to give each advertiser an extra chiseling of time. However, the program builder does have an obligation to the advertisers. The sponsor has a right to object if his paid announcement introducing a new cleansing cream is preceded by a convincing little feature chat on soap and water as the ultimate care for the skin.

The number of commercials acceptable within a given period of broadcasting time has been quite definitely indicated by the Code of the National Association of Broadcasters.[1] It is wise not to include too many commercials demanding mail returns or other direct results in the same broadcast.

Commercial copy may be furnished by the advertiser, by his agency, or by the radio station. The person conducting the program is sometimes asked to write it. This is often the wisest arrangement. This individual knows the audience and should have profited by previous experimentation in techniques for reaching the listeners and stimulating them to action. She also should have made a thorough and continuous study of audience mail on the program, watching for key words which seem to have registered and are reflected in the returns, checking on the efficiency of various mailing addresses used, and the spacing of the address in the course of the announcement, the use of a station announcer or the woman commentator to give commercials, and numerous other specific details.

The director of the program should keep in touch with the agency or advertiser responsible for the account, and frequent reports should be made on the program's progress. Once it

[1] See Chapter 4, "Control of Broadcasting."

has been accepted, the advertiser and the broadcaster should continuously work together as a team.

Up to this point the characteristics of the audience, the factors which influence program planning for women, the problems of music on the program, the place and treatment of commercial announcements, and a hint of the importance of general program pace have been mentioned. This last point should perhaps be elaborated slightly.

In any art — music, painting, drama, or a women's radio program — rhythmic form is an important element. In radio it is known as pace. Pace is a quality which is felt instinctively and which may vary within the same program from day to day. The comparative length of the several features, as well as their emotional intensity, color, warmth, and exoticism influence pace. It is radio's expression of the old artistic rules of unity and variety. It is the movement and flow which maintain interest.

There should be variety in any good program, naturally, but the transitions must be smooth. A long orchestral number should not follow a long feature talk. After three minutes of talk on preventing damage from moths, the orchestral selection should be bright and gay, as well as timed to less than two minutes and thirty seconds. The feature immediately following should likewise be short and on the side of lightness. A hard-hitting commercial announcement would be suitable in such a sequence — with a smooth-flowing musical number following fourth in line. A sentimental, poetic feature spot should never be followed by any sort of commercial. If time forces exceptions to the rules of good variation, insert a brief musical bridge of a few seconds or, if no music is available, a second or two of dead air, with a change of speed in the voice of the broadcaster, in beginning the new item, to make the transition.

A woman's program may be a regular daily series, a weekly series, or a one-time feature only. The program may be listed under the name of the personality conducting the program, as is the case with Bessie Beattie on WOR, "Around the Town" with Mary Margaret McBride on WEAF and Ann Hayes on

KCMO. Sometimes the program is established and publicized under a trade name, such as Betty Crocker on NBC, or Joanne Taylor on KMBC, for the very logical reason that the station wants to continue the over-all format of a successful program, even though the personality conducting the program may change with the fortunes of time. For example, Betty Crocker has been on the air for nineteen years under the trade name of Betty Crocker, but there have been several different women actually giving the broadcasts.

The characteristics of the commentator and the content of the program have much to do with fulfilling the social need of the listener. Listeners draw a mental picture of the person behind the microphone. Oddly enough, an extraordinarily beautiful and cultivated voice is not always an asset to a woman commentator. The feminine listener dislikes any hint of affectation, particularly in women. Occasionally she will relish sophistry, cynicism, or bombast from men, but she will shrink from the polished and perfect woman every time. She is yearning for friendliness. The normal, everyday voice and diction of the broadcaster will give her that, especially if the voice carries a note of cheerfulness and ease. It is the direct, personal, warm approach, as real and vital as a handshake, which wins the woman listener.

Neither program content nor talent are crucial determinants of the success of a woman's program if it adheres to certain basic principles. These include co-operation, imagination, patience, showmanship, personality, and promotion. In some cases, the program is built to order, after a careful analysis of the habits, needs, and interests of the community has been made. An excellent example of this type of public-service program on a local station was "Wartime Women," conducted by Clare Hays on Station KOIN, Portland, Oregon. This was designed to meet the needs of women in the area served by her station. The details as here supplied by Mrs. Hays deserve the careful attention of all those interested in planning women's programs for local stations:

The station, instead of asking one person to produce her

idea of what the community needed, assigned me to consult
with the heads of the Red Cross, the Civilian Defense Organizations, the United States Employment Service, the OPA, and
similar agencies, asking each one, "If you could have a radio
program of your own, what would you want it to be?"

It was interesting to find that all of them felt much the same
need. With hundreds of members or volunteers to contact --
often quickly — they wanted a spot on the air to which, regularly, all members could tune for announcements of meetings,
emergency notices, spot news. It would save many telephone
calls and would also make immediate notification possible.

Another thing they all wanted was a program on which the
general public could be recruited and general information
about the agency could be disseminated. These needs produced
the format of the program.

Even the hour was requested by the women themselves.
Unlike most women's programs, it comes at night, immediately
following the 10:00 o'clock news. This time was chosen because
women are so busy now. Many of them aren't home during
the day. Many agencies have instructed their members and
workers to listen to "Wartime Women" for last-minute information.

The women's audience loves to help. The commentator will
do well to let them, every once in a while, put their finger in
the pie. A program of this type can become a center in which
listeners feel that they are associating with hundreds and
thousands of other women like themselves.

Audience mail should be encouraged. It should also be read
and answered promptly. Its contents can be most enlightening
and helpful in program planning as well as in a check on the
nature of the audience. The successful woman commentator
never condescends to her audience. She studies her audience
mail with care and appreciates the sincerity of the letters she
receives from listeners of all intellectual levels.

The subject matter for women's programs is infinite. Food,
handicrafts, household hints, party plans, quilts, home sewing,
style, beauty, health, problems of child care, human-interest
stories, book reviews, interviews with interesting people, social

principles, stunts and special features. poetry, featured musical numbers, news, interior decoration, pets, the romance of common things around the house, plans for a postwar world, home canning, ways of meeting contemporary shortages and curtailment, juvenile delinquency — anything that's pertinent to the home and community life of an American woman or which can help her to be a more interesting dinner-table companion for her family has a place in choosing material for such broadcasts. Analysis of the audience will aid in deciding upon the relative value of subject matter.

Authoritative material is easily secured through the United States Department of Agriculture, professional and organizational groups, the laboratories of the great food companies, and the many industrial associations. In most instances, a simple request for all releases will place the commentator's name upon a permanent mailing list.

The station with which they are affiliated should give adequate promotion and publicity to women conducting women's programs. They should be made to feel a part of the organization for which they work, and if they are members of the staff, they should be given suitable stenographic help and office space. As Mary Mason, former director of women's activities for Station WRC, Washington, D.C., says: "This consideration will pay adequate dividends." She also found that it is of great benefit to know the local leaders in women's activities, to take part in all local civic affairs and work closely with the sales, press, and program departments of the station.

ILLUSTRATIONS OF WOMEN'S PROGRAMS

The following illustrations of women's programs are included to show informal and formal program patterns, ways of handling commercials, colorful or courageous reporting, amusing commentary, attention-getting announcements, and straightforward, matter-of-fact information programs.

One of the most courageous news analysts and commentators is Dorothy Thompson, columnist and author. Her style is well illustrated by this excerpt from a sponsored broadcast on the

Blue Network on November 21, 1943. Her first paragraph tells the story:

> This week I was down in one of the border cities of the South, speaking at an Open Forum. Just before I went on the program, I got a letter. It said: "Miss Thompson, I wanted to hear you tonight, but I can't, because I am not allowed to buy a ticket. I AM COLORED."

Miss Thompson emphasized the last three words. From that point she went on, quickly analyzing what she thought was at the bottom of the anti-Negro feeling, and then followed her point through on anti-Semitism and race prejudice as it exists today, not only in the private lives of our friends but as it crops up over and over again among the boys in the armed services.

Rich's great department store in Atlanta, Georgia, sponsors a daily women's program six times a week, with Penelope Penn, on Station WSB. The following illustration shows the standard opening and closing of Rich's commercial, the only credit given on the program — a lesson in brevity. The interview shows an effective way which was used during the war to interest women in doing their share for a scrap drive.

ANNOUNCER: Rich's clock on the corner says 8:30 A.M. – Central War Time – and it's time for Penelope Penn.

THEME: MUSIC UP AND FADE UNDER. . . .

ANNOUNCER: Every weekday morning at this time, Rich's radio reporter, Penelope Penn, brings you world news and interesting personalities.

PENN: So you, Lieutenant Patrick, were one of the men in the spearhead of the invasion. . . . They machinegunned you coming down? Was that what put your leg in the cast?

LIEUTENANT: AD LIB – Tells how bullets peppered his legs.

PENN: Captain Markrud, how soon did your Division follow the paratroopers?

CAPTAIN: AD LIB – Tells how the infantry came ashore in regular landing barges.

PENN: Was it a machinegun that got you in the arm . . . or something else?

CAPTAIN: AD-LIB – Describes what it is like to face anti-tank shrapnel . . . Describes street fighting.

PENN: What you men have been through is probably beyond the comprehension of most of us at home. But one thing is certain. The bullets in your leg, Lieutenant Patrick, and the shrapnel in your arm, Captain Markrud, might have been scrap metal once . . . that a conscientious *German* housewife turned in to *her* salvage collector. Surely, we ought to send back double for that! Look at this little needle-pointed tin tube in my hand. Did you have one of these things with you in Sicily, Lieutenant Patrick?

LIEUTENANT: I had a surette in a little cloth bag on top of my gas mask . . . every parachutist has one as part of battle equipment . . . it's full of morphine . . . you can inject it yourself, if you're wounded and need it.

PENN: Then you must have had one, too, Captain Markrud?

CAPTAIN: AD LIB — Tells how he lost his in street fighting . . . Scottish soldiers gave him one of theirs . . . very similar to ours.

PENN: Well, perhaps you didn't know that these are made from our empty tin cans. I learned that from the WPB. Our supply is so critical that the only tin we can spare to manufacture these things is what we can get from cans we've turned in. That's why we must clean and flatten and *save* them . . . and never lose even the top of one. The quota is every empty can in the country . . . and this goes on till the end of the war. That's why all grocery stores are collection stations for them. We must take them there. . . . Surettes can't be made of anything but tin. The morphine's so corrosive it eats right through other metals . . . We'd hate to think of our men being without surettes . . . or anything else needed in battle, for that matter. . . .

(Exact instructions followed regarding scrap and salvage.)

THEME: UP AND UNDER.

ANNOUNCER: Tune in tomorrow morning at 8:30 for another visit with Rich's radio reporter, Penelope Penn.

Here is an attention-getting opening, that eliminates a formal and frequently dull announcement, introducing an information program:

1. SOUND: CASH REGISTER . . . RINGS TWICE . . . CLOSE DRAWER.
2. NANCY: That's your money buying food.
3. SOUND: CASH REGISTER.
4. JOHN: That's your money paying for a home.

5. SOUND: CASH REGISTER.

6. NANCY: That's your money buying clothes.

7. JOHN: That's your money buying you a living.

8. SOUND: CASH REGISTER . . . CLOSE DRAWER.

ANNOUNCER: During the next 15 minutes, the National Broadcasting Company and its affiliated independent stations make their facilities available as a public service to the War Food Administration to present "CONSUMER TIME."

Jane Weston conducts "The Modern Home Forum" on Station WOWO, Fort Wayne. The content consists of prize-winning recipes sent in by listeners, and information on how to make pot holders, appliqued dog patterns for children, and baby-bib patterns. All have their place on the program, as well as the prize winners.

Audience participation has been a regular feature of the program several days a week. Church groups, clubs, and parent-teacher associations write in asking for a date on the "Forum." Sometimes these bookings are made as much as a year in advance. Prominent members of these groups, clubs, and organizations are interviewed on the "Forum," and refreshments are served after the program in the WOWO kitchen.

Products of the participating sponsors must be items used or consumed in the home, such as foods, furnishings, arts and crafts, needlework, and clothing. Leaflets, with recipes and patterns, are supplied to listeners on request. Miss Weston feels that the success of her program is due to its "simplicity."

Age has nothing to do with a woman's value to radio. Girls just out of college are taking their rightful place in the front ranks of radio, while programs conducted by Bessie Beattie, "Commando Mary" (Ernesta Barlow), Ruth Chilton, director of women's activities at WCAU, Philadelphia, and other veterans throughout the country continue to grow in popularity and pulling power. In her daily program, Ruth Chilton has a straightforward, factual approach in giving both information and commercial credit to her sponsors:

Colds are big business, or rather, they make big business — shame on us for having so many of them. This year the public will spend almost one hundred million dollars for pills, nose drops, chest-rubbing salves, cold syrups, cough drops, and the like. Yes, I said a hundred million dollars! There are more than 130 million of us, you know, and wouldn't you guess that an average expenditure for cold treatment would amount to a buck a year, at least? Then, there's the vitamin business. It's closely related to colds, because a great many people take vitamins primarily to build up their resistance to colds. The sale of vitamins now amounts to more than 300 million dollars a year. Tell that to some of your friends who say there are bad times ahead for this country! Remind them that every new, major discovery means a brand new industry employing thousands of people and making millions of dollars, which go to swell the national income.

NBC's "Commando Mary" (Ernesta Barlow), during the war, did a straight job of up-to-the-minute reporting on war work for women in a way that women understood. Notice Mrs. Barlow's colorful remarks about carelessness among women factory workers:

. . . Just be careless and get yourself into an accident and lose the banner for your work room, and you will find yourself about as popular as if you had thrown away a major league pennant by muffing a fly. . . .

Her description of a war-working mother was in terms that every woman understood:

. . . One particularly deft worker explained to me how she managed her home and her child and her job. The ten-hour day at this plant, with two days off, she said, was what made it possible for her. When she gets home in the evening, her daughter of fourteen has supper in the oven, most of which the mother had prepared the night before. Washing is done twice a week, and the child helps with the simple ironing . . . sounds like a grand kid, doesn't she? All shopping is done on Saturday, or one weekday evening. On Sunday, they both go to early Mass, then come back and get breakfast, clean the house, have early dinner, and then they're both off to a movie. . . . "We just have fun for the rest of the day," this mother said. . . .

Mary Margaret McBride has been on the air since 1934. Her name and style have become a legend, as have her faithful followers and imitators. Now with WEAF, she does an ad-lib show in a completely natural and unself-conscious manner.

Following are examples of the surprise element of the program and the way in which the commercials are lumped together and disposed of:

MISS McBRIDE: I hear you're married to a conductor.

MRS. SANDBACK: My husband is a conductor on the Alton Railroad.

MISS McBRIDE: I know, the C & A.

MRS. SANDBACK: Yes, the old C & A. They changed the name. (Laughter.)

MISS McBRIDE: And your father was a mule trader?

MRS. SANDBACK: My father was a farmer and a mule man.

MISS McBRIDE: Oh, my father, too.

MRS. SANDBACK: Yes, Paris, Missouri, is a place where they have lots of mules. And Shellbottom, Missouri —

MISS McBRIDE: Yes, Shellbottom — I most certainly hated Shellbottom! (Laughter.)

MRS. SANDBACK: I didn't think so much of it, myself! (Laughter.)

MISS McBRIDE: Do you want me to tell you something funny about Slater? That's where my Aunt Alameda Smith lived. Did you ever know my Aunt Alameda Smith?

MRS. SANDBACK: She was also my aunt!

MISS McBRIDE: No! You're kidding!

MRS. SANDBACK: No.

MISS McBRIDE: You know my Aunt Alameda? She weighed about 300 pounds — *my* Aunt Alameda.

MRS. SANDBACK: Well, she was *mine*. You're funny!

MISS McBRIDE: Well, that's all right. You can —

MRS. SANDBACK: I'm just getting who you are. She was a McBride.

MISS McBRIDE: Sure!

MRS. SANDBACK: Well, and she married my great uncle!

MISS McBRIDE: Can you imagine that!

MRS. SANDBACK: We're kinfolks, and didn't know it!

MISS McBRIDE: Kinfolks and didn't know it. Aunt Medy — we called her — She came to visit us — you know she was pretty fat, and our spare-room bed broke down. We heard the loud thud, and poor Aunt Medy was lying on the floor! (Laughter.)

MRS. SANDBACK: And wasn't she humiliated, as dignified as she was?

MISS McBRIDE: She didn't mind. I thought she was hurt. Her shoulders were shaking like mad, and then we found she was really laughin'.

Here follows a typical example of how Mary Margaret McBride handles her commercials:

MISS McBRIDE: I have a cute little thing here. The author of it is Florence Covell. She sends me a little sheet of paper called "Garden Memories," and every one of our products reminds her of a flower. Isn't that cute, Vincent?

ANNOUNCER: Quite an idea!

MISS McBRIDE: Sweetheart soap, for instance, reminds her of her favorite flower of all, lily-of-the-valley; has the same waxen, delicate, but long-lasting loveliness. Does Sweetheart soap remind you of lily-of-the-valley?

ANNOUNCER: I can't say the fragrance does.

MISS McBRIDE: Well, the fragrance has been called everything from a Mary Margaret McBride rose to a geranium. Anyhow, it has a beautiful fragrance and a nice oval shape. It lasts a long time, and it's economical. And it's had 6,000,000 new users in 3 years. In fact, it's six million and one, because you remember we added one!

ANNOUNCER: A brand new one, yes, that's me!

MISS McBRIDE: That's right. Then comes Od-30 right after Sweetheart soap. We don't want Od-30 running around chasing away the fragrance of Sweethcart!

ANNOUNCER: No, we don't.

MISS McBRIDE: May Glover of Norwalk, Connecticut, says: "So far, I haven't found Od-30. But what a boon it will be in a sick room!" Yes, or in a dog house, or in a house where you have lots of pets.

Like Mary Margaret McBride, Adelaide Hawley has had long experience in radio. Now with Station WEAF, New York, her program format is an intelligent combination of factual information told in dialogue form with commercial credits skillfully woven into the program:

HAWLEY: Did you hear, Clyde, about the woman who went to a
    newsreel theater and saw her husband in a picture of troops
    landing in Africa?
CLYDE: Yes, she got the theater to give her the piece of film that
    contained his picture, was that it?
HAWLEY: Yes, but the sequel is particularly interesting. She took
    those frames of film to 683 Fifth Avenue, here in New York, to
    the BACHRACH Photographic Studio, and they made a real
    portrait of her husband from that group scene — the only one
    she had of him in uniform.
CLYDE: So many of the men never have time to have a likeness
    made before they leave the country.
HAWLEY: That's why our special BACHRACH Copy Service is filling
    such a need today, and I must say it is wonderfully expert ser-
    vice, too.

Elizabeth Bemis, one of the few women news commentators
heard daily, is presented by the Columbia Broadcasting System.
Her voice is pleasing, and her straight-forward presentation of
the news, plus her ingenuity in digging up little-known facts,
as well as her amusing human interest stories, make her a
commentator to watch.

Back in the year 1832, members of Congress, in a burst
of patriotism, commissioned a young American studying in
Rome to do a statue of the Father of Our Country. And then,
in the press of business, they rather forgot about it, until they
received an urgent message asking for $1200 — to get the
statue out of the mud of an East Coast harbor. It seems that
the twenty tons of carved Italian marble had fallen through
the boat which was bringing it to this country.

You can imagine the surprise of everyone concerned when
the statue was finally unveiled in the rotunda of the Capitol.
The young sculptor had been very much influenced by the
glory that was Greece and the grandeur that was Rome; for
Washington, the Hero of Valley Forge, turned up in a wrap-
around job called a toga on his hips, sandals on his feet, and
nothing else!

The artist claimed that the light was too dim for it to be
properly seen in the rotunda, so it was moved onto the Capitol
lawn. Then a protest arose, as it was altogether too well seen.
An iron fence had to be built around it and a shelter over it.

ostensibly to protect it from the weather. Every fall, the shelter
went up, and every spring, it came down, for a matter of some
sixty-five years.

Finally, the $50,000 hunk of marble that is George Washing-
ton was moved to the Chapel, behind exhibits of printing in
the Smithsonian Institution, and there it stands to this day.
Yesterday, by the way, it had its annual bath — almost the only
attention it receives through the years now.

Elizabeth Long, director of women's activities for the
Canadian Broadcasting Corporation, is responsible for several
timely and outstanding programs for women on freedom,
money, hobbies, recreation, and postwar problems. In addition, the CBC chart of child needs, prepared especially for the
Canadian Broadcasting Corporation by the National Committee for Mental Hygiene of Canada for use on a program
dealing with the problems facing all parents today in raising
their children, has become an institution in Canadian homes.

In the spring of 1943 the National Association of Broadcasters, through Mrs. Dorothy Lewis, Co-ordinator, formed
the Association of Women Directors. The purpose of the Association was to bring together the women who were working in
the field of women's and children's programs on the hundreds
of radio stations throughout the country. Heretofore, these
women had had no opportunity to know each other or to become acquainted with the programs and activities of the
various stations. It was evident that such contact would be
invaluable and helpful both to the women themselves and to
the stations which they served. The Association has now
grown to a membership of more than six hundred and fifty.
Its constitution provides for three classes of membership:
active, for women directors actually broadcasting or responsible for women's or children's programs; inactive, for women
executives of radio stations occupying administrative, sales, or
technical positions; associate members, not connected with any
radio station, but interested in various phases of broadcasting,
such as advertising, writing, producing, editing. Both active
and inactive members must be accredited by their stations.

CHAPTER 10

TRANSCRIPTIONS AND RECORDINGS

SINCE THE DAY Thomas A. Edison put "Mary's Little Lamb" on a soft-surfaced cylinder, the recording of sound has attained to a point where it can be regarded as an indispensable adjunct to our way of life. At any hour of the day or night, hundreds of recording styli are cutting the more or less permanent footpaths of sound so that presently more hundreds of pickup needles may retranslate that sound for human ears. In a sense, the recording stylus and its reverse component have defeated time. Up until a little more than a generation ago, the sound of a word once uttered, a violin note once played, were possible treasures dropped into the none too safe repository of human memory; but the same sounds transferred to wax or plastic or film or wire can live and vibrate again fifteen minutes or fifty years from now.

The fact that it is possible to bring a controllable pause between the origin of a sound and its final impact on the ear is one of the major reasons why recordings are vital to broadcasting. Until somebody invents a good forty-eight hour day, it will be impossible to put two programs on a single wave length from a single station at one time. A recording provides the next best alternative. While a local program may be going on the air from the station's studios, recording machines are busy transcribing another program from the network lines, and the station can present it at a later available time period; or in the late watches of the night when the station transmitter is off the air and the audience is sleeping, a vital shortwave program from overseas can be fed into the runas of a recording disc and saved there for presentation with the listener's breakfast coffee.

These are only two radio uses among many that are possible through the very remarkable device Edison originated in 1877.

Before entering a general discussion of recorded sound in radio programming, it is necessary to clear up a problem in terminology because of the popular confusion that results from trying to differentiate between the expression "electrical transcription" and "recording." Actually, there is little or no difference either from the standpoint of the product itself or from the standpoint of what the dictionary has to say about the words. Either "transcription" or "recording" can be defined as "a copy of something."

As understood in the radio field, the words are synonymous. However, there is a distinction between a recording made for radio broadcast purposes and a record intended for use on a phonograph.

The mechanical differences are these: broadcast recordings are almost universally recorded at 33 1/3 revolutions per minute as compared with 78 revolutions per minute for a phonograph record; while studio reproducing apparatus can be speeded up to play a 78 r.p.m. record, very few phonographs can be slowed down to play a 33 1/3 r.p.m. recording; differences in play-back quality also exist, as in comparing the reproduction from an average broadcast recording and a low-priced phonograph record; phonograph records are almost universally confined to three or five minute segments, depending on whether the discs are ten or twelve inches in diameter, radio recordings may include anything from a fifteen-second station break to a fifteen-minute segment of a full hour's broadcast.

The idea of using recorded material for radio must have occurred at a very early date in broadcasting, although there seems to be no well-defined "first" in the annals. Originally, recording probably consisted of nothing more complex than hauling a talking machine up to the studio microphone. In the earliest days, stations often operated on a hit-or-miss schedule, depending on how much local talent could be rounded up for a performance, and it was convenient to turn over a few phonograph records while waiting for a performer to put in an appearance. Records were also a boon to stations located outside the talent centers and, indeed, were the principal source of program material available at many places.

But in time broader horizons began to appear in the recording field. As soon as methods were worked out for hooking a phonograph pickup head into the wire circuits of a station control room panel, the recording turntable was destined for a place in every radio station in the land. Then special applications broke out like a rash; the idea of recording speeches or dramatic or musical material for later use seems to have occurred to many people at once.

But whatever the genesis of various techniques, it is true that progress in the recording field was very rapid as soon as some of the basic radio applications were grasped. As with many other technological improvements, early radio recording was purged of its deficiencies because of public demand. There was a time when listeners objected in no uncertain terms to the use of recordings on the air. These objections resulted in two developments — an insistence that recordings be specified as recordings when used on the air, and a thoroughgoing research campaign to improve recording quality.

One of the milestones in this development was the introduction of "Orthacoustic" (true sound) recording by NBC some years ago. For best results, the recording "characteristic" and the play-back "characteristic" must match. The recording characteristic developed by NBC was designed to improve quality, reduce surface noises, and produce recorded sound waves with faithfulness and tonal beauty. Following its introduction, radio stations throughout the nation made adjustments in their play-back equipment so that the pickup systems would match the Orthacoustic characteristic. Equipment manufacturers, also aware of the need for matching characteristics, then started to include an Orthacoustic filter as an integral part of turntable units.

Eventually such co-operation resulted in a uniform set of recording standards which were adopted by the NAB on the recommendation of its engineering committee. The main object behind this set of standards was to put broadcast recording on a uniform mechanical and acoustical basis: it specified the number of lines per inch, the speed of rotation, the point at which sound was to start, the permissible levels of surface noise, etc.

Improvements in recording surfaces, pickup circuits, cutting heads, turntables, and other elements have resulted in recordings that today are difficult to distinguish from live studio productions. The public no longer is disturbed by the announcement that "this is a transcription," and listeners give the modern product their complete acceptance.

High fidelity and a live, studio-like quality are modern recording characteristics that have brought this acceptance. Recordings today have a frequency response ranging from thirty to twelve thousand cycles and more, a range of vibrations which includes the sounds reproduced by musical instruments of all types, from the bass viol to the top notes of a violin. This frequency response is equal to the tonal range of the best broadcast transmitter and is superior to the receiving ability of the average well-constructed home radio set.

Together with mechanical improvements, much has been done to put the art of recording production on an even footing with live studio broadcasting production. More expert handling of recordings and a greater degree of showmanship in presentation is well repaid by the noticeably greater degree of listener approval.

Before passing on to the next point, it would be well to note that a discussion of radio recording processes will be found in Chapter 24, Walter Lanterman's section on broadcast engineering.

Factors Responsible for Recording Development

Up to this point, only two reasons have been advanced to account for the usefulness of recordings as a radio device. We have noted that recordings have the capacity to put a "stop" signal in the path of time and that they are handy to have around when live talent is missing; but there are many other factors lying behind their development and use.

1. They are often the only means whereby programs can be distributed to stations. Take, for instance, a case wherein a

sponsor is unable to obtain a particular regional or national network because of time or other reasons: he can still put a broadcast on the air by sending his show to stations in recorded form.

2. Recordings have made uniform spot broadcasting possible. While a sponsor has the alternative of buying local live talent on all the stations he uses, cost considerations and a desire for uniformity in quality and talent indicate that he will probably want to use recordings.

3. Recordings bring programs of network caliber and quality which would otherwise be denied to local listeners. While it is true that many stations have and do produce live programs with local talent, most smaller stations cannot build programs on a par with recordings produced in the large talent centers.

4. Recordings offer a supplement to the coverage obtainable on a network. For example, a sponsor's live program may be recorded and shipped to stations not carrying his network show.

5. Local stations find recordings a useful device for improving program balance.

6. Recordings enable an advertiser to pinpoint his area of distribution. Often enough, a standard network hookup may not coincide with an advertiser's markets; with recordings, he can pick the specific towns where he has distribution.

7. When recordings are available, the advertiser is not held to a fixed time of day or night nor is he subject to the limitations of changing time zones. He is thus able to choose the best available local time.

8. Line costs or lack of facilities may make a particular event impossible to cover, but with a portable recorder the event can be "packaged" and brought to listeners.

9. Recordings make it possible to repeat some outstanding radio event as, for instance, on the anniversary of the event or on other significant occasions. In this sense, they may be regarded as authentic historic documents.

These are among the reasons why recordings have become vastly important to radio. The following is an outline of their modern position in the field:

TYPES AND USES OF RADIO RECORDINGS

In general, there are two types of recordings used in radio today. These are "processed" recordings, wherein multiple copies are made from a master by a pressing process, and "instantaneous" recordings, where the original disc itself is intended for some broadcasting purpose.

Uses of Processed Recordings

1. Custom-made or commercial recordings, produced to conform to a client's needs. May contain several fifteen-second station break commercials, or a full program. This type was used very extensively by the U. S. Government to further the war effort and to bring programs to U. S. forces overseas. In commercial usage, recordings are produced under best studio conditions and are shipped to radio stations.

2. "Open end," or syndicated recordings. These are program recordings, either musical or dramatic, complete in all details except for commercial announcements. Time is allowed at the beginning and at the end of the record (sometimes in the middle) for insertion of a sponsor's message by the local radio station announcer. Programs are usually made up in series of thirteen, twenty-six, or thirty-nine weeks, etc. They are developed by recording companies or by special radio production firms, and usually are sold to only one sponsor in a given market or group of markets. They offer the advantages of high caliber entertainment and expert production at reasonable cost.

3. Library transcriptions are usually musical recordings supplied to local broadcasting stations on a rental basis. The music is arranged so that it provides a complete program and, with accompanying continuity, can be used by the station as a high class sustaining feature or can be sold for commercial sponsorship. The individual selections usually run not more than 3½ minutes each and are specifically designed for radio use. Each transcription contains from eight to ten selections, and after a station purchases the basic original service, the library producer ships new recordings each month.

4. Phonograph records play an important part in the program picture. Improvements in recording have won them a continuing place in the program schedule. They are often made the basis for locally sponsored commercials and continue to be a convenient medium for filling vacant program periods.

5. Sound effects records considerably augment the station sound man's repertoire of bangs, pops, and door slams. Recording companies and organizations specializing in the production of sound effects are ready to supply anything from an authentic tree toad voice to the roar of a steamship siren. All network production centers and many stations have large recording libraries containing sound effects that would be impractical or impossible to produce by hand in the studios. To name just one category, authentic railroad train effects are available in almost limitless variety on records, but the studio would be practically crippled if it had to depend on hand methods to produce a full run of train sounds.

Uses of Instantaneous Recordings

1. A primary use is for delayed broadcasts. Stations which cannot take network service at any given time can simply direct the incoming network show through a recording circuit and play the resultant transcription later. A network may perform the recording service if, for some reason, an affiliate or affiliates cannot make transcriptions themselves at the time of a particular network airing. Shortwave broadcasts at off-air hours, or events occurring outside the studios and covered by portable recording apparatus are other phases of the same thing.

2. Network program extension is a title used to describe an occasional broadcasting situation in which a network program scheduled on a given day is to be broadcast at a later date over one or more stations. If the supplementary station list is small, enough instantaneous recordings are made by the network while the program is on the air and are shipped out the same day. This classification differs from the foregoing in that the program may be sent to stations other than network affiliates.

3. Air checks are instantaneous recordings made at the re-

quest of a sponsor or an agency. Usually, the program being checked is tuned in on a radio receiver and the output fed to a recording machine. The resulting transcription is then available so that the sponsor or his agency may check program quality, effectiveness, or transmission.

4. Reference recordings are in much the same class as air checks although they are usually made directly off a studio wire line by a station or a network, rather than being tuned in over the air. Reference recordings are made for a multitude of reasons — for recording new program ideas, auditions, discussion, etc. As the title indicates, they are for reference and file purposes.

5. Documentary recordings are usually made whenever there is a possibility that a particular program may bring up controversial issues or may inspire legal action. Such recordings are held in files against future contingencies.

RECORDINGS IN USE AT THE STATION

Putting a broadcast recording on the air involves much more than dropping a needle into the groove and letting it spin. In the first place, the turntable operator does not "drop" the needle; and before he ever gets a chance to make such a slip, there are several factors to consider about the particular recording in hand.

Primarily, the station must decide how the recording conforms with the FCC rulings about identification. If there is no announcement on the recording identifying it as a "transcription" or a "record," then the station must make a live announcement of the fact at the proper time interval as specified by the FCC.

The rule states that a recorded program of more than five minutes and not more than thirty minutes' duration must be identified by an appropriate announcement at the beginning and end of the show. Further, if the duration of such a show is longer than thirty minutes, it must be identified at the beginning, at the end, and at each thirty-minute interval. However, if this plus thirty program happens to be a single uninterrupted speech, play, church service, symphony concert, or opera, then it may be identified at the beginning and end only, without observing the thirty-minute interval announcements in between.

The FCC ruling also states that only an opening identification is necessary if the recording runs five minutes or less, and that a station does not have to identify recordings used for background music, sound effects, station identification, a program identification theme, or a sponsor identification.

With these matters decided, the station must also make a time check to see how a recording fits in with other items in the schedule. A fifteen-minute program usually times out at fourteen minutes and thirty seconds, allowing the station time for the required identification and station break announcements. A thirty-minute program generally runs twenty-nine minutes and thirty seconds, also allowing a time cushion. A so-called five minute announcement usually times out thirty seconds short, and even a one-minute announcement will shave a few seconds off the full sixty.

Although recorded programs are subject to the same NAB and labor provisions that prevail in live broadcasting, these matters are usually not subjects for station concern, but are handled by the agency, client, or recording company that produced the transcription. The NAB code prescribes the length of commercials that may be used in shows running five minutes or more. AFRA and the AFM prescribe the rates of pay that must be made to the artists and musicians who appeared on the program.

Payment for music rights is involved in almost any recording schedule where copyright music is used. The producing organization handles the details of securing permission to perform and of paying the copyright fees assessed. The ASCAP fee is twenty-five cents per selection per station per use; BMI and SESAC charge two cents per selection per record; AMP and other music copyright pools make similar charges. In addition, the radio station is required to have a "performance" license from one or more of these copyright holding organizations. In cases where a station does not have a performance license to cover the music on a recording, the producer may arrange for the license through a process known as "clearance at the source."

Because of the work and cost involved in developing a high fidelity program recording, it should be given every consideration from the time of its arrival at the station until it has fulfilled its purpose. Good business judgment would also indicate that the station should endeavor to get the best possible results out of such a program. Why sabotage a station's reputation by indifferent handling of a recorded program that has the quality and talent of a live, high grade network production?

Good playback equipment is needed, and it should be kept in perfect mechanical order. A turntable that does not revolve at the proper speed will cause "wows" and other distortion. A tone arm that does not swing freely may cause the needle to stick in a groove or to jump grooves. The weight at the point of the pickup needle should conform to the limits set by the recording company. This usually is a pressure of only two ounces. Heavier pressure will cause distortion, an increase of surface noise, and will shorten the life of the record.

Careful handling and storage are also necessary. A finger mark will introduce scratch noise, and so will dust or dirt particles that settle in the grooves. Wiping the record before use is always good practice and is routine at many stations.

As a concluding thought on station use of recorded programs, it is all-important to rehearse thoroughly such shows before broadcast time. This is particularly true in the case of open end programs and other commercial programs that require local announcing service. While all the necessary cues and copy are furnished by the producer or agency, complete familiarity with the recording and the script are essential to a smooth production on the air. And smooth productions are at the root of listener acceptance of transcribed programs.

3

THE PUBLIC SERVICE PROGRAM

CHAPTER 11

INTRODUCTION AND DEFINITION

It has often been asked, "What do you mean by public service as applied to radio?" To answer, one might include everything that is broadcast from the time a station goes on the air in the morning until it signs off at night. Broadcasting, itself, is a public service. It is the purpose of all radio stations to build programs of service to the public whether for pure entertainment and amusement or for information. Obviously, however, that is not what is meant when radio speaks of "public service."

This type of program was formerly called "educational." It still is at many stations and on some networks. The National Broadcasting Company, in using the phrase "public service," has attempted to coin a term that will be more acceptable to the public generally than the word "education," which seems to be a little austere and does not connote a type of program which might be amusing, entertaining, or easy to listen to. The public, by and large, wants to make its own decisions regarding its education. It does not want it handed out too obviously by radio. If, on the other hand, the public can acquire certain elements of education without being aware of it, can absorb information which will tend to be educational in the long run, there will be no objections, and the program has a fairly good chance of being listened to.

Doctor James Rowland Angell has said that "any program may be regarded as educational (and here we may substitute the words 'a public service') in purpose which attempts to increase knowledge, to stimulate thinking, to teach technique and methods, to cultivate discernment, appreciation, and taste, or to enrich character by sensitizing emotion and by inspiring socialized ideals that may issue in constructive conduct."

Perhaps that is a large order. The definition which has been more generally accepted throughout the industry is one presented by Doctor W. W. Charters, in 1932, while Dean of Educational Research at Ohio State University. Doctor Charters stated then: "An educational program is one which purposes to improve rather than merely to amuse, to improve the audience in the matter of information, aesthetic appreciation, and the stimulation toward proper conduct." [1] Restating this four years later at the Institute for Education by Radio, Doctor Charters said:

> This definition of educational broadcasting, therefore, implies improvement of the experience of the listener. It has, however, one technical weakness. It states that the program "purposes" to improve the audience, that the broadcaster presents the program with intent to educate. This position I am not now able to defend because, as I shall indicate, programs may raise standards of taste or increase the range of valuable information without being intended for that pedagogical purpose. I would, therefore, change the definition from "one which purposes to raise" to "one which raises." An educational program is one which raises standards of taste, increases the range of valuable information, or stimulates audiences to undertake worth-while activities. In short, an educational program is one which improves the listener.[2]

There will be many people who will take umbrage at the phrase "improve the listener," so the search continues for an all-embracing word or phrase that will describe "educational" or "public service" radio.

Not having such a definition at hand, this section, therefore, will attempt to cover the problems which arise in the planning and building of radio programs "which improve the listener" and thereby render a public service.

The radio law of the United States states that a license shall be granted to a radio station "if public convenience, interest, or necessity will be served thereby." The act does not define public convenience, interest, or necessity, and while the Fed-

[1] Year Book, *Education on the Air*, 1932, page 51.
[2] Year Book, *Education on the Air*, 1936, page 16.

eral Communications Commission has been guided by this standard, it likewise has not attempted at any time to give a precise definition.

It is a hard statement to define, but it has come to be looked upon as meaning that a certain percentage of all radio programs must be "educational," "informative," "cultural," or whatever other word one may choose to use to designate those programs which are not pure entertainment. Hence all radio stations, feeling this sense of responsibility, schedule certain programs in this particular field. No radio station is obliged by law to devote any definite percentage of time to so-called educational programs, though, because of a bill which was brought before Congress a number of years ago, there are a great many people who believe that every radio station is required to set aside at least 15 per cent of its time for educational purposes. This proposed legislation was introduced by Senator Simeon D. Fess of Ohio in December, 1931, but was never passed. Every radio station, therefore, is permitted to arrange its program schedules as it wishes without dictation from the Federal Communications Commission or any other governmental authority.[3]

The prime objective of any radio station, be it large or small, is to build programs which it believes its listeners will enjoy and listen to. In other words, radio very definitely tries to give the public what it wants. That, of course, does not mean that all of the people must like, or do like, all of the programs all of the time. But at least there must be programs on most commercial stations some time during the day that will appeal to everyone. Thus, consciously or unconsciously, through the many public service or educational programs which are scheduled, the public is coming to have a deeper appreciation of this type of program. Classical music, including symphony orchestras, for instance, are more generally accepted now than they were, say, fifteen or twenty years ago.

By giving a variety of entertainment and information, and classical as well as popular music, the radio station is soon able to decide which of its programs are acceptable and which are

3 See Chapter 4, "Control of Broadcasting."

not. After all, the public does do the deciding — that is as it should be. As Allen Miller [4] has said: "There is nothing more democratic, there is nothing more in keeping with the idea that a democracy should bring the greatest good to the greatest number than an application of that principle to radio."

In building programs for the majority of listeners, no radio station can wholly forget that there are minority groups which must be considered. They have a place in our democracy; they must also have a place in radio. No law or ruling insists on any definite percentage of time being set aside for programs for any minority group, but in proportion to their place in society, so should be their place in radio. It is in this way that program planners conceive their responsibility in arranging daily and weekly schedules.

Someone has said that all people are more truly influenced through emotion than in any other way. There is no doubt that radio has accepted that fact and used it to advantage. Advertisers as well as political leaders long ago found that it is easier to appeal to the people through the heart than through the mind. Programs built with an emotional appeal are sure to draw the largest audiences and the biggest response. Workers in the field of educational radio are loath to acknowledge this truism, maintaining that certain programs must be built to appeal to the intellect. Of course, they are right, but that is the minority appeal, and if 15 per cent of the programs were built with that intention the average would be good, but the appeal must, in the long run, be aimed at that other 85 per cent if a program is to be successful. There are exceptions, but generally speaking the foregoing is true.

A program director, or an educational director, has no assurance, of course, that any program aimed at a definite audience will catch or hold that audience. That is his intention and objective. If he is successful and the program succeeds in interesting the listener sufficiently so that future offerings will be eagerly watched for, the director can be assured that he has

[4] General Manager of KOAC, Oregon State Agricultural College radio station, Corvallis, Oregon.

accomplished his purpose. He has built a good program, has held an audience, and has enabled the station to feel that it is performing a real service to the community. That is the good will every radio station in America is looking for as it yearly renews its license.

The local and regional station, but particularly the local station, has an opportunity to serve its own community in a way a network-owned station can never hope for and, in a sense, should not be called upon to do. It should be the business of the manager of every local station to know his local government, his civic leaders, religious and lay, the officers of the local clubs; to become allied with all community activities and offer the services of his station to help, in every way possible, any activity that is intended to raise the level of the health and welfare of the town or city in which the station is operating. He could very easily be the head of the Red Cross or Community Chest drive, making the station the center of such functions; he could be a leader in any youth movement, such as the Boy or Girl Scouts. In this way, the listener comes to regard the station as part of his community life and, therefore, a part of his daily life. If only from a purely selfish standpoint, this would be excellent procedure on the part of the manager of the station; but, in addition to being good business, it is one of the most valuable ways to build continued listener interest in the station.

CHAPTER 12

TYPES OF PUBLIC SERVICE PROGRAMS

TALKS

OF ALL RADIO PROGRAM FORMS, the radio talk is the hardest to write, to give, and to make interesting and acceptable to the listening public. The first inclination of almost everyone, in turning on the radio and finding someone talking, is to switch the dial immediately until a musical program is found. That is done almost as unconsciously as breathing.

Talks, as such, are not liked. Ordinarily they are dry, academic, uninteresting in the extreme, and very hard to listen to. Why is this? In the first place, they are, in most instances, put down on paper in such form and language that they look as if they were to be published as an article in a magazine or a newspaper, not as if they were material to be broadcast. The style is likely to be the typical and accepted style to be found in books, somewhat stilted and not the easy conversational style of our everyday language. The proper radio talk should sound extemporaneous, as if the person delivering it were speaking to some friend or individual, imparting information of interest to that friend.

There are many ways of making a script come to life. Some regular broadcasters use one way, some another. Ted Malone, for instance, talks his scripts out loud and writes them down just as he speaks them, starting another line on the paper whenever he pauses, like this:

Hello there
This is Ted Malone
speaking to you from a gold and brown
frame house
one room and a hallway wide

176

and two and a half stories high . . .
on Codwise Avenue in New Brunswick, New Jersey.

Today I am speaking to you
from a small square room
on the second floor front.
It was in this room back in December, 1886
that Alfred Joyce Kilmer was born . . .
Joyce Kilmer . . .
the poet,
world-famous author of the lyric poem . . .
"Trees" . . .

Another way is to use dots or dashes, lots of them, in writing
out a script like this:

Hello there . . . This is Ted Malone . . . speaking to you from
a gold and brown . . . frame house . . . one room and a hallway
wide . . . and two and a half stories high . . . on Codwise
Avenue in New Brunswick, New Jersey.

Today I am speaking to you . . . from a small square room . . .
on the second floor front . . . It was in this room back in December, 1886 . . . that Alfred Joyce Kilmer was born . . .

Joyce Kilmer . . . the poet . . . world-famous author of the
lyric poem . . . "Trees" . . .

If, on the other hand, those same words were written down
in regular form as follows:

Hello there, this is Ted Malone speaking to you from a gold
and brown frame house, one room and a hallway wide and
two and a half stories high, on Codwise Avenue in New Brunswick, New Jersey.

Today I am speaking to you from a small square room on the
second floor front. It was in this room back in December, 1886
that Alfred Joyce Kilmer was born.

Joyce Kilmer, the poet, world-famous author of the lyric poem,
"Trees."

the speaker would be much more likely to read it rapidly making the content sound as if it were being read, thus losing the conversational style. It ceases, too, to sound so convincing.

Neither of the two styles suggested above is necessarily the one a radio speaker will adopt. Uniformity is not important. Each person must learn the form best suited to his own mode of expression. Then the script should be read aloud to see whether it sounds natural or stilted, pedantic, and dry. If it sounds stilted, it should be rewritten and rewritten until it sounds natural and conversational

Another good rule to follow is always to use simple language. No "twenty-dollar" words should be allowed, and no complex sentence structure. Sentences need not necessarily be short, but they must not be involved. The audience should always be kept in mind. They should never be talked down to. The majority of the people in the United States have had only an elementary education and have a speaking vocabulary of about two thousand words. (A well-educated person has only a speaking vocabulary of approximately nine thousand words.) It is just as important to hold the attention of the less-educated group as of the better-educated listeners. After all, the former represents the vast majority of any audience. The late President Roosevelt was a perfect example of an excellent broadcaster. His radio vocabulary was simple and direct, not full of four- and five-syllable words or long and involved sentences. He was anxious always to reach and hold the largest possible audience and he realized that he must speak their language in order to do so. This he did admirably.

On the opposite page is a photostatic copy (Figure 4) of a page from a preliminary draft of President Roosevelt's speech of December 8, 1941, to the joint session of Congress in which he asked for a declaration of war against Japan. The revisions shown on the page in pencil are in the President's own hand. Notice the wide margins; the triple spacing between lines; the short paragraphs; the fact that no words are divided at the end of the line. For instance, the word *implications* in the fifth line might very well have been divided, with the *im* at the end of the

3

Japan has, therefore, undertaken a surprise offensive extending throughout the Pacific area. The facts of yesterday speak for themselves. The people of the United States have already formed their opinions and well understand the implications to the very safety of our nation.

As Commander-in-Chief of the Army and Navy I have directed that all measures be taken for our defense.

Always ~~Long~~ will we remember the character of the onslaught against us.

No matter how long it may take us to overcome this premeditated invasion, the American people will in their righteous might win through to absolute victory.

I *believe I interpret* ~~speak~~ the will of the Congress and of the people when I assert that we will not only defend ourselves to the uttermost but will ~~see to it~~ *make very certain* that this form of treachery shall never endanger us again.

Figure 4

179

fourth line. But the whole sentence flows more smoothly when the eye can follow along the same line and not have to jump to another to complete a word. The page is not crowded, which again makes it easier to read. This form apparently is the one chosen by the late President in order to secure a smooth-flowing broadcast, a broadcast that sounded as if he were conversing with the American citizens, not as if he were reading a lecture.

Another point to remember is that a listener's attention must be caught by the first five or ten words of a talk. It is necessary, therefore, to begin with an arresting phrase or an amusing incident, maybe a sentence or two with an emotional appeal, anything that may be attention arresting. Unless that is possible, the remainder of the talk, no matter how important or interesting, is wasted. Once caught, the attention must be held by change of pace, anecdotes, vivid words and phrases, forthrightness and sincerity.

Another most important point to remember is the question of timing. It cannot be stressed too strongly. The average person speaks 155 words a minute, or anywhere from 13 to 15 lines of a typewritten page, depending of course, upon the size of the type. A radio talk should be read aloud to someone else several times to be sure the timing is correct. The point where each minute ends should be indicated on the script for guidance during the actual broadcast.

In many instances, in reading the talk during the actual broadcast, there will be a tendency to slow down, so it is always well to leave a margin of safety in the original timing — say, twenty to thirty seconds. If the program is running short, the broadcaster can slow down toward the end, as it is almost as bad to run short, making it necessary for the station to "fill," as it is to run over and have to be cut, but of the two evils, it is preferable to run short. On the other hand, a carefully timed script should come out "on the nose" every time.

It is well to change pace occasionally and slow down for emphasis, also to use different inflections and suitable pauses. All of these devices lend color and interest to a radio talk.

Listing the points to remember in writing a radio talk:

1. There must be a real purpose behind the talk.

2. The content must have general interest and appeal.

3. It must be written in conversational style.

4. It must have simple sentence structure.

5. It must be written in simple language — no four- and five-syllable words.

6. The use of contractions and colloquialisms is important if the broadcast is to sound conversational.

7. It must catch the attention immediately, or else the whole purpose of the talk is lost.

8. It must be written to inform, not to impress.

9. The broadcaster must never talk down, but rather talk *to* the listener.

10. The listener should be made to feel that the broadcaster is interested in him and really wants him to have the information being broadcast.

11. A script should be "talked" — not read. Above all else, the broadcaster should never orate.

12. The script must be timed very carefully. A well-constructed talk is built up to a perfect conclusion; if it is necessary to cut it off before that conclusion is reached, the whole object of the message will be lost.

13. It is important to change pace and inflection for emphasis.

14. It is also important to be natural.

The Interview

Probably the most frequently used, and misused, method of broadcasting information is the interview. It is misused because the interviewer so often becomes a mere stooge, asking monosyllabic questions without any knowledge of the subject under discussion. The interviewer is not, nor is he supposed to be, an authority on the subject. He should, on the other hand, be a representative of the public and as such should try to bring out in an interview any facts of interest to his listeners. Frequently radio stations schedule broadcasts of this nature on such short notice that adequate time is not available for preparation. Program directors seem to expect any announcer assigned to the broadcast to be able to act as an intelligent interviewer. This rather unsatisfactory practice has resulted in another procedure, especially in the larger cities, of the interviewee appearing at the station shortly before the broadcast time, with a fully prepared script — questions and answers all written out, in some instances by a third person, the person to be interviewed often not having seen the script until he looks it over in the studio. The interviewer and the interviewee are then supposed to present an interesting broadcast merely by running through the material once. Sometimes there isn't even an opportunity to do this, so the broadcast goes on "cold." Generally speaking, the result is a dull and expressionless broadcast. It cannot sound as if it were spontaneously conversational nor as if either of the participants were concerned with the impression the broadcast was making. This is certainly stupid procedure and not fair to either the public or the radio station.

There are, of course, instances in which outside agencies with a knowledge of radio, acting as counsels for their clients, are in a position to write intelligent radio interviews with a thorough understanding of the subject. They work with the person to be interviewed, studying his vocabulary and method of speaking, and they can, therefore, couch the material in such form that it will sound as if the person being interviewed had either prepared the material himself or was giving an ad-lib broadcast.

Where such counsel is not available, the intelligent thing is for the interviewer to get in touch with the person to be interviewed a few days in advance of the broadcast. They can then discuss the subject, making notes on sources from which further information may be obtained, so that an intelligent list of questions can be prepared, based not only on the interviewer's previous knowledge but on the knowledge he himself has acquired during this preparation.

The following script, taken at random from the files of Elizabeth Hart, shows how a successful interviewer prepares her broadcast after a conference with the person to be interviewed. Miss Hart never uses a prepared script when broadcasting an interview. Instead, whenever possible, she meets her guest a few days ahead of the scheduled broadcast and from that conference prepares a list of questions on which the interview is based. They meet in the studio perhaps thirty minutes ahead of the broadcast to go over the questions again. The person to be interviewed does not have a copy of the questions, but is free to answer them at will, taking as much time as he wishes, provided no specific number of points must be covered. Miss Hart does not like to have an answer take longer than, say, half a minute without interruption; very often it runs only fifteen or twenty seconds.

WMAQ   TUESDAY
                                   NOVEMBER 10th
                                   12 noon

ANNOUNCER: Each day at noon, ELIZABETH HART PRESENTS
HART: Today — Red Cross

Thank you — Louis Roen, and good morning. Today we honor The American Red Cross. The American Red Cross has worked nobly — for only 50 years in this country — abroad — during wartime — and during the days of peace. These days — there is, of course, an added burden put upon the Red Cross, for we are in a world-wide war. Today — we are to hear about one particular branch of the Red Cross — that needs your help — right away — that division is the Blood Donor Service. Here in the studio we have two guests — we have Mr. Arno Holm, Director of the Blood Donor Service, Chicago Chapter — and we have one of the steady — regular blood donors — Mrs. Juliette Cohen — I am happy to have them here — and happy to introduce to you — Mr. Arno Holm — and Mrs. Cohen.

(Questions to be used on Elizabeth Hart Presents November 10th)
Mr. Holm and Mrs. Cohen

Mr. Holm as director — of the Blood Donor Service here in Chicago — give some of the facts of the service — how long have we had it here in Chicago? How many in the U.S.?

Where was the first one opened? (Army and Navy increased
their quota) — What is today's quota? (2½ million pints)
How much of an increase has there been — since the time the
service was started? What is Chicago's quota in pints? (3500
pints per week) — that takes a lot of donors — how are you
meeting your quota? You've had the Army and Navy "E,"
haven't you? What are the requirements — any age (18-60)?
What if under 21 — is consent of parent necessary? What about
weight? What should you eat before donation? Take us from
the time a donor arrives at 5 North Wabash Avenue. (10th
Floor, Te. Wabash 7850.)

What is the most times any one has come back? — Is the donor
carefully checked to be sure he is all right physically? How
much blood given at a time? — What happens afterwards? —
(mention all the voluntary services there) — then — after eight
weeks — you see him again? Are there many repeats here in
Chicago? How long does the whole thing take?

HART: Now — all this time — our other guest in the studio has just
been smiling quietly to herself — so let's turn to her — Mrs.
Cohen — a regular at the Blood Donors Service — 5 North
Wabash Avenue. 10th Floor.

Where is your home, Mrs. Cohen?

How long have you been a blood donor? . . . What prompted
you to go — the first time — and make that donation? — you've
been twice — and they can count on you? — What did your
family say? — Any other member of your family donating? Be
honest with us — what about the first time — were you fright-
ened? But not for long? As you sit there waiting — do all the
donors chat? ("A lady the other day — 3rd time — a grand-
mother — is this your first time?") What about a club — of
three timers? Or four timers? What about the pins — that you
people so proudly wear? Bronze the first time — and second:
Silver the third time? And then you keep that? No gold pin —
don't need that? You feel, of course, Mrs. Cohen — that this
donation is the least you can do — more of us must feel that way
— 5 North Wabash Avenue, 10th Floor.
Thank you very much, Mr. Holm — and Mrs. Juliette Cohen —

for being with us — and all best wishes to you — and to your work.

Again on Thursday at this same time we shall have a visitor in the studio — make your plans to be with us then.

ANNOUNCER: We have just brought you ELIZABETH HART PRESENTS, and invite you to be with us again on Thursday morning at this same time.

This is the National Broadcasting Company.

WMAQ

The next example shows the way a sheet was prepared for an interview that was arranged only twenty minutes before the person to be interviewed was to go on the air. Occasionally, a famous person arrives in town unexpectedly and either the station or the organization with which the person is associated is eager to have him appear on the radio. When this happens, it is almost impossible for the interviewer to be thoroughly prepared, and the only thing to do is to throw a few fairly reliable questions at the interviewee and let him talk at will, with an occasional ejaculation from the interviewer.

If the interviewer will stick to the subject that the person to be interviewed knows, nine times out of ten there will be no trouble in getting him to answer, even though he may not be a particularly good talker. The fact that he is a famous person with an interesting background and worth-while accomplishments to his credit will be of sufficient interest to the listener and justification enough for his being interviewed on such short notice, as in the case here, when the interviewee was Sergeant John F. Bartek, who was with Captain Eddie Rickenbacker in the rubber boat "somewhere at sea."

WMAQ   WEDNESDAY
                                              FEBRUARY 24th
                                              12 noon

ANNOUNCER: Each day at noon, ELIZABETH HART PRESENTS
HART: Today — 14 minutes of news — thank you, Louis Roen and

good afternoon. When I say news today how right I am. It was to have been news from here and there — all written out — and rehearsed. But about twenty minutes ago — our NBC News Room called and said that here in Chicago — is a man who was with Captain Eddie Rickenbacker — in that jammed rubber raft — somewhere at sea. And — in the short space of 20 minutes — we have him here to talk with us. I am happy to introduce to you . . .

SERGEANT JOHN F. BARTEK . . .

HART: Sergeant Bartek . . .

Where are you from?

(The following questions were scribbled in longhand on the sheet to be used when and if necessary.)

What did you do before the war? How long in the Army Air Force? How old? What did you think about? What was your work aboard the plane? What equipment did you have aboard the plane? Conservation of food was important? Did you lose weight? Did you read the Bible? Was it hot? What about the other fellows? What did they eat? How did you feel when you were separated? How could you recover so soon? Did you ever give up hope? What are your plans? What did the raft look like? You said you don't feel like a hero?

It is usually better to broadcast from an outline than from a prepared script. It depends to a large extent both on the person to be interviewed and on the topic under discussion. When one attempts to "ad lib" there must be some surety that the person being interviewed is not subject to "mike fright," but will be able to speak fluently. The audience does not object to pauses, but it gets restless if there are long waits or much hemming and hawing. This also uses up valuable time. Interruptions are good, from either person; it makes the broadcast sound much more like a casual conversation. On the other hand, care should be taken to avoid having both participants talk at once, as this only leads to confusion. A finger raised will indicate a wish to break in. It is well to have on hand a carefully planned summary of forty or forty-five seconds, drawing together the points which have been expressed in the broadcast. It depends, of course, on the objective of the broadcast whether this summary should be in the nature of a definite conclusion or repetitious information or merely facts leading to further study and research — in other words, whether the broadcast is factual and informative or motivating and stimulating.

One great fault with all informative broadcasts, whether they be in the form of talks, interviews, or round tables, is the tendency to cram too many points into one small broadcast of fifteen minutes' duration — the average length of a talk or interview. By trying to cover everything in one broadcast, more often than not one leaves the listener totally confused, with little knowledge of the objective of the program. It is far better to drive home one point thoroughly and successfully, making sure that the listener cannot help understanding the purpose of the interview, than to try to make a single broadcast all-inclusive.

Timing is another very important point. The interviewer must watch this, as it is safe to say that the interviewee will have no idea about timing. If the program is to be ad-libbed, a very careful outline should be prepared before the broadcast to allot a certain amount of time to each question. It will then be the responsibility of the interviewer to see that this is followed. If there is a script and it has been carefully rehearsed, this should be comparatively easy to do, though it is always well to allow thirty or forty seconds' leeway, as very often the pace is slower during the actual broadcast than during the rehearsal. On the other hand, it is not quite such a simple matter if the program is to be ad-libbed, even though there has been a careful rehearsal. The person being interviewed may hesitate longer or may be reminded of a point or a story that throws the whole broadcast out of time and makes it necessary for other questions to be dropped entirely. The interviewer must, therefore, be on the alert, carefully watching the clock, to see that the program is going forward as rehearsed and that it gets off on time. This latter fact is particularly important if the program is being broadcast over a network or from a large station affiliated with a network, or when the station may be

joining a network immediately following a local program. It is
not always so important on non-affiliated stations, where there
is more of a problem of filling time than of getting off exactly
in fourteen minutes and forty seconds, the network requirement. More and more, however, time schedules are being
enforced, even on the smaller stations, and it is, therefore,
a good idea to think in terms of split seconds rather than to
be careless about timing.

A further point to be considered, both in talks and interview
programs, is the question of authority. When information is to
be imparted, the authority himself should present it if possible.
As stated before, scripts are often prepared by someone who is
an authority on the subject to be broadcast, and then read or
given by someone else. This is not the most acceptable practice. There are, of course, occasional instances when unfore-
seen accidents will keep the authority who is to broadcast from
getting to the studio at all, or from getting there on time, making it necessary for the script to be read by whoever is on hand
at the studio. This often results in a wholly expressionless
reading by someone who is, of course, totally unfamiliar with
the subject. The public's reaction, naturally, is apt to be negative, as the listener is very quick to sense both lack of knowledge and insincerity on the part of the person giving the broadcast. If the broadcaster can, however, develop a feeling of
friendliness and sincerity between himself and the listener, an
effective broadcast will result. The broadcaster must, through
his voice and attitude, convince the listener that he wants his
confidence and respect. If this cannot be achieved, the broadcaster's efforts have been in vain and the objective of the
broadcast is completely lost.

One reason why it is better to use an interview form than a
straight talk is that often the person to be interviewed can be
invited to appear on a program with an established following.
Any information the interviewee has to present will, therefore,
have a much better opportunity first, of being listened to, and
second, of achieving the results hoped for. The program, too,
becomes much more of a "duologue" than a straight interview,

with the interviewer taking a very active part in the broadcast, resulting in an all-around better program.

It is often possible when planning interview programs for use on local stations to record them in advance. This is especially helpful when the person to be interviewed is not available at the time of the actual broadcast. Then, too, interviews can be recorded with persons working on farms, in factories, or in other places where it is impossible for them to leave their work long enough to make a trip to a radio studio in order to broadcast at a particular time. This method is frequently used by directors of farm programs. It is possible to take a recording unit to the farm and pick up the conversation between the farmer, his workers, and the broadcaster with the background of farm activity coming through on the record. This, naturally, lends interest and reality to the discussion.

Let us summarize the points to remember in writing or broadcasting an interview:

1. As in the case of a talk, there must be a real purpose behind the broadcast.

2. The content, too, must have general interest.

3. The interviewer and the interviewee must get together, if possible, three or four days ahead of the scheduled broadcast to familiarize the interviewer with the subject to be presented.

4. Under no circumstances should the interviewer become a mere stooge.

5. The audience must be convinced of the interest and sincerity of both participants in the subject at hand.

6. The number of points to be covered in any one interview should be kept to a minimum in order not to confuse the listener. The interviewee should be fully conversant with the subject, but there is no reason to presuppose that the listener is, or else there would be no point to the broadcast. The broadcasters should not attempt to cram the listener's mind with too much information. If the subject is of enough general interest, it may warrant more than one broadcast. Some of the interesting points should be saved for a second broadcast.

7. If the station permits ad libbing and the person being interviewed can "think on his feet," this method is more acceptable.

8. It is permissible to pause and hesitate in answering any question, but long waits should be avoided. Time is of the essence.

9. Time is valuable. All material should be carefully timed with a stop watch in order to keep from running over or from having to cut the speaker in the middle of a sentence, and also to see that all points in the outline have been touched upon, so that the broadcast is not left "hanging in thin air."

10. No question or answer should run more than fifteen or twenty seconds, generally speaking. Change of voice and pace lends interest and keeps the broadcast "alive."

11. The person being interviewed should be an authority on the subject under discussion. If possible, too, that person should prepare his own manuscript. It is difficult to read someone else's ideas, more often than not couched in the words of the writer and not the reader. Unless there has been very careful rehearsing, this leads to a stumbling and awkward broadcast.

The following excerpt from a script of "The State Department Speaks," broadcast over NBC on January 8, 1944, is an excellent example of a well-planned and executed written interview. It is written because all public utterances of governmental employees giving factual information of vital importance must have the approval of the head of the department concerned. Here, Mr. Harkness represents the public through his questions which become a contributing part of the interview as a whole. Nowhere does the interview sound as if it had been written out; instead it has the easy give and take of an ad-lib conversation. The use of colloquialisms and contractions in the speech of all the participants naturally helps this effect. Even though some individual speeches are rather longer than is generally wise in an ordinary interview, the type of information being presented and the manner in which it is given makes them acceptable, and the length does not detract from the interest. At no point does the program become boring and hard to listen to. On the contrary, Mr. Harkness very cleverly keeps it moving from point to point in such a way that it cannot help holding the attention of the listener.

The State Department Speaks

Program Number 1

Prepared for Radio by:

Richard McDonagh

PARTICIPANTS

Mr. Edward R. Stettinius	Under Secretary of State.
Mr. James G. Dunn	Political Adviser to the Secretary of State on European Affairs.
Mr. Leo Pasvolsky	Special Assistant to the Secretary, in charge of Post-war Planning.
Mr. Michael McDermott	Chief of the Division of Current Information.
Mr. Richard Harkness	Representing the public.

The State Department Speaks

WEAF & Network
7:00-7:30 p.m.   JANUARY 8, 1943   SATURDAY

New York Announcer: For the American people, the National Broadcasting Company launches tonight a limited series of programs called . . . "The State Department Speaks." In just a moment the first of these programs will commence in Washington, but first — a word from the Honorable Edward R. Stettinius, Under-Secretary of State, who is here in New York this evening.

Mr. Stettinius.

Stettinius: A few weeks ago the National Broadcasting Company invited the Department of State to participate in four broadcasts to tell the American people more about our work in that Department of the Government, and something about the problems involved in carrying out an American foreign policy. We in the Department of State were very glad to accept this proposal, because we want to use every opportunity to keep the public informed about what its Department of State is doing to meet the international problems which face our country. As most of you know, the Department of State is the only department of your government which deals directly with foreign countries. At its head is the President's senior cabinet officer, Secretary of State Cordell Hull.

During this evening's program and the other programs in this series, Mr. Richard Harkness, NBC commentator, will undertake to represent you, the public, in putting questions to the State Department officials who appear on the program. Mr. Harkness has warned us that he is not going to be satisfied with any handouts. He says he is going to ask questions which he thinks you people would ask, if you had the chance. We have told Mr. Harkness that we would try to answer them as fully as we can.

We shall make available to him as many of the responsible officials of the Department as he wants to talk to, and his list for the four programs already includes Secretary Hull, all of the Assistant Secretaries of State, several division chiefs, special advisers, at least one Ambassador, and myself as Under Secretary. Because the Department of State works closely with Congress in the formulation of foreign policy, you will also hear from some of our Congressional leaders during the course of these broadcasts.

The National Broadcasting Company is to be congratulated for this first big effort in radio history to bring closer together the State Department as a whole and the millions of people it represents in their dealings with foreign nations. Now to Washington for Richard Harkness and the first program of "THE STATE DEPARTMENT SPEAKS."

HARKNESS: Good evening, ladies and gentlemen. This is Richard Harkness. I'm here tonight in the State Department Building as *your* representative. I'm here to find out what goes on within these walls — to try to peek behind the veil of mystery and secrecy which popular tradition says surrounds the activities of the State Department. But I can be successful as your representative only if you help me. Write me the questions *you* want answered about our State Department. I can't promise to use them all, nor to acknowledge them, but I'll use *some* of them, and in any case your questions will help guide me in laying out my interviews with the individuals Mr. Stettinius mentioned a few moments ago.

And now let's get on with the first set of them. I have found through experience that one of the best men to go to for information down here is Michael J. McDermott, known affectionately throughout the State Department and to every newspaper man in Washington as Mac. He is the Chief of the Division of Current Information, and he is right here with me now, as are two other gentlemen you will be glad to meet. The first question I want to ask you, Mac, is this: What does this job of yours consist of? Why is it necessary to have a Division of Current Information?

McDERMOTT: You're a fine one to ask that, Dick.

HARKNESS: I know, Mac, but don't forget there are a lot of people listening in who don't know as much about you and what you do as I do.

McDERMOTT: Well, you know that the State Department is always in the public eye. The newspapers and the radio people are very much interested in what goes on in foreign affairs, and in order that they may be able to interpret events, they need all sorts of information. And they are not at all fussy about the times that they need it, either, as you know, Dick, with program deadlines and newspaper deadlines to meet. They'll come after information any hour of the day or night, and it must be here for them when they come. It's my job to see to it that it is.

HARKNESS: And a good job you do, too. But tell me, Mac, does your division have any share in formulating the foreign policy of the United States?

McDERMOTT: Let me answer you this way, Dick. Every man and woman in the United States who is so inclined can have a share in formulating our foreign policy, but in order to do this, they need accurate information to guide them in forming their opinions. We help to make information on foreign affairs available to them through press and radio fellows like yourself, and so we help them to judge and analyze for themselves what is going on in the world. And, as I said before, they in turn — I am talking now about the man in the street — decide in the last analysis what our national foreign policy shall be.

HARKNESS: I see. In other words, you're saying that the work of our free press and radio has a lot to do with the actual formulation of our foreign policy by giving the people the facts on which they form their opinions.

McDermott: Right; but I know what's on your mind primarily tonight, Dick. You're interested in getting some straight dope on the Moscow Conference and what goes on in our postwar planning work. Well, here are two gentlemen, two experts, who will be able to help you out. Each of them has made a life study of international affairs. Mr. Dunn has specialized particularly in international political relations, and Mr. Pasvolsky is known as an outstanding expert on international economic affairs. And so all I can say to you, Dick, is go ahead and ask them anything you want. I am sure they'll do their best to answer you.

(GET AD-LIB GREETINGS OF MEN)

Harkness: O.K. Mac, I think I'll start with Mr. Pasvolsky, who, I understand, is a Special Assistant to the Secretary of State in charge of postwar planning. Is that right, sir?

Pasvolsky: Yes, that's right.

Harkness: Well, do you mind telling me something about what you postwar planners do, and how you got started, and what not?

Pasvolsky: Certainly, Mr. Harkness. When war broke out in Europe we knew at once we had a big job to do. It was one of the most difficult jobs of international relations the Department of State had ever faced; and one of the most comprehensive jobs, too, for it entailed not only the conduct of foreign affairs in a world at war, but also preparation for meeting the problems which this country was bound to face after the fighting was over.

Harkness: Are you saying, Mr. Pasvolsky, that our State Department's preparations for meeting postwar problems began upon the outbreak of war in Europe in 1939?

Pasvolsky: That's right. And we were actually at work early in 1940.

Harkness: How did you begin?

Pasvolsky: We started off with a group of committees to study the future implications for this country of what was happening elsewhere in the world. In February, 1941, the Department created a special research unit. Of course, both the committee and research work became real postwar planning after December 7, 1941.

HARKNESS: This postwar planning unit of yours, Mr. Pasvolsky — what kind of people are in it, and how many are there?

PASVOLSKY: There are well over a hundred specialists, drawn from all over the country, from universities, research agencies, and the professions. The unit also includes experienced officers of the Department and of the Foreign Service.

HARKNESS: And what, specifically, do they do?

PASVOLSKY: These men and women assemble and analyze a vast range of factual material for the use of the committees in preparing recommendations on policy questions. They do this, of course, in co-operation with regular officers of other divisions of the Department of State and with experts in other agencies of the government.

HARKNESS: Well, what are the main subjects these people are working on today?

PASVOLSKY: First of all, there is a group of subjects relating to arrangements necessary for the conclusion of the war. These comprise the terms to be imposed on the enemy nations after their surrender, including control of the enemy countries after they have been occupied by the United Nations forces, and the eventual definitive peace terms.

HARKNESS: I see.

PASVOLSKY: Another group of subjects relates to liberated areas. Briefly, this entails exploring the problems of re-establishment of independence in those countries which have been deprived of their freedom by the Axis invaders. Many of those countries, don't forget, will be starving and disorganized. They will need relief and other help in re-establishing their economic life.

HARKNESS: Of course. Go on, Mr. Pasvolsky.

PASVOLSKY: A third group of subjects relates to the all-important problem of providing for the future maintenance of peace and security.

HARKNESS: Now you are reaching right into the hearts of almost two billion people — two billion people who have learned now what total war is and who never want to see another one. What are our State Department's plans on how to preserve the peace, Mr. Pasvolsky?

PASVOLSKY: Well, we start with the basic assumption that the
elimination of war and the establishment of security for all
nations requires co-operative effort on the part of the peace-
loving nations, based on order under law.

HARKNESS: Yes, but how are you going to get nations to co-operate?
No one has ever yet succeeded in doing that for long.

PASVOLSKY: We know that, Mr. Harkness — only too well. But we
are not and we must not be discouraged. We believe that co-
operation between peace- and freedom-loving nations *can* be
achieved in time of peace as it has been achieved in time of
war. To do this these nations must create certain facilities and
instrumentalities for international action.

HARKNESS: Such as — ?

PASVOLSKY: Well, there must obviously be arrangements for settling
international disputes by pacific means, rather than by recourse
to war. But above all, there must be arrangements for sup-
pressing aggression.

HARKNESS: Now wait a moment, Mr. Pasvolsky. Seems to me that
was tried once before — with the League of Nations.

PASVOLSKY: Yes, it was — up to a point. But this time there must
be the *clear* certainty for all concerned that breaches of the
peace will not be tolerated — that they will be suppressed — by
force, if necessary. Secretary Hull has put it this way:
    "It is abundantly clear that a system of organized interna-
    tional co-operation for the maintenance of peace must be
    based upon the willingness of the co-operating nations to
    use force, if necessary, to keep the peace. There must be
    certainty that adequate and appropriate means are available
    and will be used for this purpose."

HARKNESS: Good! You suggested a question to me which I will
ask you later, Mr. Pasvolsky, but please continue. Sorry to interrupt.

PASVOLSKY: Think nothing of it, Mr. Harkness, we're used to interruptions. The fourth group of subjects in our postwar work
covers the problem of developing relations among nations
which will help improve their economic and social conditions.
This field includes so many ramifications dealing with trade
barriers, tariffs, cartels, aviation, shipping, labor standards, mi-
gration, education, and so forth, that I could keep you here
for hours talking about them. We are trying hard not to miss

one practical idea or plan through which international co-operation can help make this a better world to live in. I might add, Mr. Harkness, that we are not so foolish as to think we can solve these problems in the State Department alone or even in the Government as a whole. It's a tough job which will take the best thought and effort of *all* of us.

(*The program continues in this vein for thirty minutes*)

THE ROUND TABLE

The round table has come to be the accepted method of presenting any material when more than one point of view is to be expressed. This is especially true when controversial subjects are under discussion. In form, the round table is a cooperative effort combining the special knowledge of radio technicians and scholars for the presentation of a simple, informative, and generally spontaneous discussion of important contemporary problems.[1]

Three persons comprise the usual round table. In this way, as someone has said, voice is given to the right, the left, and the middle of the road. It is always wise to have one of the three members act as chairman of the group. He is supposed to keep the discussion moving, to see that the outline is followed, and to make sure that only the allotted time is spent on the various points in the outline.

To guarantee a balanced discussion, speakers should be chosen whose background and experience qualify them to represent opposing viewpoints on the subject to be presented. In general, it is better to avoid extreme points of view. Otherwise, the program may develop into a personal controversy from which nothing constructive evolves, tending to leave the listener utterly confused.

When planning a round table it is wise at the beginning to set up the objectives and build the program from there. Participants should be selected who will carry forward the objectives determined upon. The failure or success of a round table depends on the participants and on how well preliminary plans

[1] University of Chicago Round Table *Memorandum to Participants*.

Timing

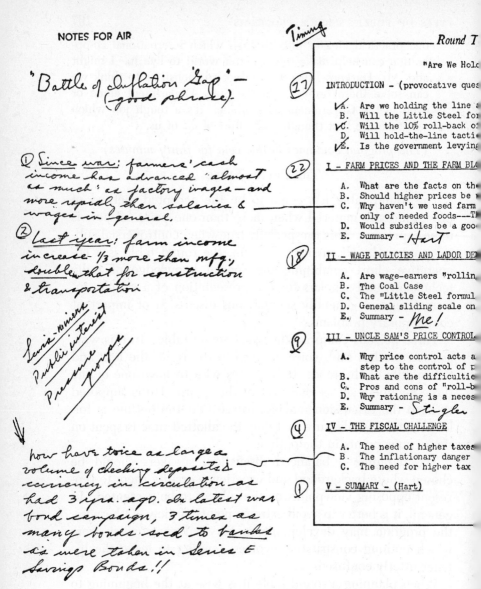

"Are We Hold

"*Battle of Inflation 'Gap'* —
(good phrase)-

⑰ INTRODUCTION - (provocative ques

✓A. Are we holding the line a
 B. Will the Little Steel fo
✓C. Will the 10% roll-back o
 D. Will hold-the-line tacti
✓E. Is the government levying

① *Since war: farmers' cash
income has advanced 'almost
as much' as factory wages — and
more rapidly than salaries &
wages in general.*

② *Last year: farm income
increase 1/3 more than mfg.,
double that for construction
& transportation*

Lewis - miners
Public interest
Pressure groups

*how have twice as large a
volume of checking deposits &
currency in circulation as
had 3 yrs. ago. In latest war
bond campaign, 3 times as
many bonds sold to banks
as were taken in Series E
Savings Bonds!!*

⑫ I - FARM PRICES AND THE FARM BLO

 A. What are the facts on th
 B. Should higher prices be
 C. Why haven't we used farm
       only of needed foods---T
 D. Would subsidies be a goo
 E. Summary - *Hart*

⑱ II - WAGE POLICIES AND LABOR DE

 A. Are wage-earners "rollin
 B. The Coal Case
 C. The "Little Steel formul
 D. General sliding scale on
 E. Summary - *Me!*

⑨ III - UNCLE SAM'S PRICE CONTROL

 A. Why price control acts a
       step to the control of p
 B. What are the difficultie
 C. Pros and cons of "roll-b
 D. Why rationing is a neces
 E. Summary - *Stigler*

④ IV - THE FISCAL CHALLENGE

 A. The need of higher taxes
 B. The inflationary danger
 C. The need for higher tax

① V - SUMMARY - (Hart)

Figure 5. This outline was prepared by the chairman of the Univer

line

Line?"

pose)

nflation?
wage control hold?
ices really work?
the inflation problem?
taxes?

c position of the farmer?
to encourage production?
o encourage production
LOC?
encourage food production?

th"? (DATA)

ess or failure?
an alternative.

tions are only a first

rcement?
subsidies?
en price control?

control can work.
bonds to banks.
ckly.

Pose questions A-C-E on behalf of Round Table listeners.

I begin thus Section I

quote Econ Stabilizer Byrnes here

Wages & salaries: up 65% in '42 over '40 ch hey industries, total pay rolls are up as much as 160% over '40. Half of this increase due to increase in employment rather than in wages. Per capita wages up 50% in '42 over '40.

quote FDR: "The only way to hold the line is to stop trying to find justifications for not holding it here or not holding it there."

pose questions here for Stigler to answer.

o Round Table, program of May 16, 1943.

have been prepared. The background, present connections, and viewpoints of each prospective participant should be known before he or she is asked to take part in the program. Also it should be certain that he is sufficiently articulate to carry on an interesting and provocative discussion.

Round tables may be broadcast from scripts, as were most such programs during the war, or ad-libbed, as is the University of Chicago Round Table. However, since a good round table, even though read, mut be broadcast as if it were being ad-libbed, perhaps it is just as well to follow the same procedures as would be laid down for an ad-libbed round table.

Written or ad-libbed, a round table must first be outlined. This helps the participants to organize their materials to convey an ordered discussion to the listener. Also it helps to assure inclusion of all points which the participants are desirous of presenting. Without an outline, too much time may be devoted to one point, so that a final and possibly more important point may be left out completely. Then it is the duty of the chairman of the round table to see that the outline is followed, so that only the number of minutes decided upon ahead of the broadcast shall be given to presentation and discussion of each point. He must be on the alert to see that none of the speakers devote too much time to any one point, as the whole balance of the program would thereby be destroyed. Naturally, if a script has been prepared ahead of the broadcast, this condition will not exist if care has been taken with timing, but it needs careful watching when the discussion is spontaneous.

Participants must guard against long speeches, technicalities, and anything remotely resembling an oration. Simplicity is the key word for any radio speech, interview, or round table; and normal. ordinary conversation should be especially easy to maintain when three persons are talking together, as in a round table. Normal conversation means normal interruptions, hesitations, asides, jokes, and spontaneous laughter, and under no circumstances technical jargon. This does not mean "talking down" to the audience; rather it implies their participation in the broadcast. For example, it is better to say, "The cost of a

can of beans would go up a nickel," than to say, "Unit cost for
the production of tinned foods would rise in an ascending
curve rapidly approaching the high index figure of April, 1922
— of 4.321 cents."

Facts and examples are always of first importance. Facts
stated simply invariably stick, and examples always tend to
impress any point on the mind of the listener. The more facts
that can be personalized, the more acceptable the broadcast.
The listener is always interested in facts obtained first-hand, in
hearing from someone who has hobnobbed with important
and famous personages in the news. It is well to remember that
one reason a round table is being broadcast is to present factual
information to the listener. He is expecting this information to
be presented by authorities; therefore, the participants must be
authorities, or else, generally speaking, they have no right to a
place on the program. They should not hesitate to assert such
authority in giving out factual information. It is much better
to say, "I saw," or, "When I talked with the Secretary of State
about this," than to say, "in recent reports" or "reliable authorities state." In this way the listener has been taken into
the confidence of the broadcaster, and he feels almost as if
he had been eavesdropping on these conversations.

Another point often neglected is the fact that the listener
cannot see the participants and, therefore, does not know who
is speaking. It takes more than a few minutes to identify for
the listener each of the three different voices, and even then
sometimes it is impossible because of the similarity of voices.
It is far better to use names frequently — last names, not first
names. The listeners are not intimately acquainted with the
participants and do not know them as "Jack" or "Robert," but
only as "Jones" and "Brown." It is, therefore, preferable to use
last names, leaving out the prefix "Mr." or "Dr." unless one
of the participants uses a title such as "general" or "President,"
but in the case of a woman, "Mrs." or "Miss" should precede
the use of the last name. It is wise also to use names frequently
when directing an answer to a specific question. For instance,
do not say, "Well, I'll tell you what I think . . . "; instead say,
"Well, I'll tell you, Jones, what I think . . . "

Frequent interruptions add interest to the program, but before such an interruption, a finger should be raised to indicate to the speaker that another participant desires to break in. The speaker should not, however, be interrupted before he has completed the thought he is expressing. Breaking in without previous indication may result in two people talking at once. One of the most annoying things that can happen on any discussion, so far as the listener is concerned, is to hear everyone attempting to talk at the same time. Pandemonium breaks loose; nobody, either the other participants or the listeners, understands anything that the other person is saying. It is both rude and confusing. It is true that in order to have a well-rounded broadcast, each of the participants must contribute his share to the program. Mrs. Roosevelt is quoted as having said that when she participated in the University of Chicago Round Table, she was so absorbed in what the other two participants were saying that she was forgetting to take any part in the discussion herself, until the director placed in front of her a card reading, "Don't be a mouse — get in there and pitch." And she did.

Naturally some subjects are more controversial than others. It goes without saying that controversy always heightens listener interest; it also serves to emphasize the arguments on both sides of the dispute. Among the listeners to the broadcast, there will undoubtedly be many on each side of any controversial question. Each group wants to hear its side presented just as forcibly as the opposite side, therefore all the participants should state their positions clearly and disagree where disagreement is expected. At the same time, it is not wise to quibble over trivialities or unimportant technical details. Such quibbling only bores the listener who is eager to have the discussion go forward.

It is also well, when possible, to use word pictures; vivid language, clever examples, and personal anecdotes, amusing incidents, and humorous stories add color and interest. The more natural a participant can be, the more human the broadcast and the larger the audience that will be built up for the program.

Depending, of course, on the objective of the round table, the participants should decide in advance whether they shall try to arrive at a definite conclusion or whether the discussion is merely to present the facts, thus motivating further study of the subject on the part of the listener. The University of Chicago Round Table has never pretended to arrive at any solutions to the problems presented each Sunday; rather, they have hoped to stimulate further thought and study among their listeners. At the close of each broadcast, the chairman takes about forty seconds to sum up the points which have been presented in the course of the discussion, but he never offers a solution. On the whole, this is the most satisfying way to end any round-table discussion. Always more than one point of view has been presented each Sunday. There are probably many listeners, each holding those different viewpoints, and if the participants, or the chairman, attempted to tie up the discussion in a neat little package, definitely drawing up a conclusion and a solution, many listeners would be dissatisfied and would accuse the chairman of being prejudiced one way or the other. With the discussion left open, each listener can think out his own conclusion without malice.

The following abstract from the May 16, 1943, University of Chicago Round Table illustrates how the outline was followed throughout the discussion:

ARE WE HOLDING THE LINE?

Mr. Cox: "I have been looking through some letters that have arrived in the last few days from Round Table listeners. It is interesting that a number of them raise questions which are the crux of the issues we had in mind to discuss today. They ask if we are holding the line against inflation. Are we?"

Mr. Hart: "Offhand, I think we have to say it's touch and go. If everything goes well, the line may hold for months; but it is entirely possible that everything may start sliding within a few days."

Mr. Cox: "Here's another question: Will the Little Steel formula for wage control hold?"

Mr. Stigler: "I hope that it will. Right now we are at the crucial point. If in the next week John Lewis loses his battle for higher wages, I have high hopes that the Little Steel formula will hold for quite a while."

Mr. Stigler: "The next question raised by listeners: Do you think that the recently announced policy of setting meat prices back 10 per cent will really work?"

Mr. Cox: "It looks pretty ambitious in view of the recent admission of the Office of Price Administration that actual prices in many areas are already a few per cent above the ceiling prices. Certainly if the prices can be rolled back 10 per cent below the official levels, and if they can be kept there, it will greatly improve the atmosphere in which wage negotiations take place."

Mr. Cox: "Another question that has been raised asks if hold-the-line tactics will solve the inflation problem."

Mr. Hart: "I do not see how we can hope that just saying that we are going to hold the line and then setting up enforcement machinery will do it alone. We still have the problem of excess spending power. The public has a lot of excess spending power that will have to be tied down if these enforcement problems Stigler was speaking about are not going to blow up in our faces. Tying those down means taxes — big taxes."

Mr. Stigler: "The last question that was sent in asks about taxes. We are going to spend around a hundred billion dollars this coming fiscal year on war. We are going to raise about thirty-five billion dollars in taxes. Is that enough taxes?"

Mr. Cox: "Certainly we are going to have a lot more taxes than are in sight in the light of action of Congress to date."

Mr. Hart: "I would go a step further. We need not only more than is in sight; we need more than anybody has been asking for officially — more than the sixteen-billion-dollar figure for extra taxes that was in the budget message and in recent Treasury announcements."

Mr. Stigler: "I might say that this fifty-fifty rule of the Treasury and the President seems to be the natural reaction of people who do not like either taxes or borrowing."

Mr Stigler: "What is the general picture? Are farmers very prosperous?"

MR. HART: "The farmer does not seem to be doing so badly. If one takes the national income statistics, one will find that from 1940 to 1942 the net income of farmers — that is, after allowing for all expenses — is up 120 per cent. It has more than doubled. That compares with a 55 per cent rise in total national income and with about a 65 per cent rise in the incomes of the wage and salary people."

MR. STIGLER: "Along with that has gone a very sharp increase in all farm prices."

MR. COX: "I am sure, too, that a great many farmers — at least those I know (and I know a good many of them personally in this middle-western area) — are fairly well satisfied with the prices that they are getting for products. They are not nearly so anxious for higher prices as certain representatives of the so-called 'farm bloc' seem to be."

MR. STIGLER: "That raises a very interesting point. What about the farm bloc? What are our chances of ever doing anything for soya beans, and nothing for cotton, when the cotton senators are so powerful?"

MR. STIGLER: "One cannot talk very long about cost of living and farm prices without going into the wage question. What is the general setting? How prosperous are the wage earners?"

MR. COX: "I think that Hart mentioned just a little while ago that wages and salary totals have gone up 65 per cent in 1942 over those of 1940. In key industries in the field of war production, total pay rolls are up as much as 160 per cent over those of 1940. Over half of this increase, however, is due to an increase in employment rather than to increases in rates."

MR. STIGLER: "That's a phenomenal increase — 50 per cent in two years."

MR. COX: "It certainly is."

MR. STIGLER: "The white-collar worker is not very happy when he thinks of that. I should say the 'frayed-collar' worker."

MR. HART: "But the white-collar worker ought to remember that the people that are doing the war work ought to be expected to be paid for it. On the whole, white-collar workers are more the passengers than the crew in the present situation."

MR. STIGLER: "I should say that that is a challenge to the War

Manpower Commission rather than a reflection on wage disputes."

MR. STIGLER: "Let us turn to a special case — the coal dispute of the present time. I am prepared to argue that the miners have done pretty well during the last four or five years. If we really go in and give them an increase, it will be an increase based primarily on the fact that they have a lot of political power."

MR. HART: "In any case, whether or not they have been having the breaks, if we start saying that now is the time to make exceptions, then, after all, everybody can put up a claim for exceptions. It simply does not mix where we're trying to make a resolute effort. As President Roosevelt said, the way to hold the line is to decide how we are going to hold the line and not to look for reasons why we should not do it yet."

MR. STIGLER: "We can always find those exceptions. I am also somewhat opposed to the idea of trying to discredit the War Labor Board. Do you not think that with it would go the Little Steel formula and that we would be pretty much at sea again?"

MR. COX: "One of the things that I dislike most is not the fact that the miners are asking for more wages, which was being done in many fields, but the tactics that have been used. Such tactics on the part of the leadership seem to me to imply trying to throw overboard the machinery which is to be looked to in holding the line."

MR. HART: "There is the alternative of putting wages on a sliding scale, but I certainly would not be for it. If we start on the principle that whenever living costs go up, one gives people more money, when the cause of living costs' going up is that they have too much money to spend already, it is plain that inflation may lie in that direction, but a rectification of living standards does not."

MR. STIGLER: "We have covered the agricultural problem and the wage discussion in our hold-the-line discussion.

We come to our third general question, which is price control. Here I would like to say, at the outset, that I think the American people have been pretty naïve in this field. In considerable part they have seemed to think that all we have to do is to announce a price ceiling. Thereafter, one goes to the stores and buys the regular quantities of goods, but just at lower prices. They do not seem to realize that price control makes rationing necessary. They do not seem to realize what an enormous task it is to enforce the ceilings and the rationing allowances."

MR. STIGLER: "Another aspect is the quality deterioration. We find that the clothes we buy are not so good as they were and that the canned goods we buy probably are not so good as they were."

MR. COX: "There has been the urgent demand from consumer organizations for grade-labeling in that direction to help the consumer enforce the prices."

MR. STIGLER: "There is, finally, one other problem I would like to raise. That is the black market. Thus far we have had just a little of it so far as we can tell, but we are likely to have more of it. What is the limit in that direction in the food line?"

MR. HART: "We really have not had too much of a test yet. These black markets that we had have showed us that there is a danger there. They have showed us that one can build up a black market very quickly."

MR. STIGLER: "I just want to add one very short note. At the present time we have about a thousand full-time inspectors in food-control pricing and rationing. Great Britain finds that it needs many more than that. My own guess is that we are going to have a terrible time getting the manpower. They have to be good people, and a lot of them — thirty thousand or fifty thousand perhaps."

MR. COX: "One thing we have already discussed in an earlier connection is the matter of subsidies and the rollback of prices that are supposed to be made possible by putting subsidies into effect on selected articles. What do you think is the advantage of that, or the disadvantage of it, from the standpoint of national policy?"

MR. STIGLER: "I might say that I am cool to that proposal, just as the farm bloc is. My reason for coolness is that it is inflationary in its direct effect. We are going to have larger governmental deficits. Secondly, I am always worried about postwar commitments in which these bonuses will keep on going a long time after the war is over."

MR. Cox: "One thing we should notice is that rationing, which we have already mentioned as a necessity for price control, will help us on the fiscal side — that is, on the side of getting more of the community's excess income in for government financing rather than for spending for price advances in the commodity market. There is also the point that if we are able by the rationing and the increase in the amount of money that people therefore save, automatically, because they can't spend it beyond their quotas, there is a chance there of improving the revenues of the government."

MR. STIGLER: "There is another point that worries me. After the war we are going to be awfully tired of price controls and rationing, and the lid may well go off. We will say that we will take our chances on inflation rather than on the OPA."

MR. HART: "Which certainly does indicate that we ought to try as far as possible to forestall that by taking money away now through taxes in a form that will not come back on us. We must say on the tax front that we have made a big gain in machinery in the past few weeks. Either the House or the Senate bill that has just gone through, whichever we get, is going to give us the machinery that it takes to collect war taxes and make them effective. But the ground has scarcely been prepared at all for the amount of revenue that must be raised. It has not been rubbed in on the public really what we must face.

We have been talking for months about the best way to forgive taxes, when we should have been talking about the best way to get revenue up several tens of billions per annum — and to do it quickly." [2]

To sum up the objectives in preparing a round table:

1. As in the case of a talk or an interview, an objective must be arrived at before asking for time to present the broadcast.

[2] This quotation was taken from the printed transcript of the Round Table which is always edited for publication purposes. All colloquialisms, contractions and participants' names, therefore, have been omitted.

2. Three participants usually present the best balanced program.

3. An outline covering points to be discussed should be prepared in order that the program shall have cohesion and balance.

4. It is the duty of the chairman of the discussion to see that the outline and timing are adhered to.

5. It is better to broadcast from script when there is any question as to the ability of the participants to carry on an ad-lib discussion or when there is not time for adequate preparation.

6. The participants should be authorities in the field to be discussed. One not familiar with the subject cannot speak with assurance.

7. Long speeches by any one of the participants should be avoided, and each one should have an equal chance to present his side of the question. No one speaker should talk more than twenty or thirty seconds at the most at any one time.

8. The broadcast should sound as much as possible like a natural conversation, even though read from a script. The use of simple words and sentence structure is always desirable. Technical jargon and "ten- and twenty-dollar" words should also be.avoided.

9. Facts and examples should be used as much as possible. Personalized, they do much to add interest to the discussion, making the listener feel he has been "looking inside" for a while.

10. The use of last names is to be preferred. It is not always easy for the listener to distinguish between voices, and he likes to know which one of the participants is talking. First names should never be used; the listener is not intimately acquainted with any of the participants, and it tends to confuse and annoy him.

11. Interruptions are also good, but some indication that there is to be an interruption is necessary so that there will not be the confusion of more than one person speaking at the same time.

12. The University of Chicago Round Table cards remind the speaker not to be a mouse but to speak up — when he has something to say. He was invited to participate for that purpose.

13. A participant should voice his disagreement when discussing controversial issues; the audience expects him to stand up for his views. Many listeners probably hold the same point of view and are eager to have as vigorous a presentation of those viewpoints as possible.

14. It is better not to draw conclusions at the end of a round-table broadcast. Instead, the chairman should draw together the threads of the discussion in a brief summation, thus allowing each listener to carry forward the discussion to suit himself.

TOWN MEETINGS

Another form for presenting controversial social, economic, and political questions by radio is the town meeting. This type of program was inspired by the early New England town meeting, one of the most typically American institutions for political education for more than a century and a half. The adaptation today is carrying forward the idea promulgated by President George Washington when he said: "Promote, then, as an object of primary importance, institutions for the general diffusion of knowledge. In proportion as the structure of a government gives force to public opinion, it is essential that public opinion should be enlightened." The idea of this type of radio program was presented first by George V. Denny, Jr., President, The Town Hall, Incorporated, to the National Broadcasting Company in 1935, and the enthusiastic response of the public has made it one of the most popular discussion programs on the air today.[1]

A town-meeting type of program consists, as is pointed out in the *Town Meeting Discussion Leader's Handbook*, "of a discussion between two or more qualified authorities about questions of immediate public interest, questions which concern each citizen of this democracy. The speeches, never more than fifteen minutes long, more often ten, are followed by a twenty- to twenty-five-minute question period in which the audience (in the auditorium of Town Hall, New York) participates. The speakers are selected because they represent conflicting views on the subject under discussion. Each speaker is asked to state his position affirmatively and to avoid, as far as possible, conventional debate technique."

[1] Heard since 1942 over the American Broadcasting Company.

Continuing, Mr. Denny points out:

The principles on which the program is based are three. The first is conflict. The result is a dramatic contest about something that concerns everyone. While, as an institution, the Town Hall never takes sides, it does make it possible for speakers holding widely divergent views to offer their solutions for many common problems. In this way we attempt to direct the listener to think constructively about the problem rather than simply to applaud the views which are naturally congenial to him. Therefore, neither speaker has been free to make irresponsible statements, as he might have done had he been on the platform alone. Then during the question period the listener is represented by 1500 citizens like himself in the audience, any one of whom may ask a pertinent question.[3] In this way, each listener feels that he has a part in the program all during the question period.

Suspense is the second important ingredient of this program. Anything may happen at these meetings, as they are completely noncensored and unrehearsed. No one knows what questions will arise, when a speaker will find himself "on the spot," or when some prominent national figure will take an unexpected stand.

The third ingredient, most essential of all, is fair play. It has been necessary to make only two rules in connection with the Town Meeting program. The first is that the questions must relate definitely to the subject under discussion, and the second that no personal or libelous attacks can be made in the guise of either statements or questions.

Mr. Denny states that

The Town Meeting of the Air is sometimes criticized for leaving the audience in an unsettled state of mind. Another complaint is that we never really solve any of the problems we discuss. True. In the first place, one of the primary objectives of the Town Meeting is to make people think for themselves. By exposing our audience to two or more conflicting views, and by carefully avoiding a commitment on the part of the

[3] During the war, there are certain restrictions governing any question period over the radio.

moderator in favor of one side or the other, the listener is
forced to think, if he has applied his mind at all to the discussion. As for arriving at solutions to these great unsolved
social and political problems, if we could solve them by an
hour's discussion, life in our democracy would be very simple
indeed. Our usefulness as a nonpartisan educational institution
would be over if we should attempt to tell our audience what
they ought to think or how they ought to act.

The same statement that no conclusions are arrived at is frequently made, of course, by persons listening to almost any of
the round-table or other discussion programs on the air.

The rôle of the moderator, or leader, in any town-meeting
program is a difficult one, and the success or failure of the
program will depend to a very great extent upon him. Mr.
Denny has laid down a few rules by which one may be guided
in choosing a moderator. He says:

A moderator must have an inherent sense of fair play, good
humor, and some knowledge of the subject under discussion.
Bearing in mind at all times the primary object of the meeting,
he should, without being officious, direct the discussion to this
end at every opportunity, by asking the speakers to answer the
same question, by bringing out points that have not been sufficiently clarified, and by pointing out the essential conflicts between the speakers. Without injecting himself too prominently
into the program, he must at the same time keep the meeting
completely within his control. He must see that the speakers
do not exceed their time limit; he must rule out unfair questions; and the audience must feel that his decisions are just
and final. In a large audience, it is sometimes desirable for
the moderator to repeat the questions from the floor, but when
the meeting is being conducted for the radio he must judge in
an instant whether the question has gone out clearly over the
air. If it has, he should not take up time repeating the question,
but let the speaker answer it immediately. For the benefit of
the radio audience he must repeat the names of the speakers
on the program frequently before they answer each question,
so that there may be no confusion in the minds of the listeners
as to who is speaking.

There might be added to the list suggested by Mr. Denny a few more "musts" in the selection of a good moderator. He must be a convincing speaker himself, able to command and hold the attention of both studio and radio audiences. He must have a good voice, clear and easy to listen to, with excellent diction and enunciation. He must, of necessity, be adept in the use of the English language, as he must not mispronounce words or the names of people or places. He must be mentally very alert, to be able to take up any slack in the question period, and so thoroughly conversant with the subject under discussion that he could ask intelligent questions of any of the speakers should there be a lack of questions from the audience. Naturally, he must like people and be able to get on with them under any and all conditions; should tenseness arise during the discussion period, he should be able to handle the situation satisfactorily to all concerned and carry forward the meeting with good will.

The choice of subjects and speakers is, of course, a difficult one and will present many problems. Practically the same traits described in the section on the round table may be applied to speakers in connection with a town-meeting type of program. A first requisite, of course, must be a good voice, coupled with the ability to project the speaker's views clearly and succinctly. He must be able and willing to answer the questions from the audience easily and convincingly and should not object to a little heckling. As the participants speak from scripts, it is not essential to choose participants who can ad-lib easily, though that, of course, is an asset when it comes to the question period.

As to the choice of subjects, it is well to keep them topical. More interest will be shown in a series of broadcasts built around current events than around abstract subjects, and while one does not particularly aim at controversy, a certain amount is sure to add interest. It is always important to see that conflicting points of view are presented sturdily and objectively, so that issues may be clean-cut.

It is difficult to present this type of program in less than an hour. If only two speakers are scheduled, forty-five minutes might be sufficient, allowing each speaker ten minutes apiece, leaving twenty-five minutes for the opening and closing and the question period. It is doubtful, however, if it is wise to attempt a program of this type in so limited a time.

It is likely to make the program more interesting and alive if there are three participants, as there are almost always more than two clear-cut points of view on any subject. On the other hand, should two well-known opponents on some very significant issue be scheduled, as in the case of the fiery Ickes-Gannett broadcast on "America's Town Meeting" several years ago, it would be better not to invite a third speaker, rather permitting the belligerent participants to fight the issue out between themselves, stimulated by the questions from the audience.

Speeches should be very carefully timed. It is not fair to assign ten minutes to each broadcaster and then let one take thirteen, thus cutting the other to seven, and such a cut would be imperative in order to maintain the time schedule. More often than not, the question period is the most interesting part of the broadcast, and it is well not to cut it, if it can be avoided. There will, of course, be exceptions.

The moderator must make it very clear during the question period that, in recognizing a questioner, he expects him to ask a short, carefully thought-out question, pointed directly at a specific speaker. "America's Town Meeting of the Air" ordinarily uses a parabolic microphone, sensitive enough to pick up the questions from the floor.[4] If such a microphone is not available, it will be necessary for the moderator to repeat the question for the benefit of the radio audience. If the question is an involved one, it is often necessary for the moderator to simplify it, more for the benefit of the audience, of course, than for the speaker. The questioner must never be permitted to make a "speech" from the floor. This is annoying to the studio audience, the speakers, and the

---

[4] During the war this method of picking up questions from the floor was discontinued in favor of small microphones held by ushers assigned to positions in the aisle.

radio audience. In any town-meeting radio program questions are welcome, but personal views would confuse the issue and not add anything to the interest of the program.

The town-meeting form of program is an excellent way of presenting local civic issues as well as national ones, especially if the local issues are at white heat. It stimulates interest in the station as well as in the community.

To summarize the points to remember in arranging and conducting a town meeting by radio:

1. The station should set aside an hour weekly out of its schedule, as this type of program, to be effective, should have at least that amount of time.

2. Subjects should be picked for discussion that are of current interest. This is only fair to the station as well as to the audience.

3. Participants should be chosen with great care. They should:

   a. be authorities in the field under discussion

   b. hold clear-cut, decisive views on the subject and be able to state their positions affirmatively

   c. have good voices, good enunciation, and good diction

   d. be able to answer intelligently the questions from the audience

   e. be able to time their scripts and hold to that timing

4. The moderator should be chosen with at least as much care as the speakers, because he is responsible for the success or failure of the program. He must:

   a. be a convincing speaker, able to command and hold the attention of both the studio and radio audiences

   b. have a good voice, clear and easy to listen to, with excellent diction and enunciation

   c. be adept in the use of the English language, as he must not mispronounce words or names of people or places

   d. be mentally alert

   e. have an inherent sense of fair play

   f. have a good sense of humor

   g. have some knowledge of the subject under discussion and thus be able to ask intelligent and pertinent questions of the speakers *h.* like people and be able to get on with them under any and all conditions, so as to handle any situation that may arise during the course of the program

5. Talks should be kept within the allotted time limits, thereby allowing adequate time for each speaker and the question period.

DRAMATIZATIONS

It has come to be a fairly well-accepted fact that the best way to catch and hold the attention of a radio audience when presenting factual or historical information is through the medium of dramatization. It does not matter whether the subject lies in the field of science, invention, art, history, literature, or any one of a hundred other fields that go to make up everyday life; those particular subjects brought to life through a story that is vital, full of human interest, conflict, and emotion in its writing plus excellent presentation becomes a moving document that cannot fail to hold the attention of anyone at all interested in the subject. It may even interest some who are not.

All information, however, cannot be dramatized successfully. It would be as fatal to try to force some material, not dramatic in itself, into the dramatic pattern as to attempt the recitation of places and dates of important historical events and expect them to be remembered. Places and dates, however, can be stamped very definitely on the mind of the listener in story form through dramatization. Statistics, a discussion of ideas in many fields, or straight factual information can best be presented through an interview or a round table. Take, for example, a proposed broadcast for National Education Week on the subject of "Education for Victory." It is readily seen that the topic lends itself admirably to the round-table form; it can be handled more forthrightly in this way than through dramatization. On the other hand, history, science, literature, and even such apparently dull topics as taxes and mathematics, will become more effective and will attract larger audiences if the broadcast is a dramatic one. A number of examples showing how well the different fields lend themselves to dramatization are given in the portions of scripts included in the chapter on "Fields of Subject Matter." The material comes alive instead of remaining a jumble of dull and uninteresting facts.

There are some instances in which a blending of the dramatic and round-table forms may be used to good advantage. Often a dramatized incident can be used as a springboard for the discussion to follow. The topic can then be pointed in such a way that it clarifies the issue in the mind of the listener, permitting him to follow the discussion with more understanding.

The following are good examples of how this combination method has been used. The first is taken from the series by the National Congress of Parents and Teachers entitled "On the Home Front," broadcast over NBC on January 17, 1942. The second is from the University of Chicago Round Table, "Economic War Between the States," broadcast over NBC on February 4, 1940.

NBC

PROGRAM TITLE: "On the Home Front"

CHICAGO OUTLET: WMAQ

(2:15 to 2:45 P.M. CST RED)   (JANUARY 17, 1942)   (SATURDAY)
           time   date   day

ANNOUNCER: "On the Home Front!"

SOUND: ICEBOX DOOR OPENS. DISHES AND PANS RATTLE AND DOOR SLAMS SHUT.

BILL (DISGUSTEDLY): A fine thing! Can't even call it a pretty kettle of fish, with not even a sardine in sight. (CALLS) Hey, Marge!

MARGE (OFF): Yes, Bill?

BILL: What's happened to our icebox?

MARGE (MOVING IN): What do you mean, what's happened to our icebox? Isn't it working right?

BILL: What difference does that make, when it's empty?

MARGE: Empty! Why, there's all sorts of stuff in it!

BILL: Stuff is right! What's a hungry man want with all that hay and junk you've got in there?

MARGE: Vegetables are good for you — and, anyway, right before you go to bed is no time to gorge yourself.

BILL: Who's going to gorge who — or whom — whichever it is? All I want is a little snack — a sandwich, maybe —

MARGE: There's a whole pound of wienies.

BILL: Who wants a cold, clammy wienie at 11 o'clock at night? Gosh, if there was just a nice wedge of cocoanut-custard pie —

MARGE: Not on *my* budget, you don't get cocoanut-custard pie, Bill Baxter!

BILL: Huh? What's happened to your budget all of a sudden?

MARGE: Welllllll . . . I used some of it to buy a war bond, if you must know!

BILL: Good enough, honey . . . only . . . we've got war bond money budgeted already —

MARGE: I know, but it just didn't seem to me that we were doing enough, Bill! When I think of Pearl Harbor — and Wake Island — and here we are, running no risks . . . you know, we *do* eat too much, and we don't *have* to have sirloin steaks and lamb chops at every meal —

BILL: Hold on, there, my good woman! When was that we had sirloins and chops at every meal?

MARGE: Oh, you know what I mean!

BILL: Sure I do, darling, but — well, we don't want to go overboard when the ship's a long way from sinking! Buying all the war bonds we can is swell — I'm for it — but robbing our stomachs to do it doesn't hit me as the soundest idea in the world. We've got a couple of husky kids on our hands — got to feed 'em right so they'll grow up right. And priorities have got me working twice as hard as I ever have before in my life down at the plant. I've got to have fuel for my boiler —

MARGE: But Bill — I was only trying to do my bit a little better! There's so little a woman who is tied down by children the way I am *can* do —

BILL: I don't know, though, Marge. Maybe you can do a lot more than you think, right here at home — and maybe with that icebox of ours, too!

MARGE: You just tell me what it is I can do, Bill Baxter, and then watch me go!

ANNOUNCER: Well, if Bill can't tell Marge what she can do right at home to help win the war, we have some very expert guests right here in the studio this afternoon who can! They are Mrs. James K. Lytle of the National Congress of Parents and Teachers, Dr. Ruth Cowan Clouse, Professor of Nutrition of the Illinois Institute of Technology, and Parker Wheatley. Radio Director of Northwestern University, who will take over the microphone.

WHEATLEY: Mrs. Lytle, Dr. Clouse, what's your advice to Marge and Bill? Mrs. Lytle?

LYTLE: There's no question, Mr. Wheatley, that Marge and Bill are doing a good job in buying war bonds, but they have just as great a responsibility to their country in seeing that their children and they themselves get an adequate diet and the proper food. I feel that in maintaining the home front — since *they* can't serve on the battle front — they're doing their duty just as much as those directly fighting our common enemy.

WHEATLEY: Dr. Clouse?

CLOUSE: Most people agree, Mrs. Lytle, that the best defense for a nation is to have a well-nourished and physically fit population. A well-nourished person is more stable emotionally — can work harder and longer — and therefore will have a better morale. And civilian morale is all-important in this time of total war.

WHEATLEY: The results of physical examinations in Selective Service have impressed upon all of us the advisability of doing something about the health of the nation as a whole.

LYTLE: They certainly have, Mr. Wheatley. And we've also been impressed by the results of lack of food in the European countries, even in countries allied with us in this war.

(*The program continues for another five minutes and ends with this final discussion:*)

ANNOUNCER: Thank you, Mr. Wheatley and ladies, and now, Marge Baxter, how about it? Do you see your way clear now to playing your part on the Home Front to better advantage?

MARGE: *Do* I! I've been making notes, and from now on you just watch the Baxter family blossom! And what's more, I think with what I've just learned, I may be able to buy a war bond now and then out of my budget, at that!

BILL: Tell you what I'll do, Marge. Looks like I'm going to save a little upkeep on the car whether I want to or not, since we won't be using it to run two-block errands so much. I'll match anything you save out of your budget, and we'll make two bonds grow where only one grew before —

MARGE: Grand, Bill!

BILL: But — if I ever find the cupboard bare again like I did tonight —

MARGE (LAUGHING): Don't worry, Mother Hubbard! From now on the Baxters will dine like royalty *can't* dine anywhere except in America!

BILL: And please God, we'll keep it that way here in America, forever!

In the foregoing illustration, "On the Home Front," Marge and Bill Baxter had a slight verbal conflict on the question of purchasing war bonds and adequate provisioning for their family of five. Dramatized through this short skit, the question seemed more alive and was brought home more fully to the listener than if the group which followed with the discussion had opened the question "cold." The same holds true in regard to the following short skit used at the opening of the University of Chicago Round Table.

PROGRAM TITLE: University of Chicago Round Table

CHICAGO OUTLET: WMAQ

(1:30 to 2:00 P.M. EWT)	NBC	(SUNDAY)
Time		Day

MR. BANE: Quarantine laws are established primarily to protect the public health and to exclude diseased goods, but these laws in their operation simply exclude goods from other states. The same thing applies to labeling. Now, there are some statutes dealing with that little commodity which we call eggs. You would think that there would be standard labeling with respect to eggs. Not true. In some of the states, eggs are fresh only if laid in that particular state. For a moment let's go to a grocery store down in Georgia.

GROCER: Good mornin', Ma'm. What's your pleasure?

WOMAN: I'd like some groceries.

GROCER: You've sure 'nough come to the best store in Camden County, Georgia. Reckon you're a stranger hereabouts.

WOMAN: That's right. My husband and I have just bought the old Chinapin place.

GROCER: Happy to have your trade, Ma'm.

WOMAN: What grades of fresh eggs do you have?

GROCER: Just one. The best Georgia eggs. Thirty-seven cents a dozen.

WOMAN: That seems a little high. Only one grade, you say?

GROCER: Yes, Ma'm. We've got other eggs but they ain't "fresh."

WOMAN: You mean they're cold storage?

GROCER: No. We've got eggs from Florida, but we can't call 'em "fresh."

WOMAN: Why not? The Florida line is only ten miles below here.

GROCER: I know that, Ma'm, but the law says that the only fresh eggs in Georgia is Georgia eggs.

WOMAN: What a strange ruling!

GROCER: Ain't it the truth? But we gotta protect our own hens. Now, do you want fresh eggs or do you want the other kind?

WOMAN: I guess I'll have to pay the price. Even if the Florida eggs are just as fresh, I don't like the idea of buying eggs that aren't called fresh.

GROCER: Them Florida hens actually ain't the quality of ours, Ma'm. You better buy Georgia since you're in the state.

WOMAN: All right, give me a dozen. But I can't see what earthly difference it makes to a hen whether she lays an egg on one side or the other of the St. Mary's River so long as it's fresh.

GROCER: The hen ain't got nothin' to say about it, Ma'm. It's just the law, that's all.

MR. BANE: And the question might also arise as to what a cow might have to say about the place in which said cow does business. We have even more laws which in their operation constitute interstate trade barriers with reference to milk and milk products.

MR. JACOBY: You are thinking, I take it, of these state milk-control acts which provide that all milk coming into certain cities must be inspected.

MR. SPENCER: And, of course, their laws are perfectly all right in terms of motives, generally speaking.

All the discussion up to this point has been on the different forms in which material may be presented and the merits of

one over the other. Nothing has been said, so far, as to how
a successful radio drama comes about. It should be taken for
granted that the writer, of course, plays the most important
part in any dramatic program. He is the creator of the script
upon which hangs the whole structure of the program. No
actor, however good, can make the lines sound alive if the
writer has not put life into them in the first place.

Albert Crews has stated in his book on radio writing: [5]

> Radio drama will become important in direct ratio to its
> ability to attract top-flight writers to the medium. History
> bears out the fact that whenever a writer appears on the
> horizon with something important to say, there will always be
> the means provided to say it. . . . The radio writer is someone to
> be conjured with. He is in a position of prestige which is en-
> viable. After all, no matter how many actors are available or
> how many production directors or how much time on the air,
> unless there is good material for these people to work on, no
> broadcast drama occurs. The radio writer is a corner-stone of
> radio drama. Everything else builds on his efforts.

Most dramatizations rely, to a great extent, on both music
and sound effects for the heightening of interest in the production. Both can, of course, be overdone, particularly sound.
Some amateur writers do not believe that a script is good
unless it is crowded with all kinds of sound effects. This is
fatal for a number of reasons. First, it may signify an inability
on the part of the writer to write a smooth or interesting script.
Second, it calls for a professional production director to make
the script play well in spite of the overabundance of sound
effects; and, in addition, it needs professional actors. Third,
more sound men and equipment would be needed than would
be available at the average local radio station. While there
might be a good production director on hand, there might not
be professional actors, or there might be a good director and
good actors, but inadequate sound equipment; and the show,
therefore, instead of accomplishing the object the writer had in

---

[5] Albert Crews, *Professional Radio Writing*. Boston: Houghton Mifflin Company, 1945.

mind, would completely fall apart. Sound must be used intelligently and, generally speaking, sparingly, and it must be handled with extreme skill to add to the effectiveness of the program. Used in any other way and in overabundance, it only tends to confuse.

Music, as well as sound, plays a prominent part in most dramatizations. It is used not only as the theme in most dramatic productions as in other radio programs, but often also to set the mood of the play and to act as the bridge between scenes. The whole score is often especially written for the script.[6]

The responsibility of selecting music for network dramatic shows falls on the production director working with the conductor of the musical unit that is scheduled to appear on the show. In local stations, where more often than not the program director acts as the production director, he or the musical director in consultation with the writer of the script, decides on the particular numbers to be used. When a writer is familiar with music, he is often able to identify the actual compositions he wishes used. Frequently, however, he is able only to indicate mood, leaving selection to whoever is responsible for putting the show on the air.

Writers have found that it is often possible to adapt the straight dramatic to other dramatic forms in presenting various types of subject matter. Thus was born the radio adaptation of the dramatic narrative. While the "March of Time" would naturally be styled dramatic, in reality it is an adaptation of both the dramatic and the dramatic narrative with, frequently, an interview included as well. More often, however, the dramatic narrative is used for the presentation of ideas or ideals, as in the excerpt from the following script heard over the National Broadcasting Company network in 1940. The program, a pageant in song and verse entitled "America Calling," was written and presented by the Mary Miller Vocational High

---

[6] For further information on the writing and production of dramatic programs of all kinds refer to *Radio Writing* and *Radio Production Directing*, both by Albert R. Crews. Boston: Houghton Mifflin Company, 1944-45.

School Workshop of Minneapolis, Minnesota. The students from this workshop came from all walks of life and have here depicted the hopes and aims of all types of Americans.

NBC

PROGRAM TITLE: AMERICA CALLING

CHICAGO OUTLET: WMAQ

(6:30-7:00 P.M. CST)	(MARCH 12, 1940)	(TUESDAY)
Time	Date	Day

ANNOUNCER:

GLEE CLUB: America calling . . . calling . . . calling . . .

BIZ: GLEE CLUBS IN LEFT, RIGHT, AND REAR BALCONIES RE-ECHO THE CALL DISTANTLY.

GIRLS' SEMI-CHORUS (IN MEASURED MONOTONE, EACH OF THE LAST TWO LINES A HALF STEP HIGHER):

"Chant me the poem that comes from the soul of America . . .
Chant me the carol of victory . . .
And sing me before you go
The song of the throes of Democracy." [7]

BIZ: GLEE CLUB (DISTANTLY): America Calling . . .
Democracy calling . . .

CHORUS: Democracy calling
Through the clamor and roar of nations,
Whose empty boasts swell their pride . . .
Calling from godless plains of the Super-State,
Where far as the eye can reach are helmeted heads,
Or arms raised to salute . . .
Men . . . young men . . .
All marching, marching, marching . . .
All numbered . . . all talked of in terms of millions . . .
There are mines and highways and forests,
There are sheep and cattle and poultry
And there are men . . . !
There must be men . . . millions . . .
Millions to feed to the god of State . . . !

[7] From "By Blue Ontario's Shore," by Walt Whitman.

FIRST ANNOUNCER: Democracy calling again . . .
CHORUS: Through blinding mists of propaganda,
    Through poverty, hunger, unemployment,
    Through persecutions of innocent hated men,
    Through the terror of war, still . . . still America . . .
    Democracy calls!

BIZ: MUSIC UP TEN SECONDS, THEN DOWN
CHORUS (WITH DIGNITY):The Constitution and the federal statutes
    Set forth the freedoms of democracy!
THIRD ANNOUNCER: First: Economic freedom! Freedom to work . . .
    To promote better working standards
    And higher living conditions for the people.
WHOLE GROUP: Democracy calls again — bitterly now — not from
    lands across the sea
    But from her own heart, the heart of America . . .
BIZ: GLEE CLUB (DISTANTLY): AMERICA CALLING . . .
CHORUS (CRESCENDO ON FIRST FOUR LINES):
    Labor strife like dark waters swirling,
    Among the common folk it's whirling,
    Broken bodies and minds it's hurling . . .
    Can't you hear?
    Listen!
    Listen to the deep mighty beat of it
    Listen to the beat — beat — beat of it!
BIZ: DURING THE FOLLOWING, THE CHORUS, WITH BODIES SWAYING
    FORWARD AND BACKWARD IN SLOW MARCHINGLIKE RHYTHM
    REPEAT THE WORD "BEAT" AT QUARTER-SECOND INTERVALS,
    DRAWING OUT THE WORD IN LOW HOLLOW TONES.
CLERK: Name?
BOY: Jimmy Mason, sir . . .
CLERK: Age?
BOY: Fifteen, sir . . .
CLERK: Experience?
BOY: None, sir . . .
CLERK: We can use a strong boy . . .
    In the mills we can use a strong boy . . .
    You'll work all day in the mills . . .
    Man's work . . . a dollar a day . . .
    While you're learning to work . . . a boy's pay . . .

CHORUS: (UP STRONG — HOLDING VOWELS: B-e-a-t; THEN DOWN)
WOMAN: My man was laid off from the mills . . . today . . .
      My boy got a job in the mills . . . today . . .
      Six for thirty they give us . . . and the rent's due,
      the grocer's due . . . It was hard before . . . now it's
      harder . . .
      Thirty dollars they took away . . . but, they give us
      six.
CHORUS: UP STRONG — HOLDING VOWELS: B-e-a-t; THEN DOWN.

SECOND ANNOUNCER: And joy and beauty and gladness
      From the garden of the world . . .
      Turn you to the abundant happy land
      And its eternal fruitfulness . . .
FIRST ANNOUNCER: America calling . . .
      America the country of play,
      America the land of happy children . . .
      Call you little girls there,
      Bouncing balls . . . playing O'Leary . . .
BIZ: GLEE CLUB (LIGHTLY)
      Seven . . . eight . . . nine O'Leary
      Ten O'Leary
      Post Man . . .
FIRST ANNOUNCER: Calling you women there,
      Knitting pinwheel afghans . . .
      This is America . . . these are her people . . .
CHORUS: Now she calls from the heat of the city . . .
      Drivers, clerks, waitresses,
      Doctors, lawyers, newsboys . . .
SECOND ANNOUNCER: This is America; these are her people . . .
CHORUS: The South . . . land of lazy charm . . .
      White cotton fields and voices singing . . .
      The air . . . heavy with perfume
      In the close-encircling twilight . . .
SECOND ANNOUNCER: This is America — these are her people . . .
CHORUS: Great snows of forceful winters
      Summer's sudden stunning heat,
GIRLS' SEMI-CHORUS: Fertile lands where the farmer
      Ploughs and plants in the sun and wind,
      Dreaming and planning with the waking earth . . .

SECOND ANNOUNCER: This is America — these are her people.
CHORUS: The Midwest beckons us . . .
  The leading farm country of the world . . .
  Red barns, exuberant corn crops, cattle-raising . . .
  The rich Midwest!
SECOND ANNOUNCER: This is America — these are her people.
CHORUS: The far West — leading the world in natural resources . . .
FIRST ANNOUNCER: In a haze of light
  The mountains loom majestically,
  Holding in their hearts stores of gold, of copper,
  and iron . . .
  The coast is an oasis of orchards
  Farther south oil wells pump forth
  A living stream from the veins of the earth . . .
GIRLS' SEMI-CHORUS: And over it all the limitless blue of the sky
  all encompassing . . .
SECOND ANNOUNCER: This is America — these are her people!
FIRST ANNOUNCER (CALLING): America calls from the living,
  lovely land that gives to Youth a heritage of timeless strength
  and beauty
BIZ: GLEE CLUB: America calling . . . America calling . . .

This program was the forerunner of many narrative and
documentary programs which have been heard increasingly
since that time. Its structure is simple enough to be used by
any local station, as it does not require large instrumental
groups or complicated sound effects. It is an excellent medium
for high schools especially, as the program can be written and
produced through the co-operation of the various departments,
such as English, History, Drama, and Music. This particular
program, "America Calling," was first broadcast over KSTP in
St. Paul as one of a series of regular school broadcasts. Many
other schools have presented programs in this form, though
not as elaborate or so long.

As was said previously, the dramatic program may be very
elaborate, written to be presented with all the available facilities of the network, large orchestras, professional actors,
sound-effects men, and expert production. On the other hand,
Alice Duer Miller's soul-stirring "White Cliffs of Dover" was

presented to radio through the use of a single voice, so dramatic in itself that it needed nothing in addition but the background of music which was especially written by Doctor Frank Black. The voice was Lynn Fontanne's. The whole broadcast was so beautifully done that NBC was forced to repeat it three times — an unheard-of event for radio.

Still another form of the dramatic narrative was used by the late Stephen Vincent Benét in his "Dear Adolf" series written for the Council for Democracy and broadcast in the early summer of 1942 over NBC. The programs were a series of letters which purported to have been written by average American citizens to Adolf Hitler. The narrator, simulating the farmer or the businessman or the laborer, read the letter, being interrupted occasionally by a "voice" challenging his statements.

One of the finest of all the dramatic narratives so far heard over the radio was the radio version of Edna St. Vincent Millay's "Murder of Lidice." Here again a teller of the tale was used, with voices, music, and dramatic incidents portraying the rape of the town. This program was broadcast over NBC in October of 1942. These, of course, are only a few of many examples which could be cited to show the various forms the dramatic narrative may take in presenting ideas over the radio.

Another offshoot of the straight dramatic form is the documentary, which was used quite extensively during the war, in programs written and produced by government agencies. Robert J. Landry, of the Columbia Broadcasting System, formerly Radio Editor of *Variety*, observed: "When the history of this war comes to be written, considerable credit will be due the so-called radio documentary programs, those lectures in dramatic form on the nature of our enemies, on the magnitude of our problems, on the challenge of our future." [8] Mr. Landry went on to point out the flexibility of the documentary programs in that they do permit "vigorous rallying voices of realism, and, at the same time, they help to articulate the new global concepts of future decency." [9]

[8] Robert J. Landry, in *Stand By* (magazine of the American Federation of Radio Artists), February, 1944.   [9] *Ibid.*

Perhaps the most outstanding of all documentary programs was the one entitled "We Hold These Truths," broadcast over the major networks on December 15, 1941, in commemoration of the one hundred and fiftieth anniversary of the adoption of the Bill of Rights of our Constitution. The script, written by Norman Corwin, featured Lieutenant James Stewart, Doctor Leopold Stokowski, and a host of other prominent artists, and portrayed through clear word pictures what the Bill of Rights means to every American today. The program closed with an inspiring message by Franklin Delano Roosevelt. The following excerpt illustrates how the subject was handled:

"WE HOLD THESE TRUTHS"

By Norman Corwin

ALL NETWORKS	10:00 to 11:00 P.M. EST
DECEMBER 15, 1941	7:00 to 8:00 P.M. PST

VOICE: We hold These Truths!

MUSIC (INTRODUCTORY PASSAGE: STRONG, HEROIC, BUT NOT ARROGANT, IT SUSTAINS BEHIND):

HUSTON (WITH QUIET DIGNITY: EACH SPACE A PAUSE):

This is a program about the making of a promise and the keeping of a promise.

This is a program about the Rights of the People.

This is a program coming to you over the combined radio networks of the United States, bringing you the voices of Americans, bringing you the voice of the President of the United States.

This is a program for listeners in all zones of continental time, for listeners on ships away from home, for listeners in uniform, for listeners on the American islands in the two great oceans.

This is a program about a guarantee made to the people of America one hundred fifty years ago . . . a guarantee that has been kept through peace and war and peace and war . . . a guarantee we call the Bill of Rights.

BARRYMORE: My name is Barrymore. I am one of several actors gathered in a studio in California, near shores that face any enemy across an ocean now Pacific in name only.

We are here tonight to join a hundred and thirty million fellow Americans in praise of a document that men have fought for, that men are fighting for, that men will keep on fighting for as long as freedom is a strong word falling sweet upon the ear.

What we enact tonight has been enacted many times before in living flesh and blood. The people we portray have walked the world. The drama is the ancient one, the endless one, the struggle for men's rights to live their lives out peacefully and profitably in a decent world.

It may be many of we people here are known to many of you people there. For with us, honored to be on this program of commemoration, are some whose names you may have heard: names such as that of Sergeant James Stewart, loaned to us for this occasion by the Air Force:

In New York City, waiting to join us, is Doctor Leopold Stokowski and a symphony orchestra; in Washington, the highest name in the land — the President of the United States, commander-in-chief of the Army and the Navy — Mr. Roosevelt.

But this is not a night of names, of personalities . . . *our* names or any names are meaningless unless *your* names are added; unless you join us, you for whom the sacred Rights were written, and to whom their keeping is entrusted; you, the guardians of what has been bequeathed to you by millions like yourselves and by the toil of centuries as dark and menacing as this we live in.

You, the People of the Federated States.

MUSIC (RESOLUTION OF INTRODUCTORY PASSAGE . . . PAUSE . . . SLOW ARPEGGIO ON HARPSICHORD INTO (SOLO) PASSAGE OF EIGHTEENTH-CENTURY FLAVOR, HOLDING BEHIND):

THIRD (OVER HARPSICHORD): One hundred fifty years is not long in the reckoning of a hill. But to a man it's long enough.
One hundred fifty years is a week end to a redwood tree, but to a man it's two full lifetimes.

One hundred fifty years is a twinkle to a star, but to a man it's time enough to teach six generations what the meaning is of liberty, how to use it, when to fight for it.

MUSIC: (HARPSICHORD SWEEPS UP INTO A (FULL ORCHESTRA) MOVEMENT OF GREAT ENERGY: NERVOUS: MODERN: METROPOLITAN:

AFTER ESTABLISHING, COMES DOWN TO BACK THE FOLLOWING:)

STEWART: Have you ever been to Washington, your capital?

Have you been there lately?

Well, let me tell you, it's a place of buildings and of boom and bustle, of the fever of emergency, of workers working overtime, of windows lighted late into the night. It's a handsome city, proud of its sturdy name, proud of the men who've stopped there and made decisions; proud of its domes and lawns and monuments. (SNEAK IN TRAFFIC BACKGROUND AS MUSIC LEVEL DROPS) Of course, too, Washington is like some other cities you have seen — has street cars, haberdasheries, newsstands, coffee shops, and slums. At busy intersections there are neon traffic signs which, when the light's against you, say:

SIGN (VERY FLATLY — LIKE A SIGN): Don't Walk.

STEWART: And when the light changes:

SIGN: Walk.

STEWART: It's a tourist's city (TRAFFIC LEVEL GRADUALLY OUT), which is proper, when you think how much of history a busy guide can cover in a day, and when you realize that the District of Columbia belongs to all the people of the states. The tourists know that here their voices have been heard from clear back home; that here their votes are put to work. The tourists go to see the sights they've seen a thousand pictures of — the sights so famous and familiar that they're thrilled to find they look just as they thought they'd look. Washington Monument, for example, or the Lincoln Memorial, (THE CITY MUSIC IS SHUT OUT — NOW LINCOLN MUSIC) where the seated and relaxed Abe Lincoln sits between two mighty murals of plain words, his own words:

LINCOLN: (ON ECHO — SLOWLY — OUT OF STONE) With firmness in the right, as God gives us to see the right, let us strive on to finish the work we are in . . . to do all which may achieve and cherish a just and lasting peace among ourselves and with all nations.

MUSIC: (LINCOLN SEGUES TO CITY MUSIC)

STEWART: The city moves on busily outside the monument . . . The tourist goes to see the Capitol, the White House, the museums; sees all about him statues and inscriptions — more sayings than he's ever seen before — wise sayings — profound sayings. At the Union Station, for example:

DEPOT: A man must carry knowledge with him if he would bring home knowledge. — Samuel Johnson.

MUSIC (FILIGREE AFTER EACH OF THESE. WE DO NOT STOP FOR THEM.)

STEWART: The Archives Building:

ARCHIVES: What is Past is Prologue.

STEWART: The Supreme Court:

COURT: Justice, the Guardian of Liberty.

STEWART: But one of the best is in the Library of Congress:

LIBRARY: The Noblest Motive is the Public Good — Virgil.

MUSIC (A RESPECTFUL CHORD)

STEWART: The tourist thinks that over —

TOURIST: "The Noblest Motive is the Public Good."

STEWART: — and with this in mind, he climbs the marble stairs inside the Library — to come at length upon a case containing a handwritten document:

TOURIST (READING SLOWLY): "The engrossed original of the Constitution of the United States of America."

STEWART: He sees the manuscript is aging, that its words are worn, as though from use. The writing's dim; it's hard to make it out . . . it's getting on in years. . . .

MUSIC (MNEMONIC STRINGS BEHIND)

VOICE (DISTANT PERSPECTIVE: SYMBOLIC OF THE FADED WRITING ON THE MANUSCRIPT): We, the people of the United States, in order to form a more perfect Union, establish justice, insure domestic tranquility, provide for the common defense, promote the general welfare, and secure the blessings of liberty to ourselves and our posterity, do ordain and establish this Constitution for the United States of America. ARTICLE ONE: Section one: All legislative powers herein granted shall be vested in a Congress of the United States, which shall consist of a Senate and House of Representatives. Section Two: The House of Representatives shall be composed of members chosen every second year by the people of the several states, and the electors in

STEWART (OVERLAPS): . . . The words are dim — but not the meaning of words.

The pens that put this down are dust — but not the marks they made.

There was a time when this was shining parchment — when the text was easier to read — when the ink was not yet dry. This can be reconstructed.

Suppose that we, stopped here in modern Washington before this shrine, were to return, go back a little north by east in time and space to one bright afternoon in Philadelphia . . . that fine fall day when deputies from twelve free states subscribed their names to a new blueprint of a new society:

each state shall have the qualifications requisite for electors of the most numerous branch of the State Legislature. No person shall be a representative who shall not have attained to the age of twenty-five years.

(CROSS ON WORD "PHILADELPHIA" IN OVERLAPPING NARRATION TO):

. . . both of the United States and of the several states, shall be bound by oath or affirmation to support this Constitution:

(VOICE FADING RAPIDLY ON BOARD — THE WRITING BECOMES CLEARED) . . . but no religious test shall ever be required as a qualification to any office or public trust under the United States. ARTICLE SEVEN: The ratification of the conventions of nine states shall be sufficient for the establishment of this Constitution between the states so ratifying the same. Done in Convention by the unanimous consent of the states present, the seventeenth day of September in the Year of Our Lord, 1787 and of the Independence of the United States the twelfth. In witness whereof we have hereunto subscribed our names . . . George Washington, President, and Deputy from Virginia.

WASHINGTON: Now, gentlemen, we are ready for your signatures: by geographical progression, north to south. The deputies from New Hampshire will please sign first.

LANGDON: John Langdon.

GILMAN: Nicholas Gilman.

WASHINGTON: The delegates from Massachusetts. . . .

STEWART: Good-looking men, these. Mostly lawyers. Two or three are surgeons.

GORHAM: Nathaniel Gorham.

KING: Rufus King.

Broom, there, Broom of
Delaware. he did surveying
for a while.

Sherman, who just signed,
he was a shoemaker before
he studied law.

The man behind Ben Frank-
lin is Alexander Hamilton.
Ben's getting old now.
Eighty-one. Slept off and
on throughout the whole
convention. But when it was
important to be awake . . .
and active.

There have been men as-
sembled in a room before.
But never to a greater purpose.

WASHINGTON: The gentlemen
from Connecticut. please.
JOHNSON: William Samuel Johnson.
SHERMAN: Roger Sherman.

WASHINGTON: And now our representative from New York.
HAMILTON: Alexander Hamilton.

WASHINGTON: The gentlemen
from New Jersey.
LIVINGSTON: William Livingston.
BREARLEY: David Brearley.

WASHINGTON: The gentlemen
from North Carolina.
BLOUNT: William Blount.
SPAIGHT: Richard Dobbs
Spaight.

WASHINGTON: The gentlemen
from South Carolina.
RUTLEDGE: J. Rutledge.
PINCKNEY: Charles Cotesworth
Pinckney.

WASHINGTON: The gentlemen
from Georgia.
FEW: William Few.
BALDWIN: Abraham Baldwin.

STEWART: Here comes the last
to sign now:

JACKSON: Attest: William Jackson, Secretary.

BUSINESS: NOW THAT THE CONSTITUTION HAS BEEN SIGNED, THE
MEETING LIGHTENS (MUSIC OUT) THERE IS GENERAL AND
AMIABLE TALK, A LITTLE LAUGHTER.

In planning public service programs with schools or with groups or organizations of any kind, there are a number of problems to be considered before the definite form of the program can be decided upon. In the first place, it is seldom that the average local station will find it possible to broadcast a complicated dramatic program. On the other hand, if the local school has a good chorus, orchestra, and dramatic department, a program such as "America Calling" might very well be written, produced, and broadcast by the school. This program did not require actors or sound effects — just voices and instruments. It could have been presented without an orchestra, using an organ or piano.

It is always well to keep in mind that where the facilities for producing elaborate programs are not readily available, it is infinitely better to keep a dramatic program as simple as possible. Otherwise, it is likely to "fall apart" completely, thus hurting the reputation of the group responsible as well as of the station.

To sum up those things to remember in preparing any public service or educational program in dramatized form:

1. Use the dramatized form in building programs only when presenting factual or historical information where conflict or emotion is present.

2. Be sure the subject has dramatic content. All types of material cannot be forced into the dramatic pattern.

3. Certain subjects lend themselves more readily to certain dramatic forms. Before planning a program be thoroughly familiar not only with the subject matter but with the various dramatic forms.

4. If the program is being written for amateur groups to be broadcast from a local station, the plot should be kept simple and the script should call for only a few characters. Amateurs are not easily coached in the technique of radio acting.

5. Remember that radio actors are not born in "Six Easy Lessons" studied at home or elsewhere.

6. When sound effects are used, they must be used intelligently and, generally speaking, sparingly, especially in programs which are being broadcast by amateurs. They must be handled with extreme care to sound natural and to be effective.

An overabundance of sound effects often tends to confuse the listener.

7. It is often better and, generally, more effective for school groups to use the dramatic narrative rather than the straight dramatic form in presenting radio programs, as well-trained voice or choral groups are more frequently found in schools than good actors.

8. Music can be used as the theme, to set the mood of dramatic programs, and as bridges between scenes, and often to suggest time and place.

CHAPTER 13

CHILDREN'S PROGRAMS

OVER A PERIOD OF YEARS, there has been a great deal of controversy regarding children's programs. This controversy has been waged to a large extent by parents who have found it difficult to accept their children's likes and dislikes in this new field of entertainment.

In the early days of radio, children's programs were rather innocuous, consisting, to a large extent, of stories told by either a "story-lady" or an "Uncle Bob." These stories were supposed to appeal to children of all age levels; or rather, age levels were never even considered. Anything in the way of a story program for children was supposed to satisfy the child from five to fourteen. Later came the various "clubs," with buttons, badges, secret signs, and codes, to which every child clamored to belong.

After ten or twelve years that fad gave way largely to other types of programs, those in which the children themselves participated. There were "juvenile theaters," "amateur hours," "quiz shows," spelling bees, and many others. This latter group, of course, is still to be found on many radio stations, and story-hours are also still popular for the small child at numerous local stations. Why not? There is definitely a need and a place for them.

Many firms began to realize at a very early date the potentialities of using children to appeal to parents. There was no better means than the radio. Then came the era of "box-tops" and "thrillers." It is not strange that the advertiser, in his search for the right kind of program to catch the attention of the largest number of youngsters, turned to the comic strips which for generations had been followed so fervently by adults as well as children. By dramatizing and thus bringing to life those favorite characters, the advertiser had a ready-made vehicle at hand.

237

The early success of these first serials for children, however, stimulated the imaginations of the script writers, who realized that all boys and girls love adventure, conflict, villains and heroes, secrets and mysteries, and before long many of the programs took on characteristics which caused parents to rise up in arms in crusade proportions. Many of the daily episodes dealt with suspense, danger, kidnapping, and situations engendering real physical fear in the minds of the listeners.

In 1937 the Radio Committee of the Milwaukee City Council of Parent-Teacher Associations adopted the following platform:

> The Committee deplores:
> 1. The overuse of suspense, especially in finishing an episode.
> 2. Programs which upset or are likely to upset proper social attitudes, viz: respect for elders, law and order, and racial tolerance.
> 3. Programs which at any time or in any way attach advantage to crime or dishonesty.
> 4. Creation of fear, physical or mental disorder caused by gruesomeness, horrible situations, violence, threats, sound effects, and other radio artifices.

Some of the criticisms were just, but, as is usual, people are often prone to generalize in their criticisms. In consequence, the good programs suffered along with the bad. Norman Woelfel, in an article prepared for the magazine *Child Study*, spring of 1942, said:

> It is of especial importance that the appeal of radio programs shall not deteriorate, but shall, if possible, be enhanced. No person in his senses would propose that the fun, adventure, mystery, excitement, and fantasy now characteristic of radio fare should be replaced by shoddy stuff supplied by educators and government bureaucrats. Unless boys and girls continue to get rich, vicarious experience from radio, they will turn from it in disgust. The problem of the script writer and the program director becomes that of adapting existing knowledge and techniques and devices to a program content derived from the

realities, values, and purposes imbedded in American democratic civilization itself.

No radio station escaped the accusation of broadcasting
stories which would terrify children, of sending those same
children shivering to bed and causing them to toss and turn in
nightmares the long night through. Not all parents, however,
were willing to condemn on such broad lines, and Mrs. B. F.
Langworthy, who was President of the National Congress of
Parents and Teachers during the time that the controversy was
at white heat, said:

> It might be well for us to sit down and analyze a bit. The
> folk tale, with its dragons breathing fire, its child-eating ogre,
> and its bloody conflicts, is as old as language. Children and
> childish adults have been frightened into being good by threats
> of the bogey man or the policeman. These tales have served
> in ancient times to stimulate and energize many a flagging
> spirit.

Often when parents or teachers were queried as to the type
of story they would prefer to hear broadcast, they inevitably
came back with a plea "for the classics," such as *Treasure
Island, Huckleberry Finn, Robin Hood,* Hans Christian Andersen's stories, Grimms' *Fairy Tales,* etc. Apparently it had been
years since they had read those tales. They had forgotten the
kidnaping episodes in *Treasure Island,* in *Pinocchio,* in *Hansel
and Gretel,* in *Snow White and the Seven Dwarfs,* in *Huckleberry Finn,* or even in the story of Joseph and his brethren in
the Bible. They also forgot about the Queen, in Andersen's
Fairy Tales, who was punished for her wickedness by being
rolled down the road in a keg of nails; or the little mermaid
who lost her tongue and danced on swords all the rest of her
life. These are the stories which make up so many of the
children's "classics." As Mary Grannon, the beloved Mary of
the Canadian Broadcasting Corporation's "Just Mary" hour,
says:

> So many parents are clinging to some favorite story in their
> own youth and measuring all children's material by it — for-

getting what the last minstrel found out in his travels, that "old times are changed, old manners gone, a stranger fills the Stuart's throne." Let's not be like the bigots of the iron time; let's be rooters for the modern.

For a while parents seemed to forget that their responsibility as parents did not cease when the child turned on the radio; rather it increased. In the August, 1938, issue of *Your Life*, Mary Linton has this to say to the parent who is blaming everyone but himself for his child's actions:

> It isn't up to the teachers in the schools, nor the Federal Radio Commissioners, nor anyone else on earth. It's up to us — it's our job! Our job to teach them right from wrong, honesty from dishonesty, a clean and intelligent attitude toward sex, a healthful fastidiousness about their own bodies. We can teach these things because we have the daily opportunity of knowing our children and their reactions. We shouldn't want anyone else to do it for us! But whether it's radio programs that upset the children, or the hundred-and-one ways that willful children upset their parents, we can begin right now. If we expect George to do our jobs for us while we groan about what the world is coming to, we can expect the next generation to grow up to be anything but real men and women.

The fine young men and women who gave such excellent account of themselves on the far-flung battlefields and in the important military posts all over the world do not seem to have been seared or in any way harmed by the "thrillers" and terror-stories heard during their childhood; and it was during their childhood that this controversy over children's programs was at its height.

In the years that have followed, many programs have come and gone, and at present there are only half a dozen of the "thriller" type left on the networks. These have, to a great extent, been revised in an attempt to meet the objections of both parents and educators. Says Doctor Harry B. Summers, Manager of the Public Service Division of the American Broadcasting Company: [1]

[1] H. B. Summers, "Adventure on The Air," *Radio Age*, April, 1943, page 10.

In the minds of the listening layman, adventure serials are a certainty for better or worse. To those experienced in radio programming, who have nursed these series through their adolescent years, they are an institution representing constructive entertainment.

In building its adventure programs, the Blue Network, which carries a heavy schedule of children's serials, has tried to find an acceptable balance between wholesome stimulation and instruction.

Working with the knowledge that, in themselves, adventure stories for the juvenile mind are not frowned upon by educators, the Blue has eliminated the recognized evils from its children's serials and has adopted a workable code of program standards.

Education, as such, we have found is resented by the child who expects entertainment and thrills in his radio dialing. Adventure, however, peppered with interesting facts, constructive ideas, and educational suggestions, is a sugar-coated pill for which American children cry. Out of the six popular children's serials still on the air, five are carried by the Blue Network.

Jack Armstrong, which made its début in 1933, is still in the foreground of popularity among boys from eight to twelve years in age. As a storied hero, the All-American Boy long ago surpassed the popularity of Tom Swift and Frank Merriwell of former days. Besides being entertaining, the program is also educational. Doctor Martin L. Reymert, an internationally known child psychologist, who scrutinizes each *Jack Armstrong* script and whose judgment is final on method of presentation and subject matter, says:

> When addressed to so young and impressionable an audience, the program undoubtedly does elicit a definite reaction toward the characters and events of the story. Since this is so, care should be taken that plot and characters strengthen rather than weaken, or even passively fail to contribute to, the training that parents are trying to instill through the influence of home and school. Thus, the *Jack Armstrong* program always reflects respect for law and order, and on the part of its juvenile characters, respect for adult authority. Further, clean living, high morals, fair play, and honorable behavior are emphasized

and are always the approved methods of meeting problems or
difficult situations.

Terry and the Pirates may sound like radio fiction, but it is
based on actual fact. The locale is present-day China, and both
the setting and characterization are pointed toward increasing
our understanding of China's life. During the war, the author,
Al Barker, not only kept his war maps of the world up-to-date
with flags marking battle lines and battle stations, but he obtained his information from government news agencies both
here and in China.

Dick Tracy has taught youngsters the dangers of black markets
and always shows, through adventure, that crime never pays.

Captain Midnight emphasizes the importance of flying and
naval activities.

The Lone Ranger, probably the most popular of all children's
serials, is the present-day version of Robin Hood. The chords
of the William Tell Overture that serve as the masked horse-
man's theme are recognized by youngsters throughout the land,
and symphony orchestras playing the number at children's
concerts are repeatedly interrupted with a shout of "Hi-Yo
Silver, Awa-a-y." The familiar cry has become such a byword
in American homes that it was used as the password by the
American troops on their entry into Algiers. The Lone Ranger
Victory Corps, dedicated to victory, responsibility, citizenship,
safety, and health, during the war enrolled hundreds of thousands of youngsters. They were given specific tasks to do, such
as collecting wastepaper, rubber, and metals, gardening, air-
raid precautions, etc. High-ranking men in defense organizations appeared frequently on the program to address this great
army of the Lone Ranger Victory Corps.

Superman. Through a series of adventures involving super-
natural strength and insight, Superman and his friend Tim
have captured the fancy of thousands of boys and girls across
the land. This program, in spite of attempts to meet objections,
still receives heavy criticism from parents.

In addition to the adventure serials, there are two network

programs participated in by children themselves which have been on the air for at least ten years: "Coast to Coast on a Bus" on American, under the direction of Madge Tucker, has presented hundreds of children in songs and dramatic sketches and has, in fact, acted as a junior training school for children who ultimately have graduated into motion pictures and to the stage. The other program, "Let's Pretend" on the Columbia Broadcasting System, has been written and produced during the thirteen years of its existence by Nila Mack. Its dramatizations of fairy tales and the favorite stories of childhood have been a delight to small children as well as adults. It has also been a springboard to fame for many young actors and actresses.

Needless to say, there is a great variety of children's programs on local stations throughout the country. Some are good and some only fair, but the same program type that is being broadcast in Pennsylvania will, undoubtedly, be found in Florida or Colorado, as every conceivable idea has been tried out during the years.

At present, the child is much more interested in real adventure, in airplanes, submarines, and tanks than he is in make-believe. He doesn't need to draw on that imagination of his for adventure. It is true, nevertheless, that he must have a variety of vicarious experiences, and these he can easily acquire through the infinite variety of radio fare he is offered.

Children themselves have refused to be classified by age levels in their likes and dislikes, deeming it their privilege to listen to and enjoy any radio program that appeals to them, whether it is labeled "children's program" or not — in fact, they are much more likely to listen to a program not so labeled than to one with the stigma of that connotation.

It is certainly true that children between the ages of ten and fourteen have tended to outgrow the juvenile programs of former years. But planners of children's programs still divide the listening habits of children into the pre-school group, up to six years of age, the intermediate group from six to nine, and the older group from ten to fourteen, and feel that programs with definite appeals to those age levels should be built and broadcast. A study of any survey covering the subject that has been made during the past few years will show the falsity of this premise except for the youngest group. It may be taken for granted that children up to six years of age are not interested in adult programs, and that broadcasts of stories can be planned with a certain assurance of reaching that particular group; Ireene Wicker's "Singing Lady" is a case in point. There is always doubt as to whether children this young do listen. It does, in almost every instance, presuppose that the parent is listening with the child, and just how much of this is done has never been accurately determined.

Because of the times, and because the child has been living in a world filled with every kind of thrill and adventure, it is safe to assume that he is not interested in the same type of radio program that amused him before the war. It is very difficult, on that account, to set down today specific criteria for children's programs based on any previous knowledge or survey. It is to be hoped, however, that the standards finally accepted as fundamental before the war may still be so considered, and that the code pertaining to those programs, drawn up by the National Association of Broadcasters and accepted by the industry several years ago, will be followed by those interested in preparing children's programs. The code reads as follows:

> Programs designed specifically for children reach impressionable minds and influence social attitudes, aptitudes, and approaches and, therefore, they require the closest supervision of broadcasters in the selection and control of material, characterizations, and plot.
>
> This does not mean that the vigor and vitality common to a child's imagination and love of adventure should be removed; it does mean that programs should be based upon sound social concepts and presented with a superior degree of craftsmanship; that these programs should reflect respect for parents, adult authority, law and order, clean living, high morals, fair play, and honorable behavior. Such programs must not contain sequences involving horror or torture or use of the super-

natural or superstitious or any other material which might reasonably be regarded as likely to overstimulate the child listener, or be prejudicial to sound character development. No advertising appeal which would encourage activities of a dangerous social nature will be permitted.

In 1942, the Federal Radio Education Committee assigned to three members of the staff of the Evaluation of School Broadcasts the task of drawing up certain suggested criteria for what constitutes a good radio program for children. In the foreword to that report,[2] Doctor John W. Studebaker, United States Commissioner of Education and Chairman of the FREC, says:

> It [the report] is based upon the insights and conclusions drawn from a series of studies of children's reactions to programs, of parents' reactions to their children's listening, and upon the various codes and standards previously developed by broadcasters, parent groups, and child psychologists. It is not a final statement, but represents an intelligent summarization of the best research findings and interpretations made to date. It deserves consideration as a worth-while example of an objective approach to a problem in which many of us are vitally interested.

The report interprets somewhat more specifically the standards set forth by the NAB code, so it may be well to quote it here:

> 1. Radio programs should convey to children, or reinforce among them, the commonly accepted moral, social, and ethical characteristics of American life.
> 2. Radio programs should contribute definitely and specifically to healthy personality development in children.
> 3. Radio programs should, by excellent showmanship, provide children with opportunities for relaxation, entertainment, and pure enjoyment.

---

[2] Howard Rowland, I. Keith Tyler, Norman Woelfel, *Criteria for Children's Programs*, page 24. Washington: The Federal Radio Education Committee, with the co-operation of the United States Office of Education, Federal Security Agency, 1942.

The judging of children's radio programs has been expanded, in the report, based on the specific criteria listed here:

1. Children's radio programs should build faith in democracy and unfaltering loyalty to the ideals of democratic living.

2. Occupational skills which are essential to American life should be honestly and sincerely portrayed.

3. The rôle of minority groups of races and of nationalities which make up modern America should be portrayed sympathetically and realistically.

4. Children's radio programs should be authentic in broad historical or contemporary interpretation, factual detail, and artistic portrayal.

5. Children's radio programs should maintain generally recognized standards of good taste.

6. Crime is not suitable as a dominant theme in a radio program directed specifically to children.

7. The rich field of children's literature should provide the main part of the content of children's radio stories, and the main cues for handling plot and character development in the stories originating from other sources.

That the emotional, intellectual, and social development of the child's personality should not be forgotten, the report suggests that the following criteria be considered in planning any children's program:

1. Radio programs should arouse in children a wide range of emotional response and avoid undue stress upon fear and aggression.

2. The child has a need for genuine characters of truly heroic proportions as imaginary playmates and models to imitate and with which to identify himself.

3. In fantasy and fairy-tale programs, the fantastic or purely imaginative elements should be clearly identifiable to child listeners as unreal.

4. Intrinsic interest, maintenance of suspense, and satisfactory resolution of suspense should be consistently observed in the development of any children's program.

5. The social problems of childhood involving friendship, gang loyalty, and respect for one's equals should be frequently and honestly portrayed on children's radio programs.

6. Family relationships, mutual respect and understanding between parents and children, and family-problem situations should be portrayed in children's radio programs.

7. The suggestive power of radio should be utilized wherever possible in leading listeners to useful hobbies, skills, interests, activities, and knowledge.

8. Humor that is within the comprehension and appreciation of children should be used more extensively as an integral part of children's programs.

Finally, the report cites those considerations relating to showmanship or entertainment values that should be stressed:

1. The specialized techniques of radio drama should contribute to the listener's visualization of the characters, situations, and the action portrayed.

2. The vocabulary and vocal inflections used in a children's radio program must be clearly comprehended by the youngest age level of intended listeners.

3. Dialogue in children's programs should not undercut, by overnarration of detail, the imaginative processes by which the listening child lives the story.

4. Sound effects, in order to be convincing, should represent things or situations which can be readily visualized by the average child.

5. Music used in connection with radio drama should communicate emotions, mood, and feelings.

Of course, it is impossible today to know how much the war colored the thinking and attitudes of the child of today; whether it is safe to assume that shortly all will be forgotten and that once again the old controversy will loom on the horizon. Just what aproach to the problem should those interested in planning children's programs have now? Can any child be interested in anything that does not include the tools of modern warfare? Is there any group that still wants fairy stories, history (dramatically portrayed), music in any form, or any of the things that appealed to him previously? Should writers be discouraged from planning children's programs? Do stations still want them, and in what form? These are questions that are difficult to answer at this time.

It goes without saying that the whole subject deserves and needs much serious thought. That there is a place in radio for programs that appeal to children should not even need to be stated. Rather, it should be as much an accepted fact as that there should be programs appealing to the adult. Mrs. Gruenberg, in an excellent study of the problem, says: [3]

> Probably the "good" effects upon children's characters are as unpremeditated as the "bad." We have not yet found any sure way through our didactic teaching or other devices to make our children "good." We may at least suspect that some of the objectionable lessons are equally ineffective in making them "bad."
>
> The radio has brought this fundamental challenge to all teaching to a clearer issue. Certainly it is a hopeful sign to find more and more parents taking the attitudes of which the following comment is representative: "I am one of the mothers who feels that radio presents no problem at all — my experience being that children grow out of the stage of listening to 'trashy' programs as easily and satisfactorily as they grow out of the pulp magazine and 'trashy' serials in their reading. Like whooping cough, it's a self-limiting disease and time takes care of it. Whether they listen or not is of less importance than the necessity that we, through our own heart interest and appreciation, consistently direct the development of taste and lead them to broader fields of interest and enjoyment."

It would require many volumes to set down the whole story of children's programs; the controversies that have evolved around them during the past decade; the surveys of the listening habits of children by many groups; the preferences expressed by the children themselves; the ideals hoped for by their parents and teachers; as well as a thorough sampling of what has been done both over the networks and by local stations throughout the years. Clearly, all these things cannot be covered in this chapter, though an instance or two showing very exhaustive study and work in this field may be added as a

[3] Sidonie Matsner Gruenberg, *Radio and Children*, page 12. Published by The Radio Institute of the Audible Arts, 80 Broadway, New York.

guide to those groups which are keenly interested in seeing that the right type of children's programs are being scheduled on radio stations throughout the country.

One of the first groups to organize for the sole purpose of studying the subject of children's programs was the Radio Council on Children's Programs, an organization of women representative of various groups interested in parent-education questions. The aim of the Council was "To aid in the promotion of more and better children's programs." It was under the auspices of this group that Mrs. Dorothy Lewis conducted a country-wide survey in 1941 and reported her extensive findings to her own organization and to the National Association of Broadcasters, who helped to finance the study.[4]

The Radio Council of New Jersey has also undertaken an extensive survey on the whole question of children's programs. Mrs. Dorothy L. McFadden, Chairman of the Children's Program Committee, says:

> Any group taking up a serious study of what radio does or could do for the child must approach the subject humbly in the knowledge that there is much to learn about radio itself and its effects on children. An individual or group, in order to be intelligently critical of radio programs, must assimilate a great deal of information and experience. The motto of the group might well be, "Learn before criticizing, then criticize constructively."

Suggested scripts are not included in this book as space would not permit a fair sampling. In the Bibliography is included a list of those books, pamphlets, and articles which should be read by anyone interested in pursuing the subject further. There are also on file in the various radio stations scripts of outstanding programs which have been broadcast, and in the United States Office of Education Script Exchange many others of interest.

The whole question simmers down to what kind of programs are wanted by whom and that, in turn, can be decided only after someone decides who is to do the deciding.

[4] Dorothy Lewis, *Broadcasting to the Youth of America.* Washington, D.C.: National Association of Broadcasters (1941).

CHAPTER 14

RELIGIOUS PROGRAMS

THE QUESTIONS of the aim of religious radio programs, the form they should take, and the gospel they should preach have long been matters of controversy. Various groups of Catholics, Protestants, and Jews have met together frequently during the past two or three years to try to formulate some list of recommendations to be presented to the broadcasting industry as a code of practices in dealing with this knotty problem.

At the Twelfth Annual Institute for Education by Radio, held in Columbus, Ohio, on May 4 to 7, 1941, the Religious Work-Study Group discussed these problems and expressed a hope that they might draw up a set of recommendations which would be fair to all religious groups in the United States and which would help, in some measure, to solve the many problems that continually arise. Such a set of recommendations was subsequently drawn up and distributed rather widely to interested persons. Within a few months a number of criticisms were received indicating that the recommendations had not been completely understood, some people even believing that they were to become regulations with the force of the Federal Communications Commission behind them. This, of course, was far from the purpose of the recommendations. They were meant to be merely what they said they were — recommendations to which religious radio groups were asked to give their voluntary consent; they were to have no regulative power whatsoever.

In order to clarify the purpose for which these recommendations were drawn, they were resubmitted to the Fourteenth Annual Institute for Education by Radio at Columbus in May, 1943. A more representative gathering finally drew up a revised set looking toward more unanimity of religious-program procedure among radio stations as a whole. The present NAB religious code states:

Radio, which reaches men of all creeds and races simultaneously, may not be used to convey attacks upon another's race or religion. Rather it should be the purpose of the religious broadcast to promote the spiritual harmony and understanding of mankind and to administer broadly to the varied religious needs of the community.

Expanding some of the implied precepts, the Columbus meeting finally adopted the following recommendations:

1. That time for the broadcasting of religious programs should be provided by radio stations on a sustaining basis, in keeping with their responsibility to serve the "public interest, convenience, or necessity" of their listeners.

2. That an adequate schedule of religious programs should be maintained by all radio stations and networks, giving fair representation to all faiths, including responsible minority groups, in the service area of the respective station or network.

3. That no regular religious radio programs should appeal over the air for contributions for the support of the radio program itself. Nor should a charge for sermons, pamphlets, or religious objects distributed through religious programs be used by the sponsor as a means of raising funds.

4. That religious programs should not be used to attack other creeds or races. The exposition of doctrine should be affirmative.

5. That religious programs, even though doctrinal and confessional, should be addressed to the public interest and understanding.

6. That religious broadcasts in wartime as well as in peacetime should not only avoid stirring up hatred against human beings of any race, nation, or creed but should seek to contribute to the understanding and good will which are basic to a just and durable peace among the peoples of the world.

The content of these recommendations speaks for itself, but it might be of some value to comment briefly on each one. The first suggests that time for religious broadcasting should be provided by radio stations on a sustaining basis. Almost any radio station recognizes as part of its obligation to the community that a certain amount of time must be set aside for the purpose

of presenting religious programs. The trouble, in most instances, has been to decide which groups in a community where
there are many denominations should have time on the air
and which should, because of lack of time, be denied the right
to broadcast. It is obvious, of course, that where there are
numerous groups it would be impossible to give each the
amount of time they probably would request. This fact being
true, many stations have resorted to the policy of allotting time
to those church groups which were willing to pay for it. With
a limited amount of time for sustaining programs at the disposal of the station manager or program director, this practice
has meant that many denominations have had no regular voice
on the air, resulting in all-round dissatisfaction; first, on the
part of the religious groups, secondly, on the part of the
listener, and eventually on the part of the station. It is scarcely
fair, therefore, to permit only those with sufficient funds to
spend to appropriate that which, in reality, is the property of
all people. On the other hand, if the station can set aside a
definite amount of time during the week for the purpose of
broadcasting religious programs and so apportion the time
that each religious group in the community is given a fair share,
with no question of money, a real service may be rendered by
the station, resulting in satisfied participants and listeners alike.

This arrangement would, therefore, cover the stipulations
set forth in recommendation number two, except that it probably would not include some small minority groups. Generally
speaking, certainly as far as the networks are concerned, the
minority groups are given occasional programs during the year.
With the limited amount of time available, it would not be
possible to arrange regular series for these groups. Undoubtedly this would hold true also as far as the operations of local
stations are concerned, except, of course, in communities where
there might be a preponderance of adherents to these minority
faiths. Then, if the station served primarily that community,
it might be better station policy to give such groups the
majority of available time. These are all individual questions
that have to be worked out in each instance.

The third recommendation, dealing with appeals for funds over the air, is included primarily to prove to the station owners that religious groups want to be entirely just and fair; that they want sustaining time exclusively for the service of religion, not for any collateral money-raising purposes. It is easy for the average listener to start speculating on how much profit a church or a minister or a group is making on the program. It has been stated that there have been religious programs on the air which were undoubtedly money-making rackets. This recommendation was, therefore, proposed to discourage such practices, with the hope that eventually they could be eliminated completely. The resolution is not intended to include special programs, such as those put on annually by recognized relief agencies, the United Jewish Relief, the Catholic Charities, the Bishop's Pence, etc.; nor is it designed to prevent public support by any religious group of such campaigns as Community Chests, the Red Cross, etc.

The fourth recommendation needs no particular clarification, except to point out that it is not intended in any way to deprive any religion of the right to expound its own doctrine; but in so doing, it should not attack any other creed or race. There have been occasional religious fanatics who have gained access to the air, preaching, undoubtedly in good faith as they believed it, in such a way as to throw aspersion upon other doctrines, races, and creeds. Eventually, the time was denied to such people, but not before some harm had been done.

The Court of Appeals in the District of Columbia said, in the Shuler case: [5]

[5] 62 F. 2d, 850.

> If it be considered that one in possession of a permit to broadcast in interstate commerce may, without let or hindrance from any source, use these facilities, reaching out as they do from one corner of the country to the other, to obstruct the administration of justice, offend the religious susceptibilities of youth and innocence by the free use of words suggestive of sexual immorality, and be answerable for slander only at the instance of the one offended, then this great science instead of

a boon will become a scourge, and the nation a theater for the display of individual passions and the collision of personal interests.

Many stations have set up their own policy codes to which they strictly adhere. The National Broadcasting Company statement of policy is typical.

> The National Broadcasting Company will serve only the central or national agencies of great religious faiths, as for example, the Roman Catholics, the Protestants, and the Jews as distinguished from the individual churches or small group movements in which national membership is comparatively small.
>
> The religious message broadcast should be non-sectarian and non-denominational in appeal.
>
> The religious message broadcast should be of the widest appeal; presenting the broad claims of religion, which not only aid in building up the personal and social life of the individual but also aid in popularizing religion and the church.
>
> The religious message broadcast should interpret religion at its highest and best so that as an educational factor it will bring the individual listener to realize his responsibility to the organized church and to society.
>
> The national religious messages should be broadcast only by the recognized outstanding leaders of the several faiths as determined by the best counsel and advice available.

The fifth recommendation merely means that Protestants, Catholics, and Jews should be conscious at all times of the fact that there are always many listeners who will not understand the specific terms and doctrines of each sect and that if such terms are used, they should be explained. For example, if the Catholics should talk about "transubstantiation," the term should be interpreted so that non-Catholics will understand what is meant.

There will always be some controversy regarding the sixth recommendation, as there are bound to be people who still believe that the only way to win a war, for instance, is to hate one's enemy. This philosophy is, of course, diametrically opposed to the Christian doctrine of "love your enemies" (see Matthew V:24). Doctor Fred Eastman, writing in the *Christian Century* for May 27, 1943, says:

> The trouble with the propagandists who are trying to build our morale out of hatred is that they do not have this faith expressed by Mr. Churchill when he said, "We believe that the spirit and temperament bred under institutions of freedom will prove more enduring and resilient than anything that can be got out of the most efficiently imposed mechanical discipline." They seem as unaware of the political and cultural ideas that underlie democracy as they are of the religious sensibilities of the American people. A radio that forgets these basic ideas, or adjourns them for the duration while it makes itself a medium for the spreading of hate, will weaken morale. It may ultimately destroy its own usefulness by destroying the people's confidence in it as a free agency of democracy. For the American people will continue to tune off dramas of hate. We know that neither our salvation nor our victory lies along that easy road. The health of democracy, not its hate, is its best propaganda. If radio will devote its power and its talent to dramatizing the ideas and values, the leaders and crises, of democracy it will contribute enormously to that health. Morale will then take care of itself.

By following the recommendations submitted at Columbus, any station manager or program director can build a well-balanced religious program designed to meet the spiritual needs of the community in a way that will prove eminently satisfactory to all listeners. It goes without saying that religious groups within a community when they approach the radio station should make every effort to co-operate with the other religious groups in the community in an endeavor to present the best possible religious program.

Doctor Max Jordan, the director of religious broadcasts for the National Broadcasting Company, said in an article in *Radio Age*: [6]

⁶ *Radio Age*, April, 1943, page 17.

Every deep faith has a certain "exclusiveness" — that is, a body of convictions and dogmas which sets it off from the other faiths. Sometimes the cleavage is sharp and deep. Yet there are also beliefs shared in common, or attitudes characteristic of every believer. Naturally, radio must seek to find these last. It cannot debate about religious matters, or bring antagonisms to the fore. To do so would mean getting entangled in a conflict which could not possibly be mitigated on the air.

There will, of course be innumerable forms which a religious program can take; for instance, broadcasting a church service, direct from the church on a Sunday morning. A different denomination might be presented each Sunday. But unless the minister is an exceptionally good speaker, able to hold the interest of his radio audience as well as those actually attending the service; and unless the music, both organ and choir, are also good, it is scarcely fair for any denomination to use the hour and a half donated by the station for this purpose. Rather, it would be better for various denominations to agree upon one of their group, known for his ability as an outstanding speaker, to represent them. From among the various churches a good choir or chorus could be gathered to take part in such a broadcast. This might represent the Protestant contribution. The Catholics and the Jews should be given a proportionate amount of time, though in some instances all three have shared in a common arrangement. These programs could be presented in thirtyminute or fifteen-minute units, depending, of course, upon the amount of time the station had at its disposal for this purpose.

If there is more than one radio station in a town or community, the religious program might be divided among them, each carrying its share, but no station should duplicate a service presented by another station.

The question of program or line costs invariably arises when the suggestion of broadcasting direct from a church is suggested. It would seem that whatever these costs amounted to, they should be borne by the group requesting the time — that is, if a church service is to be picked up frequently, the cost of the telephone lines from the station to the church should be assumed by the church. On the other hand, stations might prefer to assume these costs themselves, asking churches to take care of whatever program costs arise. These probably, in most instances, would be negligible, as generally speaking the minister would not request a fee for broadcasting; and unless the station is located in a city where there are rigid musician-union requirements, the costs for music would not be more than any group should be willing to spend as its contribution to this community religious program. On the other hand, should such groups really be unable to assume even those expenses, the station could, undoubtedly, provide appropriate recordings which could be used without cost.

Some religious organizations have sponsored dramatic radio shows, frequently based on the Bible. These are generally very popular and well received. It is infinitely better, however, not to attempt dramatizations unless such programs can achieve the same quality as similar programs broadcast over the same station; otherwise the religious dramatization will suffer badly by comparison. On the other hand, certain religious groups offer radio transcriptions, professionally prepared, which are acceptable to the station and to the general public. Still others have successfully used religious radio quizzes and transcribed dramatized spots on local stations.

In addition to religious programs presented with an adult audience in mind, many stations have worked out such programs for children. In some instances, these programs have taken the form of dramatized Sunday School lessons; in others, the presentation of actual Sunday Schools, with the children doing the majority of the broadcasting. There is a definite need for good religious programs for children. Many stations would be interested in programs of this nature, provided, of course, that the program format and participants were good. This type of program is extremely difficult to plan and carry out in such a way as to achieve its purpose; namely, to interest children. Old-time formulas have not worked. But it is a challenge to someone.

Nothing so far has been said about planning religious programs for network broadcasting. Each network has had its own philosophy on how such programs should be handled. The Columbia Broadcasting System, for instance, has built its own "Church of the Air," co-operating with all groups and denominations and picking up a different denomination each Sunday with a studio-built program. They have also broadcast for a number of years a program of spirituals by a choir of thirty-five Negro voices, with a religious talk by outstanding Negro leaders and educators. The American Broadcasting Company carries "National Vespers," the Protestant broadcast on which Doctor Harry Emerson Fosdick has spoken for a great many years, and "The Hour of Faith" presented by the National Council of Catholic Men, a series of talks by church leaders together with vocal and instrumental music, and "The Message of Israel" broadcast in co-operation with the United Jewish Laymen's Committee. Mutual presents a Chapel Service, a studio-built program, similar to Columbia's "Church of the Air," using speakers from different denominations each week, and in addition for the past year has been carrying a "Minute of Prayer" each noon, also presented by various denominational speakers. The National Broadcasting Company, in co-operation with the Federal Council of Churches, presents Doctor Ralph W. Sockman in the "National Radio Pulpit," and in co-operation with the National Council of Catholic Men "The Catholic Hour," a program of music and prominent guest speakers; also Doctor Walter W. Van Kirk in a weekly series of religious news items entitled "Religion in the News." The Jewish Theological Seminary sponsors "The Eternal Light," a half-hour series on Sundays consisting of dramatizations with occasional talks. All branches of Jewry are represented on the committee responsible for the program. From time to time all the networks have arranged special programs with a religious significance, broadcast either singly or in series; for example, NBC presented "We Believe," a program featuring the great religious music of the three major faiths.

There has always been some discussion as to who should be responsible for building and presenting network religious programs, just what form they should take, and what groups they should serve. NBC has believed that it was wiser to work with the central religious agencies, permitting them to arrange the program content. On the other hand, CBS, still working through the same agencies, prefers to build its own religious programs. Two of the programs carried over American were part of the NBC religious schedule before the networks were separated, and they have continued as originally planned, so they also follow the NBC practice of permitting the groups responsible for the programs to build them.

To summarize the points covered in this chapter, it may be taken for granted that there is a real need for radio to include a spiritual message. Doctor Harry Emerson Fosdick has said, "Multitudes of people outside the churches are religious, anxious about it, groping after it, hungry for it." The question is how best to satisfy that need by radio in a positive way without engaging in doctrinal attacks. Doctor Willard Johnson of the National Conference of Christians and Jews has stated, "All religious radio programs should be strictly affirmative and consist of guidance, stimulation, courage, and inspiration." If the builder of radio programs agrees with these premises, surely radio and religion can meet in a spiritual program beneficial to all listeners.

CHAPTER 15

AGRICULTURAL PROGRAMS

AGRICULTURAL BROADCASTING, as a phase in public-service information to the public, has been of interest to program people almost as long as radio has been in use. Radio had scarcely been perfected for listening purposes before its program planners saw what it could do to help those living in rural communities.

Radio for rural people is what might be called a "natural." The remoteness of farmers from the general run of news made radio more of an asset than any other development in their lives, aside from the automobile. No matter how remote are the people on a ranch or farm, a mere click of their radios, and they are as close to Australia, New York, or Washington as their urban cousins.

Senator Arthur Capper of Kansas once stated: [1]

> To the farmer, radio, with programs properly co-ordinated, is the sunrise devotional service, the first edition of his morning newspaper, the noonday luncheon club, the stock and grain market, and the nightly "protracted" meeting or political meeting or symphony. To the farmer's wife, radio is the cooking school, beauty parlor, household clinic, bargain counter, sewing circle, afternoon tea or musicale, community club, and evening at the theater. To the farmer's children, it is the comic strip, the home teacher, a ringside seat at big-league sports, the school of the air, and the white lights of Broadway.

Naturally, news, weather, and market reports are of paramount importance to the farmer. Before the days of radio such reports came to him by way of rural telephone party lines; by word of mouth at the crossroads store; or through newspapers two or three days old. There was no way of knowing whether

---

[1] Arthur Capper, "What Radio Can Do for the Farmer," *Radio and Education*. Chicago: University of Chicago Press (1932), pages 223-224.

there was time to harvest the grain crop before the onslaught of the hot summer winds in order to keep it from shattering on the stalk; or when to protect the stock from northwest blizzards in the winter. The winds and the blizzards were upon the farmer before he even knew of their existence. Today, with radio, all that is changed, and the advance weather reports and warnings have saved farmers millions of dollars.

With the beginning of broadcasting, back in the early twenties, owners of radio stations in the farm belt felt an obligation to furnish vital statistics to the farmer. This was particularly true of the men responsible for the operation of radio stations owned by colleges or universities, which had always provided an active extension service. Purdue, Oregon State College of Agriculture, the University of Wisconsin, Michigan State College, Cornell University, Texas Agricultural and Mechanical College, Kansas State College, and many others were leaders in broadcasting weather, market reports, and other informational programs for rural audiences. In a great many instances, the services started by those particular stations have not only continued but have expanded, until now a full variety schedule is offered by most of the educational stations.

Colleges and universities, however, were not the only groups concerned with reaching the farmer by radio; there were commercial stations as well which felt a similar obligation. The first of these was, naturally, the first radio station to be licensed for broadcasting, KDKA in Pittsburgh. It was in 1921 that those in charge of the programming activities of the station were approached by Mr. E. S. Bayard, editor of the *Pennsylvania and Ohio Stockman and Farmer*, a farm publication circulating in those two states, with the idea of using radio as an instrument to reach the farmer with market and weather reports. Mr. Frank Mullen, now executive vice-president of the National Broadcasting Company, left his position as farm editor of the Sioux City, Iowa, *Journal* to join the staff of the *Pennsylvania and Ohio Stockman and Farmer* for the purpose of supervising this new farm radio service.

Not only in the East and the Middle West were commercial

stations becoming cognizant of the part radio could play in the life of the farmer; out on the Pacific Coast, stations KPO and KGO in 1924 inaugurated a number of different agricultural programs in co-operation with the College of Agriculture of the University of California and with various state-wide co-operatives. In New York State, WGY at Schenectady established a service, under G. Emerson Markham, which has become one of the best-organized and most widely known radio farm services in the country. Instances of co-operation between commercial stations and farm groups must include mention of several other outstanding examples, such as the New England Agricultural Radio Programs, broadcast over the Yankee Network in co-operation with the Departments of Agriculture of the six New England states and various state and county extension services; "Everybody's Farm Hour," organized by George C. Biggar on WLW in Cincinnati; Art Page's "Dinner Bell" hour on WLS in Chicago; Larry Haeg's program at WCCO in Minneapolis; Everett Mitchell's "Town and Farm" on WMAQ, Chicago; and Henry Schacht's "Farmer's Digest" on KPO, San Francisco. Such co-operation has been going on since the early days of broadcasting; in fact, between 1921 and 1930 there was a mushroom growth of radio farm programs throughout the country.

With the establishment, in 1926, of the National Broadcasting Company, one of the first and paramount questions that arose was what could be done for the farmer. Mr. Frank Mullen left KDKA in Pittsburgh to join NBC as head of a newly formed agricultural department. It was proposed at that time to devote station KFKX, located at Hastings, Nebraska, and owned by the Westinghouse Electric and Manufacturing Company (one of the founders of the National Broadcasting Company), to the service of the farmer by broadcasting educational and informational programs during the daytime and entertainment and musical programs during the evening. Mr. Mullen established headquarters in Hastings and proceeded to set up a farm-program schedule. "It was soon evident, however, that it was far less practicable to render a national service from a station so remote from the sources of talent than from some more populous middle-western city. Station KFKX,[2] therefore, was closed on June 1, 1927, and a survey was made during the summer of the possibilities of maintaining headquarters and operating central studios at Chicago." [3] In the fall of 1927 such a headquarters was decided upon, and three major farm events were broadcast that autumn over thirteen middle-western stations of the NBC network — the International Livestock Exposition, the annual convention of the American Farm Bureau Federation, and the annual convention of the Illinois Agricultural Association at Rock Island.

Mr. Mullen, when in charge of agricultural broadcasting for station KDKA in Pittsburgh, had caused a number of surveys to be made to find out the best possible listening hour for farmers. Without exception, the noon hour seemed to be the time best suited to farm workers in all parts of the country. With that in mind, two services were established by NBC on October 2, 1928: the National Farm and Home Hour from 12:00 to 12:15 P.M. and from 12:30 to 12:45 P.M. and the program of the United States Department of Agriculture from 12:15 to 12:30 P.M. Both of these programs were broadcast daily except Saturday and Sunday and were carried over a network of fifteen stations in the Middle West. Co-operating with the National Broadcasting Company in the planning and broadcasting of this new farm service were many other organizations besides the Department of Agriculture; such as the American Farm Bureau Federation, the National Grange, the American Country Life Association, the American Society of Agronomy, the American Association of Land-Grant Colleges, livestock breed associations, and several state agricultural colleges. By 1929 the interest in the "Farm and Home Hour" became so widespread that the service was enlarged to six days a week and to include stations not only in the Middle West, but on the East Coast, in the South, and as far west as

---

[2] KFKX merged with KYW in 1927.
[3] From report of Merlin Aylesworth, President of the National Broadcasting Company, to members of the Advisory Council, February 18, 1927.

Denver, with the West Coast accepting the program on Saturday only. Today, with the separation of the ABC Network from the National Broadcasting Company, the National Farm and Home Hour as such no longer exists; instead, a show entitled "Farm and Home Makers" is heard Monday through Friday on American.

On January 1, 1931, the National Broadcasting Company and the United States Department of Agriculture joined forces to present, five days a week, Monday through Friday, the "Western Farm and Home Hour," originating in San Francisco. NBC furnished the orchestra; the Department of Agriculture, the speakers. This service continued in operation as a separate western farm service until December 28, 1937, when it was discontinued in favor of the "National Farm and Home Hour," which made arrangements to extend its facilities from coast to coast. However, in 1938 a new agricultural program, "Western Agriculture," was inaugurated and carried on KGO and eleven other stations on the Basic Blue until the fall of 1944.

Toward the close of the early experimental period in radio, the United States Department of Agriculture foresaw the tremendous advantage radio had over other media in getting vital market and statistical information to the farmer. Mr. Mullen had already convinced the Department of the necessity and value of making weather reports available to radio stations for broadcasts to farmers (the Weather Department at that time was located in the Department of Agriculture), and the Secretary of Agriculture, Mr. W. M. Jardine, formerly of the Kansas State Agricultural College, one of the early users of radio in connection with his activities there, decided to establish a full radio service in the Department of Agriculture. The office "was charged with the duty of making available to educational and commercial radio stations extension programs from the Department, programs, and home-making practices." [4]

At the present time the radio service of the United States

[4] Morse Salisbury, Chief of Radio Service, United States Department of Agriculture, "Contributions of Radio to Informal Adult Education," *Education on the Air* (1930), page 151.

Department of Agriculture is one of the busiest offices in the whole Department, sending out material to approximately four hundred and fifty local radio stations and to the networks each day. In most cases the station operates the farm program, inviting field people from the Department of Agriculture to participate; in others, the station turns the time over to one or more of the Department agencies, thus making the agencies responsible for filling the time.

A very complete study was made in 1936 by Edmund deS. Brunner, Professor of Education, Teachers College, Columbia University, of the radio services offered to the farmer; a study which gives, in great detail, the contributions made during the earlier years of radio by the various states.

Today, as never before, agricultural programs rank close to being first in importance in the broadcasting field. With the great demand for food production, the farmer more than ever is depending on his radio for information which will enable him to do his job with the least expenditure of manpower and in the shortest space of time. Therefore, any agricultural program built to entertain and give service to agriculturists must be laid out with considerable care and with much thought given to its contents.

First, there is the problem of the location and power of the station presenting such a program. Second, a survey should be made of the type of farmers served by the station; a program designed for dairymen, poultrymen, and livestock husbandmen would not be of much interest to farmers living in communities producing practically nothing but vegetables or cotton. With those two questions solved, the next important point for consideration is where to get the right informational program material. There are many sources besides the Radio Office of the United States Department of Agriculture; the Extension Services of the various states are also anxious and willing to send out state adaptations of the government activities, and the county agents, too, are eager to co-operate in passing on any information they have. All the radio wire services now provide special agricultural summaries. There are various groups, such as farm organizations, which cover all phases of agriculture, livestock, food packing, milk, co-operatives, etc. In addition to these, there are the rural youth groups, such as the 4-H Clubs, the Future Farmers of America, and the state youth organizations. The younger farm groups always have colorful material available for broadcasters.

There are so many aspects in presenting agricultural programs that to cover the subject thoroughly one has to think not only of the productive side, but of the business side, the living side, and economics generally. It must be borne in mind that the standard of living in the rural areas has risen rapidly in the past ten or fifteen years, and where once there was a hit-or-miss contact between dwellers in the cities and on the farms, the farmers, with their more than five million radio sets in 1945, are as well-informed on all topics as the urban listeners. The modern farmer, the farmer of today, is employing scientific methods which have lifted the running of his farm to the same standards of efficiency as that of any other industry.

A radio program must be prepared, then, that will interest and entertain a typical modern farmer and his family. It must be aimed at the man or woman, the boy or girl, who not only has the will to do a job and do it well, but one who, to be successful, must be a good agronomist, entomologist, scientist, animal husbandryman, and a keen businessman.

Some directors of rural programs have the mistaken idea that a good farm program should consist of a group of hill-billies, much laughter at one's own jokes, and such gibes and jests as once were aimed at the farmer who was called a "hick." They little realize that the tastes of the radio listeners in the rural areas differ little from the tastes of those in cities; they like good music, comedy, mysteries, etc., as well as anyone else. In addition, they do like to have their informational farm program built with the same thought and care as is given to any other type of program. They want accurate information, such as news and weather and market reports, coupled with good music, both light and classical. Whoever is in charge of the agricultural program for a station, therefore, must have a complete understanding of the content of all program material presented. Agriculture has a language of its own, and the farmer is very quick to detect any faulty presentation of farm information.

The best approach on a farm program, as on any other informational program, is one of naturalness. Never, under any circumstances, should the listener be talked down to, be he on the farm or in the city. The broadcaster will find the farmer extremely loyal to his friends and neighbors. He is quick to heed their advice and to buy on the recommendation of one whom he feels he can trust. On the other hand, he will question the statements of someone who has not proved that he has knowledge of the field.

When inviting guest speakers to participate in the program, one must be sure to seek out authorities, either professionals or farmers who have been particularly successful in some special fields of agriculture. When it is not possible to take these people to the studio, local stations equipped with portable recording apparatus may record talks or interviews directly from the farm for use at a convenient time later. This method is frequently used to pick up speakers from demonstration meetings, where it is not possible to install lines for a direct broadcast; it is also a most effective way of presenting other types of farm information, and the natural farm sounds lend color and interest to the broadcast. For example, in the fall of 1943 during an infestation of corn borer, many demonstrations of control were necessary in combating this pest. Farmers unable to attend such demonstrations received authentic information as to the method used, direct from the scene of the demonstration, by means of a series of recordings made on the spot. A natural sound effect, which could not be reproduced by studio records, accented the word picture so that the listening farmers could visualize exactly what was going on.

Farmers approve heartily of any program that gives them information on how to cut down on the time and labor involved in the chore-work on the farm as well as on production, planting, seeding, harvesting, or overhauling and the care and repair of machinery. Wherever it is possible to ferret out such information, it is wise to let the farmer who has used these short-cut methods successfully tell about them himself. The farmer may not always be the best broadcaster; but if he is natural and sincere, his broadcast will be effective and will transmit the information desired.

The time factor is, of course, all-important in building an agricultural program; the program content of a broadcast which is set up for early morning would differ greatly from one scheduled for a noontime broadcast. For instance, it is much better to discuss matters that have to do with animal health and fertilizers, extremely important subjects, both of them, in the morning program period, when one would have far less chance of offending any listeners, than to furnish such information at noon when lunch might be in progress.

Network agricultural broadcasting is more involved from the program standpoint than the broadcasting of a local program principally because of the time element, the difference in crops, and the different planting and harvesting seasons in the various parts of the country. For this reason, the co-operation of the United States Department of Agriculture is necessary in presenting national news as it affects a majority of the farmers of the country as a whole.

For the benefit of anyone interested in putting on agricultural programs, the experience of station WHO, Des Moines, Iowa, might be used as a fine example of how a local radio station can render an excellent service to its community and can plan and carry through an adequate farm program. In 1939, WHO organized as a series of ten or more farm programs "The Corn Belt Hour," with Herb Plambeck, WHO's farm editor. This particular program, broadcast at noon on Saturdays, supplements the daily features of farm news and market reports which are offered at other hours, especially in the early morning. It presents interviews with leading farm men and women of the Middle West who are authorities on various farming operations, celebrated guest speakers from all parts of the world, and popular radio stars. WHO has always felt its obligation to its farm audience to be of prime importance. Its programs of "Farm News and Farm Markets" have become daily "musts" throughout WHO's listening area.

Realizing that the middle-western farmer and his family were doing a lot of thinking about war problems of food production as well as what was going on all over the world, at the invitation of the British Ministry of Information and the Ministry of Agriculture, the station sent Herb Plambeck, in the fall of 1943, on a two months' tour of England, Scotland, Wales, and Ireland. There he observed the agricultural war efforts and needs of the British people. Every Saturday noon during his visit he broadcast a report of his observations and impressions by short wave from the British Broadcasting Corporation studios in London. His reports were beamed toward Iowa to be picked up at Des Moines and rebroadcast simultaneously during the "Corn Belt Hour" by WHO and other Iowa stations.[5] It is service of this type that convinces a station's listening audience of its sincerity in wanting to render a real public service, a conviction which goes a long way toward binding that audience closely to the station.

Early in 1944, at a meeting held in Chicago, plans were formulated by agricultural radio directors for a compact and nation-wide program to outline and extend the services of agricultural editors. The initial meeting was called to discuss the mutual problems encountered by the various radio farm departments and to crystallize the tested methods to provide better farm information service for all people, from the station owners to the listeners. Other preliminary meetings were held in New York and San Francisco. As a result, a national organization known as the Association of Radio Farm Directors was founded in Columbus, Ohio, in May, 1944. The purposes of the organization, according to their statement, are as follows:

> Closer relationship between commercial radio farm broadcasting, agencies, and farm organization; closer relationship with advertising agencies and other groups interested in reaching the farm people through the medium of radio; closer relationship and better understanding between farm radio broadcasting and station management; programming of farm radio broadcasts which will keep this type of service on a high plane; developing farm service in areas of the United States where it

[5] *Radio Daily*, January 7, 1944.

is now lacking; advancing the welfare of those engaged in farm radio broadcasting.

This chapter closes with a few points to remember in building a good agricultural program, either for a local station or for a network:

1. Define the area served by the station and see that the information that is broadcast serves the needs of that area.

2. Make contact with all farm groups within the area as sources of supply for materials to be used on the program. The mutual co-operation thus established will be of great benefit.

3. Ascertain the time best suited for listening by the farmers within the range of the station and the length of program most convenient for them and plan accordingly.

4. Be sure that all the information put on the air is from an authentic source and is both timely and helpful for the people in the territory served by the station.

5. Choose good music, not too classical nor too modern, but music that can be hummed or whistled by the listener.

6. Call attention to as many local farm activities as possible through actual participation in those activities.

7. Plan to include a well-known homemaker or home economist three or four days each week. The farm woman needs and appreciates good information on the difficult subject of housekeeping in rural areas. But, in so doing, be sure that the homemaker is known to and liked by the farm woman.

8. Be sure whenever possible to present the modern farmer himself so that he can exchange ideas with his friends and neighbors.

9. Remember that the confidence of the rural audience is invaluable to the success of any agricultural program. That confidence must be established at the outset and always be maintained. It is the only way to insure a loyal following for the program.

10. It is imperative to be natural at all times. This is true of the person regularly in charge of the program and of anyone invited to participate on it. Never talk down to the audience.

11. Present each program with the same dignity and craftsmanship as is given to the most outstanding program on the station.

4

THE SALES ORGANIZATION

CHAPTER 16

LOCAL STATION ORGANIZATION

AT FIRST GLANCE it would seem that the entire broadcasting sales problem could be covered in a single chapter. However, there are vital points of difference between conditions that surround a network time sale and a local station time sale.

Our American system of broadcasting is commercial and competitive. As such, it has been so successful that Americans own more radio receiving sets than telephones. Our plan permits continuous broadcasting operations by hundreds of radio stations at the same time with each station choosing its own programs and constantly striving to attract and hold the attention of the listener in competition with the other stations. Thus, in most American localities a listener may select a program exactly suiting his desire at the moment. He has music, drama, news, education, comedy, and thrills in never-ending variety, all because of the competition among stations for his attention.

Since competition is created through our plan of commercial broadcasts, it follows naturally that a client sponsoring a program wishes to have his program so appealing that he will have the major audience at the time his program is on the air. Thus arises the necessity for a sales force to counsel, direct, and service his advertising venture through co-operation with his advertising representatives or agency.

In 1920, KDKA, Pittsburgh began the first regular series of broadcasts in history. Soon other stations in New York, Washington, Chicago, and San Francisco had also established regular schedules, and the experiment was fascinating to those fortunate listeners who were owners of crystal sets. However, it was discovered very quickly by the broadcasters that, though they were receiving thousands of letters and columns of newspaper publicity praising their efforts, a tremendous expense was being incurred with no income. The idea of a tax on radio receivers,

273

similar to an automobile tax, was generally considered the most logical means for securing revenue. This plan was accepted by and is still used in England and virtually every country other than America. The plan most generally favored for America was a tax on the manufacturer of radio equipment for transmitters, studio, and receiving sets, and this probably would have become effective had it not been for an idea which the American Telephone and Telegraph Company, owners of WEAF, put into effect in 1922. This company believed that since people were willing to pay to transmit messages by telephone and telegraph that they also would be willing to pay for a message of general public interest transmitted by radio. So an advertisement was prepared stating that the facilities of WEAF were available for persons desiring such service. A real-estate firm, anxious to promote the advantages of a suburban development in Jackson Heights, New York City, became the first advertiser to use the service; a series of talks were given detailing the attractiveness of that new suburban section.

Although the formula of the first radio advertising service was not the best, results were secured, and a definite idea for future American broadcasting was developed. Then followed the establishment of a sales department at each radio station, and a definite rate was fixed for time periods of fifteen minutes, thirty minutes, and one hour during both the daytime and the evening periods of broadcasting. The rates were established by each station after a careful study of the approximate number of listeners who might be expected to hear the messages at the time of broadcasting. Since that time the establishment of rates on radio stations has become a science and an art. We have today rates for periods of time as low as fifteen seconds and all rates are based on a very accurate survey of the potential possibilities for attracting an audience.

Sales departments are, in general, divided into three groups — local, spot, and network. Local sales are those confined wholly to the one station with which the sales department is connected. Spot sales are those in which the same local sales force sells similar service on another station in a different locality; in other words, the sales force is acting as a representative of the distant station for the sale of its local time. When two or more stations are joined together by telephone line for the purpose of broadcasting the same program at the same time, they constitute a network, and the sales force that services the clients who use a network constitutes network sales. This discussion will deal primarily with local sales.

The local sales department of any station is organized very similarly to any other functioning department and is determined by the size and importance of the station which it represents. Personnel in general consists of a sales manager, salesmen, secretaries, and traffic and auditing clerks. The department works in conjunction and close association with the promotion, program, legal, and executive departments. Usually a large station will have from four to ten salesmen, with other personnel in corresponding numbers.

What does a sales department sell? And after the sale is made, what happens next? In the first place, the local sales department sells a definite amount of time in the station's regularly scheduled period of broadcasting, just as a newspaper advertising salesman would sell a definite amount of space in which the client's advertisement might be inserted for publication in the newspaper. The most commonly sold unit of radio time is fifteen minutes, either daytime or evening, and the sale may cover one day or all seven days of the week, with a contract usually extending for a minimum of thirteen weeks. This does not mean that the salesman calls at a prospect's office and tells him that he. has 8:30 to 8:45 A.M. available, Monday through Saturday, on WMAQ, and asks whether the prospect is interested. The salesman must be equipped with a variety of information concerning the available time period he is offering and must have a definite idea of the type of program which would be most likely to be successful at that time. Information required by the prospect will be (1) what is the type of program and who is the sponsor of the period immediately preceding the offered time; (2) what follows immediately; (3) what the other principal stations in the city are offering as competition within the period offered; (4) what evidence of a listening audience the salesman has to prove that the prospect's program has a reasonable chance of success. All this information the salesman prepares, and through consultation with the program and promotion departments he outlines a definite idea of the type of program, whether musical, dramatic, news, etc., that would be most desirable for all purposes. Auditions of the proposed program are then arranged; and if they are satisfactory, another advertiser begins his series of broadcasts.

The local sales department begins its most serious work after the client has been secured in order to keep the advertiser's service continuous. This work consists of guarding the proper scheduling of the program, assuring correct pronunciation of the client's name and product, advising against excessive length of commercials, arranging for publicity and promotion activities, and making the station's entire organization familiar with the nature of the program and its purpose. Frequent contacts are made with both the client and his advertising representatives so as to maintain good will through proof of sincere interest in the success of the advertising. In general, the local sales department of any major station is one of the most important public relations contacts of the station.

CHAPTER 17

THE NETWORK SALES ORGANIZATION

IT IS AN INTERESTING FACT that the method of financing network broadcasting was first proposed in 1925 by a national manufacturer of food products. This enterprising businessman suggested that as a return for mention of one of his concern's products he would be glad to pay whatever expenses would be involved in feeding the program over the sixteen stations of the first American network, the former American Telephone and Telegraph Company Network. Today, this formula of economic operation has financed a great industry, and the support of networks by American advertisers has made possible the present system of network broadcasting.

The net sale of "time" over the four major networks now amounts to approximately one hundred million dollars per year, an income secured and maintained in large part by the sales organizations of the networks. The broadcasting companies in turn pay a substantial portion of this income to the 598 stations affiliated with the various network systems.

As the network sales departments are responsible for the sale of time for the entire group of stations, the sales representatives act in effect as partial agents for all the affiliated stations as well as for the originating network. The network salesman, therefore, plays a vital part in maintaining the necessary income for the operation of the entire broadcasting system.

THE ORGANIZATION OF THE SALES DEPARTMENT

The sales departments of the networks are directed by vice presidents in charge of national sales, who have their headquarters in New York City. Serving each principal geographic area are sales departments headed by sales managers for each division. The Eastern divisions cover the entire Atlantic seaboard and usually the Southeast and Middle Atlantic states and New England. The Central or Western divisions are located in Chicago and cover the Mid-West and the Mississippi Valley from the Gulf to Canada and from Ohio to Colorado. The Pacific Coast divisions are responsible generally for those states west of the Rocky Mountains. In each of these sales headquarters there are network sales traffic departments and sales promotion divisions working in close conjunction with the salesmen. Throughout the country there are fewer than one hundred network representatives responsible for the sale of time on all of the four networks, and as the average amount of net billing handled by network salesmen is more than one million dollars per man, it is clear that each individual representative has a high degree of responsibility.

Usually the sales departments of each network sectional office hold meetings at least once a week in which new policies are explained, program ideas are discussed in relation to specific clients and time periods, and reports are given on prospects and on activities in connection with established clients. In these meetings, a representative of the program package sales division is usually present, as well as the network traffic manager of each division.

As there is a limited amount of time that is available for sale and each sales section of the company is making an effort to sell the open periods, constant communication must be kept between offices so that options can be registered in their proper order to avoid selling the same period to two different advertisers in different sections of the country. It is for this reason that the sales traffic department is such a vital part of each division.

The sales traffic department co-ordinates the commercial activities by contact with the traffic departments in New York, Washington, Hollywood, and Chicago and clears by teletype all options for a period, requests for station clearances, switching operations, local and sectional cut-in announcements, and the ordering of special circuits through the telephone companies for pickups outside the main originating studios of the networks. The network sales traffic manager is also responsible for the preparation of the facilities contracts, which are the agreements between the network and the advertising agency, and in general is in constant contact with other officers by wire in clearing time periods, ordering stations, advising of changes in service, procedure, and policy.

FUNCTIONS OF THE SALES DEPARTMENT

The three principal functions of the sales department are:
1. Sale of time to new advertisers
2. Sale of talent
3. Handling and co-ordinating of details in connection with established clients

The Sales of Time and Facilities. The usual practice in the network sales structure is to assign exclusive territories to the sales representatives, who call on the advertisers and agencies in their particular areas. When they are able to secure the active interest of a prospective client, the representative ascertains from both the advertising agency and the advertising department of the prospective client as much as he possibly can about the distribution and all other market factors of the client's product. The next step is to present the best time period that he has available and a list of stations which will cover the prospect's sales territories adequately. In connection with the presentation of his facilities, the salesman works with the sales promotion and merchandising department of his local office and presents not only costs but coverage maps and other statistical data which are available through the various established surveys, such as The Cooperative Analysis of Broadcasting, A. C. Nielsen and Company, and C. E. Hooper, Inc.[1]

Factors which are of paramount importance are the competition the period is faced with, as well as the preceding and following programs and the type of audience which the period will reach. Together with the presentation of the facilities and coverage is usually a report on merchandising and publicity co-operation that will be received by the client from both the network and its affiliated stations. This material is worked out

[1] See Chapter 19.

in conjunction with the press department and the promotion department, as well as with the station-relations division of the local office.

The Sale of Talent. In a good many cases, the present-day advertising agencies develop their own programs for their clients, but frequently they seek the co-operation of the net-work program and production personnel. The sales representa-tive, in these cases, arranges for meetings between the radio department of the agency and the program officials of the net-work. In the event that the advertiser has a program already planned, the sales representative must secure the approval of his program and legal departments, and after the program has been auditioned and accepted, the salesman must follow through on the assignment of studios, engineers, and other details necessary for the handling of the production.

When the client and agency do not have a particular program planned for their use, the program package sales division and program departments of the networks are consulted for the best possible production to fit the specific time period and product as well as the client's budget.

It is not generally known to the layman that in recent years the networks have discontinued their talent bureaus, and the various actors and musicians (with the exception of staff artists who are employed by the networks for sustaining programs), are now either "free lance" operators or are represented by in-dividual actors' agents. However, the networks continue to offer programs for sale to clients on a "package" basis. The term "package" indicates a program that is offered in its en-tirety, including complete cast, announcers, music, script, and production, at a blanket or flat price to cover the entire operation.

When a network has a time period available, the sales de-partment and the program package sales department discuss the best possible program that can be built on a package basis to be placed in the available period. This program becomes in effect a sustaining broadcast which is available for sale, and network representatives then attempt to sell both the time and the program as a combination package to clients and prospects.

Handling and Co-ordinating of Details in Connection with Established Clients. On the leading networks of the country, an extremely high percentage of the business handled is on a renewal basis. Therefore, the sales representatives of these organizations spend a substantial part of their time handling and co-ordinating the details of their established clients' operations with the network. Because of the natural emphasis on providing service, some of the networks have changed the name of their representatives from salesmen to account executives or contact men. In many cases, this is a more logical term, as the function of the sales representative is not only to co-ordinate the activities of the other departments as they affect the client, but also to represent the client and the advertising agency within the network itself.

For example, the network salesman is called upon to confer frequently with nine different departments in connection with the handling of an account. He has frequent dealings with the program and production details. He consults with promotion, merchandising, and press department representatives for the continued support of the program through the newspapers and point-of-sale merchandising. Network salesmen in most cases are responsible for credits in connection with losses of time or interruptions in service due to mechanical causes, and in this connection they must work closely with the accounting departments. Frequently the client wishes to add stations, which are cleared through the sales traffic department, and if there is difficulty in securing necessary time on the local outlets, the station relations department and the sales representatives exert their best efforts to clear the desired time.

There are so many specialized departments in a modern network that it is obviously necessary to have one particular department co-ordinating the various contacts with the clients, and these are handled through the network representative because he is most familiar with the clients' and advertising agencies' policies and plans. By having the sales department serve as the focal point for the various departments within the organization, considerable confusion and overlapping is avoided and more efficient service is provided for the client.

Co-ordination is especially important because of the fact that in many cases various phases of a network commercial program may be handled in two or more offices; a program may be produced in Hollywood, the client may be located in the Chicago area, and the advertising agency may be located in New York. In such a case, a sales representative would be assigned to each of the three offices affected. It is obvious that in order to provide smooth operation under these circumstances, the proper channels and contacts must be carefully maintained by the various sales representatives. In a combination contact such as is illustrated above, the sales department deals with the client as the senior authority and carries the responsibility of the account.

Because of the many multiple contacts that modern network advertising makes necessary, network representatives are seldom paid on a commission basis and are usually salaried employees. It would be manifestly difficult to apply commissions on a sale of time or talent when two or more network offices might be involved, as well as the many departments within each office.

For budget purposes in the operation of the various offices of the network, the sales are usually cleared in somewhat the following fashion: fifty per cent of the credit of the sale to the office which deals with the client; twenty-five per cent to the office in which the program is broadcast; twenty-five per cent to the office which deals with the advertising agency. Some networks deviate from this procedure and apply full credit to the office through which the order is received for the business, which in most cases would be through the advertising agency.

In addition to selling time and talent, the function of the sales representative might well be described as the responsibility for the reflection of the sum of the knowledge and experience of the various specialized departments within the network, and the co-ordination of their services for the benefit of the clients.

CHAPTER 18

ADVERTISING AND PROMOTION

SINCE THE EARLIEST DAYS of broadcasting, radio stations and networks have followed the practice of advertising their wares and services to prospective clients and to the public in general. This function of broadcasting is based upon the theory that though the world may eventually beat a path to the door of the latest mousetrap inventor, the path turns into a highway more rapidly if provided with adequate and frequent sign posts.

Broadcasting, an advertising medium, believes in the slogan "it pays to advertise," not only as applied to its clients but also as applied to itself. Even in the smallest stations the jobs of promoting and advertising the station are not left to chance. Within the time available and limited only by the ingenuity of the staff and budgetary restrictions, the station's story is told again and again. Whether the station is a two hundred and fifty watter or the clear channel key of a national network, the objectives are much alike:

> To familiarize and impress advertising agencies, clients, and prospective clients, influential individuals and organizations, and the general listening public with the station's coverage, the quality of its programs, the buying characteristics of its audience, its unusual achievements, and its constant effort to achieve perfection of operation in the public interest.

The means by which these ends are achieved are as varied as the entire field of advertising. A promotion department must be ready at the drop of a hat to create anything from a floral float in a Decoration Day parade to the design for a million match pack covers; it must be able to dig up the station's coverage story as an aid to the sales department and give the public nineteen reasons why this particular station is great in its field. Ideally, a radio station promotion director should be a combination circus barker, statistician, art director, and showman. There are few such, but the goal is there, nevertheless.

Generally speaking, the chief occupations of the promotion department will include production of mailing pieces, pamphlets, folders, leaflets, brochures, and books; presentations of the station's coverage story; advertisements in trade journals, newspapers, and general magazines; special campaigns and ideas that can be worked out in program or announcement form so that the station can use its own medium to tell its own story.

For purposes of study, this subject is one phase of broadcasting that may be safely considered from the NBC standpoint for two reasons. First of all, most promotional operations of the network have their counterparts in local stations. There will be differences, of course, but these usually hinge on considerations of degree and interpretation of basic problems. Execution of ideas can be expected to vary, too, depending on the ingenuity of the individual promotion man and his particular method of approach to a given problem.[1] For much the same reasons, a parallel will be found in the promotional activities of other networks.

Structure of the NBC advertising and promotion department is similar to that of other sections of the Company. The national director, with headquarters in New York, guides and correlates the work of the several subdivisions, including institutional promotion, network sales promotion, public service promotion, and promotion of WEAF, the New York City outlet owned by NBC. In addition to handling over-all plans for promotion on a national scale, the department also acts in an advisory capacity to develop promotion for the national spot sales department, the radio recording department, and NBC's owned and operated stations in Chicago, Washington, Cleveland, Denver, and San Francisco.

In outline, the functions of the various divisions of the promotion department may be summarized as follows:

[1] KSTP, St. Paul-Minneapolis, has done an outstanding job, found it of direct aid in overcoming what might be considered a drawback in station frequency.

Institutional Promotion Division: promotes NBC, its programs and its activities to the general public. Prepares all material of a general institutional nature, such as informational brochures about the company; also produces promotional material for all NBC departments not specifically serviced by another promotion division.

Network Sales Promotion Division: has dual function of keeping present advertisers loyal to the network and of influencing prospective advertisers to use NBC service. It supplies clients and their agencies with "success stories," listening data, reports on promotional and press activities undertaken in behalf of a client's program; prepares advertisements about NBC for trade journals and newspapers. It backs up such advertising campaigns with direct mail pieces to its clients and potential customers. It aids in making new sales by providing the sales department with factual material, listener surveys, coverage maps, market analyses for presentation to prospective clients. It also supplies stations on the network with promotional material that may be useful in local campaigns. (In particular, the NBC Parade of Stars promotion, which will be discussed in some detail later.)

Public Service Promotion Division: concentrates on special information for educational and other influential groups, dealing chiefly with the programs planned and executed by the NBC Public Service Department. Produces direct mail folders for all important program series of this nature; produces promotion aids for affiliated stations, advertisements in music and educational publications; a monthly eight-page folder "This is the National Broadcasting Company" which is sent to schools, clubs, libraries, educators, etc. for general information and reference. The division also prepares special displays for use at educational meetings and conferences.

Station Promotion Division: [2] concentrates on promoting the station as a local medium for advertisers in the local market. Audience building promotions are undertaken through extensive newspaper advertising campaigns, through exploitation in connection with local events, and through publicity campaigns

[2] Actual title is "WEAF Promotion Division," but since functions are the same at WMAQ or any other M. and O. (managed and owned) station, the general term "Station" is used to avoid duplication of material.

in co-operation with the press department. Material on the station's effectiveness is presented in trade journal advertisements, direct mail material, and in ammunition provided to the station's local sales group.

There are two subdivisions of NBC promotional activities that are not directly comparable to local station promotion departments although methods utilized are basic to any promotion campaign. The sections referred to are the national spot sales promotion division and the radio recording promotion division. The first of these has its counterpart in the promotion divisions of CBS and American which are intended to stress the value of stations these networks own or represent in spot sales. NBC has thirteen stations in this category, six of them wholly owned. The others, such as the four owned by Westinghouse, are represented by NBC as national spot sales agent.

NBC radio recording promotion, as a national network operation, has no direct parallel in other network or station advertising activities. This does not mean that other networks do not make and sell or promote their services of making and selling records. But it is a fact that the NBC recording service is considerably broader in scope than any kindred station or network operation, and promotion methods are in scale.

So much for general structure. The tools of promotion and the methods for using them will be considered next. However, it is well to insert a cautionary word at this point. No outline of promotion methods can ever be a pat formula for achieving a smash hit. Circumstances alter cases in promotion as well as in other fields; and if a given formula will not apply to a local situation, then a new one will have to be created. Thus, it takes a nimble set of wits plus certain standard promotional procedures to achieve the maximum end result. What follows here will be in the nature of "standard procedures."

MAKING TIME SALES

One of the principal ways in which a promotion department can justify its budget is through aid given in making time sales. Assistance to the sales force may come in the form of presentations, maps, market and audience statistics, and kindred types of sales ammunition.

Presentations. These may take the form of an illustrated folio or a comprehensive display marshalling all the available "reason why" copy and building up to the conclusion that the prospective sponsor should buy time on the particular station or network making the presentation. The sequence of points covered might include an introduction, a radio success story using comparable products as a yardstick, facts about the station or the network, the time period under consideration, the suggested program, program and time cost estimates, and the conclusion.

Expertly prepared presentations are brief and interesting. Attractive colors in stock and covers may be used to advantage, but care should be exercised to prevent the introduction of anything that will detract from the sales message. Every sales point is so emphasized that the reader may thumb through the presentation and understand the message without reading all the copy. Whatever copy there is in a presentation should be only an enlargement of the main headings and subheadings. It must be remembered that a prospect is not necessarily interested in what a station has to say. His attention must be snared and his interest developed by quality of thinking, method of presentation, and style of writing. The subject should be covered fully but without loss of interest.

Maps. Maps showing both day and night circulation of the station or network are essential. Advertisers co-ordinate their sales territories with the coverage of the station in order to determine its effect on sales, cost per listener, etc.

There was a time when the coverage of a station was indicated by a circle with a one hundred mile radius, the location of the station being used as the center of the circle. Now, however, advertisers insist on much more scientific and accurate circulation data, and in order to satisfy their demand various methods of measuring the listening audience of a station or network have been devised. These methods are discussed in the chapter on Audience Measurement.

It has been found that listening habits in areas where more than one station is heard are determined by the programs. In remote areas, the listening habits of the people are determined by the power of the nearest radio station. The power of the station rather than the program then determines the attention a program receives in remote listening areas. This being the case, neither a small nor a large station can claim complete coverage in its territory unless it can prove that its programs are the most desirable. In remote areas the listening habits of the people are determined by the power of the nearest radio station rather than by the programs. People usually have very little choice; they have to listen to what they can get or go without.

Market and Audience Statistics. Market and audience data should accompany station maps. Such statistics may be typed on a separate sheet, or they may be printed on the back of the maps.

The information that advertisers usually desire is the number of radio-equipped homes in the station's listening area, the potential size of the listening audience that the station enjoys, data concerning the industries that lie within the station's coverage area, the per capita wealth of the people, bank deposits, etc. These data may be secured from the local Chambers of Commerce or by special surveys made at the station's expense. The more complete the market information is the more useful it will be.

Maps showing the circulation of the station, the market covered by the station, and the cost of facilities are statistical in character and need only to be inserted in their proper places in any presentation.

Whether presentations, maps, market and listening statistics, and costs are prepared for an individual station or for a network, the procedure is the same. Even though the making of maps and the estimating of costs for a network operation is of necessity more difficult than for an individual station, the fundamentals remain the same. When an outline is sound, it may be expanded or abridged without difficulty.

KEEPING ACCOUNTS SOLD

Once the sale is made, the promotion department takes on the continuing chore of helping to keep the account sold. This portion of departmental activity is aimed at "the trade": clients, advertising agencies, sales prospects, distributors, and retailers.

The most generally useful tools to accomplish the result include (*a*) trade paper advertisements, (*b*) sales letters, (*c*) direct mail pieces, (*d*) periodical news bulletins, (*e*) courtesy announcements and radio fan programs, (*f*) newspaper advertisements, (*g*) gadgets, (*h*) progress reports. In the following paragraphs, these tools are considered in some detail.

Trade Paper Advertisements. Those publications are used extensively whose subscribers include the type of reader who would have reason to buy time on a station.

Radio station advertisements in trade papers are now made as attractive and interesting as general magazine advertisements usually are. For a long time advertisers felt that their trade paper advertisements should consist of nothing but an uninteresting tabulation of statistics. Now, however, individual programs available for sponsorship, circulation data, interesting facts about the market, and testimonials to results secured for present clients are effectively being featured in advertisements that are designed for the trade.

Sales Letters. Sales letters are a well-known form of promotion. Because they have been used so extensively, it is difficult to write a letter that will command attention and create sufficient interest to accomplish the purpose for which it is intended. A mere announcement can well be made by letter, but attractive cards that make possible a greater selection of colors and styles of type very often may be employed with more telling effect. Letters are comparatively inexpensive, but to be effective they have to be prepared with great skill. They are the simplest form of mailing piece and the most hazardous when their high mortality rate is taken into consideration.

Direct Mail Pieces. Folders, brochures, and booklets are often used to carry a special message with effective results.

But before considering this subject in detail, it is all-important to note that the best direct mail campaign will be useless unless it is sent to the right people. Before a campaign is launched, the promotion department must know exactly where the material is going to be sent. Names for the list may be obtained in a variety of places: from salesmen, from trade papers, from trade directories, etc. The list should be cross-indexed and classified so that a given section can be utilized for a given job. Classification may include such titles as clients, prospects, client agencies, prospect agencies, client key men, agency key men, industries, locations.

Getting back to the material itself, the promotion man must decide for himself which or what combination of the three forms should be utilized. Whether a single piece or a series, the major point to remember is that the message must be presented clearly, concisely, and forcefully so that the impression made on the recipient will be that for which the piece was designed.

A successful direct mail campaign is a well calculated proposition, and it is definitely not hit-or-miss. It must have continuity either in the sequence of ideas, form of the piece, color or copy style. In order to insure such continuity, all pieces in a particular series should be laid out at the same time, although it is, of course, not necessary that they all be completed and sent to the printer at the same time. As to frequency, experience indicates that not more than ten days should elapse between mailings and that mailings should be timed to reach recipients about mid-week.

The important points to consider in developing a mail piece are headlines; copy; form and size of the piece; and art work including a decision on the number and kind of colors to be employed, the printing process to be used, whether halftones or line cuts are to be used, and the character of the printing stock. A mailing piece must be attractive in order to get attention, so it is necessary to weld the various components into one attractive whole that will get the recipient's attention long enough for a perusal.

Headings are written so as to carry the complete thought that the designer wishes to impress on the reader. Thus, if a recipient glances over the folder and reads the headings, he should receive the message that the sender wishes him to get. The copy under each heading is a more complete treatment of the thought it expresses.

Art work is used to emphasize the sales points embodied in the written word. When instructions are issued to the artist who is to handle that important part of the work, he is told the number of colors that are to be used and the method of reproduction, whether letterpress, planograph, or lithograph, so that he will prepare his drawings to produce the best results from that particular method of printing.

The color of the ink is extremely important. There are many shades of red, blue, and yellow; and it is not only necessary to select each shade independently but also to study them in combination to be sure that the finished job will be sharp and pleasing. Care should be taken to avoid the combination of two colors of medium tone; it is better to choose one color that is very deep and another color light enough in weight and rich enough in tone to produce a sharp, clean contrast.

The choice of stock to be used is important. Coated stock takes halftones very well while antique paper will produce most disappointing results. The weight of the stock must be carefully considered. Will the paper fold well or will it crack and split? Is it heavy enough to give character to the mailing piece, or will it be so light when finished that it will be limp and lacking in dignity?

Periodical News Bulletins. Many a station considers it advisable to cultivate the retailers located within its primary area. They are the final link in the chain of distribution between the manufacturer and the consumer, and their good will or lack of it can materially alter the productiveness of a station's territory. Interested dealers will prominently display products advertised over the station; others may hide them and produce them only when specific requests are made by customers.

In addition to working with retailers' organizations, some

stations reach the dealers at least once a month by means of a mailing piece that is of special interest to them. A small tabloid type of bulletin or newspaper is being used by several stations for this purpose. These publications carry photographs of well-known radio stars appearing on popular programs and stories of the various features, both new and old, all of which are connected with the name of the sponsor and his products. These bulletins range in size from a double page, eight and one-half inches by eleven inches, to sixteen pages, twelve inches by eighteen inches. One station has aimed its publications at the listening audience and sells subscriptions at fifty cents a year which covers twelve monthly mailings.

Courtesy Announcements and Radio Fan Programs. Every station has a certain amount of time that is not sponsored. This time is filled with what are called sustaining programs: features, the cost of which is borne by the station. At least one sustaining feature is usually designed so that announcements may be woven into its structure; a program of this type may thus include "courtesy" announcements for new programs prior to their appearance. Two courtesy announcements each day for a week, but not in the same fifteen-minute or half-hour period, are usually sufficient to satisfy the great majority of clients. Following is a sample of this type of announcement:

> And now for the news many of you will be glad to hear. We have just received word that "Duffy's Tavern," featuring Ed Gardner, will come to Station WMAQ next Friday, 7:30 to 8:00 P.M. Be sure to tune in.

Stations have also what are called "station breaks," that is, twenty-second intervals between programs during which very short announcements are made. Some station breaks are sold to advertisers, but those that remain unsold can be used to advantage to build up the station's audience by announcing programs that are to be broadcast at later periods in the day. The following brief announcement is typical of those used in station breaks:

> The "Contented Hour" presents a salute to Great Britain at 9:00 tonight. Listen to WMAQ — 670 on your dial.

If a station has the time at its disposal, a very useful promotion device is the radio fan or gossip program, which can take from five to thirty minutes, depending on available time. Material for the show consists of feature stories and gossip items about the station's programs as well as advance promotions for shows that are due to start on the station in the near future. Preparation of material for such programs may be a function of the press department, as in the case of NBC, or it may be an assignment for the continuity branch. It should be noted that this particular device can also be classified as an audience promotion. The same quality of purpose is found in the next topic.

Newspaper Advertisements. Many radio stations have direct newspaper connections, and it is almost universal practice to have one medium aid in promoting the other. Where no such business connections exist, radio stations may find it useful to seek the arrangement of a reciprocal space-time agreement. This means that the newspaper exchanges space for time on the air. The newspaper may use its air time for a news broadcast or commentary by its news specialists; the radio station, in turn, utilizes the paper's space to advertise programs.

Gadgets. Attention getters of various sorts are used both by stations and by networks. These may consist of reminders in the way of match packs, desk pieces, pocket pieces, or some small article of worth that is not likely to be thrown away. Generally, their sales message consists of very little more than the station's call letters and frequency, and possibly a slogan such as "The Chicago Station Most People Listen to Most."

Book match manufacturers are well organized to handle consumer distribution, either nationally or on whatever kind of selective basis a station may desire. Trade distribution is generally undertaken by the station itself.

Desk pieces take many forms. A fair example is the "Hooperdroop" plaster figurine of comical lines, sent to station and agency men in connection with NBC's summer program promotion. Call letter ash trays are frequently encountered, and there are a dozen and one other omnipresent reminders.

Progress Reports. Periodic reports to the sponsor on what

is being done to promote his particular program are among the most useful devices for keeping the client satisfied with the station and its service.

While it is reasonable to expect that the client will be aware of much of the work done in his behalf, he can get the complete story only when the station hands it to him. Full reports on promotion should be compiled for the client and his agency at regular intervals. These should contain copies of station advertisements written in his behalf, copies of stories about his show prepared by the press department, copies of any pictures or newspaper mat proofs that the press department has released, copies of any air show gossip items or courtesy announcements made, all available press clippings, copies of any articles that have appeared in the station's news bulletin for retailers, and copies of any special folders that may have been issued in which the client's success story has been highlighted.

Keeping the radio audience loyal to the station is also one of the promotion department's duties. This is a responsibility shared with program and press. The creation of listener-getting devices, which can be worked out in program form, or the development of audience promotions which have useful press possibilities are offshoots of an intelligent promotion mind at work. The department is also responsible for preparing the copy that will appear in newspaper advertisements intended for public reading, as previously discussed under newspaper-radio reciprocity.

It is not sufficient to keep repeating a statement that "our station is good." Something has got to be done to prove it and to convince the audience that the statement is true. An efficient promotion department will, therefore, endeavor to arrange campaigns that help to personalize the station from the listener's standpoint. Cooking schools with audience participation, salutes to cities within the primary radiating area, fashion and garden shows with air pickups, assistance to local and outlying communities in local charity shows and bond drives, contests on the air that are designed to keep the listeners listening, arrangement of public speaking engagements for station personnel, and sponsorship of station displays at county fairs and other gatherings are the kinds of things that help to achieve a promotional goal with the audience.

In the outline of NBC's promotion department, mention was made of the company's annual Parade of Stars promotion campaign. The 1944 campaign was the third of its kind and embraced every useful standard promotion device plus a few new ones, new from a radio standpoint, at least.

The key to the campaign is the fact that a large number of NBC "name" performers return to the air in the fall months, setting the pattern and the tone of the network's programs for the succeeding months until the next vacation season. The Parade of Stars promotion is built around this annual back trek although the campaign is designed as a continuous effort which carries on week after week and simply utilizes the fall return as a substantial launching platform.

The campaign was designed for both its national and local effect. For its part on the national scene, NBC undertook an extensive program of trade paper advertisements plus considerable lineage in newspapers within the territories of the M. and O. stations. In 1944 the company utilized motion picture trailers for the first time. These were made up of existing footage from feature films in which NBC name stars had appeared, and this portion of the campaign was designed for showing in 117 NBC affiliated-station cities.

In addition, the company prepared several network radio shows, designed to display both its daytime and nighttime talent. It also utilized the regular promotion forms of direct mail, sales letters, etc. to round out the national picture.

On the local scene each individual affiliated station was provided with a so-called "bandbox," a collection of folios designed to exploit every network show carried on that station. Each folio carried a brief recorded "plug" by program personalities for use on the air, suggested newspaper stories, photographs, news mats, suggested courtesy announcements, ad copy and mats, and a collection of promotion suggestions and display layouts, car card and billboard advertising copy, etc.

The Parade of Stars campaign is mentioned here for two purposes. For one thing, it illustrates how vast in scope a modern promotion campaign can be; but probably more important though less apparent in this outline, it shows the importance of the local station promotion man. While the network can depend on its own forces for carrying out such a campaign in M. and O. station cities, these cities are far in the minority. More than one hundred promotion men, employed by the affiliates of NBC, were responsible for the actual pick and shovel work, the local inspiration, ingenuity, pavement-pounding, and money-spending that made the campaign a Parade of Stars and not a parade of stares — the vacant kind.

5

THE AUDIENCE

CHAPTER 19

AUDIENCE MEASUREMENT

EVER SINCE THE ADVENT of commercial broadcasting, there has been a demand on the part of advertisers for accurate information on the size of the listening audience that any particular program enjoys, a demand that the radio industry has honestly wished to supply. Stations and networks are interested in the size of the listening audience that they command, for that is their stock in trade; an advertiser is concerned over the size of the audience that his particular program reaches. He is paying for a certain estimated circulation and it is upon the effectiveness of his entertainment that his sales and profits depend.

During the past few years various types of survey services have been developed, all for the purpose of securing an indication of the popularity of radio programs, as determined by the relative number of people listening to each one, and also the size of the potential listening audience that is available at any specified time either day or night according to time zones. The number of telephone and other contacts made in each locality is so scientifically weighted that the result is representative of the listening habits of the people living in each area. Stations and networks use this service not only to watch the listening trends of the programs they carry but also to compare their standing with that of competitive stations or networks.

Advertisers are keenly interested in these services, because they are their only check on the manner in which the quality of their program is being maintained. If the popularity rating is going down, steps are taken to improve the program, for a loss in listening audience is usually reflected in a proportionate loss in sales and profits.

These surveys are not intended to be more than an indication. The facilities for making such measurements do not blanket the entire country, and consequently the results secured in the spots that they do cover cannot with any degree of accuracy be applied to the entire nation. Listening in remote areas does not correspond with that in the spots in which these surveys are made. The results are merely guideposts and must be regarded as such if one is to escape difficulties that are more or less serious.

These services are sold to advertisers, stations, and networks at a cost which in each case is in direct proportion to the need of the subscriber. An advertiser having one program on the air will pay less than one having two or three programs. An advertising agency having only one radio campaign running will pay much less than an agency having more than one campaign. The size of the station or network is taken into consideration when determining their respective costs for these services.

Special surveys are often made to prove a definite point. One might wish to know the number of dogs in radio homes in order to convince a manufacturer of dog food that a radio campaign would be productive. There are a number of questions that arise in the regular routine of a radio station which a scientifically planned survey may answer very accurately.

At the present time there are three independent survey organizations used generally by the radio industry, whose self-appointed task it is to measure the size of the radio listening audience at all times during the day and night. They are C. E. Hooper, Inc., 51 East Forty-Second Street, New York City; The Cooperative Analysis of Broadcasting, 330 West Forty-Second Street, New York City; and A. C. Nielsen Company, 2101 West Howard Street, Chicago, Illinois.

C. E. HOOPER, INC.

C. E. Hooper, Inc. is an independent organization which specializes in providing radio advertisers, advertising agencies, and the radio industry with measurement reports on the radio audience. They employ the coincidental telephone method of interview, a technique they have used since 1934. The coincidental method scores the average audience of every network program while the feature is on the air. The Hooper coincidental telephone survey questions are:

1. Were you listening to your radio just now?
2. To what program were you listening, please?
3. Over what station is that program coming?
4. (a) What advertiser puts on that program?
   (b) Audience composition questions

The interviews are distributed evenly and continuously over the last thirteen minutes of each fifteen-minute broadcast period.

Sample. The coincidental sample used in measuring the audience that listens to a program varies directly with the length of the program and the number of Hooper checking cities transmitting the program. The entire thirty-two-city or "National" sample is approximately as follows:

Half-Hour Programs	1320 homes called
One-Hour Programs	2640 homes called
Quarter-Hour, 3 times weekly	1980 homes called
Quarter-Hour, 5 times weekly	3300 homes called

Interviewing Schedule. The interviewing weeks begin uniformly on the first and fifteenth day of each month for the evening report. The interviewing week for the daytime report begins on the eighth of the month. (Exception: adjustments are made in interviewing dates where possible when national holidays fall within scheduled weeks.) The schedule by local time periods is as follows:

Evening Report (Sunday through Saturday)

Eastern Time Zone	6:00 P.M. – 10:30 P.M.
Central Time Zone	5:00 P.M. – 10:00 P.M.
Mountain Time Zone	4:00 P.M. – 10:00 P.M.
Pacific Coast Time Zone	3:00 P.M. – 10:15 P.M.

Daytime Report (Monday through Saturday)

Eastern Time Zone	8:00 A.M. – 6:00 P.M.
Central Time Zone	8:00 A.M. – 5:00 P.M.
Mountain Time Zone	8:00 A.M. – 4:00 P.M.
Pacific Coast Time Zone	8:00 A.M. – 3:00 P.M.

Sunday Afternoon

Eastern Time Zone	12:00 Noon – 6:00 P.M.
Central Time Zone	11:00 A.M. – 5:00 P.M.
Mountain Time Zone	8:00 A.M. – 4:00 P.M.
Pacific Coast Time Zone	8:00 A.M. – 3:00 P.M.

No interviewing is conducted prior to 8:00 A.M. local time.
All evening interviewing stops not later than 10:30 P.M. local
time.

C. E. Hooper measurement reports are based on findings
secured by calling telephone homes in the following thirty-two
cities which are geographically well distributed over the
nation:

Eastern. Detroit, Buffalo, Cleveland, Pittsburgh, Washington, Cincinnati, Richmond, Boston, Providence, New York,
Philadelphia, Baltimore.

North Central. Minneapolis-St. Paul, Des Moines, Chicago,
Kansas City, Indianapolis, St. Louis, Louisville.

Southern. Oklahoma City, Dallas, Houston, Memphis, Birmingham, New Orleans, Atlanta.

Mountain. Salt Lake City, Denver.

Pacific. Seattle, Portland, Oakland, San Francisco, Los
Angeles.

Section		Per Cent Radio Homes [1]	Per Cent Hooper Sample
Eastern	12 cities	46.4	45.2
North Central	7 cities	25.1	23.8
Southern	7 cities	15.8	16.7
Mountain	2 cities	3.1	4.8
Pacific	4 cities	9.6	9.5

[1] Based on 1940 Census – NAB projection of Radio Families, published
August, 1942.

All the regular Hooper interviewing cities meet the following requirements:

1. Local service by all four networks – American, CBS,
MBS,[2] NBC.

[2] Ogden service in Salt Lake City.

2. An adequate signal supplied by each local network station within the interviewing area.

3. A sufficiently large list of telephone subscribers.

The number of homes that Hooper calls, whether or not the telephone is answered, is regarded as one hundred per cent. If out of one hundred calls including uncompleted calls, twenty responders say that they are listening to their radio, the potential listening audience at that time is rated as twenty per cent. If out of the one hundred calls, five are listening to any particular program, the popularity percentage of that feature is five per cent. The percentage of the available audience at that time, however, is five-twentieths or twenty-five per cent for that particular program.

In the midwinter 1944 season, Hooper released the results of a survey conducted in the manner outlined above which covered eighty-nine selected cities which were representative of the 412 cities of over 25,000 population in the United States. These "U.S. Urban Hooperatings" provided for the first time the means of determining the size of radio audiences among people living in places other than very large cities, and the number of listening homes in a large and specific segment of our national population.

It is not Hooper's intention to conduct this study on a continuous basis, however, since once the relationship between the thirty-two-city rating and the eighty-nine-city rating is established, it cannot be expected to show significant variation. In addition, the telephone samples are too rapidly exhausted in the cities of smaller populations.

COOPERATIVE ANALYSIS OF BROADCASTING (CROSSLEY)

The Cooperative Analysis of Broadcasting is a non-profit organization that had its beginning in 1929 in the Radio Committee of the Association of National Advertisers. The seed was the skeptical curiosity with which this committee viewed the value of radio listening, particularly the size of program audiences. This interest, quickened by the committee's quest for information, led a handful of leading radio advertisers to finance individual surveys. The findings, which indicated the need as well as the value of continuous and co-operatively financed research, were rounded into a report which the A.N.A. published.

The report, high-lighting the usefulness of guideposts in the maze of claims and uncertainties that had mushroomed with the swift growth of the newcomer among advertising media, prompted the committee to request Crossley, Inc., which was already engaged in audience measurement research, to plan a co-operative system of investigation. Field work began on March 1, 1930, less than fourteen months after the A.N.A. Committee's first report, and has continued uninterruptedly ever since.

Supervision in the first four years of operation was exercised by the A.N.A. Committee in conjunction with a companion committee of the American Association of Advertising Agencies. A reorganization in 1934 led to the appointment of a governing committee, now the board of governors, in which both agencies and advertisers have an equal voice in supervision. Thus, the Cooperative Analysis of Broadcasting is truly representative of all the buyers of radio time and talent. The board, nominated by the American Association of Advertising Agencies and the Association of National Advertisers, contains three agency members and an equal number of advertiser members.

The cost of the Cooperative Analysis of Broadcasting is borne by the leading advertising agencies, advertisers, and networks. Operating funds are collected by dues prorated in accordance with each member's interest in radio advertising.

October, 1942, marked the introduction of CAB's latest addition to its services. It provides a dual measurement of program popularity. Until then, the CAB had measured only conscious impression. The day-part telephone technique, sometimes termed "recall," ascertained the popularity of programs that possessed memory value. But the 1942 improvement, in essence, utilized the coincidental telephone technique to measure the flow of listening irrespective of memory value. Actually the two techniques, day-part and coincidental, have been integrated.

The coincidental rating scores the average audience of every network program at the minute of the interviews. The day-part rating reports the conscious impression that every network program has created. Ratings are expressed in percentage terms — that is, a rating of 20 means that 20 out of 100 heard a program. Coincidental ratings are computed on the total number of dialings, regardless of whether the interviews were completed. Completed telephone interviews, of course, are the base for calculating day-part conscious impression ratings.

The Cooperative Analysis of Broadcasting, which uses telephone calls as the source of its information, divides each day into 32 part-days, each of which overlaps three others as shown on the chart below:

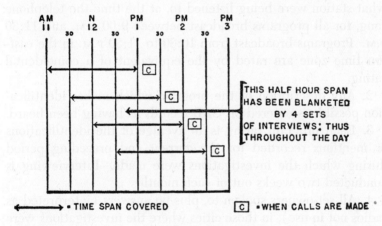

Figure 6

CAB RECALL METHOD

The primary function of this report is to measure the relative size of the radio audience that remembers having heard individual programs, and the average audience for these same programs. The information is obtained by telephone interviewing in eighty-one cities that have a population of 50,000 or over.

The size of the samples used parallels the populations, not only by geographical areas but by city size as well. That is, if fourteen per cent of the populations of cities of 50,000 or more population are in cities of 500,000 to 1,000,000, then fourteen per cent of CAB calls will be made in those cities. Thus, results provide a measure of listening in a cross-section of telephone homes in cities of more than 50,000 population.

Prior to 1944, CAB used a thirty-three-city sample and employed first the day-part of "recall" and later the coincidental interviewing techniques. The thirty-three-city sample has been discontinued and attention is now focused on various measurements made within the eighty-one-city sample.

The ratings for CAB reports are obtained as follows:

1. The listening data are obtained by interviewers asking, during the period the program is broadcast, what program and what station were being listened to, at the time the telephone rang, for all programs broadcast between 9:00 A.M. and 11:30 P.M. Programs broadcast from 10:30 to 11:30 P.M. in the eastern time zone are rated by the equivalent of a coincidental rating.

2. Any description of the program which makes identification possible is entered on CAB records as having been heard.

3. Each program rating is an average of the identifications or mentions recorded for the current and preceding period during which the investigations were made. Interviewing is conducted two weeks out of each month.

4. All set-owners spoken to, plus no answers (interpreted as radios not in use), in those cities where the investigations were made and which are also reached by the program's network, are taken as one hundred per cent.

5. The number of radio sets reported tuned to the individual program is represented by a percentage of that one hundred per cent.

6. Dialings answered by a busy signal are not included in the sample. "Don't Knows" are included as such in the final figures. They are admitted radio listeners who can't identify the program to which they are listening. As such, they are included in "Total Sets-in-Use."

7. When a program is broadcast more than once a week, the ratings for all these broadcasts are combined for an average of the week.

Total dialings for a year are estimated at over 6,300,000; they are scheduled as follows:

Half-hour programs	4,020	
One-hour programs	8,040	
Quarter-hour, five times weekly	10,050	(nighttime)
Quarter-hour, five times weekly	5,025	(daytime)

Cities where CAB calls are made are as follows:

New England — Boston, Bridgeport, Worcester, Springfield, Mass., Hartford, Providence, Waterbury, Portland, Manchester

Middle Atlantic — New York, Philadelphia, Pittsburgh, Buffalo, Scranton, Trenton, Utica, Reading, Syracuse, Rochester, Erie, Wilkes-Barre, Harrisburg, Johnstown, Schenectady, Altoona

East North Central — Chicago, Detroit, Milwaukee, Cleveland, Columbus, Toledo, Akron, Grand Rapids, Dayton, South Bend, Indianapolis, Cincinnati, Rockford, Racine, Springfield, Illinois, Springfield, Ohio, Evansville, Indiana

West North Central — St. Louis, Duluth, Wichita, Omaha, Kansas City, Des Moines, Minneapolis, St. Paul, Springfield, Missouri

South Atlantic — Baltimore, Washington, Richmond, Wilmington, Atlanta, Jacksonville, Winston-Salem, Columbia, Columbus

East South Central — Birmingham, Louisville, Memphis, Jackson

West South Central — San Antonio, Houston, New Orleans, Oklahoma City, Dallas, Little Rock, Shreveport, Tulsa

Mountain — Salt Lake City, Denver

Pacific — Los Angeles, San Francisco, Portland, Sacramento, San Diego, Seattle, Spokane, Fresno

A. C. NIELSEN COMPANY

The A. C. Nielsen Company was founded August 24, 1923, for the purpose of presenting to manufacturers indisputable facts upon which to base their marketing decisions. The company specialized in the food and drug fields until the measuring of radio listening audiences attracted their attention in the year 1936. For seven years they worked at perfecting their equipment to measure the radio audience for any particular program before presenting it to the radio industry, advertisers, and advertising agencies.

In the opinion of the A. C. Nielsen Company, the ideal radio research service must:

1. Measure the *entertainment* value of the program (probably best indicated by the size of the audience, bearing in mind the scope of the broadcasting facilities).

2. Measure the *sales effectiveness* of the program.

3. Cover the *entire* radio audience; that is:

    a. All geographical sections.

    b. All sizes of cities.

    c. Farms.

    d. All income classes.

    e. All occupations.

    f. All races.

    g. All sizes of family.

    h. Telephone and non-telephone homes, etc., etc.

4. Sample each of the foregoing sections of the audience in its proper proportion; that is, there must be *scientific, controlled sampling* — not wholly random sampling.

5. Cover a *sufficiently* large sample to give reliable results.

6. Cover all *types* of programs.

7. Cover all *hours* of the day.

8. Permit *complete analysis* of each program; for example:

    a. Variations in audience size at each instant during the broadcast.

    b. Average duration of listening.

    c. Detection of entertainment features or commercials which cause gain or loss of audience.

    d. Audience turnover from day to day or week to week, etc., etc.

9. Reveal the true popularity and listening areas of each

station and each network; that is, furnish an "Audit Bureau of Circulations" for radio.

A study was made by A. C. Nielson Company of all possible methods of meeting these specifications. After careful investigation, they decided to use a graphic recording instrument known as the "audimeter" for accurately measuring radio listening. This instrument was originally conceived by two members of the faculty of the Massachusetts Institute of Technology. In 1936, the A. C. Nielsen Company assumed the task involved in its further development and commercialization.

The audimeter is installed in radio receivers in homes. After it is properly installed, it makes a graphic record of all the times at which the set is tuned on or off and the station to which it is tuned at every instant of the day or night for a period of a month. The record actually occupies a piece of tape about one hundred feet long and about three inches wide. Approximately every twenty-eight days the completed tapes are removed and taken back to the A. C. Nielsen Company offices, where they are decoded by special apparatus designed not only for that purpose, but also for punching the listening data on tabulating cards.

Curves are then plotted according to the information contained on these tabulating cards, curves which provide a minute-by-minute picture, twenty-four hours each day, of the tuning of the radio sets in which the audimeters are installed. These curves plainly portray the effect of popular guest stars, poor or good commercials, or any other factor that either increases or decreases the listening to any particular program.

By the use of audimeters it is also possible to determine the relative size of the listening audience at any time between 10:30 P.M. and 8:00 A.M., when it is not expedient to call people on the telephone, as well as for any period during the day or evening when it is possible to gather data by telephone.

The A. C. Nielsen Company now has one thousand audimeters placed in a scientifically controlled cross-section of homes in an area extending from the Mississippi River to the Atlantic Coast, including the major metropolitan districts.

Philadelphia, Pittsburgh, Cleveland, Detroit, Chicago, Milwaukee, and St. Louis, and the small-city and rural communities throughout the area.

Eight million radio homes, slightly more than one quarter of all the radio homes in the United States, are contained in this area. Boundaries of the area have been selected in a manner which insures equal opportunity for each major network. Furthermore, time zone, urban, rural, and other characteristics have been given careful consideration. The A. C. Nielsen Company believes this area to be sufficiently big and sufficiently representative to provide the basis for accurate statistical answers to most radio questions of a national character.

CHAPTER 20

RADIO COUNCILS

WEBSTER'S DICTIONARY defines a "council" as "an assembly of persons met in consultation, or to give advice." Radio has chosen to adopt both interpretations and to add a third. A "radio council" may, therefore, be organized for the purpose of developing a co-operative relationship between radio stations and the listening public in order to encourage the presentation of better programs, which is, in a sense, "giving advice." Or a radio council may be a group organized to consult together on radio programs with no thought of passing on to the station any acquired information in the form of advice. As a third definition, a radio council, in many places, has come to be looked upon as a group organized for the purpose of developing and producing radio programs.

PRODUCING COUNCILS

Probably the first instance in which the term "radio council" was used to designate a group brought together for the purpose of developing better programs was the organization of The National Advisory Council on Radio in Education. This Council "grew out of an idea which germinated in the American Association for Adult Education. A small group of educators met in New York in the winter of 1929-1930 to discuss broadcasting and to find out whether anything could be done to utilize radio more generally as an instrumentality in education." [1] Doctor Levering Tyson, formerly of Teachers College, Columbia University, was appointed Director of the Council, which opened its doors in the summer of 1930, underwritten for three years by the Rockefeller Foundation and the Carnegie Corporation. In 1931 the Council was incorporated

---

[1] *Listen and Learn,* National Advisory Council on Radio in Education, Inc., Information Series. Number One, page 3.

under the laws of the State of New York as a membership corporation not organized for profit. The Council, in its statement of purpose and objectives, "was established to further the development of the art of radio broadcasting in American education . . . and every effort will be made to mobilize the best educational thought of the country to devise, develop, and present suitable programs, to be brought into fruitful contact with the most appropriate facilities." [2]

During the eight years of its existence, the Council, in conjunction with at least sixty co-operating American agencies, was responsible for broadcasting more than fifteen different series of programs in such fields as history, government, law, art, medicine, economics, and labor. These programs were mostly straight talks or lectures, and although they were presented by outstanding men in the various subject fields, in many instances their scope was not broad enough to compete in listener interest with the wide variety of commercial programs being offered. Early in 1937, the Carnegie Corporation withdrew its financial support, and by the close of 1938, the Council was forced to disband, as the Rockefeller Foundation had also decided to terminate its grant.

As far back as 1936, Doctor Tyson, realizing the problems the Council faced both in the production of good programs and in attracting and holding an audience, stated at the joint meeting of the Council and the Institute for Education by Radio at Columbus:

> It is still evident that the problem of finances is an enormously important one. The lack of money to do the job and to compete successfully for audiences with elaborate and attractive commercial programs seems almost hopeless. Unfortunately, there is not much chance to get money until there is some general understanding of, and agreement on, country-wide objectives to which local and regional objectives can be fitted, and until controversy over these objectives is eliminated so that a unified plan of procedure can be followed by all.

[2] *Ibid.*, page 4.

Even though the Council had to disband, it most assuredly had served a very definite purpose during its existence. It had, for one thing, drawn many dissimilar groups together in a common interest: a recognition of the need for better and more educational programs. Educators lacked a knowledge of this need quite as much as broadcasters, but until the advent of the Council, no one had made any real effort to correct the situation. In addition, the Council had held five national meetings on education by radio, attended by men and women from both fields who had had their attention focused for the first time on this new educational tool. Here was a new and vital force which could be used in adult education, if only some means could be found of doing so in the right way. It is to be regretted that a way could not be found to carry forward, through this Council, the experimental ideas that might have resulted eventually in working out new methods of education, thereby achieving the purpose and objectives for which the Council was organized.

Almost from the beginning of radio broadcasting in Chicago, both Northwestern University and the University of Chicago became associated with it, broadcasting, over one or more of the commercial stations, a series of lectures in various fields. The University of Chicago had the more ambitious program under the direct guidance of a faculty committee, with Allen Miller serving as secretary to the committee. As the broadcasting opportunities for all educational institutions in Chicago increased, Mr. Miller realized that the meager appropriations accorded to the radio activities of these educational groups would not meet the costs of building programs in the real sense of the word. At least, those funds could not compete with the monies being spent by advertisers and individual stations for quality programs. Educational radio programs as yet had not proved themselves of sufficient importance, from the educator's standpoint, to justify the setting aside by any one institution of adequate funds to defray program expenses. Knowing that such funds would have to be appropriated by the universities if they hoped to stay on the air and compete with the success-

ful commercial programs for the listener's attention, Allen
Miller conceived the idea of the University Broadcasting
Council. Membership in the Council could be composed of at
least three of the universities in Chicago, the three networks,
and any of the independent radio stations that cared to join.

Formulating the following policies and objectives, Mr. Miller
presented the plan to the educators and the broadcasters and
to both the Rockefeller Foundation and the Carnegie Corporation:

> To create, develop, schedule, and broadcast radio programs
> of an educational or cultural nature and to conduct experi-
> ments and research in education by radio.
>
> To improve the quality and broaden the appeal of educa-
> tional programs to increase their public acceptance.
>
> To establish effective co-operation with radio networks and
> stations so that the obvious advantages of their highly
> developed technical facilities and large established audiences
> may be secured for educational programs.
>
> Above these immediate objectives is the higher purpose of
> performing significant public service to the adult radio listeners
> of America.[3]

The University of Chicago, Northwestern and De Paul Universities, the National Broadcasting Company, the Columbia
Broadcasting System, and the Mutual Network, together with
the Rockefeller Foundation and the Carnegie Corporation,
agreed to finance the Council for a period of four years. The
agreement with the local stations, WLS, WJJD, and WIND,
was on a year-to-year basis. Headquarters, comprising offices,
studios, and a control room, were established and an adequate
staff was maintained to guarantee the carrying out of the aims
and objectives for which the Council was incorporated.

The control of the Council was vested in a board of trustees
with a total membership of six, each university being represented by two members, and with the director of the Council
serving as secretary of the board without power to vote. The
Council was authorized to serve as the exclusive agency for the

[3] University Broadcasting Council, Articles of Incorporation.

development, scheduling, and broadcasting of all radio programs of an educational nature presented officially under the
auspices of the universities, it being understood that such programs were to include all broadcast material other than that
in connection with athletic events. Further, the Council was
appointed as the representative of the universities with power
to act in their behalf in all matters relating to broadcasting
co-operation among the educational institutions and broadcasting stations associated in the Council. There are ample statistics to prove the success of the Council during the first four
years of its existence. Perhaps the most conclusive is the
amount of time given to Council-built programs by the networks and local radio stations. This amounted to more than
$1,500,000 in commercial value for the approximately 2500
programs broadcast. It is also interesting to note that Council
programs were never cancelled nor was their time shifted for
commercial programs, which seems to be another evidence of
the networks' and stations' good will toward the Council and
approval of its offerings.

Commenting on the University Broadcasting Council and its
activities, the *Chicago Tribune* said on February 8, 1937:

> Organized less than two years ago by Allen Miller, who now
> directs its activities, the Council is constantly demonstrating
> that Nobel prize winners may prove as exhilarating as Alexander
> Woollcott; that so-called "absent-minded professors" are as
> agile in ad-libbing as Fred Allen; that savants are more effec-
> tive word-slingers than senators; and that the night skies are
> at least as mystifying as night life. In short, the Council is
> proving every day that there is entertainment in erudition.

Even in the face of the obvious success of the Council, the
University of Chicago chose to terminate its relationship at the
close of the contractual agreement and, therefore, withdrew
its membership on September 20, 1939. Believing in the ideas
and objectives for which the Council was formed, the other
universities, the Mutual Broadcasting Company, and the local
stations continued their support for another year, as did the
Rockefeller Foundation, though the latter considerably reduced

its yearly contribution. The National Broadcasting Company and the Columbia Broadcasting System, however, also decided not to continue their support in view of the withdrawal of the University of Chicago and the cutting-down of the Rockefeller grant. With his budget decidedly curtailed, Mr. Miller realized that it was impossible to maintain the high standard of performance hitherto maintained by the Council, and that unless it were possible to do so, the networks and stations would not be interested in accepting Council-built programs. The Council, therefore, closed its doors in the fall of 1940, and each university once again established its own radio department, but with the realization that if they hoped to maintain the quality of excellence achieved by the Council, more thought, attention, and money would have to go into the preparation and presentation of any programs emanating from them.

Two of the programs originated first through the Council's auspices are still on the air today: "The Northwestern Reviewing Stand" over the Mutual Network and "Of Men and Books" broadcast by Columbia. "The University of Chicago Round Table" had been under the jurisdiction of the Council during its life, but has continued solely as a University program since the University withdrew from the Council.

During the first decade of radio broadcasting, many educators had felt some concern over the apparent monopolistic attitude of the commercial radio bodies and believed that unless they banded together to protect the rights and interests of education, the "public interest, convenience, and necessity" clause of the radio law would be forgotten as far as education was concerned. At a conference held in Chicago in the fall of 1930, with Doctor William J. Cooper, Commissioner of Education, as chairman, it was proposed that a committee should be appointed to carry out a series of resolutions drawn up by the conference, as follows:

> 1. The appointment of a committee to represent "The Association of College and University Broadcasting Stations, the Land-Grant College Association, the National University Extension Association, the National Association of State Uni-

versity Presidents, the National Education Association, the National Catholic Educational Association, the Jesuit Educational Association, the National Advisory Council on Radio in Education, the Payne Fund, and other similar groups." Commissioner Cooper was to appoint this Committee.

2. The protection and promotion of broadcasting originating in educational institutions.

3. The promotion of broadcasting by educational institutions.

4. Legislation by Congress "which will permanently and exclusively assign to educational institutions and government educational agencies a minimum of fifteen (15) per cent of all radio broadcasting channels which are or may become available to the United States."

5. The calling of "an organization meeting of this committee at the earliest possible moment."

The Committee appointed by Commissioner Cooper, with Joy Elmer Morgan as temporary chairman, was composed of the following members:

J. L. Clifton, Director of Education, Columbus, Ohio, from the National Council of State Superintendents.

R. C. Higgy, Director, Station WEAO of Ohio State University, Columbus, Ohio, from Association of College and University Broadcasting Stations.

J. O. Keller, Head of Engineering Extension, Pennsylvania State College, from the National University Extension Association.

Charles N. Lischka, from the National Catholic Education Association.

John Henry MacCracken, from the American Council on Education.

Charles A. Robinson, St. Louis University, from the Jesuit Education Association.

H. Umberger, Kansas State Agricultural College, from the Association of Land Grant Colleges and Universities.

Arthur G. Crane, President, the University of Wyoming, from the National Association of State University Presidents.

Joy Elmer Morgan (Chairman) from the National Education Association.

The Committee, financed by the Payne Fund, held its first meeting in Washington in December, 1930. Mr. Morgan had drawn up and presented the resolutions to the Chicago conference. The name of The National Committee on Education by Radio was adopted and a service bureau was established in Washington which, among other things, "would advise and help protect educational stations; and would develop research and experimentation designed to give knowledge that would make better educational broadcasting possible." [4]

Based on the knowledge that the Payne Fund grant, from which the Committee drew its support, would terminate in 1935, the Committee appointed one of its members, Doctor Arthur Crane, to survey the possibilities of its continuance and also to explore the possibilities of setting up another committee to investigate the civic and social possibilities of radio. The result of the survey was a recommendation that the Committee be continued with the objective of carrying out a "Plan for an American System of Radio Broadcasting to Serve the Welfare of the American People." As outlined, the proposal suggested a system of public councils or boards — state, regional, and national — which would develop public-service broadcasting. Stations were to be constructed and operated by the federal government to put the programs of the councils on the air. The plan, which was chiefly the idea of Doctor Crane, was a concrete development of the Committee's long-held belief that "the American states should plan an organized part in cultural broadcasting, and of their equally firm belief that the federal government should make some positive contribution to education on the air." [5]

The plan was not found to be entirely practical, but at least it had germinated the idea of state councils which, after two or three sporadic efforts in Texas and New Mexico, finally came to fruition in the Rocky Mountain Radio Council. This Council was organized in the fall of 1939, under grants pro-

[4] Frank Ernest Hill, *Tune in for Education.* New York: National Committee on Education by Radio (1942), page 17.
[5] *Ibid.*, page 76.

vided by the General Education Board, the Payne Fund, the National Committee on Education by Radio, and the Boettcher Foundation of Colorado, with Robert B. Hudson as the director. Its membership consisted of representatives from colleges, state departments of education, public schools, public libraries, women's clubs, farm groups, and educational associations, and Doctor Arthur Crane was elected chairman of the Council. The purposes of the Council were set forth in four statements on "Why a radio council?":

First. Because — The colleges and universities of the Rocky Mountain region, regardless of the sources of their support, are no longer merely seats of resident instruction; rather, they are charged with the responsibility of providing an educational service to *all* of the people, young and old alike, in their primary service areas. Radio offers to them a facility for improving a thousandfold their extra-mural services. They lack only the mastery of it.

Second. Because — The educational service organizations and important civic groups of the Rocky Mountain region are dedicated to serving the *whole* community and, through ever-continuing education, to implement democracy and perfect our American political and economic way of life. Radio reaches the people. Abuse of radio has brought ruin to nations.

Third. Because — The educational organizations of the Rocky Mountain region have literally unlimited resources of ideas, information, experience, and tested methodology at their disposal which should and can be brought into the body of common knowledge. Radio broadcasting, more effectively than any other device, can bring about this transfusion.

Fourth. Because — Both commercial broadcasters and educational interests have developed certain unchallenged skills, which lift education on the air to a higher level of effectiveness, and commercial broadcasting to a similar high level of public interest and service. For either to ignore the other is to pave the way for legislative paternalism of a sort mutually undesirable and restrictive. Both want to maintain the free principles of the American system of radio, which has achieved a position of interest and popularity above any other in the world. Co-operation is the key to this continued pre-eminence.

The Rocky Mountain Radio Council, as a pioneer in co-operative broadcasting, aims at uniting these powerful interests — commercial radio and education — with the objective of mutual growth and significance.[6]

The Rocky Mountain Radio Council, working through the Faculty radio committees and radio directors of the various colleges and universities and through radio chairmen of civic organizations,

> aids its members in the planning, editing, directing, broadcasting, and transcribing of their programs; in initiating and completing broadcast arrangements with radio stations in all parts of the region; in giving publicity to programs through radio, newspapers, and printed announcements; in obtaining copyright clearances on music and literature; in discovering and developing radio dramatic talent for use on educational programs.[7]

That the Rocky Mountain Radio Council has carried through its purpose and served its public and members well is attested in the citation presented to it by *Variety* magazine in 1941, which said:

For Regional Service
The Rocky Mountain Radio Council

> Apart from a number of news reports in *Variety*, the work of the Rocky Mountain Radio Council has been very little publicized nationally. It may therefore surprise many to hear of the Council receiving a *Variety* award. "What," such persons may inquire, "is the Rocky Mountain Radio Council?"
>
> Briefly, it is a Council of co-operating radio stations, plus colleges, plus a central staff of professional writer-directors under Robert Hudson. The formula is to draw upon the brains and artistry of the area to create programs of the kind no one station or college could organize and to share this service with any outlets that want it. The experience now behind the Council constitutes by itself an important body of evidence for

[6] Rocky Mountain Radio Council, Inc., Denver, Colorado, *Summary Report*, November 1, 1939, to July 31, 1940, page 4.

[7] *Ibid.*, page 7.

co-operative programming. The example seems certain to be part of the future organization of small-town radio in the United States. Socially it seems desirable for many reasons, among them that it is a practical method for freeing the local station from its inert attitude of reliance on either network programs or transcriptions, both the product of New York, Chicago, and Hollywood. Equally challenging to the non-network station is the possibility of obtaining through such a Council a line of live-talent programs to offset the meager diet of news, sports, and phonograph records on which too many small town stations wholly depend.

The Rocky Mountain Radio Council is for once a product of Foundation funds that is visible. Grants have set it up in Denver and kept it going. Since it deals with actual production problems, it subjects itself to the white light of public examination. It is not another semi-surreptitious for-scholars-only undertaking. The Rocky Mountain Radio Council is in direct contact with the realities of broadcasting and has made very substantial contributions to advancing the art of radio.

At the close of its fiscal year in July, 1944, the Council advised:

> During the past twelve months the Rocky Mountain Radio Council broadcast three hundred and sixty-one separate programs, a total of one thousand eight hundred and ninety-seven broadcasts, for sixteen educational and civic organizations. The time value of the four hundred and seventy-two hours and forty-six minutes used on the nineteen stations, computed at commercial rates, is forty-six thousand three hundred and thirty-eight dollars and fifty cents. The preparation of the three hundred and sixty-one programs required the time of employees of educational institutions and agencies and professional talent valued at sixty thousand three hundred and fifty-eight dollars and eighty-four cents. This amount includes Radio Council staff costs, since the activities of the staff were given exclusively to assisting in the planning, production, broadcasting, and rebroadcasting of the programs.[8]

The Council's programs have covered many fields — agriculture, history, news, biography, aviation, national and interna-

[8] *Ibid.*, August 1, 1943, to July 31, 1944, page 13.

tional affairs, vocational guidance, child study, and war activities. They have taken the form of dramatizations, talks, interviews, and forums. Where it has not been possible to use live talent on some of the smaller, more remote mountain stations, transcriptions of the broadcasts have been made and supplied to these stations.

Inasmuch as the financing of the Council has been made possible by Foundation grants which will expire within the next few years, arrangements have been suggested whereby it may become self-supporting. Such arrangements include contributions from member groups and from the radio stations through which the Council programs are broadcast; through the development of a commercial recording service by which records and transcriptions can be made for individuals and non-member organizations on a cost-plus basis; the conduct of a radio-workshop class for persons interested in radio acting and production; and gifts from local sources.

All in all, the Council has done a splendid job and is a model that might well be used by other regions in setting up a co-operative body for the production of educational and public service programs, which is the reason for the exhaustive statement of its activities included herein. With the possible exception of the Radio Council of the Chicago Public Schools, which, in a sense, is not a radio council but the radio department and workshop of the public-school system of Chicago, the three councils previously described are the only ones which have been set up purely as producing councils. The others follow more closely Webster's definition of "persons meeting to consult."

CONSULTING COUNCILS

Between 1938 and 1941 a number of such councils were organized. The Ohio Civic Broadcasting Committee, a group of sixty-two state-wide organizations with headquarters in Columbus, first came together to assist radio stations in the development and improvement of broadcasts for civic understanding. Elaborate plans were drawn up in 1939 for the New England

Council, as a division of the New England Town Hall of Boston. The Council proposed to act as a clearing-house for all educational and cultural programs; to determine sources best able to initiate programs; to prevent duplication in that area of educational programs on the air; to determine standards and audience interest. It was a noble plan, sincerely conceived, but its accomplishments were meager. On the other hand, another New England group in western Massachusetts was organized in 1939, with their main purpose to evaluate network programs and to stimulate listening. This group obtained the support of parent-teacher organizations, women's clubs, and other civic bodies. They planned regular meetings to which were invited as speakers persons active in various fields of the radio industry, and while the Council was not set up as a producing agency, it has been responsible for a few broadcasts by some of the local member groups. Recently the Council changed its name to the Pioneer Radio Council. As one of its activities it prepares and distributes a weekly radio guide to good listening.

As has been shown in the chapter on "Children's Programs," there was a good deal of agitation on the part of various organizations during the nineteen-thirties. This agitation finally was responsible for the banding together in New York of a group of men and women representing organizations and educators under the name of the Radio Council on Children's Programs. Some of the questions that confronted the Council were:

What is the actual number of children's programs broadcast over local stations throughout the country? What stations carry what programs that are sponsored and merchandised? What effects are locally-produced programs having on the children and parents in their respective communities? Are there enough good programs to satisfy the natural demands of active-minded children? Are the local programs worthy of network sponsorship to insure the American system of broadcasting?

Before defining the area in which it is to function most effectively, the Council must have the answers to these questions.

It determined to make a general survey of the country as its first constructive step and offered a plan to the National Association of Broadcasters for financing. The NAB Board of Directors approved the survey plan and allocated the sum of $1,500.00 for the project.

Mrs. Dorothy Lewis, vice chairman of the Council and national radio chairman for the National Society of New England Women, was authorized to conduct the survey as field representative of the Council. The result of that survey was a detailed report published by the NAB in 1941 under the title of "Broadcasting to the Youth of America." [9]

Early in 1942, the National Association of Broadcasters asked Mrs. Lewis to join the staff of the Association as "Co-ordinator of Listener Activities." The Radio Council on Children's Programs, with the completion of the survey and the presentation of a program of activities to the United States Office of Education, agreed to disband, feeling that they had left their objectives in good hands. Mrs. Lewis was, of course, still interested in carrying the torch for good programs for children as well as in rendering advice and aid in her new association. On her previous trips across the country she had felt keenly the need of acquainting listeners with more information on this complex new industry, and she felt too that the broadcasting station should have the benefit of knowing the opinions of its listening audience. In trying to work out those two objectives, Mrs. Lewis has been in touch with radio stations and with the public in all parts of the country. She is probably responsible for or has aided in the formation of twenty-five or thirty active radio councils in such places as Nashville, Tennessee, the Twin Cities of Minneapolis and St. Paul, Des Moines and Cedar Rapids, Iowa, Omaha, Cleveland, Kansas City, St. Louis, Portland, Oregon, Seattle, Salt Lake City, Wichita, Kansas, Reno, Nevada, and Utica, New York, to name only a few.

The Radio Council of Greater Cleveland, as an example of a live, up-and-coming group, was organized in the fall of 1940 and claims a membership of around forty sponsoring organiza-

---

[9] *Broadcasting to the Youth of America*, page 9. Washington, D.C.: The National Association of Broadcasters.

tions, with a combined membership of more than fifty thousand. In almost every instance these councils have adopted the following objectives:

1. To co-ordinate the interests of civic. religious, educational, and business organizations to encourage the presentation of more radio programs which meet with high standards of entertainment, artistry, and morality for adults and children.

2. To collect and distribute information on entertainment evaluation of current progiams.

3. To create and maintain patronage for sponsors of radio programs who broadcast programs meeting the standards recommended by this organization.

4. To create and maintain the highest individual standards of radio appreciation.

5. To become thoroughly familiar with the subject of radio by study and observation.

6. To stimulate and aid parents in assuming responsibility for children's radio entertainment.

7. To encourage by positive action of approval the presentation of radio programs which meet the recommended standards of the Council.

8. To develop a co-operative attitude between radio stations and the listening public.

9. Through open discussion to develop recommendations to radio stations of standards deemed to be desirable for broadcasting in the public interest, convenience, and necessity.

Many of the councils prepare and distribute selective listening lists, as is done by the Pioneer Radio Council of western Massachusetts, previously mentioned. In some instances, such as in Cedar Rapids, Iowa, the cost of preparing and distributing these aids is borne by some business group as its contribution toward better radio listening. "Radio Councils," said William B. Quarton, Manager of radio station WMT, Cedar Rapids, Iowa, in a talk before the NAB meeting in Chicago, August, 1944,

are simplifying the problems of public service programs for broadcasters in many parts of the country. Even more important, they provide broadcasters and community leaders an opportunity to exchange viewpoints, something that is sadly lacking in altogether too many localities. In Cedar Rapids we are demonstrating that broadcasters and organizations can work together harmoniously to the distinct advantage of the community we serve.

An ambitious program was planned by the Radio Council of New Jersey in an effort to develop children's appreciation of radio, to stimulate teacher interest, and to encourage local Boards of Education to install radios and playback and sound equipment in schools. The education committee of the Council in September, 1943, made a survey of all schools in New Jersey, public, private, and parochial together with colleges and universities. Some of the questions included in the questionnaire follow:

1. How many radios in your school?
   a. Stationary radios?   b. Portable radios?
2. How many record players are used with radios?
3. Is radio listening a part of the curriculum?
   Check types of programs used in school hours:
   Music . . . . . . Science . . . . . . Current Events . . . . . .
   Other . . . . . .
4. Is anything done about out-of-school listening to radio? Describe briefly.
5. Have pupils participated in radio programs?
   a. Actually on the air?
   b. Name of station . . . . . .
   c. Mock broadcasts within school?
6. Are any of your teachers specifically trained to work along the lines suggested in questions three to five?
7. Is the use of radio and recordings in education likely to be less or more important during the next few years? Please comment.

Following this precedent, the Des Moines Radio Council, co-operating with the Honorable Bourke B. Hickenlooper, Governor of Iowa, called a meeting at the State House on December 1, 1943, of leading educators and broadcasters of

Iowa. At this session a three-point plan was adopted, as follows:

1. That a survey of radio facilities for receiving educational radio programs in the state of Iowa be undertaken after a questionnaire has been prepared which is adapted to the needs of this state.

2. That, wherever possible, a bibliography of educational radio programs shall be made available to the teachers of the state of Iowa.

3. That, wherever possible, further and special instruction in the field of radio education shall be given to the teachers of the state through:

    a. Demonstration   *c.* Short courses
    b. Workshops   *d.* Regular training in schools and
                                       colleges

A subcommittee drew up the following questionnaire for Iowa schools, and attention is called especially to questions number 7 to 14 inclusive:

1. What radio receiving equipment is available as classroom equipment? (Indicate number.)
    a. Stationary radios . . . . . .   Where located . . . . . .
    b. Portable radios . . . . . .

2. What equipment is available for reproducing sound? (Indicate number.)
    a. Record-players for home-type records Portable . . . . . .
    Non-portable . . . . . . If non-portable, state location.
    b. Record-players for commercial or professional transcriptions (16-inch diameter, played at slow speed of 33 1/3 r.p.m.)
    Portable . . . . . . Non-portable . . . . . . If non-portable, state location.
    c. Other sound-reproducing equipment (for example, sound on film)

3. Does building have a built-in public address system? Yes . . . . . . No . . . . . . If yes: *a.* Where located? *b.* How used? (Please give details.)

4. Does building have portable public address system? Yes . . . . . . No . . . . . . If yes, how is it used?

5. Does building have equipment to make recordings? Yes . . . . . . No . . . . . . If yes: *a.* Describe equipment. *b.* State use made of it.

6. Have pupils participated in radio programs?
    a. Actually on the air? Yes . . . . . . No . . . . . . Name station . . . . . .
    b. Practice broadcasts within school? Yes . . . . . . No . . . . . . If yes: (1) Please describe. (2) How frequently held?

7. Do you have a Radio Club? Yes . . . . . . No . . . . . . If yes, describe on back of this sheet activities of such club.

8. Is any attention paid to the evaluation of radio programs? If yes, explain fully.
    a. In English classes   *c.* In social studies
    b. In music classes   *d.* Elsewhere

9. What use is made of school-made and/or commercial recordings?
    a. In English classes   *c.* In social studies
    b. In music classes   *d.* Elsewhere

10. Do you utilize radio as a means of instruction? Explain fully.
    a. In the classroom
    b. Radio Club
    c. Assigned outside listening

11. List staff members who have had training in radio educational methods. (Name – when – where – how long)

12. Do you have specific plans for the increased utilization of radio in your school? If yes: *a.* How?   *b.* When?

13. Have you found it possible to fit radio into your curriculum?
    If yes, list by name programs now being used.
    If no, do you have recommendations on how this problem may be solved?

14. List subjects you would like to have covered by radio programs. We will welcome any further, frank comment you may care to make on the back of this page.

These questionnaires may well serve as guides for Council activities.

In reporting these activities, Mrs. Lewis says:

Interest in other states has been evoked by this pioneering, as well as arousing the interest of national organizations. The following resolution favoring radio education was passed by the General Federation of Women's Clubs:

> WHEREAS, education for our youth has always been of paramount importance and is now of even greater significance, be it
>
> RESOLVED, that the (name of organization) recommends to the Federal Office of Education and all state Boards of Education that the use of radio in the classroom be recognized and made an integral part of the school curriculum under a plan which will place control in the hands of the classroom teacher, to the end that the children may be properly guided in respect to their listening habits; and that the selection of programs for classroom use be made with a view to bringing to the students an understanding of all phases of radio broadcasting, including its educational, cultural, social, news, and entertainment contributions.

Radio councils may work with radio stations and educational institutions in setting up clinics for teachers, patterned after the one developed by station KYW, in Philadelphia: "The Teachers Go to School." This practical plan, designed by Westinghouse stations to stimulate teachers and to educate them in the utilization of radio, solves many problems because it offers convenient, inexpensive training, adapted to their own requirements of time and distance limitations.

Stations KOIN in Portland, Oregon, and KMBC in Kansas City, Missouri, have also held short-termed summer radio institutes for teachers.

ORGANIZATION OF COMMITTEES

Survey Committees. The survey committees of councils have made significant studies of various kinds, both amateur and semi-professional. Some have been undertaken to explore certain program fields. One survey of daytime serials was paid for by an advertising agency and the money was given to the six hundred participants in the State University Radio Workshop for radio scholarships. Surveys of children's listening habits have been conducted frequently and have aided stations.

Production Committees. Radio councils often establish what they term production committees. However, most groups refrain from producing programs until they have adequate training, are assured of capable direction, and have sufficient funds for a worthy presentation. Any radio council program obviously would be the result of a direct need for that type of action in the particular community. In several cities the "Radio Council Presents" is a broadcast of one period or more every week by each of the participating organizations in rotation; Des Moines, Cedar Rapids, and Kansas City are cities where such a series is currently being presented. This plan relieves the station of allocating time discriminately and gives each interested group a chance to broadcast, regardless of size. It spreads such programs among the local stations more fairly and uses local personalities and council members to explore local problems with firmness and fearlessness as editors on the air. A production committee functions best by carefully balancing program material and maintaining a variety of forms, such as talks, interviews, and dramas at intervals. In Winston-Salem, North Carolina, the council secured the services of a radio director, the cost being carried by a local member organization.

War Co-ordinating Committees. During the war some radio councils established war co-ordinating committees to act as sounding boards for radio's war effort, analyzing the effect on the public of local war broadcasts and co-ordinating local organizations' requests for time for the promotion of their war drives.

Study Courses. Councils also often set up study courses when none are obtainable through local high-school or college radio workshops. It is recommended that all radio chairmen and teachers take available courses in radio appreciation, script writing, production, and the like. The councils co-operate with the Institutes of the Junior Leagues and similar study programs.

Speakers' Bureaus. Radio councils may have speakers'

bureaus or may gather lists of persons who are qualified to speak on various phases of radio. These speakers tell the fascinating story of American radio to clubs, chambers of commerce, schools, conventions, and civic meetings. In 1943, the Portland Radio Council presented "America's Town Meeting of the Air" before an audience of three thousand.

Promotion Committees. Finally, another activity of radio councils is the work of the promotion committees. The objective is to train radio chairmen by giving them specific information on radio, such as the Broadcasters' Code, and telling them of radio advertising, radio's public service, etc. These chairmen take such information back to their clubs and give short résumés at regular meetings. In addition, they attempt to devote one entire club program a year to radio. Hundreds of thousands of brochures and printed articles from the networks and the NAB are distributed by the radio chairmen to clubs, schools, and libraries.

Radio councils can educate listeners to be discriminating in their tastes and to give broadcasters the benefit of considered public opinion and thereby help to elevate and improve program standards. Radio councils aid in providing radio equipment for schools by encouraging the interest of teachers and school boards in its utilization. There is, in the American system of broadcasting, a remarkable opportunity to demonstrate a high type of democracy and to maintain one of our greatest freedoms, freedom of the air. This is what radio councils are attempting to do.

CHAPTER 21

LISTENING GROUPS

IN THE UNITED STATES

"GROUPS GATHERING TO LISTEN to radio programs are almost as old as radio broadcasting itself," says Doctor John W. Studebaker, United States Commissioner of Education.[1] What makes groups gather to listen? What impetus is back of the impulse? How does it all start? Who are the people who gather to listen? What results are noticeable from group listening that would not be apparent from individual listening? Is it a useful occupation? Is it widespread? These are some of the questions that have been raised from time to time when the question of listening groups has been brought up.

Because of very general interest in the subject and the lack of direct information on it, the Federal Radio Education Committee requested Frank Ernest Hill to make a comprehensive survey of the listening-group field. The committee felt that the findings of such a survey would be of great value to educator and broadcaster alike. Those findings might well help to decide the character of programs being broadcast, though evidence already pointed to the fact that it was, generally, the informative programs which drew groups together, the type of program that could rightfully call for discussion immediately following the broadcast.

Mr. Hill, in the report of his survey,[2] says that benefits from group listening accrue to three classes of persons: the educator, the broadcaster, and the listener himself. Assuming that most group listening is done for educative purposes, he believes that the educator benefits in five ways:

1. People listen more attentively in groups.
2. An educator wants an audience. If he knows that there

[1] Foreword to *The Groups Tune In*, by Frank Ernest Hill, issued by the Federal Radio Education Committee.
[2] *Ibid.*, pages 17-18.

332

are organized groups listening to him, it gives him more confidence that his message is being heard. Without such groups, there is no way of telling beforehand whether he is talking to one person or ten thousand, or to himself in the studio.

3. He likes to know that there is a possibility of a two-way communication with a part of his audience, with which he may make contact from time to time.

4. Group listening can indicate the effectiveness of a broadcaster. People would not gather to listen unless they were interested either in the broadcaster or in the content of his subject.

5. Groups can justify the service of listener aids, which, in themselves, mean more effective listening.

The broadcaster, Mr. Hill believes, profits indirectly in all the ways in which the educator profits, and in addition, "all groups and most registered listeners act as agents for spreading the fame of the programs they hear." [3]

Lastly, the listener benefits in ways too numerous to mention in their entirety, but Mr. Hill points out first the obvious reason that, by listening in a group, the hearer pays more attention to the broadcast, and, therefore, derives more profit from it. In the second place, listening in a group invariably means discussion following the broadcast, which, as Mr. Ojemann points out in the following paragraph, is bound to clarify issues and ideas and in many instances makes it possible to carry forward applications to local situations. Still another reason, which has not been stressed, but which nevertheless has much merit, is the idea that participating in group discussion gives many people the self-confidence which they have lacked heretofore in their ability to express themselves or to present their ideas before other people. Such meetings do much to make people tolerant of opposing points of view. Finally, in many small or isolated communities a group meeting to listen to a broadcast often provides the only opportunity for any social gathering.

Doctor R. H. Ojemann of the State University of Iowa, commenting on the reasons for group listening, at the Institute for

[3] *Ibid.*, page 18.

Education by Radio in Columbus in 1936, stated that he saw five reasons why people got together in groups to listen to the radio.

1. Intention to discuss. "He is not so likely to assume a passive attitude when he is in a group as when he is at home in his easy chair."
2. Discussion within a group helps to clarify confused ideas.
3. "Group discussion also provides the opportunity to complete ideas."
4. "The group presents an opportunity for applying generalizations, especially to problems which have local significance."
5. In cases where examples are used by the speaker which do not resemble the problems met by the groups, the discussion may supply real examples, thus enhancing the meaning of the principles presented.

The idea of forming groups for the purpose of listening to a single broadcast, or preferably to a series of broadcasts, probably was first thought of, with the hope of furthering adult education, by educational institutions owning radio stations, stemming from extension divisions of such universities or colleges. Parent-teacher groups as far back as 1928 were meeting to listen to authorities on child care and health education. Doctor Jessie Allen Charters, in her report on the radio activities of the Division of Parental Education at Ohio State University, of which she was director, stated at the Institute for Education by Radio in 1930: "We had developed a considerable mailing list of parents interested in parental education. To most of these we were sending mimeographed monthly programs, either by direct mail or through a study-group leader." [4]

One of the best known of the early series on parental education and child care was the program arranged for listening groups in Iowa under the joint sponsorship of the State College at Ames and the Iowa State Teachers College. The talks given in this series were planned especially for the use of discussion

[4] *Education on the Air*, Ohio State University, 1930, page 168.

groups. In 1935, three series were presented, one for parents of pre-school children, a second for parents of elementary-school children, and a third for those of high-school age. Various methods of publicizing the series were used, and suggestions were sent out for organizing and conducting group meetings. In reporting on this effort at Columbus in 1935, Tracy F. Tyler said: [5] "An indication of the value of this series is found in a report dated January 22, 1935. At that time there were 144 local clubs with a total enrollment of 2262 individual members. These clubs represented 62 Iowa communities." Mr. Tyler in that same report pointed out numerous places where the same type of co-operation was being carried on by radio stations and parent-teacher groups, most notable of which was a New Jersey project organized in 1932, with more than three hundred groups by 1935.

Another interesting listening project in Iowa was outlined at the 1930 Columbus meeting by Mr. W. I. Griffith, Director of Station WOI, Ames, Iowa, known as the WOI Radio Book Club.[6] This club was started early in 1930 in response to numerous requests, following the station's popular book-review programs, for information as to where the books might be purchased or borrowed. While the club was organized primarily as a service to individual members, it was found that the idea had expanded and that in farms and villages study groups were being formed, where the books could be read and discussed while members were busy with sewing, knitting, or other forms of handicraft.

The National Congress of Parents and Teachers over a period of years have had a good deal of evidence of special meetings being called by local associations scattered across the country for the particular purpose of listening to the various series of programs sponsored by them in co-operation with the National Broadcasting Company. Every indication points to a growing acceptance of listening-together by local membership groups. In Los Angeles the local association reported a mem-

[5] *Ibid.*, 1935, pages 171-172.
[6] *Ibid.*, 1930, pages 241-244.

bership of one hundred thousand listening to the 1943-44 series of "The Baxters."

More important than the listening projects outlined above is the ability of radio to bring together other people who have not had even the advantages of the farm folk in rural areas of Iowa, Kansas, and other farm-belt communities; people, for example, tucked away in the hills and mountains of southeastern Kentucky, where life is more primitive than in any other part of our country. These people had not had, until the turn of the century, much contact with the outside world. They were still spinning their own thread, and even their efforts to raise their own crops frequently met with little success. In 1933, the University of Kentucky's Agricultural Department determined to see how they might help to interest these people in improving their living conditions as well as to stimulate them mentally. Battery radio sets were installed in fifteen different locations throughout the area where information on farming was most needed. These were set up in mountain community houses maintained by various church organizations, in mountain schools, and in general stores, in charge of the director of the community house or the storekeeper. Through word of mouth the news of this "talking-box" traveled up and down the creeks and the mountain-sides; gradually the inhabitants sauntered in to see what it was all about and stayed to listen. It finally became the habit of groups to congregate at those times when programs put on especially for them were being broadcast. At first they learned about soil and crops, later local and national news was tuned in and was a favorite. Then programs of good music were made available. These people are, of course, the descendants of the early Scotch-Irish settlers, and their music had been the ballads of those early days; they knew nothing of swing and jazz, so it is not to be wondered at that they preferred the classics to the popular music of the day.

In discussing these listening centers, the man who was responsible for the project, Elmer Sulzer, Director of Radio at the University of Kentucky, said:

An exposition of this system would be rather incomplete without at least briefly outlining the values that have been derived from this system. It appears that radio has brought the outside world closer and made it more real. The groups are amazed at the immensity and diversity of the United States and the world, as revealed by the geography broadcasts. Many of the people had the impression, of course, that every place was just the same as their own neighborhood. It has enlarged their restricted mental horizons, as most of them had no idea of modern ways of living and of farming. It seems highly conceivable that, using the radio sets, these centers will in a short time develop into the real cultural centers in the mountains.[7]

Group listening has not, of course, been confined to primitive or rural areas. Attempts have been made by various groups to stimulate listening to good radio programs, as touched upon in the chapter on "Radio Councils." Other projects, not quite so ambitious as some sponsored by the councils, have been started by groups brought together by such organizations as the American Association of University Women of Wisconsin. This association is responsible for the Better Listening Committee, with headquarters in Madison, and is made up of numerous groups scattered over a wide area in southern and central Wisconsin. All member groups come together about twice a year to discuss their findings and to present reports on numerous programs, calling attention to those which they consider particularly worth while. For several years they have had charts of news programs printed, to be distributed to all interested persons for ten cents. The committee has done much to stimulate listening to many good programs, both educational and entertaining.

In Oklahoma, Doctor Alice Sowers, Professor of Family Life Education at the University of Oklahoma, organized the "Family Life Radio Forum," which was broadcast weekly over the University's radio station as a program for all the families in Oklahoma; indeed, as she says, "for all individuals and

7 *Education on the Air*, Ohio State University, 1934, pages 148-155.

groups interested in education for family living." [8] The program was followed weekly by many diverse groups, among them large numbers of students listening in their classrooms or laboratories, either called together for the purpose of hearing the program or listening while in their sewing classes. Invariably a discussion period followed. In other instances, colleges appointed official listeners who would present a résumé in class the next day and lead a discussion. WPA, NYA, and AAUW groups, although organized for other purposes, often met in groups to listen and discuss the program, and probably the most unique of all the groups were in the prisons, where the teachers among the inmates would listen and discuss the problems among themselves afterward.

Before the transportation problem became acute, three high-school students would be selected each week from different towns as far away as two hundred and fifty miles to come to the University in order to participate in this half-hour, informal discussion program. Each year complete printed programs, listing the topics and giving three leading questions pertinent thereto, were distributed throughout the State of Oklahoma as well as to neighboring states within the listening range of the University station. Frank Ernest Hill,[9] in commenting on Doctor Sowers's efforts in connection with her program, states:

> Doctor Alice Sowers can point to her groups as an evidence of widespread interest in her work. It is safe to say that owing to the groups she was able to establish the Family Life Forum, has convinced the university authorities of the vitality of the program, has got more radio stations throughout the state to carry it, has gathered a larger number of individual listeners, and, as a result of groups already established, a larger number of groups; for the knowledge that bodies of radio listeners exist stimulates the formation of new ones. Moreover, Doctor Sowers has undoubtedly had an easier time in getting speakers to appear on the program because of the serious popular sup-

8 Frank Ernest Hill and W. E. Williams, *Radio's Listening Groups*, page 87. New York: Columbia University Press, 1941.
9 *Ibid.*, page 116.

port that her groups indicate, and she has been able to influence her speakers to prepare more carefully. She gives a sheet of instructions to each expert before he appears, and it is safe to say that participants usually pay more attention to these instructions because they know of the listening bodies which the program attracts, and are inclined to feel the importance of their rôles more than they would were they appearing before a radio audience which, to their knowledge, was composed only of scattered individuals.

Presumably the program which has been responsible for the organization of the largest number of listening groups is "America's Town Meeting of the Air." This program, presented first in 1935 over NBC by George V. Denny, Jr., and now heard over American, has well over twelve hundred groups associated with it. These groups, scattered in all parts of the country, generally meet to listen to the program and then stay for a discussion period. The groups and their members are registered with Town Hall and for a fee, depending on the type and amount of service, can receive various aids and informational services. Such groups naturally aid in spreading the fame of the program and in so doing are acting as salesmen for the local station over which the program is heard. Mr. Denny is convinced that these discussion groups have had an important part in stimulating the growth of knowledge of local, national, and international affairs which is evidenced in national polls on all current topics.

In Great Britain

Realizing the potentialities of adult education through group listening, but also realizing that very little effort had been put forth to discover what was being done in the way of establishing listening groups, the National Advisory Council on Radio in Education asked the British Institute of Adult Education for a report on similar activities being carried forward in Britain. The report was published by the Council in 1933 with a foreword by the Council's Director, Doctor Levering

Tyson, now President of Muhlenberg College. Doctor Tyson states:

> In spite of an often expressed belief that study clubs, college classes, worker's education centers, and various adult education groups ought to be able to use certain types of broadcast programs in their own interest, there really has been little progress in America toward organized listening of this sort. There are several reasons why more progress in group listening has not been recorded. In the first place, the lack of an intelligent system of program planning for radio in the United States, in turn traceable to the instability of our whole radio machinery and practice, makes it difficult if not impossible to co-ordinate the requirements of groups with programs designed for a national audience. Then there is the ever-present difficulty of the time differential in various parts of the country. A network program that is broadcast at eight-thirty o'clock in the evening for a group located in the eastern time zone would be broadcast on the Pacific Coast as early as five-thirty P.M., practically eliminating the program's usefulness for groups operating in the western provinces.
>
> Contrasting what we face in America with what we find in Europe, the only continent where group listening has been developed at all, other difficulties are emphasized. In a country like Great Britain, for example, conditions seem more favorable for this type of thing. There the broadcasting service is compactly organized, and audiences of certain types are more clearly defined than they are here. There are no time changes. The territory to be covered does not offer a serious problem as it does for us.

In discussing the setup in Great Britain, Mr. W. E. Williams, of the British Institute of Adult Listening, says: [10]

> A Central Council for Broadcast Adult Education was set up in 1929 for a period of five years. It included a Central Council for Broadcast Adult Education and four Area Councils, each with its Education Officer. (The Home Counties, Wales, and Scotland were not included in this development until 1934-1935, when three additional Area Councils and

[10] Hill and Williams, *op. cit.*, pages 171-172.

Education Officers were appointed.) During these five years the Central Council planned and supervised substantial programmes consisting of five concurrent series of ten or twelve talks, each broadcast at the fixed hour of 7:30 P.M. each evening from Monday to Friday throughout the year, with the exception of the three summer months.

In 1934, the machinery for stimulating and organizing groups was revised; in fact, it was dissolved and a much smaller Central Committee for Group Listening was set up in its place. They were not responsible for program content, leaving that to the British Broadcasting Corporation, but were instead acting as educational administrators. Mr. Williams further points out:

> However, between 1935 and 1937 it became clear that the development of groups would never be soundly based unless the administrative aspects were supervised by specialists with the necessary training and knowledge. Since school broadcasting had already secured the services of a distinguished Director of Education to look after the administrative side of school broadcasting, it was decided early in 1937 to put the administration of group listening under the same supervision. As Secretary of the Central Council for Group Listening he was assisted by a group of educationists, who continued to act as an advisory body on programmes for the B.B.C. and had, indeed, a programme subcommittee which continued to work in close contact with the responsible programme officials.
>
> The B.B.C. officers were now free to devote their whole attention to programmes, while experienced educationists (that is, the Central Committee for Group Listening) were able to go ahead with the work of organizing groups and training leaders. . . . The war has, however, played havoc with this foreshadowed development, and owing to the curtailment of programme alternatives for defence reasons the whole system of talks-broadcasting has had to be modified almost out of recognition.

IN EUROPE

In half a dozen European countries [11] before the war some

[11] Hill and Williams, *op. cit.*, page 209.

more or less sporadic efforts had been made to organize groups
for listening. For example, Sweden did some effective work
with languages, claiming as many as 50,000 listeners to various
courses, and Czechoslovakia probably was on its way to establishing the most successful listener-group set-up of any country
on the continent, with a total of 4128 groups having an aggre-
gate group membership of 173,000 people for a series on "What
Can You Do For Your District?"

In Russia, for many years, radio has been used in factories
for the discussion of technical problems by employers and for
the purpose of answering questions put to them by the workers.
Loud-speakers are found in town and city squares so that announcements of national importance can be made on short
notice by the heads of the government. People, of course,
gather in groups around these loud-speakers to listen and discuss
what they have heard. Back in 1930 or 1932 there seemed to
be a rapid growth in the formation of discussion groups in
Germany, especially in rural areas, where people were eager
for education and information on all subjects. With the advent
of the Nazi régime, such activities, of course, were done away
with, and it remains to be seen whether or not they will be
resumed.

Mr. Williams sums up his observations on group listening in
Europe as follows: [12]

> 1. Group listening in the European democracies has proved
> an innovation of slow growth. This modest development must
> be attributed, for the most part, to certain very real disad-
> vantages inherent in the group-listening principle.
> 2. Of these disadvantages the principal one is that group
> listening can provide only a one-track system of discussion.
> With this disadvantage there is closely linked the question of
> group leadership. This substitute leadership of ideas pro-
> jected by the broadcaster is at best a natural disability of the
> system.
> 3. Group listening has not established itself as a well-defined
> new colony of adult education. It has depended largely for its

[12] Hill and Williams, *op. cit.*, pages 164-165.

existence so far on the support accorded it by the adult educational organizations, yet wherever these are already well developed, group listening has not proved a particularly important collaborator.

4. As an educational method there is some risk of the overvaluation of discussion. To be effective, discussion must be based on possession of a body of knowledge by the participants; and group listening often ends by beating the air or in ignorance.

5. The limited appeal of group listening in Europe contrasts with the volume of "serious" broadcasting there. The interest in educational talks, radio discussions, and features is considerable in most European countries; so, too, is the demand for such types of educational broadcasting as courses in foreign languages.

6. The special programmes designed for group listening must not be assessed merely from the formal point of view of the adult educator; they are proved to possess what may be called a diffused value, and in this way are shown to be a social influence of considerable and diverse value.

FORMING NEW GROUPS

There is no doubt, apparently, that recently there has been much more interest in this country in the establishment of listener groups than in any other part of the world, as evidenced by the claim that there are at present more than fifteen thousand such groups meeting regularly, with a membership well into the hundreds of thousands. This, of course, cannot take into account the untold numbers of informal groups which are probably meeting just as regularly in homes everywhere to listen to such programs as the opera or the symphony. They can certainly be called listening groups as well as those other groups which meet for the purpose of listening and discussing. It is impossible, however, in this short chapter to touch upon all the types and forms these latter groups may take, nor to cite all the places where group activity is being carried on. Many radio stations have been helping such groups over a period of years. The most extensive survey

on the whole subject that has been made is reported by Frank
Ernest Hill in *Radio's Listening Groups,* from which numerous
quotations have been made in this chapter. A careful study of
the contents of this book will give the reader as complete a
picture as is now available of what has been done, as well as of
the quality and worth-whileness of this whole activity.

It follows logically that the next question must be, how does
one go about forming a listening group? A few suggestions
may be set down as a guide:

1. It should be apparent that there must be a well-organized
radio program available, carried consistently by the local
station at a definite hour.

2. There must be sincerity of purpose back of the starting of
such a group.

3. If the group is being formed for the purpose of discussion
following the listening period, an able leader must be available
for the discussion.

4. Membership in the group should probably be decided
after the aims and purposes in forming the group have been
determined.

5. A group may be started by an individual or an organization, such as a parent-teacher association, a woman's club, a
luncheon club, a library, a church, or any other local organization. But unless there is an able leader, intensely interested
in the idea and the program, interest on the part of the members is liable to sag, and before too long, individuals drop out
and the group disbands.

6. It is desirable to have the membership of any discussion
group as representative as possible — a clergyman, a doctor,
a librarian, a banker, people from various trades — to insure a
fair sampling of all schools of thought and opinions. This is
sure to make for a more interesting and provocative meeting.

7. It is well to keep most discussion groups fairly small in
number, say, fifteen or twenty persons. Forums, of course, may
run to fifty or more members, but it is difficult to keep a discussion moving in a constructive and objective vein if the
group is too large. Many people who are hesitant about expressing their ideas before a large audience will gladly enter
into the discussion when the group is small.

8. It is helpful if some members of the group can take notes during the broadcast, so that no points will be ignored when it comes time for the discussion period. Otherwise, only the points or topics brought out toward the end of the program will be remembered and discussed.

Frank Ernest Hill has so ably summed up the part listening groups can play in our democracy that it seems fitting to close this chapter with his words:

They serve society as a whole. They promote leadership, they make for a better informed electorate, they encourage the habit of discussion upon which a democracy must rest, and they break down prejudices and increase tolerance. Moreover, they already do these things on a greater scale, in proportion to the effort expended, than any non-radio agencies can hope to do them; and they hold the possibility of exerting much more power than they have already manifested. Radio and its groups may be as important to the democratic process as the railroad and motor cars are to transportation. They can be multiplied and immeasurably improved. If they are, they may become the instruments of a constructive and significant revolution, a revolution not only in educational techniques, but also in important social habits.[13]

[13] Hill, *The Groups Tune In*, page 22.

6

SERVICING THE PROGRAM

CHAPTER 22

PRESS AND PUBLICITY

"PUBLICITY" is a term generally used to describe the end product of a process that brings a name, an article, an idea, a cause, or a service to public attention. In the all-inclusive sense, publicity is anything in the way of prepared words or illustrations that makes a calculated impact on the public mind.

The foregoing observation is placed here solely for the benefit of those individuals who insist that any study must begin with a definition. From the standpoint of the job to be undertaken by a radio-station publicity man, it is much more practical to begin with the assumption that everybody knows what publicity is and to proceed immediately to an analysis of what publicity can do for a radio station. The next logical step is to plan how to do what must be done — and then do it.

PURPOSES OF PUBLICITY

From the standpoint of a radio station, publicity has the primary purpose of helping to build and keep the station's audience. As between two stations of equivalent coverage and programs, publicity can be the margin that gives one station a better and more consistent audience than the other.

The second purpose of station publicity is to keep the station, its people, and its service on a respectable footing with the public.

A third purpose is to help to build and maintain a commercial advertiser's good opinion of the station. This purpose can be of direct aid in the sales column through helping to retain sponsors already on the air and to cultivate new sponsors. It is obvious that this particular purpose borders very closely on station promotion, but since the publicity director at many local stations is also the director of sales promotion, consideration of the topic is logical under the publicity heading.

OUTLETS

In planning a station's publicity campaign, work begins with a complete review of possible outlets. The next step is to determine what kind of material must be provided for those outlets. The third consideration is purely physical — a determination of how much time can be spent on the job and how much effective material can be turned out in that time. Consideration of the time element is highly important. Any experienced publicity man will testify that mass of material has very little to do with end results, especially if quality is low. A station publicity man would be well advised to spend the bulk of his time planning and placing a few good stories rather than in turning out a quantity of mediocre copy.

Radio Stations. In setting out to survey available outlets, the one thing a station publicity man should *not* do is to overlook the possibilities of his own station as a channel for his efforts. Strange as it seems, many radio publicity men have completely missed this point. It is a complete mystery why a few lines in a newspaper should be regarded by a publicity man as more worth while than a quarter-hour chance at a station audience, but this has often been the case.

As an illustration of what may be done along the line of using one's own station as a publicity outlet, ever since the fall of 1938, WMAQ has presented a weekly, quarter-hour radio gossip show, prepared by the Press Department of the NBC Central Division. Under the title "Radio Parade," this program has built a good audience for itself and has furnished a valuable means of giving extended coverage to many radio stories. Aside from radio gossip and feature material and program news, the broadcast has been utilized also to present interviews with radio performers.

An interesting offshoot of this technique may be found in a somewhat similar program launched by the NBC Press Department, but currently off the air. This particular program followed the assumption that the normal operations of the station itself might be interesting to the listener, and so it proved. Over a period of time, the program presented on-the-spot interviews with station and network personnel in sound effects, program, continuity, engineering, music, recording, and various other broadcasting departments.

Illustrating the technique involved on an individual show was the program demonstrating a station's short-wave equipment. The broadcast opened in the studio for a quick standard program summary. The announcer then transferred to a portable microphone and "walked" the program out to the studio roof. Across the Chicago River, at a spot easily visible from the announcer's post, was another NBC announcer with a pack transmitter, and the program jumped over to pick up a conversation between this man and the captain of a Chicago fire boat anchored at that spot. The broadcast next jumped to the short-wave station located in the Civic Opera Building for a brief chat with the operator on duty there, and wound up with some conversation carried on with a man in the NBC mobile unit, cruising the Chicago waterfront. From such programs as these, listeners were able to gather an adequate picture of behind-the-scenes operations at the station and an understanding of broadcasting problems that no studio tour would ever convey.

Along the line of gossip shows, station publicity men will be interested to know that the NBC Press Department in New York prepares and syndicates an ably written fifteen-minute weekly script designed for use as is or for incorporation with similar material prepared by local stations. "Your Radio Reporter" is the name of this program, and it is available for the asking.

Newspapers. Inevitably, for reasons which are so obvious that they need no repetition here, any talk of publicity must include a consideration of newspapers. Before studying the how and why of this highly important topic, there is need for a slight digression into the field of publicity ethics. No honest publicity man will ever tell a deliberate lie to a newspaper. He will not bore newspaper people with stories and items that have no news merit. He will reciprocate favors whenever possible and will do his best to give the papers a break whenever they give him a break. There should be no one-way traffic in the relationships between stations and newspapers. Failure to "give something for something" is often the basic irritation that brings on a case of newspaper-radio friction.

Publicity material intended for newspaper use falls into two types: stories of national importance transcending the local scene, and stories that are chiefly of interest to papers in the station's territory. The first type of story is not very common. The fact that Roy Acuff, rustic fiddler and singer of the WSM staff, had been qualified by fans for the Tennessee gubernatorial primaries in 1944 was of more than local interest; coming as it did in a hot election year, that story should (and did) carry the national news wire services. The fact that Roy Acuff had purchased a vacant lot in Nashville for a future home may be of interest to the real-estate editors of Nashville, but hardly to anyone else — except possibly Roy Acuff.

Chief grist of a station's publicity mill will be radio program and personality material and straight news of interest to the local area, to be sent to papers in the station's primary coverage area. With the aid of newspaper directories and station-coverage maps, a listing of all papers in the territory should be made. The next step in setting up coverage for the field is to get a copy of every weekly and daily paper listed. A close study of these papers will develop two facts: first, the study will tell what kind of radio material is being used; secondly, the study will uncover a number of papers not using radio information which might do so if given the right kind. The net result is an abundance of specific information and a mailing list.

Magazines. In the magazine field, a station publicity man will be chiefly concerned with the trade press and, to a much smaller degree, with fan magazines and those of general circulation. One of the chief benefits of a trade magazine is its value in presenting the station's story to a sponsor or an advertising agency. The leading publications in this field are *Broadcasting and Broadcast Advertising, Radio Daily, Adver-*

tising Age, Tide, the *Advertiser, Billboard, Variety,* and *Motion Picture Daily.*

Currently, there are only two radio fan magazines: *Radio Mirror* and *Tune-In.* These offer occasional opportunities for stories on artists and programs, but stories should be of more than local interest. General magazines or trade magazines in other fields will accept specialized stories now and then and should be kept in mind.

After deciding where material can be sent, the next point to decide is what kind of material is available at the station and how it should be prepared, packaged, and shipped. For the newspaper list, routine program timetables, best-bet suggestions, program paragraphs (short items in news style giving program facts in detail), program corrections, and follow-up items on new program developments are all part of the basic service. A local station would probably issue such basic service once a week, with follow-up correction service at intervals between. Program stories in general should have an eight- or ten-day deadline if possible, and corrections should follow as soon as they develop.

PREPARING AND PRESENTING COPY

Material. It is vital to the success of any long-term publicity project that basic newspaper principles should be followed in preparing and presenting copy. The copy must be honest. It must be accurate. It must be brief. It costs money to set news material in type, so brevity is far better than bulk. In writing a story for the papers, come to the point immediately, be brief, don't editorialize, follow news style, put in a period, and quit. Be regular about it, too. If material reaches a radio editor's desk at regular intervals, he will come to look for it and depend on it at those intervals. Also, keep the copy clean, and try to make it a bit distinctive if possible. These are small considerations, but they fall into the same bracket as the question of whether you like a crisply ironed napkin or a crumpled one when you sit down to eat.

Material for trade papers should be sent out in the form of

a weekly roundup, mailed to reach these magazines not later than Tuesday of each week. A special last-minute story has some chance if wired no later than Thursday. In general, the trade press will be interested in news of station personnel, visitors from the industry, new business sold, stories about special promotions, new equipment, etc.

Requirements for other magazines are too detailed to be covered here. The best recommendation is to study the magazines closely and then follow their pattern in developing stories.

Aside from routine program releases, there is good opportunity for station publicity in special-feature stories. Depending on the nature of the material, such stories may be sent out in the regular releases to newspapers or they may be routed to magazines or other outlets. In general, there are three types of features to look for at a station: biographical or historical articles on artists, station personalities, or programs; magazine-length features which tell a vital story; experience stories with a twist or snapper ending or with comedy features.

Pictures. Pictures are certainly not to be overlooked, and if a budget for pictures is available, a regular mailing list for photographs and/or mats should certainly be set up. It is earnestly recommended that station publicity personnel should study papers and magazines for a clue as to what is being used before burning up valuable flash bulbs and negative stock. Several general suggestions can be offered here.

It's a good idea to make a complete portrait file of all important station personnel. The file should also contain pictures of the studio layout, the lobby, the transmitter, etc. There is constant call for this kind of material, and it is well to have it on hand.

In pictures intended for newspaper use, avoid wide compositions. Pictures should be made to print in one column, or in two at the widest. Many newspapers will use nothing but half-column heads.

Obviously posed pictures should be avoided like bubonic plague. Natural shots with good candid quality have the best chance for getting into print.

Pictures should always be taken with the idea that they are

going to be used. It is impossible to justify a photograph budget if the pictures end up in somebody's scrapbook or pin-up collection.

Write the best caption possible. A bad caption can spoil the chances of a good picture. Conversely, a good caption sometimes helps a fair-to-middling pose to get into print.

If the budget will stand it, set up a regular mat mailing list for smaller papers that do not want to be burdened with engraving expense.

Stunts. Now comes a consideration of stunts (or "gags," if the reader prefers). Whether intended for development in photographs, news features, or magazine stories, the stunt is one of the oldest and best devices of publicity. At a time when there may be nothing startling or newsworthy about a station, an active publicity man will use his wits and concoct a stunt.

In general, the stunt must be completely authentic or completely absurd. Avoid the so-called "press agent's pipe-dream," in which the participant in a stunt never knows about his participation therein until he reads about it in the papers next day. If the facts of a stunt do not already exist, take steps to make them exist.

Another fact to remember is that stunts must be suited to the participants. Never make an actor look silly unless he is a comedian and, therefore, entitled to look silly. The ordinary run of people in stunts may appear crestfallen, chagrined, or amazed by events, or happy about the whole thing.

There are many kinds of stunts, and a few are classified here:

Informative gags: Pictures or stories that connect a station personality with some angle of a national or local project. An example of one such stunt is a picture strip of a radio actress illustrating how to prepare tin cans for salvage.

"He was there when" gags: Pictures of station people participating in civic events, sports events, etc., any kind of circumstance where juxtaposition of the individual and the event has combined publicity and news value.

"On the Lot" gags: There are plenty of picture possibilities in station events. Example of one such gag is the occasion on which WMAQ dedicated a new group of studios. The pic-

ture had a pretty girl and the chief engineer breaking an old power tube over a corner of the audiorack, launching the new setup.

Goofy gags: An out-and-out gag that is obviously a gag gets some of the best attention. An example of this is a picture of comedian Red Skelton nursing a finger that, apparently, had just been chewed by a hot dog equipped with legs and a set of false teeth. The caption was: "No News. Dog Bites Man."

CO-OPERATION

Any person who has been in publicity for a reasonable length of time knows that much is to be gained from co-operative effort and that two or more groups can often combine for a joint effort that is far better in effect than what each might do individually. Co-operatively planned publicity can produce excellent results through wider coverage and through unification of effort.

For such co-operation the local station publicity man can often depend on sponsors and their advertising or publicity agencies. In particular, local stations can rely on the network press departments for much help, especially in connection with establishing metropolitan publicity contacts and in aiding the circulation of station stories that have national importance.

Of particular value to the local man is the co-operation he can obtain from working with newspapers in his territory. Practically all newspapers at one time or another indulge in special promotions, and many of them would appreciate a helping hand from the local station. Also of great importance are co-operative programs, such as "Meet the Press," which was aired over WMAQ weekly during most of 1942 and 1943. This was a fifteen-minute broadcast, presenting newspapermen of the Chicago area in an "old shoes" type of interview about themselves, their jobs, and their papers. Another variation of this idea, used by several stations, is to send a recording crew around the station's territory to interview newspaper editors for a series of delayed ET shows.

In essence, the success of any station publicity campaign depends on money, time, and ingenuity. Generally speaking, a healthy budget will produce healthy publicity results, although it is possible to do a fine job on even a small budget. Time is necessary for the development of plans because, while a lot of publicity is the result of split-second thinking, most successful campaigns are the result of plodding, careful thought. Most important is ingenuity. With a small handful of outstanding ideas, cleverly thought out and cleverly promoted, a station can achieve practically all the goals of publicity.

CHAPTER 23

TRAFFIC AND COMMUNICATIONS

NETWORK

IN GENERAL, the traffic department is the contact between a network and its affiliated stations for all routine matters in connection with the availability of both commercial and sustaining programs. The traffic department also is charged with the arrangement and co-ordination of all wire and overseas facilities that may be required for the transmission of programs to the affiliated stations from various program origination or pickup points, as well as from the studios.

A network consists of many thousand miles of specially engineered telephone circuits leased from the telephone company. These circuits are available for the network's use twenty-four hours a day, and the time they are used varies from sixteen to eighteen hours a day in different sections of the country. In addition to these circuits, traffic operations places several hundred orders a month for temporary facilities, primarily for program transmission for pickups outside of the studios. Such temporary facilities consist of specially engineered telephone circuits and the overseas communications facilities and are purchased on a per-pickup basis.

Many details are involved in the handling and routing of network programs and arranging for program pickups, and the seven huge traffic operations boards — at NBC, for example, one for each day in the week — in the traffic operations office provide a graphic picture of the network setup with all current and future program information that has been received for the entire day. These charts provide a visual picture of operations and act as a "bible" for all operational activities.

Network operational information is transmitted twice daily to the telephone company, via teletype, and is simultaneously forwarded by the telephone company to all their operational points throughout the United States. This information is also sent to the operating personnel in various cities which are the primary operating points of the network.

The Commercial Traffic Division. This division is the general source of station information for all details concerned with the scheduling of network commercial programs in accordance with information received from the sales department. This covers such points as the starting and ending dates of programs; the program content of commercial programs; their availability for use by a station; various program and product changes; contests and offers, etc.

The Sustaining Traffic Division. The sustaining traffic division similarly advises the stations relative to sustaining programs in accordance with advice received from the program department. While commercial programs are available only to those stations ordered by the advertiser through the sales department, sustaining programs are made available to all affiliated stations in accordance with the availability of network line facilities. The acceptance of such programs is entirely the choice of the individual station.

As it is necessary to keep detailed records of the handling of commercial programs by affiliated stations, wire reports are received daily from the stations covering their handling of the previous day's schedule. Supplementing these daily reports a mail report is received from every affiliated station covering every broadcast for the previous week. Not so much detail is required for sustaining-program records. A weekly report is received from each affiliated station covering its schedule of sustaining programs for the previous week.

From these reports and records the station reports division sends "certificates of performance" certifying to the advertising agencies handling the sponsors' accounts that the required stations have or have not carried their programs as ordered, together with any details relative to any breaks or interruptions in service that may have occurred. The station reports division also prepares a monthly chart showing one week's schedule of programs available to and carried by the affiliated stations.

The Communications Division of the Traffic Department.
This division is responsible for the sending, receiving, and
delivery of all telegrams and communications. Teletype is used
primarily in communicating with the affiliated stations. All networks have a leased teletype circuit for a specified number of
hours' service per day. This circuit is like a private-line telephone circuit and is entirely for the use of each individual
network. Teletype service to affiliated stations is called TWX
(timed wire exchange service). This service is handled like
any long-distance telephone call with the communication in
writing instead of by voice. Provisional points act as relay
points for the affiliated stations in their own areas or geographical divisions. This cuts down the cost of TWX operation,
inasmuch as the necessary information can be relayed to provisional points on the contract circuits.

In addition to TWX communications with affiliated stations,
regular telegraph service is often used and, of course, for communication with foreign countries the overseas facilities of the
various communications companies are used. Approximately
125,000 thirty-word messages pass through the communications office of NBC each month, which is comparable to the
telegraph traffic of a good-sized city.

LOCAL INDEPENDENT STATIONS

The title of traffic supervisor in a small local, independent
station is usually borne by someone, who, in addition to being
the keeper of the time chart, must be responsible for a dozen
other odd jobs, including responsibility for the handling and
scheduling of all programs; and in most cases that person is a
woman.

Either the program director or the sales manager who is
interested in booking a new program requests "availabilities"
of the traffic supervisor. In other words, he is interested in
finding out what time periods on the daily schedule are "open."
And by "open" is generally meant what times are not filled by
a commercial program. Unfortunately, most sustaining programs are not given the same consideration as the commercial

programs and almost always are moved at will if a commercial program is being offered to the station. It is the business of the traffic supervisor to keep the daily and weekly schedules up-to-date at all times so that "availabilities" may be seen instantly.

If the request is for a sponsored or commercial program, the traffic supervisor must know the nature of the product wanting time, as the policy of the station, in all probability, makes it imperative to see that there is at least a fifteen-minute interval between sponsors of competing products. The same is true of spot announcements. As a rule the scheduling of the spot announcements is left entirely to the traffic supervisor, with the salesman indicating whether the announcement is to be heard during daytime or evening. As most of the revenue of the local, independent station is derived from these short commercial announcements put on by some local shop wanting to announce a sale, it is not unusual for requests for time to come through on the day they are to be heard — sometimes as many as five or ten for one company. It is then the job of the traffic supervisor to see that they are placed where they will not compete with other similar products. In a small town this is likely to be a ticklish job. The traffic supervisor is also responsible for handling all sustaining programs, and in many instances creates and writes the shows to fill any vacant spot, just as many of the salesmen are often not only responsible for getting the orders for commercial shows but must write the shows as well.

A schedule chart is kept at every station, as shown in Chapter 6. This schedule is handled and typed daily by the traffic supervisor, who is also responsible for seeing that it and all copy for the announcers and engineers are gathered together in a "copy book," and dire consequences result if one item is missing. Not infrequently, a large part of the copy used at small stations is standard and is used from day to day. The traffic supervisor must see that this copy is filed properly and checked, so that each piece of copy goes on at the right time on the right day.

In some instances announcers "ad-lib" the copy used on sustaining recorded programs. It is then the duty of the traffic supervisor to make up the lists of records and keep them in order, so that the same numbers will not be heard too frequently.

In addition to keeping the schedules and copy books straight, the traffic supervisor is responsible for keeping an accurate record of all commercial programs, future and past. Future programming information is generally kept on large wall boards made up, sometimes, six months in advance, each board representing a separate day. The type of program usually is marked on the board with different colored pencils, red for commercial, for instance, blue for sustaining news, and green for all other sustaining programs, with perhaps yellow for participating programs. Since this chart is the reference for all the station personnel, sales and program, it must be kept absolutely accurate and up-to-date.

Transcribed commercial programs and announcements are also the traffic supervisor's responsibility. They must be very carefully handled, especially these days, when they are likely to be of glass. Each announcement must be played through and checked before it is broadcast to see that no mistake has occurred in the recording; typed copy for checking accompanies each recording. These transcriptions are put on the air by the engineer, who, in addition to handling the control panel, also is responsible for the broadcasting of all transcriptions. The traffic supervisor must see that these records are sent to the engineer and later returned either to be filed or to be sent back to the company from which they came.

NETWORK AFFILIATES

In a network affiliated station, the traffic department generally consists of two or three persons instead of one, as at a small local independent station. Then, in addition to the jobs indicated above which will come under the traffic department, the supervisor or the department as a whole is responsible for seeing to it that all the network offerings are sent to the right people in the station, and, if accepted, are properly scheduled. The department is also in charge of scheduling all local "cut-ins" (when a local distributor or dealer makes an announcement as to where the product advertised on the network show may be purchased), timings, and network cues, and seeing that they are properly indicated on the schedule and included in the copy book.

The traffic department of the affiliated station must supply "availabilities" to the network when queried and must see that the network programs are properly scheduled. Also accurate records have to be kept of the scheduling of all commercial and sustaining programs for the weekly reports which must be sent in to the networks. If there have been interruptions during the broadcasting of any commercial program, such interruptions must be indicated, with the exact amount of time lost and the reason for the interruption or delay.

7

ENGINEERING

CHAPTER 24

RADIO ENGINEERING

ANY DAY at any radio broadcasting station there are visitors, most of whom just drop in to "see broadcasting." After seeing and hearing some of their favorite orchestras, entertainers, and announcers, they also hope to learn something about how radio works. The usual visitor's conception of the latter is pretty vague: in some way the microphone picks up sound waves, and in some mysterious manner "electricity" conveys the sound waves to their loud-speakers at home. Even seeing the equipment does not help much. The guide points out a row of black panels and says that they are amplifiers, but the visitor sees nothing familiar nor very interesting except perhaps a few vacuum tubes projecting from the panels. There is no sound or visible evidence to indicate what (if anything) the amplifiers are doing, and the visitor walks on unimpressed; to him the workings of radio remain as much a mystery as ever.

Modern radio apparatus, in fact, consists mostly of silent, motionless devices that show no outward signs of being in operation. In the following pages an attempt will be made to outline briefly the mechanism by which programs are broadcast.

BASIC PRINCIPLES

First in the sequence of things is the studio where the program is performed, in which a microphone "picks up" the sounds. Sound consists of waves of air particles in to-and-fro motion. The microphone has a sensitive metal-foil ribbon which the moving air deflects back and forth slightly in passing. The microphone is also a miniature electric generator, and the vibrations of the metal ribbon cause a weak electric current to flow through it, fluctuating exactly as the air particles did. The program has now lost completely its identity as an air sound wave and has been converted into an electric current whose variations in strength represent the original sound. But the current produced is only about one-millionth as strong as that required to operate an ordinary electric lamp bulb! To be useful, it must be amplified to much greater strength, but without altering the nature of its variations.

Adjacent to the studio is a control booth to which the currents from the microphone are conveyed by wires. The output of each microphone passes through its individual volume control, called a "fader," and then all the outputs from microphones in that one studio are mixed together. After mixing, the currents pass through the master volume control and thence, still being conveyed by wires, to the amplifiers.

An amplifier is an electric circuit which "makes" large currents of small ones. The heart of the amplifier is the vacuum tube, which acts as a sort of shutter and controls large currents by application of weaker ones. Thus, the feeble currents from the microphone are made to control slightly stronger currents, and these in turn are applied to another tube to control still larger currents, and so on, as many times as are necessary to obtain the current strength desired. Each vacuum tube may amplify the current forty- or fifty-fold. In all, the total amplification between the microphone and the control-room lines is about ten billion times! Still the current is relatively weak — the energy is about equivalent to the amount that is required to light one small flashlight bulb.

In the main control room, where the final amplifiers are located, there are sundry control and switching devices for switching from one studio to another for successive programs and for doing the dozens of other things necessary for the smooth, continuous flow of programs.

Up to this point the program has actually had no connection at all with radio, for it has traveled from one point to another in the form of currents carried by wires. The currents — and the entire process, in fact — are very similar to those flowing in telephones.

Not until the program reaches the transmitting station, however, is it actually put "on the air." The station itself is usually located in a rural district away from the city and studios and consequently is seldom seen by visitors. It consists of more silent, motionless panels of electrical equipment and vacuum tubes, this time of larger dimensions to enable them to handle more electric power, and an antenna. Here the program is broadcast into space. The way in which this is accomplished is relatively simple. If an electric current is caused to flow in a long straight wire, and it is also made to reverse its direction of flow many thousands of times per second, the electrical energy literally refuses to be confined to the wire. Some of it radiates into surrounding space, spreads out in all directions, and keeps going at a speed of 186,000 miles a second. The number of oscillations or current reversals in one second of time is the frequency of the station. We usually express this in kilocycles, meaning the number of thousands of times the current reverses each second. (Another method of expressing the same thing is in terms of wave length. Wave length is measured in meters and is equal to three hundred million divided by the frequency in cycles. Thus, a station operating at one thousand kilocycles, or one million cycles, has a wave length of three hundred meters.)

Amplified currents from the microphone are also oscillating many times per second, corresponding to the original vibrations of the sound waves. It will probably occur to the reader, then, that these currents themselves might be put into an antenna and thus be made to radiate directly. But the trouble is that their frequency, or number of oscillations, is not great enough for radiation to take place, so that it is necessary to use a separate current of higher frequency to accomplish the radiation.

When some of this released energy encounters other wires in its travels through space — receiving antennas, for example — it produces minute currents in them. These currents oscillate at the same rate as the parent current in the transmitting antenna. They also take on other features of the transmitter current; if the latter changes in strength or frequency, they follow faithfully. Now, the only reason for complicating things by introducing high-frequency current into the system is to achieve the necessary radiation to carry energy through space from the transmitting antenna to the receiving antenna, whence it receives the name "carrier." It serves the same purpose as the blank paper upon which this page was printed: namely, to carry information.

To make use of the carrier to convey information — that is, the program — the information must be imprinted upon it, just as the type is imprinted on the paper. This is accomplished by arranging things in the transmitter so that the amplified program currents from the studio will control either the carrier strength or the carrier frequency. In other words, the nature of the carrier energy being radiated is "molded" to conform to the fluctuating program currents.

In the receiving antenna, the current induced reproduces the fluctuations of the carrier. In the receiver itself, the carrier is removed, having served its useful purpose, and is discarded; only the currents corresponding to the original program sounds are retained. These are amplified and passed through the loud-speaker, which reverses the job done by the microphone and converts the electric currents into air sound waves again. Except for minor shortcomings of the entire system, the reproduced sound is identical with the original studio program.

Utilizing these physical principles, radio broadcasting has grown to full stature as a public service. It provides a medium for the distribution of entertainment, news, and information unmatched by any other. Now let us observe the elaboration of these basic principles into a complete modern broadcasting station.

THE STUDIOS

A medium-sized broadcasting station will usually require several studios. For best acoustic results, there is an optimum size of studio for each size of group: a five-piece orchestra in a large empty studio *sounds* like a five-piece orchestra in a large empty studio. So an assortment of different-sized studios is needed. One or two for small groups may be about the size and shape of an ordinary living room, while another is large enough to accommodate an orchestra of thirty or forty pieces plus an audience of two hundred or three hundred people. In addition, there may be one or more smaller studios for recorded or transcribed programs, news broadcasts, and the relaying of network programs.

Usually the studios are located for convenience in a building in the downtown section of a city, where — unfortunately — traffic and street noises are most intense. Besides these noises, which are transmitted through the air, the building itself is subject to vibrations produced by passing streetcars, trains, and other heavy traffic and by machinery within the same or neighboring buildings. Both of these kinds of disturbances have to be excluded from the studios so that they will not be picked up by the microphones; sound isolation is therefore a necessity. This is provided partly by the sound-absorbing material which reduces reverberation, as explained in the following paragraph, and partly by the use of double walls and flexible suspension of floors, walls, and ceilings on springlike mountings.

If an ordinary room with bare plastered walls were used as a studio, the large amount of reverberation or echo of sound reflected from the walls would create an unpleasant annoyance to a listener inside the room. If a microphone is placed in such a room and connected to a loud-speaker in another room, the disturbing effect of reverberation as heard through the loud-speaker is even more objectionable. For this reason, the walls and ceilings of broadcasting studios are covered with sound-absorbing material to reduce the reverberation to a satisfactory degree.

Sometimes, however, an excess amount of echo is desired for some special effect. For this purpose, specially constructed echo chambers with hard plaster walls, floors, and ceilings are used. The program is reproduced in the echo chamber by a loud-speaker and bounces around from wall to wall and ceiling to floor until it is picked up again by a microphone at the opposite end of the room. Thus, a hollow or "empty barn" effect can be added to any part of a program to create the illusion of a cave, a tunnel, etc.

Microphone Placement. In the studio proper, one or more microphones are carefully placed for the best pickup of the program. Normally, best results are obtained by using only one microphone at a time, although several may be set up in different locations for various parts of a program. In a typical studio setup, for example, there may be one microphone for the orchestra pickup, a second for a soloist, a third for a quartet, and a fourth for an announcer. Nevertheless only one should be "live" or "faded in" at any one time, because sound reaches different parts of the studio at different times, and if the same sound is picked up by two microphones at different locations, interference results. Directional microphones help to reduce this effect and, if properly used, permit the operation of two or more microphones at once to pick up separate parts of the same performance.

Proper use of microphones requires some knowledge of their characteristics, plus experience and experiment. Figure 7 shows a typical studio setup with microphones placed for orchestra, vocal soloist, and announcer; the orchestra seating is arranged so that a good balance of instruments is observed when heard on a monitoring loud-speaker. This usually calls for placing the lighter instruments nearest the microphone, with the brass and bass instruments farther to the rear. The soloist and his microphone are then placed in the "dead" area of the orchestra microphone. The soloist's microphone is oriented so that its "dead" side faces the orchestra.

Often a part in a dramatic program calls for the effect of an overheard telephone conversation. For such purposes, there are special amplifiers whose reproduction is deliberately distorted to sound like a telephone. When such an amplifier is used in connection with one of the studio microphones, anything said into it will create the illusion of having been heard through a telephone.

Studio Control Booths. Adjacent to each studio is a control

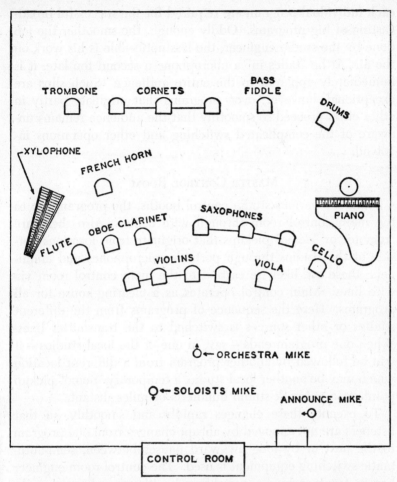

*Figure 7. Diagram of typical orchestra setup in studio showing micro-
phone placement. Arrows indicate direction toward which each
microphone is sensitive. Soloist's and announcer's microphones have "dead" sides toward orchestra.*

and monitoring booth. Here the studio engineer balances the
orchestra and mixes the output currents of the microphones.
He also controls the over-all volume from his studio, watching
a volume-indicator meter and adjusting the volume to keep it
within required limits. Years of previous experience on the
part of the studio engineer as well as hours of rehearsal for

each individual program are required for the successful broadcasting of big programs. Oddly enough, the smoother the job
done by the studio engineer, the less noticeable is his work on
the air. If he "fades in" a microphone a second too late, it is
immediately apparent to the entire audience. Such slips are
exceptional, however; even programs that originate partly in
other cities proceed so smoothly that the audience remains un-
aware of the complicated switching and other operations involved.

MASTER CONTROL ROOM

From the various studio control booths, the programs go to
the main control room through wire cables. Also there are
"remote" or "nemo" pickups that originate from locations outside of the studios through portable microphones and amplifiers; these are likewise carried to the main control room via
wire lines. Main control operates as a clearing-house for all
programs. Here the sequence of programs from the different
studios or other sources is switched to the transmitter lines.
When one program ends — say, in one of the local studios — it
will be followed by another program from a different location
which may be another local studio, a temporary "nemo" pickup
point, or a network studio hundreds of miles distant.

To execute these changes rapidly and smoothly, so that
listeners are not annoyed by abrupt changes from one program
to the next or by long awkward pauses between, semi-auto-
matic switching equipment is used. The control-room engineer
has in front of him a switchboard with several score push-
button keys and signal lights. This board is called the master
control desk and looks somewhat like an oversized organ con-
sole. It is frequently called the "nerve center of broadcasting"
(although some people who try to operate it prefer the name
"nervous center").

By pressing certain keys, the control engineer starts a chain
of automatic magnetic-switch operations which disconnect
and reconnect until all circuits are properly set up for the next
program. The signal lights "report" back to him the progress

of events, and one final light indicates completion of the switch. The entire operation has required about one second, and everything is in readiness for the next program to start.

Assuming that the station is affiliated with a network, there may be at the master control desk the controls for reversing the network lines. Sometimes the network will feed programs to the station; on other occasions, a station may feed its programs to the network. Network lines transmit in only one direction at a time, because one-way amplifiers must be used at intervals of about fifty miles to provide the high-fidelity transmission required. However, the direction of transmission can be reversed if all of these amplifiers are "turned around" electrically in the circuit. To do this manually at each point would require several minutes, so that automatic magnetic switches are installed, which are under the control of the control-room engineer. Then the engineer can reverse the entire circuit of perhaps two thousand miles merely by pushing a button, and the whole operation requires only from two to six seconds in place of minutes.

Even different parts of the same program may originate in different cities. Here again the reversible network lines come into use. Thus, when the announcer says, "We take you now to Hollywood," the control engineer has received a cue to reverse the entire line, and in such a few seconds that the pause is hardly noticed, the program continues from another studio hundreds or thousands of miles away.

In the main control room, or in an adjacent equipment room, are the many vacuum-tube amplifiers through which the program currents are increased in strength. Amplifier input and output wires are connected through jacks like those on a telephone switchboard. Then if an amplifier becomes defective while in use, such as by the burning-out of a tube, the control engineer is able to disconnect it and connect a spare one in its place by means of switchboard cords. These cords have plugs at each end which make electrical contacts when inserted into jacks, and they are called "patch cords."

On another side of the control room will be found a small

telephone switchboard, where private lines come in from the studios, nemo points, network repeater offices, the transmitter, etc. Over these lines, or order wires, the control engineer talks to any of the points involved in producing the broadcast, to give instructions or to obtain information.

Other equipment in the control room serves many diverse purposes. There are equalizers, for instance, which correct the unbalance of high and low tones caused by transmission of program currents through long lengths of wire lines. There is equipment for testing the performance of amplifiers, lines, and other apparatus. There are innumerable rows of magnetic switches, called relays, to do the switching of programs. There are clocks for accurate timing of programs, and a teletype machine for communication with the network control room in another city. There are several loud-speakers for monitoring various programs at the same time and amplifiers to operate them.

Visitors often wonder how the control engineer can listen to three or four loud-speakers at once. The secret is that he really doesn't — he develops a sort of deaf ear to any normal program, so that even in the presence of the mumble-jumble from several different loud-speakers, he is really not hearing any one of them. But let a program on one loud-speaker be interrupted, or let a stray noise occur in one of them, and his critical ear notices it immediately. Broadcast engineers probably have the most critical ears of anyone who ever listens to a radio program.

AIR CONDITIONING

Broadcasting studios must be quiet and free from unwanted noises. Therefore, the use of open windows for ventilation is out of the question because of street noises, and artificial ventilation or air conditioning is a necessity. Studios are built virtually airtight except for air ducts leading to and from the large circulating fans. Fresh air taken in from outside is blown through a water-spray chamber, which washes out dust, smoke, and odors, and then is cooled to about forty degrees to condense out excess moisture. It is then reheated to room temperature by steam radiators and distributed through the duct system to the studios, control room, and offices. Not only does this provide a comfortable atmosphere for the artists, audience, and personnel working in the studios, but it also holds the air at the correct humidity content and temperature to keep musical instruments in pitch and to protect amplifiers and other apparatus from the effects of dust and excessive humidity. Even the dust stirred up by persons walking in the studios and corridors amounts to several pounds a month and would cause trouble unless filtered out!

FIELD BROADCASTING (NEMOS)

When a field or nemo broadcast is to originate from a point outside the studio proper, a special circuit is installed from the control room to the site of the pickup, and portable amplifiers and microphones are taken to the outside location. In the early days of broadcasting, field pickups were quite an engineering problem, owing to the unavailability of especially designed equipment. Generally it was necessary to use heavy and cumbersome standard studio equipment, either installed semi-permanently or built into special carrying cases which were wired together at the pickup location. The setup usually included two or more storage batteries and a large number of heavy-duty B batteries or a motor-generator set for power supply. Owing to the non-portability of the equipment involved, the amount of time required to set it up, and the lack of microphones that would give trouble-free operation when taken outside the studio and subjected to various changes in temperature and humidity, field broadcasts were something to be avoided whenever possible.

At the present time light, compact equipment specifically designed for use outside the studios is available, and most stations make a considerable number of field broadcasts. These programs range in scope from night-club dance-band broadcasts or the pickup of market quotations from a remote point to the broadcasting of an entire opera from the stage of an opera house or a complex special-event program that requires short-wave transmitting and receiving equipment.

Field engineers assigned to these broadcasts install, operate, and dismantle the equipment used. Many of the broadcasts, particularly those handled by networks, are from out-of-town locations, and the engineers involved spend a large amount of time in traveling.

The majority of field broadcasts are of a routine nature. They are generally from locations in the same town or near the station's studios where equipment is often installed on a semi-permanent basis, with the apparatus being set up and left at the pickup point. Such routine pickups include dance music from cafés, pickups from remote studios or theaters, baseball parks, or other locations where the programs are on a recurring schedule.

All other field broadcasts are treated as "special" and include "one-time" pickups at locations in or out of town, or recurring pickups where it is not worth while to leave semi-permanent or permanent equipment at the pickup point. These include variety, musical, news events, sports, or short-wave relay programs, and recording pickups for later broadcasts from the studios.

Most of the programs that originate in the field are fed to the control room of the station via special telephone lines. In addition to the circuit used to transmit the program to the studio, an order wire or talk circuit provides communication between the studio and the pickup point.

The equipment used on remote broadcasts, like that in the studios, consists of one or more microphones connected to a mixer and an amplifier to increase the minute currents generated by the microphones up to a value that may be transmitted satisfactorily by telephone lines without interfering with other telephone services. If there are no telephone lines available to reach the exact pickup point, a short-wave broadcast transmitter is connected to the output of the amplifier, and the program is relayed to a short-wave receiver at the studios or at a point where it can be connected to the lines.

PLATE 1

Transmission engineer making equalization measurements on telephone lines for a "remote" pickup. The electronic oscillator (center of nearest panel) produces currents of audio frequency, and is adjustable over the range of audible tones. Current from the oscillator is fed to the lines via the patch cards and jacks in front of the engineer, while he talks by private line phone to the outside pickup point.

PLATE 2

Courtesy NB

ABOVE: Studio control booth panels, containing volume indicator meter, microphone faders and master volume control, and other controls for the studio.

PLATE 3

BELOW: Medium-sized broadcasting studio showing acoustic tile wall panels for sound absorption. Control booth is behind window at rear. *NBC Phot*

In addition, a second transmitter is often used at the receiving point to transmit instructions and cues to the pickup location. Another receiver is required at the pickup location to receive this "cue" transmitter. There are many variations in program requirements, and this relatively simple setup is a mere example of the technique used on field broadcasts.

Any of the types of microphones used in the studios are suitable for use in the field, although certain types are more adaptable because of their more rugged design, special directional characteristics, lighter weight, or lower susceptibility to wind noises when used out-of-doors. The ones best suited for field use are those of the so-called dynamic or inductor type and the modified ribbon type having unidirectional response. Bidirectional ribbon microphones are used extensively on indoor pickups, where the bidirectional response pattern can be used to advantage or where extraneous noise pickup from the unused side is not objectionable. Various types of highly directional microphones are used for outdoor pickup of distant bands or other sound sources, among these being the parabola reflector and the "machine-gun" type.

Amplifiers may either be battery operated or may obtain their power from the public power lines. The battery-operated type is preferable for special broadcasts, as it is not dependent on commercial power sources. Most of the amplifiers used have sufficient amplification so that with the microphones connected to the input, the telephone line can be fed directly from the output. The mixer and volume-indicator meter are contained in the portable case housing the amplifier, to form one compact unit. Previous to going on the air, the field engineer checks his volume-indicator meter with the one in the control room by speaking into the microphone and calling off the meter readings. The word "woof" is especially appropriate for this purpose, since it produces a sustained deflection of the meter. Other features of field amplifiers include connections for headsets or loud-speakers for monitoring, line and microphone connections, and switches. The microphones and lines and other miscellaneous equipment are connected to the amplifier by flexible rubber-covered cables equipped with plugs and jacks.

Various accessories are required, depending on the elaborateness of the pickup. Monitoring headphones, microphone stands, and fixtures are necessary on all pickups. A monitoring loud-speaker is sometimes used in a quiet room located at or near the point of pickup. If the program is to be fed to a public-address system, proper connecting devices must be used. Extensive broadcasts from a theater stage may require the use of a soundproof portable control booth in which the equipment is installed and where the program may be monitored by means of a loud-speaker. In order that the producer in the booth may pass instructions to the artists or musicians on the stage, a talk-back system is required. This consists of a separate microphone and loud-speaker system, the microphone being located in the booth and the loud-speaker on the stage.

Modern field equipment is designed to be as compact and sturdy and of as light-weight construction as possible, with each component part contained in a suitcase type of case so that it may be carried easily. Although many reductions in weight have been made, any piece of equipment that is supplied with handles is considered portable. As the field engineer sees it, sometimes excessively heavy equipment becomes "portable" merely by the attachment of handles!

If it is necessary to use a short-wave link to transmit the program to the control point or studio, various kinds of low-powered transmitters are available, the power output being between two and twenty-five watts and most of the transmitters working on frequencies between 1600 and 3000 or 30,000 and 41,000 kilocycles. The lower-powered types are usually of pack or similar construction so that they may be readily transported. Commercial or composite short-wave receivers of conventional design are used; however, in the near future it is expected that most relay broadcast equipment will be of the frequency-modulated type in order to take advantage of the superior qualities of this form of transmission.

Because of the elaborate setups sometimes required for short-wave relay broadcast operations it is often desirable to build a large amount of short-wave equipment into a car, truck, or trailer on a permanent or semi-permanent basis. These "mobile units" contain one or more short-wave transmitters and several short-wave receivers, complete with antenna systems and an independent gasoline-engine power supply. Some also include recording equipment, so that transcriptions for delayed broadcast purposes may be made at out-of-studio locations.

Field engineers never lead a dull existence because of the many special programs that are booked from various in-town and out-of-town locations, few of which are identical as to equipment requirements. Because it is necessary for engineers handling this type of work to install, operate, and maintain a large amount of radio and audio equipment of different types under different conditions, the qualifications for field engineers must include a diversified knowledge of all phases of radio broadcasting and a large amount of self-reliance and ingenuity. The field engineer is "on his own" when at a remote location, and he alone is responsible for the proper operation of the equipment and therefore for the success of the broadcast.

RECORDING

When the announcer says, "The next program comes to you by electrical transcription," what does he mean? Has he stopped at the music store on his way back from lunch and bought a few of the latest releases in phonograph records? Or is he referring to some unusual type of record that is entirely unlike ordinary ones? The answer is, neither. Electrical transcriptions are fundamentally the same as any disk type of phonograph record. They are different in two ways, however. They are larger in diameter (16" instead of 10" or 12"), and they run at slower speed (33 1/3 revolutions per minute instead of 78), in order that a full fifteen-minute program can be recorded on one side of a transcription in place of the usual two and one half or three minutes on a standard record.

Although many stations broadcast programs using ordinary

phonograph records, they are always announced as such and involve nothing special from the technical standpoint. Therefore, the following discussion will describe recording processes with particular emphasis on their application to electrical transcriptions.

Recording consists of inscribing a spiral groove in the surface of a disk of soft material, using a sapphire cutting needle. This groove is about four-thousandths of an inch wide and about two-thousandths of an inch deep. Several different disk materials are in use; the two most common are a special soaplike compound (frequently misnamed "wax") and a lacquer coating over a glass or metal base. These serve different purposes, as will be explained later. The cutting needle is caused to vibrate sideways in both directions — or vertically by some recorders — by means of an electrically operated cutter head which is controlled by amplified currents from the program source. From this comes the name "electrical transcription."

The result is to convert the smooth spiral grooves into wavy lines in which the waves represent the vibrations of the original sound waves. In reproduction, these waves in the grooves deflect the needle of the pickup head, which generates electric currents in much the same way that a microphone does.

Transcriptions serve two general purposes: they permit delayed broadcasts of programs on the one hand, and on the other, they make possible the advance recording of programs, copies of which can then be distributed to any number of stations for broadcasting at times convenient to their individual time schedules. In the first case, the transcription serves to store temporarily a program that is performed before it can be broadcast. A station affiliated with a network, for example, may have a conflicting program schedule at the time of a network program. If the latter is recorded, it can be played back for broadcast during the next time period available. For this purpose the lacquer-coated disks are used, since they are soft enough to cut nicely and at the same time are hard enough to permit direct play-back without any processing. From this quality they derive the name of "instantaneous recordings."

Such transcriptions usually are played back once only, although they can be reproduced up to twenty-five times without appreciable loss in quality.

When more than two or three copies of the same record are required, however, as for the second purpose mentioned above, either the lacquer-coated or the compound disks may be used for cutting the original. In this case the original record itself is not played back, but is used as a "master" for the manufacture of copies. First, its surface is covered with a thin layer of gold by a process of evaporation and condensation. Then a heavy backing of copper is electroplated onto the gold, and finally, the metal is stripped from the record. The result is a matrix on which is reproduced in metal the surface and grooves of the master record, except that they are in reverse, or "inside out"; that is, the grooves of the record are represented by ridges on the metal. The metal disk is then trimmed and installed in a hydraulic press, in which it is used as a "stamper" to press out from a plastic material exact duplicates of the original. As many as five thousand to ten thousand copies can be made from one stamper if desired, although more than a few hundred copies of a transcription are rarely needed.

Another important function of recording in a broadcasting station is for reference use, when programs are recorded solely for the purpose of obtaining a permanent record of their contents. These can be reproduced at will for legal or other purposes, to check what may have been said or what musical selection may have been played on a particular program. For this service, where high fidelity is not an important consideration, slower record speeds and other expedients are used to increase the running time of each record to a maximum. Thus, a full hour's program can be recorded on each side of a sixteen-inch record.

For broadcast purposes, however, the reproduction from a transcription should have the highest possible fidelity to the original program, as mentioned before. In order to take advantage of the full-range capabilities of the type of reproducing machines built for broadcasting use, the tone-frequency compensation that is used for transcriptions differs considerably from that used for ordinary phonograph records. As a result, the quality of reproduction is hardly distinguishable from the original live-talent studio program. (Naturally, the reader will wonder why these refinements are not extended to home phonographs and records. They could be, but the differences in size and speed of records, number of times they are to be played, and ruggedness and possible abuse of reproducing equipment, etc., make it impracticable to do so, at least at the present time.)

TRANSMISSION ENGINEERING

This branch of engineering deals, not with the radio transmitting station, as the reader is likely to infer from the title, but with an entirely different thing. The transmission engineer's job is to keep the studio and control-room equipment in adjustment, so that the program currents from microphones to amplifiers are maintained at their proper values and so that no distortion occurs. He also tests the wire lines which carry the programs from point to point in the studios and control room, from the field or nemo pickups to the control room, and from the control room to the transmitter. In other words, he is constantly measuring and testing to keep the quality of transmission through all the lines and equipment up to the high standards required.

To understand how he goes about doing this, it is necessary first to explain that all sounds — and this includes speech and music — are composed of mixtures of frequencies of vibration ranging from about twenty per second up to fifteen thousand per second. After the sound waves are converted into electric currents by microphones, the currents have exactly the same frequencies as did the sound waves. If, through some defect in any of the equipment through which they flow, all of these currents are not amplified to the same extent so that they retain their original relations to each other, distortion will result, because the reproduced sounds will not be identical with the original ones. For example, assume that in a studio a pipe organ is being played, using the full range of tones from the deepest bass to the highest treble. If the amplifier through which this program is passed does not amplify the bass tones to the same extent as the treble, then part of the original music is lost. Obviously, such conditions cannot be tolerated when high fidelity of reproduction is the objective.

To test the performance of each piece of apparatus in the system, and thus avoid such distortion, the transmission engineer uses an electronic oscillator, a device which generates a steady electric current of one frequency, which can be connected to any apparatus to be tested. The frequency is adjustable to cover the whole range of musical frequencies. By connecting a volume-indicator meter to the output of the apparatus, the amount of amplification at each frequency can be measured accurately. Such measurements made throughout the range of sound frequencies indicate the performance of the amplifier.

As has been mentioned before, wire lines such as are used to carry program currents from the control room to the transmitting station do not deliver currents of different frequencies in the same proportions. The higher frequencies suffer more loss than the lower ones. To correct this type of distortion, the transmission engineer installs at the end of such a circuit an electric filter called an "equalizer." This device has an effect opposite to that of the line: it attenuates low frequencies more than high ones and is adjusted so that it just compensates for the action of the line. The over-all result is no discrimination against any frequency. To make such adjustments, the transmission engineer uses his oscillator and meters in a manner similar to that used for testing amplifiers.

Similar tests and adjustments are required for most of the other electrical equipment of the studios and control room. Apparatus used for recording, for example, frequently requires readjustment to maintain its high standard of reproduction. All such work falls to the lot of the transmission engineer, who is thus responsible for the proper transmission of programs through the many pieces of apparatus and through wire lines to their destination at the transmitting station.

The Transmitting Station

Up to this point many things have happened to our program currents, but they have so far been carried from one place to another by means of wires. Thus, no radio listener would have been able to hear them, since they have not yet been broadcast or put "on the air." Finally, we have arrived at the point where actual broadcasting takes place; usually, as previously stated, this is at some location in the country.

Twenty years ago nearly all broadcasting stations were located atop tall buildings in the center of large cities. The reason for this was to reach as many listeners as possible with the limited power outputs then available. Later, as the art progressed and higher power became available, it became necessary to relocate the transmitting plants in less populated areas. One of the reasons for this was to reduce to a minimum the interference to the receiving sets in thickly populated areas, thereby enabling all to listen to the station of their choice. Another reason for moving away from the city was that the tall buildings in the business districts absorbed a great deal of the energy radiated from the antenna system. This made the transmitting plants less efficient, and reception in the metropolitan areas was poor and very spotty.

Now most transmitting plants are located outside the cities. The location of plants in outlying areas and the use of sensitive receivers make possible reception of programs over a large area reasonably free from interference.

At the transmitting plant the wire lines bringing in the programs are connected to special line amplifiers, to make up for the volume loss in the lines between studio and transmitter and to restore the program volume to the same level as when it left the studio.

In order to broadcast the programs that arrive at the transmitter through the lines from the studios, a radio-frequency carrier current must be generated, and upon it must be superimposed the voice and music, as explained previously, by a process called "modulation" of the carrier. There are three different ways of producing modulation, bearing the technical names of "amplitude," "frequency," and "phase" modulation, respectively. The latter apparently offers little practical advantage over the other two and its use to date has been limited to experimental and a few communication applications.

Amplitude modulation, which is used by the "standard" broadcast transmitters in the 550- to 1500-kilocycle band and also by short-wave broadcast stations, employs a carrier of constant frequency but of variable strength or amplitude conforming to the program. But disturbances caused by atmospheric electricity (static) and some kinds of electrical machinery may also produce additional variations in the carrier amplitude as it arrives at the receiver antenna. Once this has occurred, the receiver circuits, which translate the variations in carrier strength back into currents of the same nature as those produced by the studio microphone and eventually into sound waves, cannot differentiate between program and disturbance, and the latter appears as noise inseparable from the program. Fortunately, such interference is not continuously present; on occasion, however, it may become so violent that the program itself is obscured.

In contrast, the frequency-modulated carrier is of constant strength, but its frequency is caused to change back and forth between arbitrarily fixed limits by the program currents. Thus, if the latter happen to be oscillating at the rate of one thousand times per second, they sweep the carrier frequency up and down, one thousand times per second, about a central or nominal value. While static and other disturbances may produce amplitude variations in the signal, the frequency-modulation receiver does not convert them into noise, because it responds only to the changing frequencies and ignores the amplitude variations. Hence, for the most common and serious types of electrical interference, the frequency-modulation method has an advantage over the amplitude method in eliminating noises.

Satisfactory operation of frequency modulation requires a frequency spread of 150,000 cycles for each station. If stations in the "standard" broadcast band (which is only 950,000 cycles wide) used this system, there would be room for only six stations! Consequently, for practical purposes, frequency modulation is confined to stations of much higher carrier frequencies, where 150,000 cycles represents a lower percentage of variation. These high carrier frequencies, for reasons which have nothing to do with the type of modulation, do not travel as far as the lower ones, but have a limited range of about the distance to the visible horizon as seen from the transmitter antenna. Hence, the coverage of stations using frequency modulation, and therefore confined to the high carrier frequencies, is limited practically to a radius somewhere between thirty and a hundred miles, depending on transmitter power and antenna height.

The equipment involved in the generation of a radio frequency carrier for a high-powered transmitter is very complex. The primary source is a vacuum tube oscillator, which, except for frequency modulation, is controlled by a quartz crystal that is accurately ground to the operating frequency of the broadcast station. The crystal is contained in an oven in which the temperature is controlled to within one-tenth of one degree. Such a crystal can maintain a station on its assigned frequency to within one part in a million, well within the limits prescribed by government regulations, which permit a tolerance of twenty cycles (about twenty parts in a million).

The amount of energy delivered by the oscillator is very small, so this energy must go through five stages of amplification before it reaches the final amplifier. The latter amplifies the signal to the full power output of the station, which may be from one hundred watts to fifty thousand watts. (One thousand watts is about the amount of power used by an electric iron.)

In the meantime, the program from the line amplifier goes to a high-powered audio amplifier, thence to a modulator, which in turn is connected to the second radio frequency amplifier preceding the final amplifier. This is the point at which the program and carrier are combined, in such a way that the program controls or modulates the carrier as previously explained.

The radiator or antenna is an electrical conductor which, when connected to a transmitter, is capable of transmitting energy through space to the receiving antenna. Between the transmitting and receiving antennas, the radiated waves must travel through space over land and water; their mode of travel through space is exceedingly complex and involves a great number of still unknown factors. Conditions change from day to day. Day and night conditions are different, because sunlight affects transmission; programs can be received at nighttime over greater distances than in daytime owing to the waves' being reflected back to earth from the ionosphere (a layer of the upper atmosphere that reflects radio waves). Distance reception is usually better in winter than in summer, owing to the absence of static, which is caused by electrical storms and disturbances in the atmosphere.

The antenna proper is usually a tower ranging in height from one hundred to more than eight hundred feet. The height depends upon the operating wave length of the station; the longer the wave length, the higher the tower. In some cases transmitting plants are located along air routes, where the Federal Communications Commission and Civil Aeronautics Authority limit the height of towers to not more than five hundred feet so that they will not present too much of a hazard to aerial navigation. In order that stations assigned to longer wave lengths and located along air routes may operate as efficiently as possible, the tower is divided some distance down from the top, and the sections are insulated from each other. At this broken section a coil is inserted which tunes the electrical length of the tower to the desired wave length.

In a preceding paragraph it was mentioned that the equipment was involved and complex. A transmitter consists of thousands of parts, such as condensers, resisters, coils, relays, transformers, generators, and a multitude of other items. In a 50,000-watt transmitter and associated equipment there are approximately seventy tubes in operation at one time — of forty-three different types. Failure of any one of these parts could cause interruption of the program.

Although many broadcasting stations are on the air seven thousand or more hours a year, the total loss of time because of failures during a year may total only about ten minutes. Time out for changing tubes is usually the greatest cause of such shutdowns. This low percentage of failures speaks well for the design of the equipment, the rigid maintenance of it, and the personnel who operate it.

One of the most important considerations in the operation of a transmitting station concerns safety to the operators, because of the high voltages employed. All doors to the transmitter and high-voltage enclosures are protected by interlocking devices which automatically shut off all power upon being opened.

It is important that all personnel be highly trained in the handling of high-voltage equipment, skilled in the art of artificial resuscitation, and capable of meeting any emergency. At the transmitter, *"It's safety first always."*

MAINTENANCE PROBLEMS

An old story relates the musings of two tramps about the thing they hated most: work. "Wouldn't life be easy," said one, "if there were a machine to do all the work? Then we could do everything just by pressing buttons."

"Maybe," reflected the second tramp, "but who would push the buttons?"

Had these fellows been better versed in technical matters, they might have had even greater concern about the question of who would fix the machine when it wouldn't run. Even the best of machines fails once in a while, and the invention of bigger and better machines to ease man's work always creates the new job of keeping the machinery itself adjusted and running.

In a broadcasting studio, as we have seen, there are so many automatic devices which do things when buttons are pushed that the tramps' dream seems very near to realization. Behind the microphones, control knobs, push-buttons, and indicating lights in the control room, there are numerous amplifiers, volume indicators, automatic electric switches, and many other complex gadgets.

But sometime the control operator may push a button and nothing will happen; somewhere something does not function. He immediately transfers the new program to a spare circuit to avoid any further delay. Then he picks up a special "SOS" telephone, which connects him immediately and directly to the maintenance room, and reports the failure. He might say, for instance, that "channel 3 on switchback 4 studio C did not operate," and maintenance engineers would promptly go to work to locate and clear the trouble. It may be only a speck of dust which has lodged between the electrical contacts of an automatic electric switch (called a "relay") and is preventing its operation, or it may be a blown fuse; or perhaps a tube has burned out in an amplifier.

In the control room, there are many amplifiers and relays, plus many other varieties of apparatus. The maintenance engineer must be familiar with the location and functioning of them all. He must be able to trace complex electric wiring quickly with the aid of circuit blueprints. Many such blueprints are required to record all the circuits in the studios and control room.

Good maintenance, like good doctoring, requires the ability not only to locate and fix troubles after they occur, but to anticipate them and make repairs before the failure happens. In the studios and control rooms, maintenance engineers make numerous routine tests on all apparatus at regular intervals. They put things "through their paces" literally by duplicating all of a day's operation in an hour or so, keeping an expert eye on the indicating lights, and listening to the loud-speaker with a critical ear. The slightest irregularity is detected and further checked. Of course, no such tests can be carried on while programs are in progress; therefore, most testing must be done at night when the station is "off the air."

Another important job of the maintenance engineer has to

do with time; he is literally paid to "watch the clocks." Correct
time is an essential item in any radio studio. Many stations
use in their studios and control rooms electric clocks especially
constructed for extreme accuracy, and these must be accurate
to the exact second at all times. In some control rooms, even
the slight variations of frequency of the public power lines,
which are unnoticeable to the average user, cannot be tolerated. Special tuning forks and amplifiers are used to secure
this extreme accuracy. Such systems do not vary more than
about one second in a week. Nevertheless, the master clock
is checked regularly four or five times a day by radio time
signals from the Naval Observatory. When any deviation is
noted, the tuning forks are slowed down or speeded up to
reset all clocks to exact synchronism.

Amplifiers which carry the program must also be tested
frequently. Tubes may be wearing out, batteries may be losing
their voltage, or occasionally even the more permanent parts
of an amplifier may become defective in operation. At the
transmitter, the higher-power apparatus requires even more
critical testing and adjusting.

Thus, the radio maintenance engineer is the man who fixes
the machine which does not run when the button is pushed.
In radio studios the "machine" consists of many electronic and
other electrical devices, from amplifiers to storage batteries.
To be able to handle any situation, the maintenance engineer
must be a combination general repairman, radio operator,
chemist, mechanical engineer, electrical engineer, radio
trouble-shooter, telephone man, electrician, and mechanic. In
addition, he must be a sort of "technical detective," anticipat-
ing when the machine threatens to stop and fixing it before it
does.

TELEVISION

While this discussion has been intended to deal primarily
with the art of sound broadcasting, it would be incomplete
without a brief description of the closely allied subject of television. For the listener's best interpretation and maximum

enjoyment, a program, unlike the proverbial ideal child, should be both seen and heard. Television makes this possible by adding a visual picture to the sound picture of ordinary broadcasting. Its equipment and technique are at the same time similar to and in contrast with those of sound broadcasting.

It is different in that it is the varying shades of lightness and darkness of objects making up a scene, rather than sound waves, which must be translated into electric currents. It is similar in the ultimate use of the resulting currents to modulate a radio transmitter for their transmission through space.

When an artist wants to enlarge a picture, he sometimes rules off parallel horizontal and vertical lines on the small original, forming squares, and then draws the contents of each square in the corresponding square of a larger card, which is similarly ruled with larger squares. The process of television is quite similar, except that the content of each square of the scene is viewed in sequence by a photoelectric mechanism and is transformed into electric currents which are proportional to the brightness of each square.

In the television studio, we find a light-sensitive vacuum tube which, with its associated equipment, makes up the television camera. This corresponds to the microphone in a sound pickup. In brief, the sensitive tube consists of a flat plate of insulating material upon which is sprayed a thin layer of minute globules of silver. Through a lens system an image of the scene to be picked up is focused on the plate. The plate is continuously "scanned" by a sharply pointed, fast-moving beam of electrons which produces a minute current from each globule in passing. The exact amount of current depends upon the brightness of the light in the part of the image where the silver droplet is located. Thus, the currents produced by the process of scanning all the droplets in the entire image in rapid succession represent electrically the variations in light intensity in the scene, just as the currents produced by a microphone are electrical equivalents of the sound waves that actuate the microphone ribbon. After amplification, these currents from the camera are made to control or modulate a radio transmitter in exactly the same manner as in sound broadcasting.

At the receiver, the varying currents delivered by the carrier must be reconverted into a picture. A special vacuum tube is again employed, in which another sharp electron beam is caused to scan a large flattened glass surface coated with a phosphorescent material. This coating glows wherever the beam strikes it, with a brilliance that depends upon the strength of the beam. The varying currents representing the picture are arranged to control the intensity of the electron beam, and thus each point of the sensitive surface emits an amount of light corresponding to the brightness of the corresponding globule of silver in the camera. The rate of scanning is so rapid that the observer at the receiver sees all the glowing areas as a composite picture which reproduces the lights and shadows of the scene in the studio.

RADIO OF THE FUTURE

These are the means through which we hear (and see) programs in our homes. Born in the laboratory and developed, applied, and expanded, simple electrical phenomena have been combined to give us modern radio entertainment and service for millions of people. What future things radio will bring us, no one can foretell, but their origin and technical pattern will be the same. Engineers will take the discoveries and inventions of scientists, add a dash of the new and a portion of the old, and build our studios, our control rooms, our transmitters, and our receivers of the future.

PLATE 4

ABOVE: A modern broadcasting transmitter. Here the program is received from the master control room through telephone lines. This equipment generates the high frequency carrier, modulates it with the incoming program, and amplifies the modulated carrier, which is then fed to the transmitting antenna to be radiated into space.

PLATE 5

BELOW: Equipment for recording electrical transcription. Cutting lathes shown in foreground and amplifier panels at rear.

PLATE 6

Master control desk, through which the programs from the studios, outside "nemo" pickup points or networks are routed. Here they are monitored, and switched to the transmitter lines in sequence. Push buttons, which can be seen in the center panel, perform these operations through relays mounted inside the desk, or in another room.

8

EDUCATIONAL BROADCASTING

CHAPTER 25

THE EDUCATIONAL STATION

FROM THE EARLY DAYS OF RADIO, when universities, colleges, and other schools owned two hundred and two radio stations, the number had dwindled to a mere twenty-six in 1945.[1] Some of these stations are operated exclusively by the educational institutions themselves, while in other instances the stations have leased part of their facilities to commercial interests, retaining certain periods during each day for their own use.

The history of the educational station has been long and stormy.[2] Most of the pioneer educational stations were built for experimental purposes by engineering or physics departments, their interest lying primarily in technical development. Very little, if anything, was done by the school to keep up with modern broadcasting practices. Small sums were set aside by uninterested administrative bodies for the upkeep of equipment, studios, and programming. This resulted, of course, in these stations being wholly unprepared to meet the competition of the upsurge of the commercial stations in the early and middle twenties.

In 1927, with the advent of the Federal Radio Commission, strict requirements for technical equipment and better broadcasting services in the interest of the public made it almost prohibitive for some of the educational institutions to continue operations on the limited budgets allotted to them. It is not to be wondered at, therefore, that many such stations discontinued operation. Commercial stations, too, were clamoring for the channels occupied by those stations, on the grounds of ability to serve the public more adequately. This resulted in long and expensive hearings in Washington. The costs of the

[1] A list of these stations is given on page 403.
[2] The history of the educational stations has been written by S. E. Frost, Jr., in *Education's Own Stations*. Chicago: University of Chicago Press (1937).

hearings were easily and gladly paid by the commercial interests, but the educators found them almost impossible to meet. At about that time, William J. Cooper, Commissioner of Education, set up the National Committee on Education by Radio under the chairmanship of Joy Elmer Morgan, of the National Education Association. This committee represented the Association of College and University Broadcasting Stations, the Land-Grant College Association, the National University Extension Association, the National Association of State University Presidents, the National Education Association, the Jesuit Educational Association, the National Advisory Council on Radio in Education, the Payne Fund, and other similar groups.

It was the purpose of the committee to carry out the resolutions drawn up in Chicago at a conference of all these representative groups, called together by Commissioner Cooper. Those resolutions advocated:

1. The protecting and promoting of broadcasting originating in educational institutions.

2. The promotion of broadcasting by educational institutions.

3. Legislation by Congress "which will permanently and exclusively assign to educational institutions and government educational agencies a minimum of fifteen (15) per cent of all radio broadcasting channels which are or may become available to the United States."

With headquarters established in Washington, the committee set out to acquire all possible information on the subject of educational broadcasting and its responsibility to the nation as a whole. It was its purpose also to keep abreast of all governmental regulations, in order to be in the best possible position to aid educational stations in their fight for existence. The history of the committee and its accomplishments during the years of its existence, from 1930-1941, have been set forth by Frank Ernest Hill in his report, entitled *Tune In for Education.* The committee was instrumental in many instances in helping an educational station to stay on the air. Notable was the case of KOAC, the Oregon State Agricultural College at Corvallis. The committee also was instrumental in forcing a congressional study of broadcasting in general, which resulted in the appointment of a new body to replace the Federal Radio Commission. This new body, known as the Federal Communications Commission, was created by an act of Congress in 1934.

As the years wore on, it became evident that commercial interests were doing their utmost to improve their educational broadcasts and were showing more willingness to co-operate with all public agencies as well as with the schools themselves. It, therefore, seemed less necessary that any fixed percentage of time or facilities should be set aside for "educational institutions and government educational agencies." On the other hand, the Commission felt that all groups should secure adequate representation by radio and that, accordingly, the co-operation between broadcasters and interested groups should be under the direction and supervision of the Commission itself. So was born in 1935 the Federal Radio Education Committee, a body with a membership of forty representing educational stations, independent educators, networks, and local commercial educational stations. Doctor John W. Studebaker, United States Commissioner of Education, was appointed head of this new committee and is still acting in that capacity. The membership of the committee itself has been reduced to an executive committee of fifteen instead of forty, though it still represents the original groups.

With the appointment of the Federal Radio Education Committee, the National Committee on Education by Radio felt that the purposes for which it had been set up would be duly carried out and protected. Those educational stations which had survived the depression of the early thirties and the inroads of the commercial interests now seemed to be well able to look after their own interests; thus, with representation on the Federal Radio Education Committee, there was no likelihood of education's voice not being heard in the future. It remained for the original committee only to put its affairs in order and disband. This was done in 1941.

The ability of the educational stations to maintain themselves was not always as simple as it seemed. While many school administrators were viewing radio from a promotional standpoint only, the commercial stations were winning audiences through a variety of interesting programs. It was difficult for some of the persons responsible for programming on the educational stations to realize that a station to be successful must actually render a service to the community in which it operates. More often they held to the thought that any program service should promote first, little thinking that unless a program can stimulate interest, it cannot promote. In most instances administrators now recognize this fact through the establishment of more adequate radio budgets and through the appointment of trained personnel in the radio departments and studios with ability to create a program schedule interesting enough to hold the audience in their community in competition with the commercial stations.

This is not meant to imply that the aim of all educational stations should be to try, constantly, to compete with the commercial stations for listener interest. There are, of course, many services the educational station is in a position to render a community that cannot and should not be duplicated by other stations. When unlimited time is available to an educational station, a wide diversity of subject fields can be presented in series that a commercial station would not be able to carry. Then, too, emphasis is placed on entertainment by the commercial station; the educational station, as Harold B. McCarty, Director of the University of Wisconsin radio station WHA points out, definitely "seeks to advance the public taste and elevate existing wants, not merely satisfy them." [3] Mr. McCarty continues that "as universities and colleges are constantly reaching out for new truths and new interpretations, so it is possible for educational stations to do likewise." He might have added, without the pressure of having to make every minute count financially.

On the other hand, the educational station must be ever

[3] *Education on the Air*, 1937, page 60.

mindful of its obligation to broadcast in "the public interest, convenience, or necessity." This means that while the greater portion of its radio fare will probably appeal to a more limited audience than that commanded by the commercial station, it must not confine its appeal to that smaller audience, but should consider the whole audience. There are frequent programs on both networks and local commercial stations appealing to minority groups of listeners, but the popularity of any commercial station would be short-lived indeed should it build its entire program with only these groups in mind.

Toward the end of the war, the problem of maintenance was very difficult for some of the small and medium-sized commercial stations, as well as for some that were college-owned. The latter were in the more difficult position, however, because the commercial station generally has sources of revenue to which the educational station does not have access.

There are, naturally, exceptions to this statement, notably the University of Wisconsin, which owns the oldest educational radio station in the country. (See Figure 8.) The administration has realized its importance from the beginning and made every effort to establish it on a firm foundation. The operation of the station is conducted by the Division of Radio Education, a department of the university. It is not, however, a part of any college or school in the university. It has a faculty radio committee of seven representatives from various divisions of the university: music, agriculture, speech, etc. This committee serves as an advisory and policy-making body. The station has an adequate staff, with radio training and a consciousness of what the public served by the station wants to hear. Its program schedule is planned first with the listener in mind, and, secondly, with the idea of what that service may do for the university, realizing, of course, that a good program means good publicity.[4]

Space will not permit an exhaustive statement here of the relative merits of all those educational stations which have be-

[4] *Education on the Air*, 1930, pages 284-290; 1932, pages 67-68; 1933, pages 276-280; 1934, page 167

DIVISION OF RADIO EDUCATION U. of W.

ORGANIZATION CHART

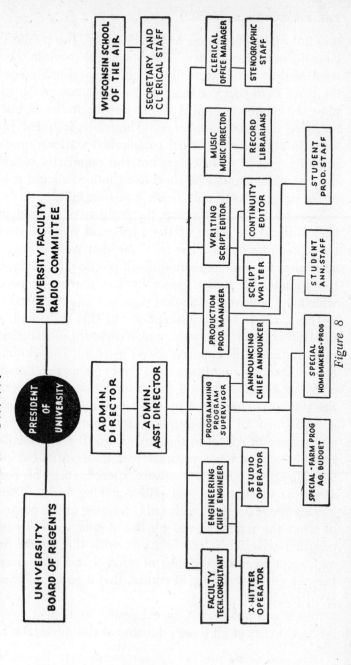

Figure 8

AMERICAN EDUCATIONAL RADIO STATIONS

(LEGENDS: D — daytime operation only; LS — Local sunset; N — Night.)

FLORIDA	Gainesville	WRUF	850	5000 watts	University of Florida
GEORGIA	Atlanta	WGST LS N	920	5000 watts 1000 watts	Georgia School of Technology
ILLINOIS	Urbana	WILL D	580	5000 watts	University of Illinois
INDIANA	Lafayette	WBAA LS N	920	5000 watts 1000 watts	Purdue University
IOWA	Ames	WOI D	640	5000 watts	Iowa State College
	Decorah	KWCL D	1240	250 watts	Luther College
	Iowa City	WSUI	910	5000 watts	State University of Iowa
KANSAS	Lawrence	KFKU LS N	1250	5000 watts 1000 watts	University of Kansas
	Manhattan	KSAC LS N	580	1000 watts 500 watts	Kansas State College
MICHIGAN	East Lansing	WKAR D	870	5000 watts	Michigan State College
MINNESOTA	Minneapolis-St. Paul	WLB D	770	5000 watts	University of Minnesota
	Northfield	WCAL D	770	5000 watts	St. Olaf College
MISSOURI	St. Louis	WEW D	770	1000 watts	St. Louis University
NEW YORK	Ithaca	WHCU	870	1000 watts	Cornell University
	Troy	WHAZ	1330	1000 watts	Rensselaer Polytechnic University
NORTH DAKOTA	Grand Forks	KFJM LS N	1440	1000 watts 500 watts	University of North Dakota
OHIO	Columbus	WOSU	820	5000 watts	Ohio State University
OKLAHOMA	Norman	WNAD D	640	1000 watts	University of Oklahoma
OREGON	Corvallis	KOAC LS N	550	5000 watts 1000 watts	Oregon State Agricultural College
PENNSYLVANIA	Grove City	WSAJ	1340	100 watts	Grove City College
SOUTH DAKOTA	Rapid City	WCAT D	1230	100 watts	South Dakota School of Mines
	Vermillion	KUSD	920	500 watts	University of South Dakota
TEXAS	College Station	WTAW D	1150	1000 watts	A and M College of Texas
	Port Arthur	KPAC	1250	500 watts	Port Arthur College
WASHINGTON	Pullman	KWSC	1250	5000 watts	State College of Washington
WISCONSIN	Madison	WHA D	970	5000 watts	University of Wisconsin
	Stevens Point	WLBL DS	930	5000 watts	Wisconsin Department of Agriculture

come an integral part of the community they serve, nor is it possible to list their outstanding programs. Suffice it to say that they are rendering exceptional service in many fields by providing a service not found elsewhere in radio.

THE EDUCATIONAL FM STATION

FM, or frequency modulation, is a method of transmitting radio waves differing from AM, or amplitude modulation.[5] In 1938 the FCC decided to open up the forty-megacycle band for public broadcast service, and after many tests and hearings in 1940 adopted standards and rules providing thirty-five channels for commercial stations between forty-three and fifty megacycles for use by FM stations. The band between forty-two and forty-three megacycles was set aside for educational stations. These stations are now required to use FM unless a special need for the use of AM can be shown.[6]

In reporting on this assignment, William Dow Boutwell, then Director of Information and Radio Services, United States Office of Education said:

> This allows for five educational channels. The allocation of the education band adjacent to that of commercial FM broadcast stations places the educational stations on an entirely independent basis, yet gives them the benefits of developments in the service rendered by commercial stations. Since regular FM receivers provide for the reception of both services, any home which has an FM set will be able to hear the

[5] See page 387.

[6] On January 16, 1945, the FCC allocated ninety channels to FM. Of the ninety, twenty have been earmarked for educational services with the retention of the 200 kc. channel width. It was indicated at that time that FM was to be moved from its coveted 50 mc. area to 88-106 mc., but the move provides more than twice the number of channels presently reserved for FM. Mr. R. R. Lowdermilk, United States Office of Education radio specialist, suggests in the FREC January, 1945, bulletin that, though the shift may work some hardships on the five educational FM stations already in operation, there is technical evidence to suggest that they may be able to supply much better service at the newly-assigned frequencies because this portion of the radio spectrum is not subject to certain imperfections known to exist in the old FM band. There may be exceptions to the proposed allocations filed, so that it is quite possible that certain compromises of a minor nature may be made before the final allocation pattern has been determined.

broadcasts of noncommercial educational stations. Thus, there is established a sound basis for the parallel growth of non-commercial educational and of commercial broadcasting with this new and superior form of transmission at these frequencies.

Approximately seventy FM stations had been authorized when the war required the restriction of construction, and at this time some forty-five FM stations are in operation and providing a high quality, noise-free broadcast service. Since any single FM frequency channel may be assigned to a number of stations so long as they are separated by intervals of sufficient distance to eliminate interference, the total number of educational stations which may be established is very large, although the maximum number erected in any one locality is small. Actual separation to avoid interference need be as little as twenty to twenty-five miles for low-power stations and one hundred to one hundred and forty miles of stations one kilowatt and up.

Recent studies by the United States Office of Education reveal that all schools in a state like Ohio could be served by judicious location of eighteen or twenty major transmitters using all five available channels.

While education has five FM channels, only every other channel may be used in any given locality. This is required in order to make certain that there will be no interference between stations operating on adjacent frequencies.

At present there are five educational FM stations. Four are in large city school systems: Chicago, Cleveland, New York, and San Francisco; one is at the University of Illinois. As this book goes to press, four more stations are under construction and eight applications are on file, while approximately one hundred and sixty educational institutions have expressed interest in this service.

Cleveland schools have for many years been pioneers in educational broadcasting, first using the services of the regular commercial station and later their own station WBOE, established in 1938. With the opening of the FM band by the FCC in 1940, Cleveland shifted from AM to FM, and has been gratified by the superior quality of the broadcast reception.

Mr. William Levenson, Department of Instruction, Board of Education, Cleveland, in writing to Doctor Boutwell said, "Today we feel that school reception is no longer the 'bottle-neck' of classroom radio."

The Chicago Board of Education fortunately purchased their FM equipment just prior to Pearl Harbor and so were in a position to go ahead with their plans even after the war had started. Their station WBEZ began operations in the spring of 1943. Because of their previous broadcasting experience, the trained radio staff found no difficulty in shifting their activities from AM to FM broadcasting. About one hundred and fifty FM receivers had been purchased for the schools before the war and were installed and ready for use by the time the station was completed. In reporting this activity in the *Journal of the Association for Education by Radio*, September, 1943, Mr. George Jennings, Acting Director of Radio for the Chicago Board of Education, said:

> Reception on FM receivers is considerably better than over standard sets. Man-made and natural static is not transmitted through the FM receiver. With fixed-tuning sets (which will eventually be used in every school) there will be no interference, no fishing for the broadcasting station at the last minute before the program time. A click of the switch will bring in WBEZ.

It does not require much imagination to foresee the strides which education by radio can make through this new home of its own on the air. During the past two decades hundreds of schools all over the country have been gaining experience through testing this new medium. The field of subject matter and the uses which the school systems and colleges are now making of radio is a slight indication of things to come. In the October, 1943, issue of the *AER Journal*, Doctor Boutwell presented a list of uses which may be helpful to teachers interested in planning such programs:

> News and current events programs adapted for age levels.
> Subject motivation programs.

Supplementary aid programs.
Teaching by radio.
Story-telling.
Guidance programs.
Library programs.
Talks by prominent guests.
In-service teacher training.
Adult education programs.
Music for special activities, such as dancing.
Announcements.
Student-talent programs.
Forums and discussions.
Sports programs.
Community co-operation programs.
Holiday and special events programs.
School public relations programs.
Programs for handicapped children.

The FCC has established the following basis of eligibility for receiving a license to operate an FM radio broadcasting station:

Section 4.131. The term "non-commercial educational broadcast station" means a high-frequency broadcast station licensed to an organized non-profit educational agency for the advancement of its educational work and for the transmission of educational and entertainment programs to the general public.

Section 4.132. The operation of, and the service furnished by, non-commercial educational broadcast stations shall be governed by the following regulations in addition to the rules and regulations governing high-frequency broadcast stations.

(a) A non-commercial educational-broadcast station will be licensed only to an organized non-profit educational agency and upon a showing that the station will be used for the advancement of the agency's educational program.

(b) Each station may transmit programs directed to specific schools in the system for use in connection with the regular courses as well as routine and administrative material pertaining to the school system and may transmit educational and entertainment programs to the general public.

(c) Each station shall furnish a non-profit and non-com

mercial broadcast service. No sponsored or commercial program shall be transmitted nor shall commercial announcements of any character be made. A station shall not transmit
the programs of other classes of broadcast stations unless
all commercial announcements and commercial references
in the continuity are eliminated.

Section 4.136. The transmitting equipment, installation, and
operation as well as the location of the transmitter shall be in
conformity with the requirements of good engineering practice
as released from time to time by the Commission.

At the September, 1943, meeting of the FREC, James
Lawrence Fly, then Chairman of the FCC, said:

Much progress has already been made in the direction of
introducing "listener interest" in educational programs. If the
new FM stations are to succeed, that progress must continue.

It is certainly not too early to begin plans for these five educational channels. During the war period, of course, equipment and man-power shortages are preventing immediate expansion. After the war, however, equipment will be freely
available; plans should be laid now to get going at the earliest
possible date. For, inevitably, after this war, there will have
to be a reshuffle of frequency assignments. Whole new portions of the spectrum formerly deemed useless have been
opened up through wartime research, while the expanding
need for world-wide communications and especially the vast
new aviation uses of radio will in all probability crowd the
postwar ether even more tightly than the comparatively smaller
spectrum was jammed before the war. In such a reshuffle the
friends of educational radio will certainly want to hold their
own. If their plans are ready and they can show both the real
use to which educational frequencies are being put and the
proposed use for which plans have been fully laid, the necessary frequencies will no doubt remain available. But if lethargy
prevails and others seeking to expand their own services are
able to show that the channels reserved for educational stations
are going to waste, then it will almost certainly be either
difficult or impossible to continue the reservation of unused
frequencies.

Many educational institutions across the country have made plans for the installation of FM stations in this immediate postwar period. Some states, notably Michigan, have even gone so far as to set up the structure for state-wide FM networks, so that each school may be in a position to contribute a specific type of program to the daily program schedule. In this way a well-rounded and interesting program schedule may be maintained. Other states have also indicated an interest in the same type of service. It would seem that through these new channels education by radio has finally come into its own.

CHAPTER 26

BROADCASTS TO SCHOOLS

NETWORK

THE EDUCATOR has been slow to acknowledge radio's contribution to education through programs aimed at the student, whether broadcast by the networks or by local stations. Norman Woelfel [1] makes the statement:

> To most teachers and school administrators radio has no special significance. If educators think about nation-wide school broadcasts at all, it is to regard them either as one more applicant for time in an already crowded course of study, or as something for a department of audio-instruction to plan for. The rich educational potentialities of a nation-wide school broadcast seem to have been completely overlooked both by educators and civic leaders.

This statement seems somewhat severe in the light of the efforts made consistently by networks and local stations alike to build programs of educative worth for classroom listening. With the formation of the National Broadcasting Company in 1926, a committee was appointed, headed by Doctor Edwin A. Alderman, then President of the University of Virginia, to study ways and means of best presenting education by radio. The slowness of educators to realize the possibilities of this new medium is also indicated in Doctor Alderman's subsequent reports to the Advisory Council of the National Broadcasting Company. In the face of this apparent apathy, however, Doctor Walter Damrosch, encouraged by the response of children and adults alike to a series of three concerts sponsored by the Radio Corporation of America in 1927, presented the first series of the "NBC Music Appreciation Hour" in the

[1] "Radio Over U.S.A.," Bulletin Number 62, IV. "Radio and the School," November, 1941. Evaluation of School Broadcasts. Columbus, Ohio: Ohio State University.

autumn of 1928 under the title of the "R.C.A. Educational
Hour." The object of this series was to stimulate interest in
good music, especially among children, with the ultimate hope
that they would come to love it. Ernest LaPrade, reporting
on the program at the Institute for Education by Radio at
Columbus, Ohio, in 1930 stated: [2]

> It was not his [Doctor Damrosch's] object to give instruc-
> tion in theory or practice of music, for he believes that can be
> handled better in class. Certain educators have proposed that
> radio should not attempt to teach anything that can be taught
> in the classroom. . . . I should say that, at any rate, radio
> should not attempt to teach anything that can be taught *better*
> in the classroom. Appreciation of symphonic music seems to
> be one thing that can be taught better by radio than in any
> classroom, because it is impossible to introduce a symphony
> orchestra into a classroom.

Going on that assumption, Doctor Damrosch built an hour
program of music appreciation for children of different age
levels, divided into two half-hour periods, broadcast on alter-
nate weeks. Series A was originally intended for use in grades
three and four; series B in grades five and six; series C in grades
seven, eight, and nine; and series D in high-school and college
classes. It was suggested that teachers should disregard this
set pattern in the use of the program, and, instead, use each
series according to the background of the pupil, regardless of
age level. Study aids in the form of student notebooks and
teachers' manuals were available for use in connection with
the broadcasts.

The Damrosch Hour, as the program soon came to be called,
was broadcast by the National Broadcasting Company, and
later by the Blue Network, from 1928 through the spring of
1942, when Doctor Damrosch chose to retire and the network
refused to carry on the program without him. As far as is
known, this was one of the first, if not the first, network program prepared and broadcast for classroom use.

[2] *Education on the Air,* 1930, page 218.

On the Pacific Coast, also in 1928, October 18, to be exact, the Standard Oil Company of California undertook the "Standard School Broadcast." This was a weekly musical lecture prepared by Arthur Garbett, then Educational Director of the Western Division of the National Broadcasting Company, and given on the same day as the evening "Standard Symphony Hour." The lectures dealt in simple terms with the elements of music, fully illustrated by instrumental music. In each of the lectures the principal compositions of the evening concert were analyzed and passages from them were played. The thought, of course, was that the student, through these lectures, would acquire a higher appreciation and understanding of orchestral music. The program was and still is broadcast over the Pacific Coast network as a service to schools. Now in its fifteenth year, it is still one of the finest of classroom broadcasts, and the Standard Oil Company has lived up to its promise that there would be no effort to advertise products; instead, advertising is limited to the mere mention of the Standard Oil Company of California as sponsor of the program.

In 1930 the Columbia Broadcasting System first presented the "American School of the Air" under the sponsorship of the Grigsby-Grunow Company, manufacturers of radio sets. After one year, however, the sponsors abandoned the series and from that time on the program has been offered by CBS on a sustaining basis. This was the first attempt by any network to present a daily program to schools; and each day was devoted to a different subject. In 1940 the network enlarged the field of operation of the "American School of the Air" to include all of the twenty-two nations of the Western Hemisphere, changing the title to the "School of the Air of the Americas." The programs, to quote from their manual, "are designed to supplement and vitalize the work of the teachers, by bringing into their classrooms the living world in the form of important national and world events and of fine dramatic and musical talent. They are planned to broaden the horizons of students and inspire them to increased reading and greater interest in their work."

In addition to broadcasts for pupils in the elementary and secondary schools, the networks have pioneered in attempting to present educational content in broadcasts aimed at the college level. As early as the spring of 1930, the National Advisory Council on Radio in Education was organized "to promote the more effective utilization of the art of broadcasting in the general field of American education." [3] Functional committees were formed to devise radio programs in various subject fields. Actual broadcasting started in 1931 and continued through 1937, presenting programs in art, history, labor, agriculture, and economics over both the National Broadcasting Company network and the Columbia Broadcasting System. Lack of further appropriations by the Carnegie and Rockefeller Foundations forced the Council to disband. As the programs presented by the Council were only a part of the adult-education features offered by the networks, with the discontinuance of this service the networks assumed the entire responsibility of carrying forward educational programs on an adult scale.

It would be impossible to list here the vast number of such programs broadcast on this level by the networks. Over the years many series of outstanding caliber have been presented. How great a following those programs have had in the classrooms of colleges or universities it is difficult to say. With the establishment of the "Inter-American University of the Air" by the National Broadcasting Company in 1942, some attempt was made to ascertain whether such a service was desirable. The support of teachers was asked in order that assigned listening outside the classroom might be encouraged. The two programs offered in the framework of this new service were a historical series, "Lands of the Free," and a study of the music of the Western Hemisphere known as "The Music of the New World." Enough interest was manifested by the New York City Board of Education so that a course in the use of radio in teacher training was inaugurated in the late winter of 1943. Listener and study material was provided from which the "in-

[3] National Advisory Council on Radio in Education, Inc., Information Series, Number 1, 1936.

service" teachers could receive credit. It is too early to appraise the results that are being accomplished both by the program itself and by the teacher-training courses. That it is an interesting experiment goes without saying.

The Canadian Broadcasting Corporation, always interested in educational and informative programs, launched a series of broadcasts for schools in the fall of 1942. In 1943, all Departments of Education throughout the Dominion were invited to co-operate in preparing and broadcasting the programs for in-school listening under the title of "National School Broadcasts Series." Today this series includes programs devoted to conservation in Canada and the presentation of Canadian literature and painting, with the addition of a brief review of the week's news. In addition to this special daily series, the regional networks carry a number of provincial school broadcasts in English and French. As in the case of both the "Inter-American University of the Air" and the "School of the Air of the Americas," the Canadian Broadcasting Corporation offers a handbook for teachers to be used in connection with the broadcasts.

The whole question as to whether a network can perform a satisfactory service to schools through broadcasting programs for in-school listening is a matter of opinion, with at least two points of view. There are some people, and those having to do with the public-service programming of the National Broadcasting Company are among them, who believe that because of the wide differential in time across the continent, it is not practicable to try to present a daily series of programs for classroom listening by pupils at various grade levels; and that it is too difficult for each school to attempt to integrate the program into the curriculum. Also there are those who believe that only persons closely associated with the schools themselves are capable of planning broadcasts suitable for classroom use in the various states, cities, towns, and hamlets where they might be received.

On the other hand, there are and have been many programs prepared and broadcast by several of the networks for elementary- and secondary-school consumption, as has been shown previously in this chapter. Evaluation studies made from time to time by disinterested groups have shown that the majority of those programs have been acceptable in the schools where reception has been possible. Many teachers with an interest in radio have been able to use the programs in numerous ways, even though, in some instances, a particular program was not directly correlated with the subjects being studied at the time. It is, therefore, purely a matter of opinion and conjecture whether in-school broadcasting by networks is the answer to education by radio.

State and Regional School Broadcasting

In addition to programs presented by the large networks, many other educational features are now being broadcast over state and regional networks. The "Standard School Broadcasts" of music appreciation, previously referred to, are still carried by the Pacific Coast network; and the "Texas School of the Air," established in 1941, is probably the largest state school of the air in the United States, covering 20,000 square miles with a claimed listening group that year of 2765 schools, or 20,000 teachers and 500,000 pupils. This radio school, made possible by funds set up by the Texas Legislature, functions in co-operation with many state-wide educational and social organizations, including the State Department of Education. "The Texas School of the Air" is exactly correlated with the state's school curriculum and is supervised by the twenty-four regular state school supervisors. Teacher-training has been an integral part of this school program; eleven hundred teachers enrolled for eighteen courses in the in-service training in the summer of 1941.

There have been other state-wide uses of radio through various schools of the air, notably the "Ohio School of the Air," founded in 1929 with the co-operation of the Ohio State Department of Education and financed in part by the Payne Fund, and the "Wisconsin School of the Air," established by the University of Wisconsin in 1931, supported by state funds.

The "Ohio School of the Air" was broadcast both by the Ohio State University Station WOSU at Columbus and the Crossley Station WLW at Cincinnati. One half-hour was set aside daily by WLW at no cost to the State Department of Education in order that this program might serve the schools of Ohio and adjacent states. Almost every subject field offered in the public schools was covered during the twelve years' existence of the "Ohio School of the Air."

In order that the University of Wisconsin might better serve the state as a whole educationally, its newly reorganized station, WHA, established the "Wisconsin School of the Air" in 1931. It was found that WHA could not be depended upon to cover the northern portion of the state, and so arrangements were made to broadcast simultaneously over WLBL at Stevens Point, a station also owned by the state, with coverage in the north. Thus the state was able to give additional educational opportunities to the schools throughout Wisconsin. As in the case of the "Ohio School of the Air," the Wisconsin radio program was and still is broadcast daily and, in the course of the week, many subject fields are covered, with programs for all grade levels, from the kindergarten through the high school.

Without doubt the University of Wisconsin, through these two stations, has been in a position to render an invaluable service educationally. This they have done over a period of years, since the School of the Air was founded, endeavoring always to live up to the objectives expressed by the late Doctor Glenn Frank, former President of the University of Wisconsin,[4] which might well be used as a guide by others interested in the field:

1. To serve the agricultural interests of the state by furnishing technical and market information, and sound guidance in economic organization.

2. To serve the households of the state by furnishing technical counsel on the construction, care, and conduct of the efficient home.

[4] Glenn Frank in *Education by Radio,* June 23, 1932.

3. To serve the adult citizenry of the state by furnishing continuous educational opportunities.

4. To serve the rural schools of the state by supplementing their educational methods and materials, by sending over the air the best teaching genius we can muster.

5. To serve public interest and public enterprise by providing them with as good radio facilities as the commercial stations have placed at the disposal of private interests and private enterprise.

6. To serve the interests of an informed public opinion by providing a state-wide forum for the pro-and-con discussion of the problems of public policy.

One of the first objectives of the Federal Radio Education Committee after its formation was to ascertain the value of broadcasting to schools, by networks as well as by local stations. For the purpose of securing factual information in that field as well as in many others, the Bureau of Educational Research at Ohio State University was asked to make a series of studies under the general heading of "The Evaluation of School Broadcasts." J. Wayne Wrightstone, a member of the group assigned to make the studies, stated at that time: [5]

> Some of the unsolved questions about school broadcasts are: What are the expressed and implied educational objectives of typical school broadcasts? How can school broadcasts contribute to the realization of a comprehensive range of educational objectives? What procedures before, during, and after the broadcasts seem to produce most fruitful results? How much do such techniques of presentation as talks, interviews, round-table discussions, symposiums, spot broadcasts, or dramatic sketches contribute toward each of the several educational objectives and outcomes of broadcasts? How can or should school broadcasts be integrated with school curriculums? What are the differentiating criteria for nation-wide, regional, and local school broadcasts?

In August, 1941, a report of the findings of this study [6] was

[5] *Education on the Air*, 1938. J. Wayne Wrightstone, *Evaluation of School Broadcasts*, pages 87-88.

[6] Seerley Reid, *Evaluation of School Broadcasts*, Ohio State University, Bulletin Number 35.

brought out. The introduction by Doctor I. Keith Tyler
carried this first paragraph:

> Radio networks have a significant and unique contribution
> to make to public school education. Through school broad-
> casts, centrally produced and widely distributed by affiliated
> stations throughout the country, it is possible for schools of
> varied types located in all parts of America to utilize common
> curriculum elements. All American children, rural and city,
> southern and northern, Negro and white, poor and wealthy,
> have a similar heritage, face common problems, and need a
> better understanding of each other. It is clear that programs
> dealing with these common elements can enrich, enliven,
> stimulate, and unify the education of the boys and girls of
> America.

While the number of programs considered was small, the
study was very thorough in its attempt to evaluate three of the
programs broadcast regularly by CBS in the "American School
of the Air" series. Those findings and suggestions are so adequately stated in the report that they bear repetition here as a
guide for teachers and broadcasters in the preparation of network programs for in-school listening.

Concerning School-Broadcast Writing and Directing

By and large, the weaknesses of the individual broadcasts
in the three series, other than those of curricular defects and
deficiencies, seemed to have been attributable to (1) a failure
to recognize the realities of classroom listening conditions, and
(2) a lack of understanding of the intellectual and emotional
maturity of students nine to fourteen years of age (grades four
to nine). The following suggestions for the writing and producing of school broadcasts are based upon teachers' criticisms
of certain aspects of the broadcasts, their commendations of
other aspects, and their suggestions for improving the broadcasts; upon a comparison and contrast between the most valuable and least valuable broadcasts; and upon a detailed
examination of the scripts of all the forty broadcasts. Although
they are primarily applicable to the writing and production of
a network series, for which dramatic talent and complete studio
equipment are available, many of them are equally applicable

to any series, state or local, of broadcasts for classroom consumption.

1. Plan the broadcast, both in content and in form, so that it will be clearly understandable to listeners of the *lowest* grade in that span of grades for which the series is intended. If the series is planned and designated for students in grades four to nine, then the broadcasts should be clear and comprehensible to fourth-grade listeners.

2. Organize the content of the broadcast into a simple and coherent structure of pattern, one which students can discern without difficulty. The broadcast structure should be so clear to listeners that they can outline or synopsize the content without difficulty.

3. Follow a consistent pattern in the structure of broadcasts from week to week throughout a series. Knowing what to expect from week to week gives both teachers and students a feeling of security in using this new medium of communication, radio; a broadcast pattern varying, sometimes inexplicably, from week to week gives listeners the feeling that the series is confused both in direction and destination.

4. Present few scenes and episodes, developing each one fully, rather than including many scenes and events, no one of which can be developed adequately. In a thirty-minute broadcast, five or six scenes are usually sufficient; in a fifteen-minute broadcast, three or four scenes.

5. Avoid sudden or extreme shifts in time or place from scene to scene. In most instances, a simple chronological sequence of events is preferable to one crisscrossing backward and forward through time. Prologues, epilogues, and historical flashbacks should be used sparingly.

6. Choose vocabulary — words, phrases, numbers, statistics, and concepts — appropriate to the intellectual and emotional maturity of student listeners. One of the standard graded word lists should be used in determining the suitability of words for a particular audience, the advice of experienced teachers in deciding upon the comprehensibility of ideas and concepts. If numbers and statistics are used, they should be related to some understandable standard, and, if possible, translated into verbal "pictograms." Avoid the technique of presenting facts and statistics through a succession of quotations by anonymous voices.

7. Use language and situations universally understood and appreciated throughout the country, avoiding expressions, situations, or conventions peculiar to one locality (unless, of course, the purpose of the broadcast is that of sensitizing the whole nation to the localisms of one group or community. Even in such a broadcast the language and behavior must be within the comprehension of *all* listeners).

8. Present only a few major characters in the broadcast in order that listeners may be able to identify one from another and also that they may be able to understand the motives and actions of individual characters.

9. Use dialect very sparingly in school broadcasts, only when logically the character would be speaking English with an accent, i.e., a German refugee in America, or when, because of incomplete characterization in the script, two characters must necessarily be distinguished from each other. In classroom situations, clear, understandable dialogue is of paramount importance.

10. Make sure that the transitions from scene to scene establish clearly in the minds of listeners the locale of each new scene and its time-place relationship to the preceding scene. In general, use a simple and obvious technique, such as a narrator's unadulterated explanation or the time-place identification characteristic of the "New Horizons" broadcasts, rather than a lengthy one of explanation or a subtle one of sound alone. Avoid voice fading as a means of indicating transitions.

11. Employ sound judiciously and sparingly in school broadcasts. Make sure that the sound effects do not make the dialogue unintelligible, and remember that overly loud sound effects force teachers in classrooms possessing small or unsatisfactory radio receivers to adjust the volume of their radio sets continuously in order to hear the characters' voices and yet not be blasted by the sound effects or music. Noisy broadcasts are not good school broadcasts.

12. Avoid voice fading except, possibly, when that fading is a logical part of the action, i.e., a character leaves the scene, talking as he goes. Remember the realities of classrooms, the fact that station fading and deliberate voice fading are often indistinguishable, and that frequently students in corners of classrooms must exert themselves to hear the radio program over the small set on the teacher's desk.

13. Relate in every way possible the content, problems, and situations in the broadcast to real or easily imagined experiences of student listeners. Making one of the major characters approximately the same age as listeners will usually increase the degree of relationship between the broadcast and the interests and experiences of students.

14. Make use of humorous situations and dialogue, whenever they are an integral part of the broadcast content or story, in order to heighten listeners' enjoyment and sustain their interest throughout the program. Such humor should be simple, within children's comprehension and appreciation, never adult or sophisticated.

15. Dramatize the programs, whether they be in the field of literature, social science, science, or even music. Understandings can be developed, insights deepened, appreciations heightened, attitudes changed, thinking stimulated, and even information learned when facts, ideas, and concepts are presented in a social situation involving the fears, hopes, conflicts, and emotions of human beings. Dramatizing subject-matter materials not only makes a broadcast more interesting to students, but also, in many instances, makes those materials more realistic and more meaningful in terms of their effects upon men, women, and children. In dramatizing a school broadcast, make every effort to have the program conform to simple dramatic standards: life-like characters, natural dialogue, believable situations, strong characterizations, intense conflict, and a convincing conclusion. A broadcast should be emotional rather than conversational.

16. Try to so organize the broadcast, or plot the story, that listeners' attention will be caught immediately and maintained from beginning to end. Lengthy explanations, detailed listings, verbose dialogue, or irrelevant materials all reduce students' attention. No teacher supervision or disciplinary measures should be necessary during the broadcast.

17. Avoid romantic or sentimental scenes and episodes in school broadcasts, especially those intended for students in grades four to nine. Youngsters nine to fourteen years of age giggle and groan and are embarrassed in group situations when they hear expressions of endearment or protestations of affection. School broadcasts should be free from "love and stuff."

LOCAL BROADCASTING

Almost from the beginning of radio broadcasting some far-visioned educators and station managers realized that before too long a time radio could become a potent force in elementary and secondary education. While there were instances in the early days of teachers who were fearful of adopting radio as an adjunct to their teaching, thinking that by so doing they were sounding their own death knell, there were many others who welcomed this new medium as a means of supplementing their own teaching, with no thought that it would ever take the place of the classroom teacher.

During the first decade, from 1922 to 1932, twenty-two public school systems secured licenses to broadcast. Of that number only one remains in existence today — KBPS in Portland, Oregon, owned by the Polytechnic High School. Educators unskilled in the uses of radio soon found that not only was it impossible to secure adequate funds to staff and present programs of value to the student body and the community, but that the costs of maintenance of the radio station itself were far in excess of their ability to finance. The prime object of most educators using radio during those days was to stimulate interest in the schools through promotional talks by the superintendents; programs written and broadcast by the pupils, covering the work in the schools; and the presentation of sports and other student-body activities. Little thought was given to how radio might vitalize and stimulate the regular class lesson.

Without adequate staffs of radio-trained personnel, educators soon found that they could not maintain regular broadcasting schedules and that there was little interest on the part of the public in the so-called public-relations programs being presented. This became increasingly true as managers of commercial stations acquired more skill in ferreting out types of programs which were of real interest to the community as a whole.

With the disappearance of the school-owned station, some

schools turned to these commercial stations for co-operation in building and broadcasting their programs. In most instances they found the stations ready and willing to listen to their ideas, though often the ideas were better than their execution.

In other instances it was the commercial station which made the advances, offering the facilities of the station to the school, though they too often found the school apathetic. Frequently it was a question of the schools' not being equipped with radios or with only one radio in an auditorium, or of principals and teachers alike being unwilling to rearrange standard curricula in order to integrate the radio program with the daily schedule. Teachers questioned the ability of the station program people to prepare fitting programs for school use, while on the other hand they were reluctant to do it themselves. A number of experiments were tried as far back as 1923 and 1924 in the school systems of New York, Chicago, and Oakland, California. Some radio sets were installed in a few schools and daily program schedules were maintained for several months. These were sporadic efforts, however, that blew hot and cold, depending primarily on the interest of the person in charge of the experiment. It was not until the early thirties that radio really began to get a foothold in the schools and educators gradually became awakened to its possibilities.

Back in 1926, the Cleveland, Ohio, schools pointed the way with a program twice a week that was planned for the primary and intermediate grades, but even there the interest lagged and the experiment was discontinued in 1928, to be revived in 1929 with a totally new and different idea, that of using a master teacher. Doctor Ida M. Baker was one of the foremost teachers of arithmetic in Ohio. What better use could radio be put to, thought Mr. R. G. Jones, superintendent of schools, than for Miss Baker to broadcast arithmetic lessons for pupils and teachers alike? The second grade was selected for the experiment, principally because second-grade children "are beginning to acquire certain habits and abilities in the processes in arithmetic." [7]

[7] Ida M. Baker, "Radio Lessons on the Air," *Education on the Air*, page 158. Columbus, Ohio: Ohio State University, 1931.

In reporting on the experiment at the Institute for Education by Radio, at Columbus, Ohio, in 1931, Miss Baker said: [8]

The material has been carefully planned, organized, and constructed so as:

1. To allow the child to participate as well as to listen. During the teaching period the child has a printed lesson sheet on his desk. Combinations to be studied, activities to be carried out, drills on hard abilities, problems to be solved, and spaces for writing dictated exercises are arranged in rows on the lesson sheet. In this twenty-minute teaching period the broadcaster gives directions; the child studies number facts or works examples or solves problems, and always corrects his own paper as the answers are called out. At the end of the teaching period he knows where his difficulties are. Drill sheets furnish practice in the learning material presented in the radio lesson. They also provide for individual difference and furnish remedial drill.

2. To appeal to the child's interests in order to secure the maximum of effort and attention.

3. To connect each process with its most common uses.

4. To utilize and suggest activities that build up habits of reasoning.

5. To provide for individual differences and to furnish remedial drill.

6. To measure achievement at regular intervals.

7. To take care of the various habits needed for each process; to give special drills on difficult processes; to give the combinations the proper amount of repetition; to build up habits and abilities according to the best-known laws of learning.

The school administrators and teachers were eagerly following the experiment to ascertain (a) if radio teaching was the modern way of supervising the teaching of arithmetic, and (b) if it takes care of the necessary habits and also allows time for the teacher to pay attention to individual children and to activity work. At first there were eight teachers in one school co-operating in the experiment. At the end of the first series, one of them remarked: "We teachers of Tremont School feel that we have received as much benefit from this series of

[8] *Ibid.*, pages 159-160.

radio lessons as we would have gained from a course in methods of teaching arithmetic." [9]

Miss Baker also reported:

> The people connected with the radio experiment at Cleveland were not interested in spectacular work over the radio. They were interested rather in finding out whether carefully planned teaching material and learning material presented to the many children directly by the builder is more effective than such material coming through the supervisor, the principals, supervisory assistants, and the many teachers to the children.[10]

The experiment was considered successful enough to warrant trying out other subject fields, alternating from one to another. Careful work sheets and detailed records were kept to show progress of the radio-taught group over the group not receiving the benefits of this new form of teaching. Not only were the benefits to students checked, but the benefits of this master training to the teachers. Mr. H. M. Buckley, assistant superintendent of schools, in commenting on the progress of this program, said:

> Our broadcasts have been aimed directly at the classroom in the form of model lessons which, in general, project the work of a week. My own prediction in 1928, to the effect that the radio would prove more effective as a means of supervision even than as a mode of instruction, seems to have been borne out in our experience here. Or, to put the matter differently, a model lesson directed at pupils is the best form of supervision.[11]

This first project was worked out with Station WTAM in Cleveland, but was later continued and enlarged over the Cleveland Board of Education's own frequency modulation station, WBOE, licensed in 1938, and still in operation today

[9] *Ibid.*, page 161.
[10] *Ibid.*, pages 161-162.
[11] Carroll Atkinson, *Development of Radio Problems in American Public School Systems*, pages 71-72. Edinboro, Pennsylvania: Edinboro Educational Press, 1939.

as one of the most successful elementary educational projects in the country.

Also among the early pioneers was the Chicago Board of Education. While at first, back in 1926, there was little support given to an experiment conducted by Station WMAQ in a three-times-a-week program, when a half-hour daily was offered to the schools in 1932 they were quick to accept it. The teachers planned and presented the programs, working in co-operation with the program staff of the station. During the summer of that same year, when no schools were open owing to a slump in the finances of the school budget, a summer school of the air for pupils was planned and broadcast for eight weeks, also over WMAQ. Very comprehensive work-study books were written by the teachers and printed by the station for the use of the student body. Certificates of promotion were given to many of the pupils who successfully passed tests based on the work of these summer sessions.

Even with these successful experiments behind them, there was little radio activity in the Chicago public schools between 1933 and 1937. In the latter year an epidemic of poliomyelitis delayed the opening of all schools for three weeks. During this time seven Chicago radio stations gave time in fifteen-minute periods throughout the day, five days a week, for the presentation of lessons for all the grades from the lower third through the eighth. The teachers themselves broadcast the lessons and prepared tests which were given when the children eventually returned to school. It was estimated that more than three hundred thousand children received these radio lessons, but no checks were made to determine whether the results were particularly objective. The broadcasts, however, made possible the establishment of a radio department in the Chicago Board of Education, with a radio-minded principal, Harold Kent, as director and an adequate staff to work out an integrated program. This has proved to be both valuable and effective, increasingly so with each succeeding year. At first the radio program of the Chicago schools was broadcast only over commercial stations, but in 1942 the school system was licensed to construct and operate an FM station of its own, which went on the air as Station WBEZ in the spring of 1943. This short-wave transmitter is now used, in addition to the local commercial stations, for broadcasting programs to the schools.

The Chicago radio schedule for schools has always been a full one, the administrators believing that "the radio must be harnessed and put to use directly in the accomplishment of the important educational objectives toward which we strive in our classrooms. Only thus can we derive the maximum value from the new tool. Only thus can we avoid some of the miseducation for which radio is also responsible." [12] Believing that radio has much to offer as a tool of education, the Chicago Radio Council has indicated eight ways in which radio can serve the pupil: [13]

1. Its power of instantaneous communication is of tremendous importance in obliterating isolated remoteness, in removing frontiers, and in disseminating knowledge and culture. Specifically, it broadens the scope of a child's experience.

2. Radio dramatizes and makes the past live in relation to the present to give new emphasis and meaning to the student.

3. Radio introduces history in the making through words of living participants or commentators actually present.

4. Radio brings great music into the school.

5. Radio can make the child sensitive to the problems of other peoples, other classes, and other races in a way that would not otherwise be possible.

6. Radio stimulates critical thinking and discrimination on the part of the student.

7. Radio exemplifies good speech.

8. Radio cultivates the power of attention.

The programs which the Council broadcasts weekly have been built with these eight principles in mind. Beginning with the lower elementary grades, for which a story-teller program

---

[12] Quoted from a mimeographed pamphlet, *Why Radio?* (page 12), prepared for the use of the teachers by George Jennings, Director of the Chicago Radio Council.

[13] *Ibid.*, page 2.

is presented each Monday, the radio program offers a wealth of material through the intermediate grades, with their social studies programs, and finally to the upper grades, where a diversified program in the fields of literature, social studies, languages, current events, and science is presented weekly. That this well-thought-out and integrated radio program has met the needs of teachers and pupils alike is evidenced by the fact that in 1943, according to a survey, there were more than one hundred thousand children in three hundred and sixty-two schools in Chicago listening to the twenty-five weekly programs offered.

The local stations in Chicago have always been most cooperative in this radio venture, which may also be said of the stations in Detroit, where broadcasts have been arranged for classroom listening over all the stations ever since 1935. Ten programs were broadcast weekly during 1935 over three commercial stations, with the prime object of interpreting the schools to the community. Finally, however, the radio staff realized the greater benefits that could accrue to their pupils through programs planned particularly for them, and in 1936 a well-rounded schedule was devised with the following objectives in mind:

1. To supplement and enrich the regular instructional program.
2. To bring events and personalities into the classroom.
3. To provide some instructional materials that are not readily available otherwise.
4. To portray certain school and community relationships.
5. To present different viewpoints on current issues.
6. To develop in students discrimination in radio listening.
7. To interpret the work of the schools to the public.

Warren E. Bow, former Superintendent of the Detroit Board of Education, said, in a talk before the American Association of School Administrators, Chicago, February 21, 1943:

Teachers in the Detroit public schools have always been interested in using every possible device that accelerates learning. Many Detroit public school radio programs produced by the Department of Radio Education deal with current materials and often contain information that will not be available in textbook form for some time to come. In order that teachers may make all possible use of this material, annotated listings of the scripts have been prepared from which teachers select those they desire for use in the classroom.

These scripts, together with transcriptions of professional broadcasts, are offered through the Radio Script and Transcription Exchange. Mrs. Kathleen Lardie, in charge of radio for the Detroit schools, reports that eleven hundred packages of scripts and transcriptions are available, and at least twenty-five per cent of the schools are using them every day.

A committee of forty Detroit teachers evaluates the programs and reports the number of pupils actually listening daily. This committee also acts as an advisory group on program content, meeting frequently with the radio staff to discuss student reception as well as the elements of the program itself. The programs are carried on five commercial Detroit stations; and while listening is voluntary on the part of the individual schools, Mrs. Lardie says that surveys indicate that their smallest listening audience one day totaled ten thousand pupils and that they have found ninety per cent of the pupils in schools of two thousand listening to a single broadcast. All participants in the Detroit public school broadcasts are students who have been auditioned by staff members in cooperation with the teachers in charge of radio in the various schools. Of course, staff members are regular participants on the program.

Following closely on the heels of these pioneers, the school systems of Akron and Toledo, Ohio, ventured into this new field, broadcasting their programs over the local stations. The schools in Minneapolis and St. Paul followed suit, as did those in Omaha, Nebraska; Los Angeles and Alameda, California; and Indianapolis, Indiana.

In Rochester, New York, Paul Reed, the director of audio and visual education, has presented an outstanding and am-

bitious program ever since the fall of 1929, using local commercial stations entirely. It was in that year that an interested
radio listener presented thirty radios to the Board of Education
so that children could hear the symphonic concerts being presented weekly by the Rochester Civic Orchestra Association over
the National Broadcasting Company network and carried locally
by WHAM. The interest manifested by teacher and pupil
alike in this new experience led Mr. Reed to develop a full
program schedule, covering such subjects as science, literature,
art, current events, social behavior, and general guidance.
Because of the widespread interest, it was not difficult to persuade the three local stations to co-operate. The relationship
has been a cordial and profitable one from the beginning.

In reporting on the School of the Air of the Akron Board
of Education, Miss Josephine French, Director of Radio Education, states:

> In Akron the school radio programs are intended to supple-
> ment classroom work. No curriculum change was made with
> the introduction of radio lessons. In several buildings, how-
> ever, the principals changed the timing of the period bells,
> shortening all periods, in order to include a separate period for
> radio according to the radio schedule.
>
> Since the broadcasting time was the same every day, 10:30
> to 10:45 A.M., this extra period made it possible for the children
> to receive the radio lesson without missing fifteen minutes of
> any one subject every day.
>
> We did not think of radio in terms of its contribution to
> school subject matter. We were more concerned with its con-
> tribution to general educational objectives. It has been our
> experience in Akron that the children look forward to their
> daily fifteen-minute program of education by radio with keen
> interest and anticipation. In our radio programs we have not
> attempted to follow any course of study or to teach any par-
> ticular subject or grade. Rather, we have embarked upon a
> course of enrichment.
>
> We have tried to stimulate and intensify the pupil's interest
> in old as well as in new subject matter and to vitalize class-
> room instruction by supplying new points of view. We have

aimed to enrich the curriculum with current supplementary material as well as with supplementary material that is accumulated and assimilated only after exhaustive research, which the average teacher has not time to do. By means of radio interviews of men and women in various walks of life, we have brought to students much experience and first-hand information.

There are many radio programs of interest and worth coming over the air after school hours, as well as on Saturdays and Sundays. We have made an effort to guide the home listening of the pupils, thereby developing their appreciation of good radio programs. We have also tried to encourage collateral listening by suggesting certain programs that might add information to our classroom work, and have even given out assignments for home listening. We feel that collateral listening should be encouraged as much as collateral reading is encouraged.

Inasmuch as we have taken the responsibility of the pupil's home listening upon our shoulders, we have felt that it was our obligation to supply part of the programs for them to tune in at home. Accordingly, we presented a half-hour program every Monday, Wednesday, and Friday nights. The participants in many of these programs were the groups producing high-school programs.[14]

One of the latest instances of the wholehearted support being given to local school systems by radio stations blossomed into fruition in the summer of 1943, when a newly organized radio committee of the Philadelphia schools launched a schedule of interesting programs over two local stations, KYW and WFIL. The most unusual of the programs is the "Junior Town Meeting," the first program of its kind in the country. It is a half-hour program presented in co-operation with Catholic and private schools every Thursday morning. After three secondary-school pupils have presented their opinions on some current topic, a group of boys and girls from several schools have a chance to ask questions of the speakers on the panel. In

[14] *Local Broadcasts to Schools*, pages 156-157, edited by Irvin Stewart. Chicago: University of Chicago Press, 1939.

this way young people, while they learn how to build today for a better tomorrow, begin to realize the great privilege which is theirs of free speech in a free country.

The list of towns and cities broadcasting in co-operation with local schools is a long and worthy one, and where educators, in former days, approached stations for time on the air without adequate knowledge of its value or how best to use it, they are now becoming increasingly conscious of their obligation to present to the stations the best-planned program possible before accepting the time. Stations, too, realizing their obligation to the community, are still anxious and willing to aid the schools and, in spite of crowded commercial schedules, are lending their help in the planning and production of more acceptable programs. The day is fast disappearing when the schools can ask for time without any idea of how it should be used; and stations are no longer interested in giving time merely for children to recite pieces in order that their doting parents may hear them over the radio, as only the doting parents are interested — not the station's diversified audience.

It would seem from all the evidence that broadcasting to the classroom by the local school staff through the local radio station is generally more satisfactory from every point of view than for the networks to attempt to render this service. There is no doubt that networks can offer the schools a richer program by presenting outstanding personalities from every field of activity, but the community's own school system, broadcasting over the local station, can prepare and present a better all-around, daily, integrated program.

CHAPTER 27

RADIO WORKSHOPS

THERE HAS FREQUENTLY been some confusion as to just what is meant by the term "radio workshop." What is a radio workshop and what does it purport to do? Is it set up by a high school or a college for the purpose of (*a*) training students for professional radio, (*b*) training for teaching and directing radio school activities, (*c*) training for the development of discriminatory listening, (*d*) training to develop better educational programs, (*e*) stimulating experimental research in the program field, or, as a final objective, given by the Syracuse University Workshop (*f*) encouraging interest in local educational programs to the end that these eventually may be organized into a community radio project? To all of these purposes, George Jennings, of the Chicago Radio Council, in his introduction to radio workshop units,[1] adds: "To awaken within the student a realization of the power of modern radio as a medium of propaganda, of education, and of cultural dissemination as well as a medium for entertainment and advertising."

To carry the query still further, does a radio workshop continue to be a workshop if, as in the case of Northwestern University, it is the laboratory for the student body registered in the courses of the regular department of radio? Or should the workshop be divorced from the college or high-school course in radio and be, in turn, the agency responsible for the planning and broadcasting of such programs as are regularly scheduled on a local station?

It would seem that schools should be allowed to interpret the definition as best suits their particular situation. The words "radio workshop" were probably first used by Philip Cohen,

[1] *Radio Workshops in the High School.* Chicago: School Broadcast Conference, 1943.

now Director of American Broadcasting Service in England, but then manager of the Radio Workshop at New York University, in 1935. He was describing an intensive laboratory course in radio. This particular venture into broadcasting techniques was set up through the United States Office of Education by Doctor John W. Studebaker, Commissioner, to enable a limited number of educators to participate in the activities of the educational radio programs being broadcast, under the direction of William Dow Boutwell, by the educational radio project of the Office over the National Broadcasting Company and the Columbia Broadcasting System.

The Radio Workshop offered to those enrolled for it an opportunity to improve their ability in writing, planning, and directing radio programs, with a view to the advancement of the use of radio in the interest of education. The first session ran for six weeks during the summer of 1936. Classes were given by a professional radio staff in script writing, production, and music analysis, with the objective of offering these six main learning opportunities:

1. Practice under expert supervision in script writing, production, acting, and music.
2. Observation of various radio programs arranged for the students, so that they could see in action what they were to learn to do.
3. An opportunity to rehearse and produce under expert supervision programs written in the script classes.
4. An opportunity to hear lectures by prominent men in the various branches of radio.
5. Individual conferences on personal problems of the students.
6. Co-operative study among the students of the major problems facing education by radio.

The results of this first six weeks' study were gratifying enough so that the Workshop was continued for two successive six-week periods. Great stress was laid on the fact that the function of the Workshop, as it was conceived and developed, was not to train an individual for any single field in radio. It was felt, rightly, that this could not be done in six weeks. The purpose was rather to give an over-all view of the entire field so that students could learn the interrelationships of the various aspects of radio and what obstacles they might face in entering the field.[2]

There is no doubt that the success of this workshop pointed the way to the establishment of many others in all parts of the country, though courses in radio were being given in many colleges and universities prior to 1936. In a bulletin issued in 1937 by the National Broadcasting Company, radio courses were listed as being given during that summer in fifty colleges and universities by people who had been working in the field for a number of years. In almost every instance the term "workshop" was used in referring to the radio summer school. The object of the courses was "to train for greater and more intelligent production and writing of radio materials for the coming year. The courses are planned to provide background for active participation in radio production, as a stimulation of the creative faculties and a widening of broadcast experience."[3]

In some instances those who were doing the teaching had had "practical experience," as designated by commercial radio stations, but in most cases the instructors were college faculty members whose experience had been gained solely from working with radio on the campus. When the college or university had a definite tie-up with a commercial station, such as is the case at Syracuse University, the experience would be considered more practical than when the experience had been gained merely through broadcasting educational programs over a college station. This is true only because program standards generally are more exacting on a commercial station than on an educational station. It would probably be fairer to state that that was true in 1937, while today, with the competition so great for listener attention, the director of radio activities

[2] Report prepared by Philip H. Cohen for the United States Office of Education.

[3] *The National Broadcasting Company Bulletin*, July, 1937.

for an educational station has had to revise his program standards upward. The difference in the production quality of the
programs now offered by the educational station and by the
average local station is not nearly so great as it was back in
1937.

That the courses offered and the laboratory work given in
the various workshops throughout the country have had much
to do with the raising of these standards should not be questioned. There has been a constant interchange of ideas between the people working in both fields; there also has been
more opportunity for the educator to become acquainted with
commercial broadcasting activities, so the information offered
in schools is now more authentic as regards actual production
standards than it was a few years ago.

Thomas D. Rishworth, then educational director of Station
KSTP, St. Paul, and later public service director of the National Broadcasting Company, discussed radio workshops before a meeting of the National Council of Teachers of English.
Mr. Rishworth referred to the work being done in high-school
radio workshops throughout St. Paul and Minneapolis and
used the Mary Miller Vocational High School of Minneapolis
as an example of the way in which radio through a radio workshop may be integrated with all the courses and activities of
the school. He outlined the accomplishments of the young
people of that school in their workshop, which was entirely a
voluntary activity with no credit offered for the work accomplished. Even though these boys and girls were learning trades,

> they were no less eager to know something of the arts of
> speech, music, and literature. They began their study of radio
> with the use of recordings. They listened to the best radio
> had to offer, recordings of radio plays by Archibald MacLeish,
> for example. They practiced new techniques in the use of the
> school radio system and in actual broadcasting over local radio
> stations. They discussed their problems as American youth —
> problems in job-getting, education, social adjustments, home
> conditions, propaganda, war. They decided, in the final
> analysis, that American youth had certain rights and responsi-

bilities, that opportunity in a nation like ours was not lost merely because of the state of being young. They went to the poems of Walt Whitman, Carl Sandburg; they studied Erskine Caldwell's *I Have Seen Their Faces*. They read the newspapers and magazines. They were concerned over the reports of the Marian Anderson incident at the Lincoln Memorial. They read Adolf Hitler's *Mein Kampf*. And finally, they chose for the theme of a broadcast an article, "Calling America," in the *Survey Graphic* magazine. The result was a half-hour broadcast, "America Calling," which received first honors from the Institute for Education by Radio at Columbus, Ohio, as one of the nation's most distinguished programs of the year.[4]

The script for this broadcast was the product of the imaginations, dreams, ideals, victories, defeats, and hopes of a young generation. It was written in free verse entirely by the students themselves and read by a verse-speaking choir, with musical interpolations by the student choral club. Here was the voice of youth learning the practical art of radio, applying their knowledge to the expression of their deepest convictions. Here was the radio workshop at its best, as an actual producing unit, as a motivating force in the development of interest in the several arts associated with radio, as a course in discriminating listening.

Mr. Rishworth believes that the functions of a radio workshop, either in a high school or a college, can be divided according to its purposes and states:

A radio workshop can take any form, depending on the size and character of the school. There are schools equipped with the most expensive types of intraschool broadcasting systems, for example, a loud-speaker in every room, a central control board, and an actual studio within the school. There are schools conducting their own radio stations, either on the regular or "long" wave bands or on the "short" wave bands. There are thousands of schools equipped with only a single radio receiver or with none at all. However, the radio workshop is adaptable to any school, to every school. The smallest rural school can, with some imagination, equip its own

[4] For an excerpt from the script of this broadcast, see page 224.

"studio," using a tin can, if necessary, as a microphone. The workshop itself can be either a separate course in the curriculum, with credit granted toward graduation; a unit of a course in English, journalism, speech, or other related subjects; or an extra-curricular activity meeting after school hours.

Mr. Rishworth's long experience with radio workshops has led him to formulate very succinctly their objectives and functions. He says:

> The first function of a radio workshop is to develop familiarity with the radio offerings of local and network broadcasts. Through assigned listening after school hours and later reports during class hours on the programs heard, a critical appreciation of radio can be developed which should become an important factor in the listening habits of these young people as they grow older. It is obvious that radio cannot offer everything of value to the classroom during school hours. Assigned listening may supplement the work of the teacher in many fields: civics, economics, international relations, sociology, journalism, literature, music, art, vocational guidance, and others. The "University of Chicago Round Table," "America's Town Meeting of the Air," "Cavalcade of America," "The Human Adventure," "Invitation to Learning," "Of Men and Books," "Doctors at War," the great symphonies and the opera, and many others scheduled during after-school hours are designed for supplementary education of this type. And the wise teacher will not confine his assignment to the serious programs alone. He will permit students free discussion of all types of programs.
>
> The second function of the radio workshop is the development of further analytical powers through the study of transcriptions or recordings of outstanding programs of the past. Many of radio's best offerings have been recorded for later reference, and schools having the necessary playback equipment can tap these resources as a significant factor in providing the necessary background for future practical applications of the broadcasting art. The United States Office of Education, the networks, many college and university stations, independent educational and professional organizations, and local broadcasters have recordings available on either a loan or purchase basis. This phase of radio workshop activity can be

used to train script writers, actors, announcers, producers. It can supplement the work of the creative writing class, the history class, and a score of others.

In one of our Minneapolis high schools, an experimental project in the use of recorded programs of the "Art for Your Sake"[5] series was developed. With the co-operation of the Walker Art Center, study questions were provided for the use of the teacher in leading the preliminary classroom discussion. The National Broadcasting Company also made available a series of pamphlets on the lives and work of our great artists. Reproductions in full color of each masterpiece, to be discussed during the broadcast series, were also supplied. Following the classroom discussion, the students heard a transcription of one of the programs in the series. This in turn was followed by another discussion of the broadcast itself and of the artist and his work. The students were then given an assignment. For example, in the use of the program on Franz Marc, the class was told to do a sketch in crayon or fresco of a scene of animals or of people, using blue for strength, green for treachery, yellow for loyalty, and red for fertility in the manner of the artist himself.

The results were interesting in that certain techniques proved more successful than others. On several occasions, the assigned creative work was delayed until a day or two following the broadcast. On these occasions, the results were unsatisfactory. In other instances, the preliminary or follow-up discussion was omitted, and the creative work was again unsuccessful. Regardless of the occasional change in the conditions of the experiment, however, the use of classroom listening resulted at the end of the semester in marked improvement in both range of knowledge and scope of appreciation.

In his analysis of the workshop, Mr. Rishworth assumes that it is not intended to develop professional broadcasters, feeling that that is the function of the college curriculum in radio, plus long and arduous experience in the radio studio. In this Sherman Lawton, formerly Director of the Stephens College Radio Workshop, concurs when he says: "For the most part, radio

[5] "Art for Your Sake" was a series of programs broadcast by NBC in 1939-1940 in co-operation with the National Art Society.

courses in the workshop at Stephens College are training in radio appreciation and are not intended to prepare students for the radio profession." Both men are agreed that radio may discover talent which later may find its outlet in professional radio. That it does perform this function in many instances has been proved over and over, as can be verified through the placement offices of many high schools, colleges, and universities in which radio courses and workshops have become a recognized educational activity.

Mr. Rishworth believes:

> Emphasis should be given to the fact that a radio workshop, although it cannot substitute for actual studio experience, can and must insist on the highest possible standards if it is to be effective as a production unit. It is realized, of course, that some in the group will not meet those standards. If the work includes all the functions here described, even these students can become better consumers of radio, though not producers. No one has given a satisfactory answer as yet to the question of limitation of enrollment in the workshop.

> I am one who prefers the broader view of the responsibilities of the workshop. I should go so far as to say that no budding journalist of today is completely equipped unless he knows something of news broadcasting and of the special functions of the news reporter for a radio station. Anyone who intends to indulge himself in the art of public speaking should be familiar with the technique of radio delivery. The advent of new writing techniques for radio demands of the creative writing student a knowledge of scripts as a special art. The student of international affairs must certainly become a critical listener if he is to be informed.

> These problems necessitate a dual function for the production activities of a radio workshop. First, the group must familiarize itself with the "gestures" of radio through practice within the school. Let the workshop produce programs for school consumption alone. If the school is properly equipped, the workshop may produce a daily program of announcements, news, and other features. If the school lacks a centrally controlled system, perhaps the public address equipment in the assembly hall may provide a substitute. The group may produce an occasional assembly program.

Most certainly, a variety of efforts must first be undertaken within the four walls of the workshop itself, each student criticizing every other student's work, before any display to a larger public is attempted. And no actual broadcast must be permitted until the group has proved its right to go on the air. Too many school broadcasts, supposedly educational, are educational to neither participants nor listeners. Similarly, no workshop should receive a hearing on the air unless it has something worth saying.

The fourth function of the radio workshop is the actual production of broadcasts from a local radio studio. Talent can be discovered in these groups, frequently superior in quality, and if these exceptional young people can be allowed to express themselves in terms within the realm of their own experience, they should most certainly be given an opportunity. Youth has something to say and it should be heard. But youth too is frequently imitative and not itself. I dislike the workshop broadcast that permits young students with immature voices to play adult rôles. [Here, of course, Mr. Rishworth is referring primarily to high school workshops.] I do not believe in a George Washington leading his soldiers across the Delaware with the voice of a sixteen-year-old. If a given group finds it impossible to read lines without stumbling or as if they were a vocabulary test, then let them speak extemporaneously. If they cannot express themselves extemporaneously, then let them remain silent as far as the air waves are concerned.

In a completely effective high-school workshop broadcast, all of the work should be done by students: sound effects, musical transitions, acting, announcing, and writing. It is with this function of radio, and with in-school programs as well, that the co-ordinated activities of an entire school can be used. The choice of the music and its presentation becomes the responsibility of the music department. The preparation of the script is the task of the workshop or the English classes. The planning of sound effects may well be the work of the manual training department. The typing of the script is assigned to the business department. The choice of an announcer may come from the speech department, and the actors may be selected from the drama classes. Research work involves the school library. The material, if not the partici-

pants, in a round table discussion may be drawn from the
civics, economics, or history classes. The journalism class is
concerned with the publicity and promotion of the program.
The vocational guidance division may provide the background
for an interesting discussion of youth employment. The athletic division will, of course, have its part to play in an occasional single broadcast or an entire series. The art department provides the posters for bulletin board announcements.
Radio, as it reaches into all phases of modern life, is a democratic function both in and out of school.

George Jennings, of the Chicago Radio Council, also believes
that each department in the high school may play some part in
this learning-through-doing process of the workshop, but he
adds this word of caution:

> In dividing the radio field into such definite departments,
> we must not forget the average listeners, that, after all, most
> of our students are. Consider the program from this view-
> point as well as the more specialized side. Points to be looked
> for, among others, are: purpose of the program; to whom is it
> addressed; why is the program done; of what value is it other
> than as a means of presenting a sales message; consider the
> "why" of the sustaining program.

The College Radio Workshop

Colleges and universities, as well as high schools, have become increasingly aware of the need of acknowledging that
radio has gained a rightful place in the curriculum. Northwestern University has been long a pioneer in this field with
a well-integrated radio department and workshop. In commenting on the place of the radio workshop in the curriculum,
Armand Hunter, chairman of the radio department, School of
Speech, Northwestern University, has this to say:

> The American concept of a college education as a process
> designed for the development of both skill and wisdom comes
> primarily from the feeling that an education should be prac-
> tical as well as cultural. In other words, American schools and
> universities have gradually joined the practical arts with the

liberal arts, until today, the majority of them present many systematic and carefully planned degree programs that are definitely a combination of professional training and cultural education.

This being the case, we can expect radio courses and training on the college level to be designed in such a way as to fulfill both of these functions because radio is an industry and a profession as well as a medium of communication and expression. Any complete and well integrated radio curriculum will offer studies in the social, economic, political, and artistic significance of the medium as well as courses in specialized skills, techniques, and professional operations.

Since college courses in radio are designed, either explicitly or implicitly, to fulfill the objectives of both professional skills training and a broader cultural application, the radio workshop at this level finds its chief function as a laboratory for the development of practical skills. As such, it provides an outlet for all professional training activities; it serves as a proving ground of the student's abilities; and it becomes the chief medium wherein the experience, the knowledge, and the training necessary for future professional application are acquired. In other words, the radio workshop becomes the point of synthesis for all of the practical training courses in the radio curriculum. It brings the students and instructors together in a learning process that cannot be equaled under any other conditions; and through the process of planning, writing, producing, and broadcasting programs, it develops the highest professional standards and performance criteria.

Obviously, this practical workshop requires an experienced teaching staff, equipment and facilities equal to the average radio station, and students with ability and intelligence as well as interest and enthusiasm. Given these, the college radio workshop under this definition is the finest answer to the professional training problem for industry that education and the university can offer.

Leonard Power, formerly radio consultant and co-ordinator of research of the Federal Radio Education Committee, comments on the college radio workshop:

The college radio workshop should be a real radio studio

with facilities to meet the most exacting requirements for satisfactory production of musical or dramatic programs of a high quality. The directors of the workshops should be so experienced in broadcasting that their productive abilities are appreciated and valued by the station managers with whom they work. In addition to supplementing the production departments of the stations, the college radio workshops may serve as research laboratories for experiments with various forms of radio programs. The directors of the workshops, due to their broad training and to their membership on a college faculty, are in an excellent position to aid the station in conducting listener research studies. Thus it is seen that in several ways a well-equipped and completely staffed college radio workshop is a valuable asset to all parties concerned.

It should be stated at the outset that none of the radio workshops has sufficient personnel at present to do much more than scratch the surface of the need for better civic broadcasting. Each workshop is in charge of a director who must rely upon such assistance as he can get from students. In addition to the programs which are produced for nonprofit groups, the workshop must produce all of the programs that are needed by the educational institution of which it is a part, and the director must teach all of the radio courses that are offered. When one considers the amount of time that is required to prepare and produce a single good program, it is easy to understand the limitations under which these workshops operate.

The principal workshop limitation is lack of professional personnel to assist the director and his student staff. If the full services of radio workshops in universities and colleges are to be realized, they will eventually be staffed by a sufficient number of persons to meet most of the social service broadcasting needs of the community.[6]

That there is a need for radio workshops on various educational levels is certainly evident. That they have much to offer to both the student and the radio station is likewise obvious. But that they must be adequately staffed and financed before

[6] Leonard Power, *College Radio Workshops*, pages 7-8. Washington, D.C.: Federal Radio Education Committee, United States Office of Education, 1940

they can meet the exacting requirements of an industry that has, in a few short years, set high standards for itself, is realized only too well by those who have been working in the field of radio over a period of years. Gradually, the old-style educator is becoming aware of this new tool and the many opportunities it can offer as an adjunct to the educative process, and it is safe to assume that more and better-equipped workshops will become as integral a part of high school and college courses as any of the so-called extra-curricular activities that have at long last become part of the regular curriculum.

APPENDIX

GLOSSARY

AAAA: American Association of Advertising Agencies.

Ad lib: To extemporize lines not written in the script, or in music to play parts not in the score, entirely at the speaker's or musician's discretion. Music or lines so delivered.

AFM: American Federation of Musicians.

AFRA: American Federation of Radio Artists.

AGRAP: American Guild of Radio Announcers and Producers.

AIRS: Association of Independent Radio Stations.

AMP: Associated Music Publishers, Inc.

ANA: Association of National Advertisers.

ASCAP: American Society of Composers, Authors, and Publishers, which licenses public performances of the music of its members.

Audio: The electric circuits — microphones, cables, lines, and amplifiers — used in radio transmission. A word used to differentiate the actual sound circuit from the power circuits and from the radio frequency circuits used in reception. Also refers to a range of audible frequencies.

Audition: A trial of artists or musicians under actual broadcasting conditions.

Background: A sound effect, musical or otherwise, designed for use behind dialogue or other program elements.

Balance: The arrangement of musicians in a studio so as to produce a transmission of equal volume from all instruments or voices and so as to effect the most artistic relationship between instrumentalists and vocalists.

Beam:

   (a) The direct line running perpendicularly from the face of the microphone or the loud-speaker.

   (b) The small angle with the face of the microphone or loud-speaker within which that instrument functions at its greatest efficiency.

Bit: A small part in a dramatic program. A performer who plays a "bit" part is referred to as a "bit player."

449

Blasting: Piling more volume into the microphone or other transmitting equipment than it can take, resulting in distortion.

Blurb: A statement handed out for publicity purposes.

Board: The engineer's control panel connected with the studio.

Breaks: Interruptions in radio program transmission.

Bridge: Music or sound effects used by the director in dramatic
shows to indicate scene transitions.

Bring it up: Increase the volume.

C.A.B.: Co-operative Analysis of Broadcasting.

Call letters: Initials assigned by the Federal Communications Commission to identify a station.

Canned music: Recorded music or transcriptions.

Carbon: A carbon microphone, the earliest type used by radio
broadcasters.

Chain: Two or more stations linked together for the joint transmission of programs.

Character: An actress or actor with an older voice (of thirty-five
to sixty years) who can do dialects or who has eccentricity of
speech and characterization.

Chimes: Musical notes used on some stations or networks for
identification, and for reversals by the telephone company.

Circuit: A complete electrical channel used for telephone or transmission purposes.

Clambake: A program for which preparations are filled with uncertainties, and rehearsals filled with errors, with changes and
failures, and which is likely to result in a bad performance.

Clear a number: To obtain permission from official sources to make
use of a certain musical selection.

Clear the rights: To obtain permission to broadcast literary or
musical material.

Cold: The opening of a radio program which begins without theme
or musical introduction or background.

Coming up: The ten-second warning cue before going on the air.

Commercial: A program sponsored by an advertiser; also the sales
talk on a radio program.

Commercial credit: Specific mention of the client or his product.

Continuity: Prepared copy for programs.

Control room: Housing for the monitoring equipment from which
the show is both directed and controlled.

Corn: Unsophisticated show treatment. Simple and obvious musical or dialogue arrangement.

Credit: The commercial copy mentioning the advertiser or his product. Acknowledgment of sources and ownership of program material.

Cross-fade: To fade in one sound from one source while sound from another is faded out.

Cross-fire: Interfering telegraph transmission.

Cross-talk: Interfering conversation originating at a point other than that of program origin.

Crowd noises: The sound of a crowd, produced by an effect record or by a number of people in the broadcasting studio.

Cue:

(a) The closing words of an actor's speech as a signal for another actor to enter.

(b) A sound, musical or otherwise, or a manual signal calling for action or proceeding.

(c) A phrase designating the transfer of the point of program origin; or, as in the case of network identification, a line such as, "This is the Columbia Broadcasting System," "This is the National Broadcasting Company," "This is the Mutual Broadcasting System," as a signal to radio and telephone operators for the switching of channels.

Cue sheet: An orderly tabulation of program routine containing all cues.

Cushion: A portion of the program near its end, composed of a musical number or sequence of sound or an announcement which can be lengthened or shortened according to time requirements.

Cut:

(a) To stop transmission or any part of the program abruptly, either by stopping performers or by use of an electrical switch on the control board.

(b) Deletion of program material to fit a prescribed period of time.

Dead mike: A microphone not connected or out of order.

Definition: Clear-cut transmission and reception, making possible the complete identification of the various musical units in an orchestra, in chorus, and sounds from the effects table.

Dress: A program rehearsed for the last time exactly as it is to be broadcast.

Dynamic mike: A type of microphone designed as an improvement on the condenser microphone and having a higher degree of efficiency.

Echo chamber: A reverberant room used to add hollow effects and actual echoes (that is, the repetition of sounds). These effects may be produced both mechanically and electrically.

Eight ball: A pressure-actuated microphone characterized by non-directional pickups and having a 360-degree beam.

Engineer: A technician who designs, operates, or controls the electrical radio equipment.

Fade: A diminution of volume either by moving the sound source away from the microphone or turning down the volume control.

Fade-out: The manual and electrical diminution of volume to zero.

FCC: Federal Communications Commission.

Feed: To transmit a program over telephone lines to stations or groups of stations or to any listening point.

Feed-back: The coupling of input to output of amplifiers either electrically or acoustically, resulting in a squeal or howl.

Fill:

(a) The transmission of a stand-by program to meet the requirements of an unused portion of an assigned program period.

(b) To add program material to complete an assigned period.

Fill-in: One who stands by to perform in case a program change has to be made immediately. See stand-by.

Filter: An electrical device used to change tone characteristics by eliminating frequencies.

FTC: Federal Trade Commission.

Gain:

(a) Control of volume used in transmission.

(b) The monitoring equipment used in this control.

Hold it down: An order for the studio engineer to reduce the volume.

Ingenue: A female performer with a youthful, pleasant voice.

Jumping a cue: An actor coming in earlier than he is supposed to.

Juvenile: An actor whose voice carries an age quality of seventeen to twenty-four.

Lead: The most important male or female rôle in a dramatic program.

Leg: A branch of a radio network feeding stations in a region not served by the main lines.

Level: The amount of volume audibly noted or electrically measured.

Live mike: A microphone in which the current is flowing.

Make local: To announce the call letters of the local station carrying the program.

MC: Master of ceremonies on certain types of programs.

Master control: Technical direction center.

Middle breaks: Station identification in or near the middle of a program.

Mix: To combine the input of two or more microphones to effect a complete balance.

Mixer: A panel for controlling and blending the sounds picked up by microphone.

Monitor: To check the program by means of audio equipment.

MPP: Music Publishers Protective Association.

NAB: National Association of Broadcasters.

NABET: National Association of Broadcast Engineers and Technicians.

NAEB: National Association of Educational Broadcasters.

Nemo: A corruption of "remote." Any program originating outside the broadcasting studio or requiring portable equipment.

Off mike: A performer's position away from the center of the microphone.

On the air: The actual period during which a broadcast is being transmitted on its wave length.

On the cuff: A service for which artists receive no compensation.

On the head: The starting of a program on scheduled time, made possible by the proper timing of the preceding broadcast.

On the nose: The ending of a program exactly on the second.

One shot: A single program, not one of a series.

PA: Public address or talk-back system.

Pancake turner: Any technician controlling the playing of double-faced records.

Panel: The control board of one or more units.

Patch: A temporary and removable connection in studio equipment.

Peak: Maximum amplitude of sound in electrical energy formed while flying through a circuit. The maximum point of the needle swing on a volume indicator "kick."

Peaks: The distortions resulting when the amplitude is too great for the apparatus. Sometimes applied to performers whose uneven voice control causes peaks.

Pickup:

(*a*) Location of microphones in relation to program elements.

(*b*) Acoustical value of program.

(*c*) Origination point of a broadcast.

(*d*) A device containing an electro-mechanical member which vibrates when in contact with a moving phonograph record; a modulated electric current for the purpose of making the record audible from a loud-speaker.

(*e*) Colloquially, the process of gathering material for broadcasting a particular event, other than the actual radio transmission thereof.

(*f*) Primary apparatus used to convert sound to electrical energy.

Pick it up: A term used in instructing a musician or actor to speed up his delivery.

Pick up a cue: Be prompt in speaking lines immediately after the preceding speaker has concluded.

Piped program: A program transmitted via wires.

Playback: The playing of a recording for audition purposes immediately after it is made.

Producer:

(*a*) One who originates and presents a program.

(*b*) The individual or the broadcasting company that offers a program for observation or consideration, or that brings a performance before the public.

Production: The building, organization, and presentation of a radio program.

Production director: Individual in charge of a radio studio program.

Program monitor: A loud-speaker or radio set over which the quality and the character of a program may be checked.

Ribbon: A velocity microphone.

Ride gain: To control the volume range of a program electrically in order to transmit it over lines and equipment within proper limits.

Scoop: To outwit a rival network or station in the broadcasting of a special event or a program of public interest.

SESAC: Society of European State Authors and Composers, similar to ASCAP.

Setup: Arrangement of musicians, performers, and sound effects in a studio to achieve the most favorable acoustical effect.

Short: A show lacking sufficient material to fill the allotted time.

Show:
> (a) A radio program or broadcast.
> (b) A conceited performer.

Signature: The musical number or sound effect which regularly identifies a program.

Sneak in: To bring music in softly and swell it to full behind dialogue.

Song plugger: A music publisher's representative who promotes his firm's songs.

Sound panel: A movable panel of rock wool for sound absorption, or a hard surface for reflection.

Sound track: A graphic record of sound produced on film or on sensitized paper for reproduction.

Sour: An off-pitch voice or instrument.

Sponsor: One who pays the cost of a program broadcast to advertise a product or cause.

Sponsored program: A program or series of programs the cost of which is assumed by an advertiser.

Spread: To stretch any part of a broadcast for the purpose of filling the time allotted for it.

Stand-by:
> (a) A substitute program ready to go on the air in any emergency.
> (b) A warning to performers to get ready to take the air.

Step it up: Increase the volume.

Stretch: Same as "spread." Also, to play at a slower tempo the last musical number of a show in order to finish at the scheduled time.

Sustainer or sustaining program: A program put on by a station or network, unsponsored by an advertiser.

Take a balance: To test the sound level and quality of any portion of a program.

Take it away: The cue from the studio engineer to the engineer of the succeeding program. A cue to proceed given by one engineer or announcer to the engineer or announcer in another studio.

Talking down: Condescension on the part of a radio speaker, considered an unpardonable sin in good broadcasting.

Tight show: A program timed accurately to fit its allotted period. Also a program which, in rehearsal, times a few seconds over the allotted time and should either be cut or played rapidly, if the material permits a rapid treatment.

Time check: Synchronizing the timepieces of all concerned in a broadcast.

Transcription: An electrical recording made for the express purpose of broadcasting in contradistinction to a recording that is made for general or home use.

Transition: The change from one dramatic scene to another. The music, sound, or silence that is used to suggest this change.

Tying-in: Coming into a chain program which may already be in progress.

Visual show: A radio program which is also being presented before a studio audience.

BIBLIOGRAPHY

GENERAL

Archer, Gleason, *Radio History*. New York: American Historical Society, Inc., 1938.

Archer, Gleason, *Big Business of Radio*. New York: American Historical Society, Inc., 1939.

British Broadcasting Corporation, *Handbook*. London: British Broadcasting Corporation, 1938 to date.

Broadcasting and Broadcast Advertising, Yearbook. Washington, D.C.: Broadcasting Publications, Inc., 1935 to date.

Brunner, Edmund de S., *Radio and the Farmer*. New York: Radio Institute of the Audible Arts, 1935.

Buehler, Ezra C., *American vs. British System of Radio Control*. New York: H. W. Wilson Co., 1933.

Cantril, Hadley, and G. W. Allport, *Psychology of Radio*. New York: Harper and Brothers, 1935. (Reprinted, New York: Peter Smith, 1941.)

Columbia Broadcasting System, Inc., *What the New Radio Rules Mean*. New York: Columbia Broadcasting System, Inc., May, 1941.

Dryer, Sherman H., *Radio in Wartime*. New York: Greenberg Publisher, Inc., 1942.

Dunlap, Orrin E., Jr., *Story of Radio*. New York: Dial Press, Inc., 1935.

Ethridge, Mark, *A Fair Deal for Radio*. Washington, D.C.: National Association of Broadcasters, May, 1941.

Federal Communications Commission, *An ABC of the FCC*. Washington, D.C.: Superintendent of Documents, 1940.

Federal Communications Commission, *List of Radio Broadcast Stations as of March 29, 1941. By Call Letters, by Frequency, and by State and City*. Washington, D.C.: Federal Communications Commission, 1941.

Federal Communications Commission, *A Public Primer*. Washington, D.C.: Federal Communications Commission, 1941.

Federal Communications Commission, *A Short History of Radio*

Regulation. Washington, D.C.: Federal Communications Com
mission, 1941.

Federal Communications Commission, *A Report of the Committee
Appointed by the Commission to Supervise the Investigation
of Chain Broadcasting.* Washington, D.C.: Federal Communications Commission, June, 1940.

Federal Communications Commission, *Report on Chain Broadcasting.* Washington, D.C.: Superintendent of Documents, May,
1941.

Federal Council of the Churches of Christ in America, *Broadcasting and the Public: A Case Study in Social Ethics.* New York:
Abingdon Press, 1938.

Friedrich, Carl Joachim, and Evelyn Sternberg, *Congress and the
Control of Radiobroadcasting.* Cambridge: Radiobroadcasting
Research Project, 1944 (No. 5 in *Studies in the Control of
Radio*).

Friedrich, Carl Joachim, *Controlling Broadcasting in Wartime: A
Tentative Public Policy.* Cambridge: Radiobroadcasting Research Project, 1940 (No. 2 in *Studies in the Control of Radio*).

Frost, S. E., Jr., *Is American Radio Democratic?* Chicago: University of Chicago Press, 1937.

Fundamentals of Radio: Edited by William L. Everitt. New York:
Prentice-Hall, Inc., 1944.

*Harvard Graduate School of Business, The Radio Industry: The
Story of Its Development.* New York: A. W. Shaw Company,
1928.

Hill, Frank Ernest, *The Groups Tune In.* Washington, D.C.: Federal Radio Education Committee, 1940.

Hill, Frank Ernest, *Listen and Learn: Fifteen Years of Adult Education on the Air.* New York: American Association for Adult
Education, 1937.

Hill, Frank Ernest, and W. E. Williams, *Radio's Listening Groups.*
New York: Columbia University Press, 1941.

Huth, Arno, *Broadcasting Today.* Switzerland: Geneva Research
Center, 1942.

Institute of Social Research, *Studies in Philosophy and Social
Science,* vol. IX, no. 1. ("Remarks on Administrative and
Critical Research," by Paul F. Lazarsfeld; "Radio as an Instru-
ment of Reducing Personal Insecurity," by Harold D. Lasswell;
"On Borrowed Experience. An Analysis of Listening to Day-

time Sketches," by Herta Herzog; and "Radio and Education," by Charles A. Siepmann.) New York: Institute of Social Research, 1941.

Landry, Robert J., *Who, What, Why is Radio?* New York: George W. Stewart, Inc., 1942.

Lazarsfeld, Paul F., *Radio and the Printed Page.* New York: Duell, Sloan and Pearce, 1940.

Lazarsfeld, Paul F., and Frank Stanton (eds.), *Radio Research, 1941.* New York: Duell, Sloan and Pearce, 1941.

Lewis, Elmer A. (comp.), *Radio Laws of the United States.* Washington, D.C.: Government Printing Office, 1941.

Lohr, L. R., *Television Broadcasting.* New York: McGraw-Hill Book Company, Inc., 1940.

MacLatchy, Josephine H. (ed.), *Education on the Air.* Columbus, Ohio: The Ohio State University, Year Books of the Institute for Education by Radio, 1930 to date.

Miller, Neville, *The Code Preserves Free Speech.* Washington, D.C.: National Association of Broadcasters, 1939.

National Association of Broadcasters, *The ABC of Radio.* Washington, D.C.: National Association of Broadcasters, 1941.

National Association of Broadcasters, *The NAB Code.* Washington, D.C.: National Association of Broadcasters, 1939.

National Association of Broadcasters, *Radio Reaches People.* Washington, D.C.: National Association of Broadcasters, 1940.

National Broadcasting Company, *Statement by Niles Trammell before Senate Interstate Commerce Committee, June 17-18, 1941.* New York: National Broadcasting Company, June, 1941.

Radio Annual, New York: *Radio Daily,* 1938 to date.

Reck, Franklin M., *Radio from Start to Finish.* New York: Thomas Y. Crowell Company, 1942.

Roberts, Holland, Helen F. Rockford, and Elizabeth Goudy, *Airlines to English.* New York: McGraw-Hill Book Company, Inc.

Rolo, Charles J., *Radio Goes to War: The "Fourth Front."* New York: G. P. Putnam's Sons, 1941.

Rose, C. B., Jr., *National Policy for Radio Broadcasting.* New York: Harper and Brothers, 1940.

Sarnoff, David, *Principles and Practices of Network Radio Broadcasting.* New York: RCA Institute Technical Press, 1939.

Sayre, Jeannette, *An Analysis of the Radio Broadcasting Activities of Federal Agencies.* Cambridge: Radiobroadcasting Research Project, 1941. (No. 3 in *Studies in the Control of Radio.*)

Sergio, Lisa, *Radio — The Conquest of Our Time*. New York: The Town Hall, Inc., 1939.

Sterner, A. P., *Course of Study in Radio Appreciation*. New York: Educational and Radio Guides, Inc., 1941.

Summers, Harrison B., *Radio Censorship*. New York: H. W. Wilson Company, 1939.

Thomas, Lowell, *Magic Dials: The Story of Radio and Television*. New York: Polographic Company of America, 1939.

Variety Radio Directory (Annual). New York: Variety, Inc., 1937-1938; 1938 to date.

Wylie, Max (ed.), *Best Broadcasts of 1938-39*. New York: Whittlesey House, McGraw-Hill Book Company, Inc., 1939.

Wylie, Max (ed.), *Best Broadcasts of 1939-40*. New York: Whittlesey House, McGraw-Hill Book Company, Inc., 1940.

ADVERTISING AND AUDIENCE STUDIES

Beville, Hugh M., Jr., *Social Stratification of the Radio Audience*. New York: Princeton Radio Research Project, 1939. (Now Office of Radio Research, Columbia University.)

Borden, Neil H., *The Economic Effects of Advertising*. Chicago: Richard D. Irwin, Inc., 1942.

Chappell and Hooper, *Radio Audience Measurement*. New York: Stephen Daye, 1944.

Connah, Douglas D., *How to Build the Radio Audience*. New York: Harper and Brothers, 1938.

Cooperative Analysis of Broadcasting, *Ten Years of Network Program Analysis*. New York: Crossley, Inc., 1939.

Cooperative Analysis of Broadcasting, *Program Popularity 1938 to Date*. New York: Crossley, Inc.

Dunlap, Orrin E., Jr., *Radio in Advertising*. New York: Harper and Brothers, 1931.

Dygert, Warren B., *Radio as an Advertising Medium*. New York: McGraw-Hill Book Company, Inc., 1939.

Felix, Edgar H., *Using Radio in Sales Promotion*. New York: McGraw-Hill Book Company, Inc., 1927.

Friedrich, Carl Joachim, and Jeannette Sayre, *The Development of the Control of Advertising on the Air*. Cambridge: Harvard Radiobroadcasting Research Project, 1940. (No. 1 in *Studies in the Control of Radio*.)

Goode, Kenneth M., *Advertising*. New York: Greenberg, Inc., 1941.

Goode, Kenneth M., *What About Radio?* New York: Harper and Brothers, 1937.

Grumbine, E. Evalyn, *Reaching Juvenile Markets.* New York: McGraw-Hill Book Company, Inc., 1938.

Hettinger, Herman S., *A Decade of Radio Advertising.* Chicago: University of Chicago Press, 1933.

Hettinger, Herman S., and W. J. Neff, *Practical Radio Advertising.* New York: Prentice-Hall, Inc., 1938.

Howard, Kenneth S., *Methods of Sales Promotion.* New York: McGraw-Hill Book Company, Inc., 1940.

Lumley, Frederick H., *Measurement in Radio.* Columbus, Ohio: The Ohio State University, 1934.

National Association of Broadcasters, *Manual of Radio Advertising.* Washington, D.C.: National Association of Broadcasters, 1942.

National Association of Broadcasters, *Results from Radio.* Washington, D.C.: National Association of Broadcasters, 1939 to date.

National Association of Broadcasters, *Urban Radio Listening in the United States.* Washington, D.C.: National Association of Broadcasters, March, 1941. (In co-operation with CBS and NBC, based on a study conducted by Crossley, Inc.)

CHILDREN

Clark, Weston R., "Radio Listening Habits of Children," *Journal of Social Psychology,* August, 1940, XII, 131-149.

De Boer, John J., *The Emotional Responses of Children to Radio Drama* (Doctor's Thesis). Chicago: University of Chicago, 1938.

Eisenberg, Azriel L., *Children and Radio Programs* (A Study of More than Three Thousand Children in the New York Metropolitan Area). New York: Columbia University Press, 1936. See "Recommendations to Educational Organizations and the Broadcasting Industry," pp. 195-200.

Evaluation of School Broadcasts, *National Morale and Radio.* Columbus, Ohio: Evaluation of School Broadcasts, Ohio State University, 1941.

Frank, Josette, *What Books for Children?* New York: Doubleday, Doran and Company, Inc., 1941. See chapter on "Children's Radio Programs."

Gruenberg, Sidonie M., *Radio and Children.* New York: Radio Institute of the Audible Arts, 1935.

Grumbine, Evalyn S., *Reaching Juvenile Markets* (How to Advertise, Sell, and Merchandise Through Boys and Girls). New York: McGraw-Hill Book Company, Inc., 1938, pp. 197-235.

Herzog, Herta, *Survey of Research on Children's Radio Listening.* New York: Office of Radio Research, Columbia University, 1941.

Jersild, Arthur T., "Writing Scripts for Children," *Education on the Air*, pp. 129-140. Columbus, Ohio: Ohio State University, 1936.

Jersild, Arthur T., "Children's Radio Programs," *Talks* (April, 1938), III, 41-45.

Lewis, Dorothy, *Broadcasting to the Youth of America* (A Report on Present-Day Activities in the Field of Children's Radio Programs). Washington, D.C.: National Association of Broadcasters, 1941.

Lewis, Dorothy, *Radio Patterns for Children's Programs.* New York: National Association of Broadcasters, 1943.

Reid, Seerley, and Norman Woelfel, *How to Judge a School Broadcast.* Columbus, Ohio: The Ohio State University, Evaluation of School Broadcasts, Pamphlet Series no. 2, 1940.

Reymert, Martin L., *Standards for Children's Radio Programs* (as applied to the scripts of the "Jack Armstrong" program). Unpublished.

Rowland, Howard I., Keith Tyler, and Norman Woelfel, *Criteria for Children's Radio Programs.* Washington, D.C.: Federal Radio Education Committee, 1942.

DRAMA

Boyd, James (comp.), *The Free Company Presents.* New York: Dodd, Mead and Company, Inc., 1941.

Corwin, Norman, *Thirteen by Corwin.* New York: Henry Holt and Company, Inc., 1942.

Corwin, Norman, *We Hold These Truths.* New York: Howell, Soskin, 1942.

Coulter, Douglas (ed.), *Columbia Workshop Plays.* New York: McGraw-Hill Book Company, Inc., 1939.

Huber, Louis J., *Short Radio Plays.* Minneapolis, Minn.: The Northwestern Press, 1938.

Kozlenko, William (comp.), *100 Non-Royalty Radio Plays.* New York: Greenberg, Inc., 1941.

Lawton, Sherman P., *Radio Drama.* Boston: Expression Company, 1938.

MacLeish, Archibald, *Air Raid.* New York: Farrar and Rinehart, Inc., 1938.

Morris, James M., *Radio Workshop Plays.* New York: H. W. Wilson Company, 1940.

Oboler, Arch, *Fourteen Radio Plays.* New York: Random House, Inc., 1940.

Oboler, Arch, *Ivory Tower and Other Radio Plays.* Chicago: W. Targ, 1940.

Oboler, Arch, *Plays for Americans.* New York: Farrar and Rinehart, Inc., 1943.

Oboler, Arch, *This Freedom: Thirteen New Radio Plays.* New York: Random House, Inc., 1942.

Oboler, Arch, *Oboler Omnibus.* New York: Duell, Sloan and Pearce, Inc., 1945.

Riley, D. W., *Handbook of Radio Drama Techniques.* Ann Arbor, Michigan: Edwards Brothers, Inc., 1938.

Weiser, Norman S., *The Writer's Radio Theatre, 1940-41: Outstanding Plays of the Year.* New York: Harper and Brothers, 1941.

Ziebarth, Elmer W., and R. B. Erekson, *Six Classic Plays for Radio and How to Produce Them.* Minneapolis, Minnesota: Burgess Publishing Company, 1939.

EDUCATION

Association for Education by Radio, *Journal of the AER.* 228 North La Salle Street, Chicago.

Atkinson, Carroll, *Radio Network Contributions to Education.* Boston: Meador Publishing Company.

Atkinson, Carroll, *Education by Radio in American Schools.* Nashville, Tennessee: George Peabody School for Teachers, 1938.

Atkinson, Carroll, *American Universities and Colleges that Have Held Broadcast Licenses.* Boston: Meador Publishing Company, 1941.

Atkinson, Carroll, *Development of Radio Education Policies in the American Public School Systems.* Edinboro, Pennsylvania: Edinboro Educational Press, 1939.

Barr, Ariel S., and Henry L. Eubank, *Radio in the Classroom.* Madison, Wisconsin: University of Wisconsin Press.

Bartlett, Kenneth L., *How to Use Radio.* Washington, D.C.: National Association of Broadcasters, Inc., 1938.

Barry, Lola, *Radio Development in a Small City School System.* Boston: Meador Publishing Company.

Belville, H. M., and Cuthbert Daniel, *Classification of Educational Radio Research.* Washington, D.C.: Federal Radio Education Committee, 1941.

Cairns, Huntington, Allen Tate, and Mark Van Doren, *Invitation to Learning.* New York: Random House, Inc., 1941.

Charters, W. W., *Research Problems in Radio Education.* New York: National Advisory Council on Radio in Education, Inc., 1934. Bulletin no. 4.

Cleveland Board of Education, *Report of Radio Activities 1938-39. Station WBOE.* Cleveland, Ohio: Cleveland Public Schools, 1939.

Darrow, Ben H., *Radio Trailblazing.* Columbus, Ohio: College Book Company, 1940.

Dykema, Peter W., *Radio Music for Boys and Girls.* New York: The Radio Institute of the Audible Arts, 1935.

Education on the Air. Columbus, Ohio: The Ohio State University, 1930-1944.

Educational Radio Script Exchange Catalog. Washington, D.C.: Federal Radio Education Committee. Fourth Edition, 1943.

Educational Radio Script Exchange, *Handbook of Sound Effects.* Washington, D.C.: United States Office of Education, 1938.

Federal Radio Education Committee, List of pamphlets put out by Evaluation of School Broadcasts Project. Forty-five different items dealing with different phases of broadcasts to schools and the use of radio and various programs in the schools.

Federal Radio Education Committee, *Service Bulletin.* Washington: Federal Radio Education Committee.

Federal Radio Education Committee, *Radio in Education: A Syllabus for a College Course in Radio for Teachers, Supervisors, and School Administrators.* Washington, D.C.: Federal Radio Education Committee, 1941.

Friedrich, Carl Joachim, *Radiobroadcasting and Higher Education.* Cambridge: Radiobroadcasting Research Project, 1942 (No. 4 in *Studies in the Control of Radio*).

Frost, S. E., Jr., *Education's Own Stations: The History of Broadcast Licenses Issued to Educational Institutions.* Chicago: University of Chicago Press, 1937.

Gaudet, Hazel, and Cuthbert Daniel, *Radio Listener Panels.* Washington: Federal Radio Education Committee, 1941.

Gruenberg, Sidonie M., *The Use of the Radio in Parent Education.* New York: National Advisory Council on Radio in Education, Inc., 1939. Bulletin no. 19.

Harrison, Margaret, *Radio in the Classroom.* New York: Prentice-Hall, Inc., 1937.

Herzberg, Max J. (ed.), *Radio and English Teaching.* New York: D. Appleton-Century Company, Inc., 1941.

Hill, Frank Ernest, *The Groups Tune In.* Washington, D.C.: Federal Radio Education Committee, 1940.

Hyders, Faith H., *The Library and the Radio.* New York: National Advisory Council on Radio in Education, Inc., 1938. Bulletin no. 18.

Levenson, William B., *Teaching Through Radio.* New York: Farrar and Rinehart, Inc., 1945.

Lowdermilk, R. R., *The School Radio Sound System.* Washington, D.C.: Federal Education Committee, 1941.

Lowdermilk, R. R., *Teaching with Radio.* Columbus, Ohio: The Ohio State University. 1938.

MacLatchy, Josephine (ed.), *Education on the Air.* Columbus, Ohio: The Ohio State University, 1930 to date.

Marsh, E. S. (ed.), *Educational Broadcasting.* Chicago: University of Chicago Press, 1936.

Marsh, C. S. (ed.), *Educational Broadcasting.* Chicago: University of Chicago Press, 1937.

McFadden, Dorothy L., *Guiding Our Children's Amusement Tastes.* National Parent-Teacher, June, 1941.

National Advisory Council on Radio in Education. New York: National Advisory Council on Radio in Education, Inc., 1936. Bulletin no. 1.

Overstreet, Harry A., and W. Bonaro, *Town Meeting Comes to Town.* New York: Harper and Brothers, 1938.

Parker, L. W., *School Broadcasting in Great Britain.* New York: National Advisory Council on Radio in Education, Inc., 1937. Bulletin no. 17.

Power, Leonard, *College Radio Courses.* Washington, D.C.: Federal Radio Education Committee, 1941.

Power, Leonard, *College Radio Workshops.* Washington, D.C.: Federal Radio Education Committee, 1940.

Power, Leonard, *Cooperation with Radio Councils.* Washington, D.C.: Federal Radio Education Committee, 1940.

Power, Leonard, *Local Cooperative Broadcasting.* Washington, D.C.: Federal Radio Education Committee, 1940.

Power, Leonard, *Local Station Policies.* Washington, D.C.: Federal Radio Education Committee, 1940.

Power, Leonard, *Radio Advisory Committee and Audience Preparation.* Washington, D.C.: Federal Radio Education Committee, 1940.

Power, Leonard, *Schools of the Air and Radio in the High School Curriculum.* Washington, D.C.: Federal Radio Education Committee, 1940.

Power, Leonard, *Small Station Cooperation.* Washington, D.C.: Federal Radio Education Committee, 1940.

Present and Impending Applications to Education by Radio and Allied Arts (Revised, July, 1936). New York: National Advisory Council on Radio in Education, Inc., Bulletin no. 5.

Reed, T. H., *Four Years of Network Broadcasting* (Report of the Committee on Civic Education by Radio). New York: National Advisory Council on Radio in Education, Inc., 1937. Bulletin no. 16.

Reid, Seerley, *Radio and the Teaching of English.* Columbus, Ohio: The Ohio State University, Evaluation of School Broadcasts, 1941.

Reid, Seerley, and Norman Woelfel, *How to Judge a School Broadcast.* Columbus, Ohio: The Ohio State University, Evaluation of School Broadcasts, Pamphlet Series No. 2, 1940.

Reid, Seerley, and Norman Woelfel, *How to Judge a School Broadcast.* Columbus, Ohio: The Ohio State University, Evaluation of School Broadcasts, 1941.

Rowland, Howard I., Keith Tyler, and Norman Woelfel, *Criteria for Children's Radio Programs.* Washington, D.C.: Federal Radio Education Committee, 1942.

Sauer, Julia L. (ed.), *Radio Roads to Reading.* New York: H. W. Wilson Company, 1939.

School Broadcast Conference, *Proceedings of the Annual Meetings.* Chicago: School Broadcast Conference, 1937 to date.

School Broadcast Conference, *Radio Workshop in High School.* Chicago: School Broadcast Conference, 1941.

School Broadcast Conference, *The Teacher and the Radio Program.* Chicago: School Broadcast Conference, 1941.

School Broadcast Conference, *Utilization Practices in Educational Radio.* Chicago: School Broadcast Conference, 1941.

Sheats, Paul M., *Forums on the Air*. Washington, D.C.: Federal Radio Education Committee, 1939.

Sound Recording Equipment for Schools. New York: Committee on Scientific Aids to Learning, 1940.

Stewart, Irving (ed.), *Local Broadcasts to Schools*. Chicago: University of Chicago Press, 1939.

Tyler, I. Keith, and R. R. Lowdermilk, *Aids to School Use of Radio*. Columbus, Ohio: The Ohio State University, 1936. Bureau of Educational Research, Radio Bulletin no. 12.

Tyler, Tracy F., *An Appraisal of Radio Broadcasting in the Land-Grant Colleges and State Universities*. Washington, D.C.: National Committee on Education by Radio, 1933.

Tyler, Tracy (ed.), *Radio as a Cultural Agency: Proceedings of a National Conference on the Use of Radio as a Cultural Agency in a Democracy*. Chicago: University of Chicago Press, 1934.

Tyson, Levering (ed.), *Radio and Education: Proceedings of the 1st-5th Assemblies of the National Advisory Council on Radio in Education*. Chicago: University of Chicago Press, 1931-1935.

United States Office of Education, *Let Freedom Ring*, 13 scripts. Washington, D.C.: Government Printing Office, 1938. Bulletin 1937, no. 32.

United States Office of Education, *Let Freedom Ring: A Manual Adapting to Use . . . The Radio Series, "Let Freedom Ring,"* etc. Washington, D.C.: Government Printing Office, 1938. Bulletin 1937, no. 33.

Woelfel, Norman (ed.), *How to Use Radio in the Classroom*. Washington, D.C.: National Association of Broadcasters, 1941.

ENGINEERING

Dashiel, Francis B., *The Beginner's Story of Radio*. Cleveland: Radex Press, 1935.

Duncan, Rudolph L., *Foundations of Radio*. New York: John Wiley and Sons, Inc., 1931.

Hathaway, K. A., *Modern Radio Essentials*. Chicago: American Technical Society, 1936.

Hubbell, Richard W., *Four Thousand Years of Television*. New York: G. P. Putnam's Sons.

Hubbell, Richard, *Television Programming and Production*. New York: Murray Hill Books, Inc., 1945.

Langdon-Davies, John, *Radio: The Story of the Capture and Use of Radio Waves*. New York: Dodd, Mead and Company, 1935.

468   APPENDIX

Morgan, A. P., *Getting Acquainted with Radio.* New York: D. Appleton-Century Company, Inc., 1940.

Porterfield, John, and Kay Reynolds, *We Present Television.* New York: W. W. Norton and Company, Inc., 1940.

Siepmann, Charles A., "Radio and Education," *Studies in Philosophy and Social Science,* IX, no. 1 (1941), p. 120. This issue also includes an excellent article by Herta Herzog.

Strayer, Ralph, *Dictionary of Radio and Television Terms.* Brooklyn, New York: Chemical Publishing Company, Inc.

MUSIC

Ewen, David, *Music Comes to America.* New York: Thomas Y. Crowell Company, 1942.

NEWS AND SPECIAL EVENTS

Howe, Quincy, *The News and How to Understand It.* New York: Simon and Schuster, Inc., 1940.

Kaltenborn, H. V., *I Broadcast the Crisis.* New York: Random House, Inc., 1938.

Murrow, Edward R., *This Is London.* New York: Simon and Schuster, Inc., 1941.

Saerchinger, Cesar, *Hello America!* Boston: Houghton Mifflin Company, 1938.

Schechter, A. A., *"Go Ahead, Garrison!": A Story of News Broadcasting.* New York: Dodd, Mead and Company, Inc., 1940.

Schechter, A. A., and Edward Anthony, *I Live on Air.* New York: Frederick A. Stokes Company, 1941.

Swing, Raymond Gram, *How War Came.* New York: W. W. Norton and Company, Inc., 1939.

TECHNIQUES AND CAREERS

Abbot, Waldo, *Handbook of Broadcasting.* New York: McGraw-Hill Book Company, Inc., 1937. (Second Edition, 1941.)

Barnouw, Erik, *Handbook of Radio Writing.* Boston: Little, Brown & Company, 1939.

Bartlett, Kenneth G., and Douglas W. Miller, *Occupations in Radio.* Chicago: Science Research Associates, 1940.

Bender, J. F. (comp.), *NBC Handbook of Pronunciation.* New York: Thomas Y. Crowell Company.

Carlile, John S., *The Production and Direction of Radio Programs*. New York: Prentice-Hall, Inc., 1939.

Carlisle, Norman, and Conrad C. Rice, *Your Career in Radio*. New York: E. P. Dutton and Company, Inc., 1941.

Crews, Albert, *Radio Writing*. Boston: Houghton Mifflin Company, 1944.

Crews, Albert, *Radio Production*. Boston: Houghton Mifflin Company, 1944.

De Haven, Robert, and Harold S. Kahm, *How to Break into Radio*. New York: Harper and Brothers, 1941.

Dunlap, Orrin E., Jr., *Talking on the Radio*. New York: Greenberg Inc., 1936.

Ewbank, H. L., and S. P. Lawton, *Projects for Radio Speech*. New York: Harper and Brothers, 1940.

Gibson, Pauline, *Handbook for Amateur Broadcasters*. Pittsburgh: Scholastic Publications, 1937.

James, Arthur L., *Broadcast English, I-VII*. London: British Broadcasting Corporation, 1928-1939.

James, Arthur L., *The Broadcast Word*. London: Kegan Paul, Trench, Trübner and Company, Ltd., 1935.

Keliher, Alice V. (ed.), *Radio Workers*. New York: Harper and Brothers, 1940.

Lawton, Sherman P., *Radio Continuity Types*. Boston: Expression Company, 1938.

Lowell, Maurice, *Listen In: An American Manual of Radio*. New York: Dodge Publishing Company, 1937.

McGill, Earle, *Radio Directing*. New York: McGraw-Hill Book Company, Inc., 1940.

Seymour, Katharine, and John T. W. Martin, *Practical Radio Writing*. New York: Longmans, Green and Company, 1938.

Whipple, James, *How to Write for Radio*. New York: McGraw-Hill Book Company, Inc., 1938.

Wylie, Max, *Radio Writing*. New York: Farrar and Rinehart, Inc., 1939.

MAGAZINE ARTICLES OF SPECIAL INTEREST

Angell, James Rowland, "International Relations in Broadcasting," *Bulletin of the Pan American Union*, February, 1939.

Antrim, D. K., "Music Master to Millions: Walter Damrosch," *Reader's Digest*, April, 1940.

Aylesworth, Merlin H., "Broadcasting in the Public Interest," *Annals of the American Academy of Political and Social Science,* January, 1935.

Barnouw, Erik, "Radio and the University," *Columbia University Quarterly,* December, 1940.

Bartlett, Kenneth G., "Trends in Radio Programs," *Annals of the American Academy of Political and Social Science,* January, 1941.

Beville, H. M., Jr., "The ABCD's of Radio Audiences," *The Public Opinion Quarterly,* June, 1940.

Black, L., "Radio and Children," *Education,* June, 1940.

Columbia Broadcasting System, *Fortune,* June, 1935.

Corey, Herbert, "Radio is Censored"; Judgment of Broadcasting Station Owners Not So Free as that of Newspaper Publishers — The License Club. Editorial, *Public Utilities Fortnightly,* May 11, 1939.

Corey, Herbert, "Radio's Growing Pains: The FCC and Control in the Public Interest," *Nation's Business,* February, 1939.

Crane, Vernon, "Are the Programs They Like Bad for Them?" *Parent's Magazine,* April, 1940.

Curtis, Alberta, "Radio and Reading: Do Broadcasts Compete with Books?" *Saturday Review of Literature,* June 8, 1940.

Damrosch, Walter, "Music and the Radio," *Annals of the American Academy of Political and Social Science,* January, 1935.

Davis, Elmer, "Broadcasting the Outbreak of War," *Harper's Magazine,* November, 1939.

Dempsey, William J., and William C. Koplovitz, "Radio Economics and the Public Interest," *Annals of the American Academy of Political and Social Science,* January, 1941.

Denison, Merrill, "Freedom, Radio and the FCC," *Harper's Magazine,* May, 1939.

Denison, Merrill, "Radio in Canada," *Annals of the American Academy of Political and Social Science,* January, 1935.

Denison, Merrill, "Soap Opera: Daytime Serials," *Harper's Magazine,* April, 1940.

Durstine, Roy S., "The Future of Radio Advertising in the United States," *Annals of the American Academy of Political and Social Science,* January, 1935.

Ernst, Morris, and Alexander Lindey, "Freedom of the Air," *Saturday Review of Literature,* January 6, 1940.

Ethridge, Mark, "The Government and Radio," *Annals of the American Academy of Political and Social Science*, January, 1941.

Federal Communications Commission, *Fortune*, May, 1938.

Fly, James Lawrence, "Regulation of Radio Broadcasting in the Public Interest," *Annals of the American Academy of Political and Social Science*, January, 1941.

Fortune, Surveys Relating to Radio: "Abuse of Power," January, 1936, p. 144; "Favorite Recreations," January, 1938; "Newspapers vs. News Broadcasts," April, 1938; "Abuse of Power," August, 1938, p. 72; "Industries that Satisfy," August, 1938; "Newspaper Radio Columns," April, 1939; "The President on the Air," April, 1939; "Uncle Sam as Censor," June, 1939; "The Press and the People," August, 1939; "Movies vs. Radio," November, 1939.

Frank, Glenn, "The Radio as an Educational Force," *Annals of the American Academy of Political and Social Science*, January, 1935.

Frank, Josette, "These Children's Programs!" *Parent's Magazine*, February, 1939.

Gruenberg, Sidonie Matsner, "Radio and the Child," *Annals of the American Academy of Political and Social Science*, January, 1935.

Hard, William, "Radio and Public Opinion," *Annals of the American Academy of Political and Social Science*, January, 1941.

Hays, Arthur Garfield, "Civic Discussion Over the Air," *Annals of the American Academy of Political and Social Science*, January, 1935.

Herring, James M., "Broadcasting and the Public Interest," *Harvard Business Review*, April, 1940.

Hettinger, Herman S., "Marketing of Radio Broadcasting Service: Selling Time and Programs to Sponsors," *Harvard Business Review*, April, 1939.

Hettinger, Herman S., "Organizing Radio's Discoveries for Use," *Annals of the American Academy of Political and Social Science*, January, 1941.

Hill, Frank E., "Democracy Rules the Airwaves: Radio's Forums Have given Understanding of Public Issues," *Current History*, February, 1940.

"Is There a Monopoly in American Radio?" *Congressional Digest*,

December, 1938. **Fact material and** pro and con discussion.

Kaltenborn, H. V., "An American View of European Broadcasting," *Annals of the American Academy of Political and Social Science,* January, 1935.

Kaltenborn, H. V., "Covering the Crisis," *Current History,* October, 1939.

Kerby, Philip, "Radio's Music," *North American Review,* June, 1938.

Keyhoe, D. E., and J. J. Daly, "Treachery in the Air: Fighting the Radio Fifth Column," *American Magazine,* September, 1940. (Abr. *Reader's Digest,* November, 1940.)

Kirstein, Louis E., "Radio and Social Welfare," *Annals of the American Academy of Political and Social Science,* January, 1935.

Landry, Robert J., "Radio and Government," *Public Opinion Quarterly,* October, 1938.

Landry, Robert J., "Radio: Key to National Unity," *Atlantic Monthly,* April, 1942.

Landry, Robert J., "Wanted: Radio Critics," *Public Opinion Quarterly,* December, 1940.

Michie, A. A., "War as Fought by Radio," *Reader's Digest,* June, 1940.

Miller, Clyde R., "Radio and Propaganda," *Annals of the American Academy of Political and Social Science,* January, 1941.

Miller, Neville, "Place of Radio in American Life: A Free People Can Never Tolerate Government Control," *Vital Speeches,* September 15, 1938.

Miller, Neville, "Self-Regulation in American Radio," *Annals of the American Academy of Political and Social Science,* January, 1941.

Muller, Edwin, "Radio Versus Reading: How Powerful is Radio in Forming Public Opinion?" *Reader's Digest,* March, 1940.

Muller, Edwin, "Waging War with Words," *Current History,* August, 1939. (Abridged in *Reader's Digest,* August, 1939.)

Paley, William S., "Broadcasting and American Society," *Annals of the American Academy of Political and Social Science,* January, 1941.

Paley, William S., "Radio and the Humanities," *Annals of the American Academy of Political and Social Science,* January, 1935.

Peter, Paul F., "The American Listener in 1940," *Annals of the*

American Academy of Political and Social Science, January, 1941.

Reed, Paul C., "Radio as an Aid to Learning," *Annals of the American Academy of Political and Social Science,* January, 1941.

Saerchinger, Cesar, "Radio as a Political Instrument," *Foreign Affairs,* January, 1940.

Sarnoff, David, "Broadcasting in the American Democracy," *Vital Speeches,* January 15, 1937.

Sarnoff, David, "Possible Social Effects of Television," *Annals of the American Academy of Political and Social Science,* January, 1941.

Seldes, Gilbert, "The Nature of Television Programs," *Annals of the American Academy of Political and Social Science,* January, 1941.

Seldes, Gilbert, "Radio for the Future," *Atlantic Monthly,* April, 1941.

"Shall We Have Public or Private Censorship?" *Public Utilities Fortnightly,* January 19, 1939.

Siepmann, C. A., "Radio's Big Chance," *New Republic,* January 12, 1942.

Siepmann, C. A., "Radio and Education," *Studies in Philosophy and Social Science,* IX, no. 1 (1941).

Streibert, Theodore, and Fulton Lewis, Jr., "Radio as a News Medium," *Annals of the American Academy of Political and Social Science,* January, 1941.

Strombert, R. E., "Should the Government Control Radio Profits?" *Public Utilities Fortnightly,* February 29, 1940.

Tallents, Stephen, "British Broadcasting and the War," *Atlantic Monthly,* March, 1940.

Taylor, Davidson, "Breaking into Radio" (Interview), *Etude,* May, 1940.

Taylor, Davidson, "Good Radio," *Theatre Arts Monthly,* March, 1941.

Titterton, Lewis H., "Radio and its Progeny," *American Scholar,* October, 1941.

"Toscanini on the Air," *Fortune,* January, 1938.

White, Paul W., "Covering a War for Radio," *Annals of the American Academy of Political and Social Science,* January, 1941.

RADIO AND ADVERTISING TRADE PERIODICALS CONTAINING RADIO SECTIONS

Broadcasting and Broadcast Advertising, 870 National Press Building, Washington, D.C.

Radio Daily, 1501 Broadway, New York, New York.

Variety, 154 West Forty-Sixth Street, New York, New York.

INDEX

Abbott and Costello, 124
AFM, 65, 66. *See also* American Federation of Musicians
advertiser, advent of in American broadcasting, 32; how charges and discounts to are fixed by network, 36; factors governing charges to, under FCC rulings, 37; factors governing choice of programs, 123; attitude toward women's programs, 146; attitude toward children's programs, 237; his relation to radio publicity, 349
Advertiser, The, a publication, 353
Advertising Age, a publication, 353
advertising, limited in state-owned systems, 4; importance of in small radio stations, 19; restrictions in use of, 49; in early broadcasting, 274; rates, 274; origin in network, 277
advertising agencies, radio, absence of in BBC, 6; as source of commercial programs, 57; function, 58
Advertising Federation of America, 61
affiliated-stations, number, 20; multiple affiliation, 21; program function, 22; as source of network features, 22; program control in, 103; and sustaining programs, 359; wire reports of, 359
AFRA, 66. (*See also* American Federation of Radio Artists)
agencies, advertising, 57, 58; production, 61; band-booking, 62, 63; transcription, 63
Agriculture, U.S. Department of, as source of program material, 150; daily farm programs, 264, 268
agricultural programs, importance, 260; Senator Capper on, quoted, 260; and state universities, 261; history of, 261-64; broadcasts of major farm events, 263; problems in presenting, 265; sources, 265; aims of, 266; time-factor and, 268; of WHO, Des Moines, 268, 269; building of, 270
air checks, 165
air-conditioning, in studio, 376
Akron Board of Education, School of the Air, 430
Album of Familiar Music, 128
Alderman, Dr. Edwin A., 410
Allen, Fred, radio show, 124
"America Calling," script, 224-227
American Association for Adult Education, 311
American Association of Advertising Agencies, 60
American Association of Land-Grant Colleges, 263

American Association of School Administrators, 428
American Association of University Women, of Wisconsin, 337
American Broadcasting Company, 130, 240, 243, 258, 259, 339
American Communications Association, 67
American Council on Education, 317
American Country Life Association, 263
American Farm Bureau Federation, 263
American Federation of Musicians, 65
American Federation of Radio Artists, 66
American Medical Association, weekly programs of, 135
"American School of the Air," 412
American Society of Agronomy, 263
American Society of Composers, Authors, and Publishers, purpose of, 64; disagreement with networks, 64
American Telephone and Telegraph Company, early rôle in network broadcasting, 31; first to advertise radio services, 274
"America's Town Meeting of the Air," 135; effect of, 339
"Amos 'n' Andy," 124; origin as sustaining program, 135
amplifier, construction of, 368; to produce distortion, 372; in reversing network lines, 375; types of, 379; testing of, 392
amplitude modulation, 387
Angell, Dr. James Rowland, 171
announcer, duties of, 119
Annual Institute for Education by Radio, 250, 251
antenna, described, 388; height of, 389
"Army Hour, The," 136, 137
"Arthur Hopkins Presents," 125
ASCAP, referred to, 64, 65, 167. (*See also* "American Society of Composers, Authors, and Publishers")
Association of Land Grant Colleges and Universities, 316, 317, 398
Association of Radio Farm Directors, 269
Association of Women Directors, 158
Associations of College and University Broadcasting Stations, 316, 398
audience participation program, origin and development, 131; defined, 133
audience, radio, influence, on American programs, 8; on British programs, 7; in selection of daily programs, 71; contrast between network and local, 73; women in, 142; mail from, 149
audimeter, 309
auditions, of radio scripts, 115; of programs, 276

475

482

Smith, Kate, 128
"Soap operas," see Dramatic serials
Society of European Stage Authors and
Composers, 64
Sockman, Dr. Ralph W., 258
sound, defined, 120, 367; amplification of,
368; acoustic control, 371; distortion,
for special effects, 372; wave nature of,
384
sound effects, recordings of, 165
sound technician, 118
Sowers, Dr. Alice, 337
special events programs, 134
sponsors, absence of in BBC, 6; in early
networks, 32; and opera and symphony
broadcasts, 128; and news broadcasts,
130
"spot" announcements, 145; scheduling
of, 361
Standard Oil Company of California, 412
"State Department Speaks," 191–97
State University of Iowa, 333
station breaks, 292
station identification, FCC regulations
regarding, 47
stations, defined, 13, 14; affiliated, 18;
option regulations, 34, 35; policies of
discussed, 40; station coverage maps,
288, 352. (See also Affiliated-stations
and "Non-affiliated stations")
station-time, 35
Stettinius, Edward R., 191
Stewart, James, 229
Stokowski, Leopold, 229
Studebaker, John W., 245, 434
studios, radio, 370
Sulzer, Elmer, 336
Summers, Dr. Harry B., 240
Summers, Mrs. Leda P., 126
"Superman," children's program, 242
surveys, in commercial broadcasting, 34;
of daytime serial listeners, 126; ratings
of programs, 127; as advertiser's check
on program, 299; costs of, 300; of children's programs, 324; committees for,
329
sustaining programs, in relation to commercial programs, 77, 78, 134; defined,
123; solicitation of funds on, 133; role of
in war, 136
Swing, Raymond Gram, 130

talks program, limitations of, 176; writing
of, 181
"Teachers Go to School," radio clinic, 329
"Telephone Hour," radio feature, 128
telephone survey, of radio audiences, 300
telephone wires, in network broadcasting,
31; in field broadcasts, 378. (See also
Wire lines)
teletype, 358, 360

television, 393–94
"Terry and the Pirates," children's program, 242
testimonials, use of, 55
"Texas School of the Air," 415
Thompson, Dorothy, 130, 150
Tide, a publication, 353
time, allocation of, 14; sale of, 31; sale
to political parties, 133; sale of, to
churches, 139; sales units of, 275; syn-
chronization of clocks, 392
timing, of programs, 180, 181, 187, 189,
268
"Today's children," radio feature, 135
Tomlinson, Edward, 130
Toscanini, Arturo, 128
"Town and Farm," radio feature, 262
Town Meeting Discussion Leader's Handbook, 210
town meeting, type of program, 210; rules
for running of, 215; moderator of, 213
traffic department, defined, 358; commercial division of, 359; sustaining
division of, 359; communications division of, 360; of network affiliates, 36
traffic supervisor, of local stations, 360
transcriptions, electrical, restrictions on
use of, 47; agency transcriptions, 63;
vs. phonograph records, 160; early forms,
161–62; development of, 162–63; processed, 164–65; instantaneous, 165–66;
FCC regulations regarding, 166–67;
NAB code provisions, 167; care of, 168;
apparatus for, 355; for short wave relay,
381; making of, 382; master copies,
383
transmitting station, described, 369; location of, 386
"Treasure Chest," audience participation
program, 131
Tucker, Madge, 243
Tune-in, a publication, 353
Tune in for Education, 398
TWX (time wire exchange service), 360
Tyler, Dr. I. Keith, 418
Tyler, Tracy F., 335
Tyson, Dr. Levering, 311, 312, 340

Umberger, H., 317
Union Internationale de Radiodiffusion
(UIR), 11
union organizations, relation to networks,
67
United Jewish Laymen's Committee, 258
United Jewish Relief, 253
United Press Service, 19
University Broadcasting Council, policies
of, 314; disbanded, 316
University of California, College of Agri-
culture, 262
University of Chicago, early interest in